Rivers in the Desert

Rivers in the Desert

MEDITATIONS AND PRAYERS FOR REFRESHMENT

Edited by Rowland Croucher

AN ALBATROSS BOOK

© Rowland Croucher, 1991

Published in Australia and New Zealand by
Albatross Books Pty Ltd
PO Box 320, Sutherland
NSW 2232, Australia
in the United States of America by
Albatross Books
PO Box 131, Claremont
CA 91711, USA
and in the United Kingdom by
Lion Publishing
Peter's Way, Sandy Lane West
Littlemore, Oxford OX4 5HG, England

First edition 1991

National Library of Australia
Cataloguing-in-Publication data

Croucher, Rowland
Rivers in the Desert

ISBN   0 86760 137 X (Albatross)
ISBN   0 7459 1709 7 (Lion)

1. Meditations   I. Croucher, Rowland

242

Front cover photograph: Galvan's Gorge, Kimberley Region
 Copyright: Trevern Dawes
 Courtesy of Horizon International
Back cover photograph: John Waterhouse
Printed by Kyodo Printing Co. Ltd, Singapore

Contents

Preface

One of the few generalisations we can make of all the great biblical leaders is that they spent a disproportionate amount of their lives in deserts (or prisons).

Deserts are dry, idol-less, sometimes fearful places. But, as Carlo Carretto reminds us, we must go there to discover God and ourselves more truly. In *The Desert in the City* he says the desert does not mean the absence of other humans; it means the presence of God. In his *Letters from a Desert* he reminds us that we are what we pray. Our ability to love is our ability to pray.

A desert is a place of aloneness with God (and without telephones!). Even in dryness and in barrenness, our prayer is, as Julian of Norwich put it, well pleasing to God.

The forerunners of this volume, *Still Waters Deep Waters* and *High Mountains Deep Valleys*, proved surprisingly popular. It is gratifying that so many want to 'go deeper' in their devotional life. Wives and husbands tell me they read selections to each other. Preachers use this material for their sermons, and quotes in their church bulletins.

Royalties from this book are divided between World Vision and John Mark Ministries (which seeks to encourage pastors, ex-pastors, church leaders and their spouses).

Thanks again to Grace Thomlinson for her administrative and editorial assistance, to David and Christine Jones, Hugh Linaker and Yvonne Wake for checking the proofs and, as always, to my wife Jan and daughters Amanda and Lindy for their very special love and encouragement.

Rowland Croucher
John Mark Ministries
7 Bangor Court
Heathmont
Australia   3135

Theme: Provision and growth

Rivers in the desert

The poor and needy search for water,
   but there is none;
   their tongues are parched with thirst.
But I the Lord will answer them;
   I, the God of Israel, will not forsake them.
I will make rivers flow on barren heights,
   and springs within the valleys.
I will turn the desert into pools of water,
   and the parched ground into springs.
I will put in the desert
   the cedar and the acacia, the myrtle and the olive.
I will set pines in the wasteland,
   the fir and the cypress together,
so that the people may see and know,
   may consider and understand,
that the hand of the Lord has done this,
   that the Holy One of Israel has created it.
                           Isaiah 41: 17-20, NIV

Words and silences

I know that you are all-powerful:
  what you conceive, you can perform.
I am the one who obscured your designs
  with my empty-headed words.
I have been holding forth on matters
  I cannot understand,
  on marvels beyond me and my knowledge. . .
I knew you then only by hearsay;
  but now, having seen you with my own eyes,
I retract all I have said,
  and in dust and ashes I repent.
May the words of my mouth and the meditation of
my heart be pleasing in your sight, O Lord, my Rock
and my Redeemer.
Be not rash with your mouth, nor let your heart be
hasty to utter a word before God, for God is in heaven,
and you upon earth; therefore let your words be few.
A time to keep silence, and a time to speak.
A word fitly spoken is like apples of gold.
Study to be quiet.
The kingdom of God is not a matter of talk, but of
power.
Then a great and powerful wind tore the mountains
apart and shattered the rocks before the Lord, but the
Lord was not in the wind. After the wind there was
an earthquake, but the Lord was not in the earthquake.
After the earthquake came a fire, but the Lord was not
in the fire. And after the fire came a gentle whisper.
When Elijah heard it, he. . . went out and stood at the
mouth of the cave.

Be still, and know that I am God.

I tell you this: there is not a thoughtless word that comes from your lips but you will have to account for it on the day of judgment. For out of your own mouth you will be acquitted; out of your own mouth you will be condemned.

(Job 42: 2-6, JB; Psalm 19: 14, NIV; Ecclesiastes 5: 2; 3: 7; Proverbs 25: 11 – all RSV; 1 Thessalonians 4: 11, AV; 1 Corinthians 4: 20, NEB; 1 Kings 19: 11-13, NIV; Psalm 46: 10, AV; Matthew 12: 36 and 37, NEB)

Many people are looking for an ear that will listen, writes Dietrich Bonhoeffer. But he goes on to say that they often won't find that listening ear among Christians, because Christians are talking when they should be listening.

Many of us are great talkers. Word merchants. Offering an endless stream of wordy advice. We are so afraid of silence that we must fill every empty space with words, whether we have something to say or not. But people in trouble don't need our words as much as they just need us: our presence and our love.

To test whether clergy fail to listen, a psychologist arranged an experiment. He went to visit a number of clergymen, presenting himself as someone with a serious problem seeking counsel and help. He had a stopwatch in his pocket to note the time when the minister intervened with advice while he was pouring out his story. In his visits to ten clergymen, the longest time he was allowed to speak before being interrupted was five minutes!

Words, words, words. We place such value upon them, giving them a weight which they do not justify. The apostle Paul wrote to the Corinthians, challenging their wordy self-importance: 'The kingdom of God is not a matter of talk but of power.' The power of love, the power of grace, the power of prayer, the power of the Spirit. Often it is the quiet forces that have the greatest power.

Henry Gariepy, in his studies on the book of Job, *Portraits of Perseverance*, reminds us that sunbeams, unheard by the human ear, bring energy and blessing; that the dew which falls silently at night refreshes the earth; and that it is the silent power of the force of gravity which holds the planets in their orbits.

Why are we afraid of silence? Why can't we find the power that comes in the quietness, in the readiness to listen, whether to another human being or to God? As Dietrich Bonhoeffer says, 'If you can no longer listen to another, you will soon no longer be listening to God either.'

Jesus knew when to speak and when to keep silent. He didn't waste words. He didn't really talk a lot. When he taught, it was always concise, clear and admirable in its restraint, yet gripping mind and heart with a quality that made the words memorable, unforgettable. I believe this was because he spoke only the words his Father gave him to speak.

Where did he find those words? In the silences, in the secret place where he communed with God. Again and again in the gospels we read of those times and places of meditation and prayer, still veiled in sacred silence, where he found the wisdom and the words.

It is in the secret place that we find the balance, the rhythm of the spiritual life between being and doing, between contemplation and action, between words and silence. Richard Foster in *Freedom of Simplicity* writes, 'We devour people with our words. Silence is one of the deepest disciplines of the Spirit simply because it puts a stopper on that.'

It is in the discipline of silence that we learn to fine-tune our receptivity to God's presence, his will and his word. This is not a negative, empty silence but, as Anthony Bloom points out, the positive disciplined silence of a sentry at the post of duty or of a bird-watcher motionless and attentive to the slightest sound or movement in the bushes. We need to be still through the discipline of silence and listen to what God is saying to us. Then what we say to others will have the sensitivity, the conviction and the restraint which marked the powerful words of our Lord.

The endless cycle of ideas and action,
Endless invention, endless experiment,
Brings knowledge of motion, but not of stillness;
Knowledge of speech, but not of silence;
Knowledge of words, and ignorance of the Word.

Where is the Life we have lost in living?
Where is the wisdom we have lost in knowledge?
Where is the knowledge we have lost in information?

T.S. Eliot, *Choruses from the Rock*

Many people are looking for an ear that will listen. They do not find it among Christians, because these Christians are talking when they should be listening. But those who can no longer listen to others will soon be no longer listening to God either; they will be doing nothing but prattling in the presence of God, too. This is the beginning of the death of the spiritual life, and in the end there is nothing left but spiritual chatter and clerical condescension arrayed in pious words. One who cannot listen long and patiently will presently be talking beside the point and be never really speaking to others, albeit without being conscious of it. Those who think that time is too valuable to spend keeping quiet will eventually have no time for God and other, but only for themselves and their own follies.

Dietrich Bonhoeffer, *Life Together*

Discipline yourself so that your words are few and full. Become known as a person who has something to say when you speak. Maintain plain speech. Do what you say you will do.

Go another step. Try to live one entire day without words at all. Do it not as a law, but as an experiment. Note your feelings of helplessness and excessive dependence upon words to communicate. Try to find new ways to relate to others that are not dependent upon words. Enjoy, savour the day. Learn from it.

Richard Foster, *Celebration of Discipline*

Jesus' speech was admirable in its restraints, therefore always potent for good. It may truly be said that we should be better understood if we said less. There are some, it is true, with whom slowness of speech has become taciturnity, but for most of us the important thing is to impart a sense of judgment and fitness to the torrent of our words. God will surely count a prudent silence unto us for righteousness. Certainly, before speaking publicly about God, we ought always to be sure that God's word is in our very bones, burning for expression. Thousands of our words will not equal a few of God's words.

Albert Osborn, *The Silences of Christ*

Silence frees us from the need to control others. One reason we can hardly bear to remain silent is that it makes us feel so helpless. We are accustomed to relying upon words to manage and control others. A frantic stream of words flows from us in an attempt to straighten others out. We want so desperately for them to agree with us, to see things our way. We evaluate people, judge people, condemn people. We devour people with our words. Silence is one of the deepest disciplines of the Spirit simply because it puts the stopper on that.

Richard Foster, *Freedom of Simplicity*

Sometimes words are inappropriate, an intrusion on the deepest and most sacred experiences of life. There are times when all we can offer to one in deep sorrow is our presence and the sacrament of silence.

When Job's three friends saw his horrible plight, his calamitous losses, his disfigurement and isolation, 'They sat on the ground with him for seven days and seven nights. No-one said a word to him, because they saw how great his suffering was' (Job 2: 13). Seven days was the customary mourning period for the dead. His three friends grieved as though Job were dead.

The seven-day silence of Job's friends was far more eloquent than any words they could have spoken.

Henry Gariepy, *Portraits of Perseverance*

'A word was secretly brought to me,' said Eliphaz (Job 4: 12) as he claimed a vision from God. He vividly described his experience: '. . .the hair on my body stood on end' (Job 4: 15). After all, who can debate the authority of someone who says, 'God has spoken to me'? It leaves no room for discussion. Thus Eliphaz spoke with absolute dogmatism.

He rubbed salt into Job's wounds by suggesting his sin had caused the loss of his children (Job 5: 3-4). Job's afflictions were attributed to the corrections of God, and he was advised 'not to despise the discipline of the Almighty' (Job 5: 17).

Eliphaz broke all the rules of offering counsel and comfort. From him we can learn the negatives to avoid when people are hurting. His arrogance instructs us not to be dogmatic, judgmental, insensitive, theologically naive and superficial. Often, people in trouble do not need our words and our philosophies; they need us. They need our love, our caring, our compassion, our affirmation, our practical support and our encouragement.

Henry Gariepy, *Portraits of Perseverance*

Discipleship begins with silence and listening. When we listen to someone we think we are silent because we do not speak; but our minds continue to work, our emotions react, our wills respond for and against what we hear. We may even go further than this, with thoughts and feelings buzzing in our heads which are quite unrelated to what is being said.

This is not silence as it is implied in discipleship. The real silence towards which we must aim is a complete repose of heart and mind and will; the silence of all there is in us, including our body, so that we may be completely aware of the word we are receiving, completely alert and yet in complete repose.

The silence I am speaking of is the silence of the sentry on duty at a critical moment; alert, immobile, poised and yet alive to every sound, every movement. This living silence is what discipleship requires first of all, and this is not achieved without effort. It requires from us a training of our attention, a training of our body, a training of our mind and our emotions so that they are kept in check, completely and perfectly.

The aim of this silence is the perceiving of what will be offered to us, of the word that will resound in the silence. And this word we must be prepared to hear, whatever it may be.

Anthony Bloom, *Meditations on a Theme*

I have been impressed very much in pondering over Jesus' silent contemplation of his passion. Imagine the scene; endeavour to catch the spirit of awe, of inspiration, the foreboding and misgiving of the disciples, together with the kingly confidence of the Lord. 'And they were in the way going up to Jerusalem; and Jesus went before them: and they were amazed; and as they followed, they were afraid.' See him drawing away from his followers so that he may ponder the fulfilment of his great consecration without interference. As he ponders, so great is the tension that the disciples are first amazed, then afraid. Many of our decisions are wrong because we have such a multitude of counsellors.

Great resolves are often best taken alone, with God only for counsellor. No matter how good or well-intentioned the disciples were, if their advice or opinion had been asked, which of them would have seen a kingdom beyond the cross?

So may it be said of our spiritual constraints. The world's 'twelve good men and true' would almost invariably condemn our proposed consecrations as unremunerative and impolitic; but we must not ask their opinion, although we shall be troubled enough by them whether we ask or no. Let us resolve to go up to our cross bravely, silently and triumphantly.

Albert Osborn, *The Silences of Christ*

Under the silent watchful eye of the Holy One, we are all standing. . . In that Centre, in that holy Abyss where the Eternal dwells at the base of our being, our programs, our gifts to him, our offerings of duties performed are again and again revised in their values. Many of the things we are doing seem so important to us. We haven't been able to say 'no' to them, because they seemed so important.

But if we 'centre down', as the old phrase goes, and live in that holy silence which is dearer than life, and take our life program into the silent places of the heart, with complete openness, ready to do, ready to renounce according to his leading, then many of the things we are doing lose their vitality for us. I should like to testify to this as a personal experience, graciously given. There is a re-evaluation of much that we do or try to do, *which is done for us*, and we know what to do and what to let alone.

Thomas Kelly, *A Testament of Devotion*

Father,
Knowing the empty-headedness of so many of my words, I am silent before you. . .
Forgive me that so often I talk first instead of waiting patiently on you. Forgive me, too, that I seek the counsel of others before first bringing my concerns to you.
Teach me, Lord, the beauty of being silent in your presence, enjoying your company, being enfolded by your love and enraptured by your glory, awaiting those deep insights which you are so ready to give.
Teach me too, Lord, the discipline of a controlled tongue as I go out into my workaday world. Give me an awareness of when to speak and when to be silent. May I, and all your servants, eschew a wordy ministry, but live, speak and act in the style of our Master, Jesus Christ. Then at the close of this day, I will know it has been a day well spent and acceptable in your sight.

A Benediction
Into your hands we commit our spirit.
Into your hands, the open and defenceless hands of love,
into your hands, the accepting and welcoming hands of love,
into your hands, the firm and reliable hands of love,
we commit our spirit. Amen.

Rex Chapman

2

Our first responsibility

God, the Lord God, has spoken
and summoned the world from the rising to the setting
sun.
    God shines out from Zion, perfect in beauty.
To whom then will you liken me,
whom set up as my equal?
asks the Holy One.
    I am the Lord, I myself,
and none but I can deliver.
I myself have made it known in full, and declared it,
I and no alien god amongst you,
and you are my witnesses, says the Lord.
I am God; from this very day I am he.
    Tell out, my soul, the greatness of the Lord,
rejoice, rejoice, my spirit, in God my saviour;
so tenderly has he looked upon his servant,
humble as she is. . .
    His name is Holy;
his mercy sure from generation to generation
toward those who fear him. . .
Holy, holy, holy is God the sovereign Lord of all, who
was, and is, and is to come!
    Thou are worthy, O Lord our God, to receive glory
and honour and power, because thou didst create all
things; by thy will they were created, and have their
being!
    O depth of wealth, wisdom and knowledge in God!
How unsearchable his judgments, how untraceable his
ways! Who knows the mind of the Lord? Who has
been his counsellor? Who has ever made a gift to him,

to receive a gift in return? Source, Guide and Goal of all that is — to him be glory for ever! Amen.

What we have seen and heard we declare to you, so that you and we together may share in a common life, that life which we share with the Father and his Son Jesus Christ.

Be still and know that I am God.

(Psalm 50: 1-2; Isaiah 40: 25; Isaiah 43: 11-13; Luke 1: 46-48a,49b,50; Revelation 4: 8b,11; Romans 11: 33-36; I John 1: 3 — all NEB; Psalm 46: 10, AV)

Some forty years ago, the Australian Methodist Church conducted a national evangelistic campaign with this theme: 'If God matters at all, he matters most.' It was a sentiment so obviously right, it could almost have been called trite. Of course God is the most important reality with which we have to do. How could it be otherwise? After all, God *is* God!

But is it really that simple? Not if we think for a moment about how we actually conduct our lives, even those aspects of them that we would call specifically religious.

In the 1920s, Evelyn Underhill, a laywoman, gave a series of talks to Anglican priests in England. Speaking of their ministry, she said '. . .the Christian revelation, the work done by Christ in our souls, has. . . as its main object the promotion of God's glory, the shining out of his reality more and more fully through our acts; the increase of our wide-open, loving, selfless adoration, the deepening of our creaturely awe, the expanding of our consecration in service. . . [this] means that attention to God must be your primary religious activity, and this for the strictly practical reason that without that attention to God, all other religious activities will lose their worth. . .'

When I read those words not long ago, I found them disturbing. They sound so plainly right, and yet they describe an attitude and a state of affairs that is surely a long way from where we actually are. Here is someone who is saying that the fundamental ministry of the church is the worship and adoration of God, and that the primary business of the ordained among us must therefore be to lead the church in that practice. By implication, she is saying, too, that it is the primary business of all of us to look to such things in our own lives. If God matters at all, he matters most.

Unfortunately, this kind of language doesn't remind me of too many church communities I know — I fear it doesn't especially remind me of myself. Take, for example, how we commonly prepare our people for ordination. We try to ensure that they become exegetes, historians, theologians, ethicists, preachers, administrators, educators and counsellors. We might even be concerned that they turn out to be effective evangelists. But where in the curriculum and in our educational structures do we press the point hard that they should also be people of *prayer* who are able to lead others in the disciplines of their communion with God?

Or consider the same notion from the standpoint of the laity. We ready ourselves thoroughly for the daily work to which we are called. We are intent upon being good teachers, or lawyers, or business people, or home makers, or farmers, or miners. We read, we study, we discuss, we think about what it all means. But aren't we also supposed to be fulfilling our vocation as the Body of Christ in the world?

Where does that get the same amount and degree of disciplined attention? Nor is it enough to point to the fact that we are very busy with the affairs of the church or with religious matters. The issue is not how active we are, but how much our lives are in fact concentrated on God. How much is 'wide-open, loving, selfless adoration' our primary business, in order that God's glory and reality may shine out more and more fully through our daily presence? If in everything we do day by day we are meant to be women and men and communities of *God*, isn't it both strange and alarming that we spend so little of our average week being occupied with what it is like to live with God?

The union of human beings with God is the goal of Christianity.

Gerhardt Ladner, *Theologie und Politik*

Come now, little person, fly for a moment from your affairs, escape for a little while from the tumult of your thoughts. Put aside now your weighty cares and leave your wearisome toils. Abandon yourself for a little to God and rest for a little in him. Enter into the inner chamber of your soul, shut out everything save God and what can be of help in your quest for him and, having locked the door, seek him out. . . speak now, my whole heart, speak now to God: 'I seek your countenance, O Lord, your countenance I seek.'

St Anselm, *Proslogion*

Unless the whole of your priestly life is a movement of praise and adoration, unless it is instinct with awe, the work which that life produces won't be much good. And if that be true, it follows that the Christian revelation, the work done by Christ in our souls, has also as its main object the promotion of God's glory, the shining out of his reality more and more fully through our acts; the increase of our wide-open, loving selfless adoration, the deepening of our creaturely awe, the expanding of our consecration in service. And all this must happen in you, before you can give it to your people, mustn't it? You have to show them in your own person the literal truth of the. . . great Ignatian saying: 'I come from God — I belong to God — I am destined for God!'

This, then, seems the first consideration which should be before the mind of the priest, in planning your personal devotional life. It means that attention to God must be your primary religious activity, and this for the strictly practical reason that without that attention to God, all other religious activities will lose their worth; that the life of the minister of religion depends almost entirely for its value on the extent to which it is bathed in the Divine Light. . .

It is the ultimate object of all those devoted, ceaseless

and changeful activities of yours, to bring into the lives of those for and with whom you work, something of that changeless temper of Eternity. If you, with your special facilities and training, do not manage to do this, it is not particularly likely that anyone else will do it; and your power of doing it depends upon your possession of it.

Evelyn Underhill, *Concerning the Inner Life*

It is true. . . that in thinking of prayer we must guard against the inclination to regard it chiefly as a way of getting strength and help; of making use of God. Nevertheless, it is for the priest the unique source of pastoral power. Other things — intellectual and social aptitudes, good preaching, a capacity for organisation — help this work, and help much. None of these, however, is essential. Prayer is. The person whose life is coloured by prayer, whose loving communion with God comes first, will always win souls; because they see in that life and person the attractiveness of reality, the demand, the transforming power of the spiritual life. . .

It follows from this that the priest's life of prayer — communion with God — is not only the priest's primary obligation to the church; it is also the only condition under which the work of the Christian ministry can be properly done. The priest is called, as the Book of Wisdom says, to be a 'friend of God, and prophet': and will only be a good prophet if also in reality a friend of God. For the priest's business is to lead us out towards eternity; and how can this be done, unless it is a country in which the priest is also at home?

Evelyn Underhill, *The Parish Priest and the Life of Prayer*

The very first thing we need to do is set apart a time and place to be with God and him alone. The concrete shape of this discipline of solitude will be different for each person, depending on individual character, ministerial tasks and milieu. But a real discipline never remains vague or general. It is as concrete and specific as daily life itself. . . Ministry can be fruitful only if it grows out of a direct and intimate encounter with our Lord. Thus the opening words of St. John's first letter echo down through history: 'Something. . . we have heard, and we have seen with our own eyes; that we have watched and touched with our hands: the Word, who is life — this is our subject' (I John 1: 1).

Henri J.M. Nouwen, The Way of the Heart

Devotion is neither private nor public prayer; but prayers, whether private or public, are particular parts or instances of devotion. Devotion signifies a life given, or devoted, to God.

William Law, A Serious Call to a Devout and Holy Life

Grant, Lord, that we may hold to you without parting,
Worship you without wearying,
Serve you without failing;
Faithfully seek you,
And for ever possess you,
The only God,
Blessed, now and for ever.

St Anselm, Prayers

O God, let your Holy Spirit fasten me to you until I learn that to adore and love you is to give everything else I do its point and meaning. This one thing is what is really necessary. But since every good I possess is your gift in the first place, grant me henceforth the grace of an adoring, loving heart, that I may be set just where I should be.

A Benediction

To him who loves us and freed us from our sins with his life's blood, who made of us a royal house, to serve as priests of his God and Father — to him be glory and dominion for ever and ever! (Revelation 1: 5b-6 NEB).

The grace of our Lord Jesus be with you always. Amen.

3

Memory therapy

You have forgotten me.

Does a young woman forget her jewellery, or a bride her wedding dress? But my people have forgotten me for more days than can be counted.

Hope is gone once God is forgotten.

Remember what the Holy One has done and give him thanks.

Remember that I, the Lord Almighty, am holy; I am the one you must fear.

Lord. . . You welcome those who find joy in doing what is right, those who remember how you want them to live.

Remember the prophets who spoke in the name of the Lord. Take them as examples of patient endurance under suffering.

The thought of my pain, my homelessness, is bitter poison; I think of it constantly and my spirit is depressed. Yet hope returns when I remember this one thing: The Lord's unfailing love and mercy still continue, fresh as the morning, as sure as the sunrise. The Lord is all I have, and so I put my hope in him.

By the rivers of Babylon we sat down; there we wept when we remembered Zion. . . May I never be able to play the harp again if I forget you, Jerusalem! May I never be able to sing again if I do not remember you, if I do not think of you as my greatest joy!

I am worn out, Lord, waiting for you to save me; I place my trust in your word. My eyes are tired from watching for what you promised, while I ask, 'When will you help me?' I am as useless as a discarded wineskin; yet I have not forgotten your commands.

Mary remembered all these things and thought deeply about them.

Just then a cock crowed, and Peter remembered what Jesus had told him: 'Before the cock crows, you will say three times that you do not know me.' He went out and wept bitterly.

The Lord says: 'I am the one who strengthens you. Why should you fear mortal man, who is no more enduring than grass? Have you forgotten the Lord who made you, who stretched out the heavens and laid the earth's foundations? Why should you live in constant fear of the fury of those who oppress you, of those who are ready to destroy you? Their fury can no longer touch you.'

Remember the Lord in everything you do, and he will show you the right way.

Do this so that you will remember me.

All nations will remember the Lord.

(Ezekiel 22: 12; Jeremiah 2: 32; Job 8: 13; Psalm 30: 4; Isaiah 8: 13; Isaiah 64: 5; James 5: 10; Lamentations 3: 19-24; Psalm 137: 1,5–6; Psalm 119: 81-83; Luke 2: 19; Matthew 26: 74–75; Isaiah 51: 12–13; Proverbs 3: 6 – all GNB; Luke 22: 19b, Barclay; Psalm 22: 27, GNB)

There is a religious crisis in the Western world today. It's not that people no longer believe in God. All the surveys show that the great majority still do. We believe in God, yet take our decisions as if he didn't exist!

Conscious acts of remembering God and what he tells us in the Bible foster ongoing spiritual development in three ways. First, they help us to believe. It is as we remember Jesus' incarnation, life, death, resurrection and ascension that he and these great events become the foundation on which we rest our hope.

Of course, faith is not a once only, initial experience. It is an ongoing commitment. And in order to grow, our faith requires nurturing with the spiritual food found in the Bible. Jesus reminds us that we need every word that

God speaks in order to live (Matthew 4: 4). He himself was able to live by faith in very difficult circumstances during his temptation and rebut the devil because he was able to quote the scriptures from memory.

Secondly, remembering God helps in our Christian discipleship. As disciples we are learners, called to a lifelong apprenticeship in the way of Christ. Our Christian discipleship will progress as we build up a memory bank through reading, listening to and meditating upon the Bible.

A Christian disciple is more akin to a craft apprentice than to a college student. Our learning experience is designed to be more practical than theoretical. We are called on to be 'doers of the word' (James 1: 22) — practitioners, not academics. But we can hardly be doers of words we cannot remember!

Thirdly, remembering who God is and what he says is vital to one's sense of Christian identity. Just as victims of amnesia have no conscious identity, so the absence of an active biblical memory inevitably means we can spend hours, days and weeks without any awareness that we are the people of God! Biblical memory informs us about who we are. Not only are we reminded about the fact that Jesus Christ died and rose again for us, but that *we* died and rose with him (Romans 6). A day-by-day conscious Christian identity is impossible without an active biblical memory!

Forgetfulness of God is an acid which corrodes religious vitality and inexorably saps our ability to resist the secularising processes all around us. On the other hand, remembrance of God matures faith, encourages discipleship and facilitates a Christian lifestyle in an age which increasingly demands that we take up our cross if we want to follow Jesus.

❧❧

Life without memory would be meaningless. Imagine the terror and confusion of having all your memories wiped out, from birth to the present. You would have no identity, no knowledge, no life history, no recognition of friends or family. Your past would be a total blank. In a very real sense we are our memories.

Denis Coon, *Introduction to Psychology*

Christians tramp well-worn paths; obedience has a history. This history is important, for without it we are at the mercy of whims. Memory is a data bank we use to evaluate our position and make decisions. With a biblical memory we have two thousand years of experience from which to make the off-the-cuff responses that are required each day in the life of faith. If we are going to live adequately and maturely as the people of God, we need more data to work from than our own experience can give us.

Eugene Peterson, *A Long Obedience in the Same Direction*

Christ Jesus, being both Saviour and Lord, supplies those who are guests at his table, not only with spiritual energy for their ongoing needs, but also with special guidance and strength to meet the historic situation in which their lot is cast.

John A. Mackay, *The Presbyterian Way of Life*

Partaking the death of Christ, Paul has come to share in his risen life. On the cross he owned his Saviour — owned his wound, his shame, his agony of death, and felt himself therein shamed, wounded, slain to death. Thus joined to his Redeemer, as by the nails that fastened him to the tree, Paul is carried with him down into the grave — into the grave, and out again! Christ is risen from the dead: so therefore is Paul.

G.G. Findlay, *The Expositor's Bible: Galatians*

I felt as though I had looked into his future and it was that of a man who died in the middle of his journey because he did not know just where he was going and had almost forgotten where he started from.

Ciro Alegria, *The Golden Serpent*

The only person too many Christians consult is themselves and the only experience they evaluate is the most recent ten minutes. But we need other experiences — the community of experience of brothers and sisters in the church, the centuries of experience provided by our biblical ancestors. A Christian who has David in his bones, Jeremiah in his bloodstream, Paul in his fingertips and Christ in his heart will know how much and how little [reliance] to put on his own momentary feelings and the experience of the past week.

Eugene Peterson, *A Long Obedience in the Same Direction*

Memory, in the biblical perspective, is more than simply the capacity of the mind to recall facts and information; it involves also understanding. In the conception of some people, human memory is rather like a computerised filing system; data from the past can be recalled at the console operator's command.

But such a computer has no *perception*, and *perception* is crucial to the biblical understanding of memory. For truly to remember is first to recall the facts, and second to understand them. . . Personal memory recalls not only the events of an individual's life, but also the reasons lying behind the successes and the failures. True memory is a branch of wisdom.

Peter C. Craigie, *The Daily Study Bible: Ezekiel*

God remembers his people; he pleads with them in their turn to remember him. When the Bible says God remembers his people, it does not think of a vague ineffective thought passing through his mind. It means that God *acts*. He puts out his hand to save them. Then later he asks them to remember what he has done. Not because he has a petulant and small-minded desire for their adulation, but because he is their Father, and loves them. He wishes them to love him and trust him; he knows that it will be their greatest joy and liberty if they do so. He wishes to bless them in the future, and he can only give them the fullness of his gifts if they are grateful. For God's people to forget him and his kindness is the great inhumanity, the cardinal sin.

David Cairns, *In Remembrance of Me*

A Christian with a defective memory has to start everything from scratch and spends far too much. . . time backtracking, repairing, starting over. A Christian with a good memory avoids repeating old sins, knows the easiest way through complex situations and, instead of starting over each day, continues what was begun in Adam.

Eugene Peterson, *A Long Obedience in the Same Direction*

While it is true that we humans change from century to century in many respects — those who lived before the discovery of the wheel were very different from those, like ourselves, who live in the space age — yet, beneath these surface differences lie certain characteristics which do not change from millennium to millennium — our need for love, for forgiveness, for happy community relations, for light on the basic problems of human existence and on life after death, and so on.

Donald Coggan, *Convictions*

Lord, we believe, we accept, we adore.
Less than the least though we be.
Fire of love, burn in us, burn evermore
Till we burn out for thee.

Amy Carmichael

Lord, forgive my forgetfulness of you. So often I allow the pressures of living to crowd you out! Help me to develop a biblical memory which your Holy Spirit can use to guide me day by day in the way of life everlasting. May I remember in order that I might render glory to your name! Amen.

A Benediction
Come and see what the Lord has done;
See what amazing things he has done on earth.
The Lord Almighty is with us;
the God of Jacob is our refuge.

4

The faithful God

Know therefore that the Lord your God is God; he is the faithful God, keeping his covenant of love to a thousand generations of those who love him and keep his commands.

For the word of the Lord is right and true; he is faithful in all he does.

I will sing of the love of the Lord forever; with my mouth I will make your faithfulness known through all generations.

The Lord is faithful to all his promises and loving towards all he has made.

For his compassions never fail. They are new every morning; great is your faithfulness. . .

I will betroth you to me forever. . . I will betroth you in faithfulness. . .

God is faithful; he will not let you be tempted beyond what you can bear.

The one who calls you is faithful.

The Lord is faithful, and he will strengthen and protect you from the evil one.

If we are faithless, he will remain faithful, for he cannot disown himself.

Jesus Christ. . . is the faithful witness.

(Deuteronomy 7: 9; Psalm 33: 4; Psalm 89: 1; Psalm 145: 13; Lamentations 3: 22b–23; Hosea 2: 19–20; 1 Corinthians 10: 13; 1 Thessalonians 5: 24; 2 Thessalonians 3: 3; 2 Timothy 2: 13; Revelation 1: 5 — all NIV)

If I had to name one quality of God that means more to me than any other, it would be his faithfulness.

In time of gloomy doubt or nagging unbelief, of plunging despair or bewildering confusion, I have found security in the knowledge that the faithfulness of God is deeper and more fundamental than all of these. In practical terms, it means that no matter what else had happened or is happening or is about to happen, God is there.

My favourite biblical statement about God's faithfulness is found in *Lamentations*. For two and a half chapters, the prophet pours out his griefs and disappointments to God. Unspeakable things have happened in his beloved Jerusalem (2: 20). People scoff and mock its inhabitants (2: 15).

He himself feels crushed and rejected. It is as if God has imprisoned him (3: 7), shut out his prayers (3: 9), mangled him (3: 11), used him for target practice (3: 12), filled him with bitterness (3: 15) and trampled him in the dust (3: 16).

But in the depths of his heaviness, one thought stands out like a flashing piece of opal in the secret womb of the earth: 'But this I call to mind and therefore I have hope. . . his compassions never fail. They are new every morning; great is your faithfulness' (3: 21-23).

This triumph of trust over tragedy has often been an inspiration to me. When I was nineteen, as the result of a motor cycle accident, I found myself hovering for several dark days, face to face with death. Less than ten years later, my wife and I became involved in a business arrangement that brought us to the brink of bankruptcy. On many other occasions, I have experienced the chilling disillusionment of being let down or criticised or misunderstood. In all these things, I have learned more and more to remind myself that God never changes: he is always faithful.

Another biblical writer who discovered the blessing of God's faithfulness was the Psalmist Ethan the Ezrahite. In a time of questioning, he found that the faithfulness of God was the only thing that made sense. Ethan's difficulty was that God seemed to have broken his promise that there would always be a descendant of David on Israel's throne. Although God had declared that David's line would endure forever — as eternal as the heavens, in fact, and as constant as the sun and the moon in the sky (Psalm 89: 29,36-37) — Israel's throne was overturned and the nation plundered.

'Where is your former great love,' Ethan demanded of God, 'which in your faithfulness you swore to David?' (Psalm 89: 49).

At this point, when you read the psalm, you expect an answer to this question, a justification on the part of God for the apparent breaking of his covenant. But suddenly the psalm ends. The last verse reads simply, 'Praise be to the Lord forever! Amen and Amen.' (89: 52).

Have we missed something? Surely the Lord vindicates his position? No. He does not. That is the only answer the psalm gives. And Ethan emphasises the point with a double affirmation. Amen and Amen. So be it. So be it. In other words, we don't understand how God's covenant can apparently be fractured like this, but we trust him anyway. So all we can do is praise the Lord!

Of course, we now know that God did not break his covenant. Through the Messiah, the anointed One, David's dynasty has been secured forever! (Luke 1: 32; Acts 2: 24ff). But Ethan did not know that — he had to trust the Lord anyway.

It is easy to trust God when things are going well. But to trust him when everything has crumbled around us — ah! that is a different proposition! The truth is, however, that only then do we really trust him.

God cannot deny himself. He is truly faithful. And I don't know anything about God that means more to me than that.

❧

Great is thy faithfulness!
Great is thy faithfulness!
Morning by morning new mercies I see;
All I have needed thy hand hath provided —
Great is thy faithfulness, Lord, unto me.

Thomas Chisholm

'And now,' said Gandalf, turning back to Frodo, 'the decision lies with you. But I will always help you.' He laid his hand on Frodo's shoulder. 'I will help you bear this burden, as long as it is yours to bear.'

J.R.R. Tolkien, Lord of the Rings

What God has promised, it is his will to perform. If you have a promise of God, then you have the will of God, and to know God's will is to know that you have the petition you desire of him.

Leo Harris, God Heals Today

John Wesley, who had helped so many to overcome fear of death, lay happily awaiting his departure. . . By March 1 he was sinking, yet that morning he surprised them by starting to sing a hymn. A little later he asked for a pen and ink but his fingers would not respond.

'Let me write for you, sir,' said Elizabeth Ritchie. 'Tell me what you would say.'

'Nothing — but that God is with us.'

By Wednesday morning, March 2, 1791, the end was plainly near. . . Once Wesley cried out in a remarkably strong voice: 'The best of all is, God is with us!'

John Pollock, John Wesley

Trust in God alone, and lean not on the needs of human help. Be not surprised when friends fail you: it is a failing world. Never count on immutability in others: inconstancy you may reckon on without fear of disappointment. . .

Any simpleton can follow the narrow path in the light: faith's rare wisdom enables us to march on in the dark with infallible accuracy, since she places her hand in that of her Great Guide.

Charles Spurgeon, Lectures to My Students

All will be well, and all will be well, and all manner of things will be well.

Julian of Norwich

All good belongs
to the Lord who is God Most High and supreme.
Every good is his.
So let us thank him
from whom all good things come.

Francis of Assisi

The Witch was just turning away with a look of fierce joy
on her face when she stopped and said, 'But how do I
know this promise will be kept?'

'Haa-a-arrh!' roared Aslan, half rising from his throne;
and his great mouth opened wider and wider and the roar
grew louder and louder, and the Witch, after staring for
a moment with her lips wide apart, picked up her skirts
and fairly ran for her life.

C.S. Lewis, *The Lion, the Witch and the Wardrobe*

Now a little before it was day, Good Christian, as one half
amazed, broke out in this passionate speech: 'What a
fool,' quoth he, 'am I, thus to lie in a stinking dungeon,
when I may as well walk at liberty! I have a key in my
bosom called Promise; that will, I am persuaded, open any
lock in Doubting Castle.'

Then Christian pulled it out of his bosom, and began
to try at the dungeon door; whose bolt. . . gave back, and
the door flew open with ease: and Christian and Hopeful
both came out.

John Bunyan, *The Pilgrim's Progress*

The Fourth Man had come to help Shadrach, Meshach and
Abednego in the urgency of their need. He had subdued
the crackling flames, robbed the fire of its sting, torn off
the bonds of his servants, lifted them up and, while the
old king watched, he was walking arm-in-arm with the
three Hebrew children right in the middle of the flames.

Oral Roberts, *The Fourth Man*

And it is of no slight importance for you to be cleansed
of your blind love of self that you may be made more
nearly aware of your incapacity; to feel your own in-

capacity that you may learn to distrust yourself; to distrust yourself that you may transfer your trust to God; to rest with a trustful heart in God that, relying upon his help, you may persevere unconquered to the end; to take your stand in his grace that you may comprehend the truth of his promises; to have unquestioned certainty of his promises that your hope may thereby be strengthened.

John Calvin, *Institutes of the Christian Religion*

'Not at all,' answered Redgum. 'God's love and faithfulness are never a reward for the good we do. We would receive precious little of his love if that were the case.'

'I guess you're right,' said Spindles quietly.

'God's love is always given to us freely,' Redgum went on. 'So whether we do good or bad, he loves us. That's why I told you that he is always faithful, no matter where we are. For he did not choose you because you are particularly good — but just because he loves you.'

Barry Chant, *Spindles and the Children*

Oh, trust in this unchangeable God!

Thomas Watson, *A Body of Divinity*

Lord, I want your heart to be in my heart. For in you I come alive, moving ahead from boring death to exciting life!

In your promises, I will move from discouragement to hope.
In your pardon, I will move from shame to glory.
In your power, I will move from weakness to strength.
In your providence, I will move from failure to success!
Thank you, Lord. Amen.

Robert H. Schuller, *Success is Never Ending;*
Failure is Never Final

Heavenly Father,
Thank you for your faithfulness.
In a changing world,
it is encouraging to know
that you are changeless;

In a fickle society,
  it is reassuring to believe
  that you can be trusted;

In a crumbling community,
  it is comforting to remember
  that you are always near;

In a despairing age,
  it is exciting to recall
  that you give hope for the future;

In my sin-scarred life,
  it is liberating to understand
  that, through Jesus,
  you have dealt once and for all with my sin,
  and made me clean — totally;

In my human weakness,
  it is stimulating to know
  that I am God's workmanship,
  and that I can do all good things through Christ,
  who died for me,
  and rose again,
  and now dwells within me
  by his Spirit!

For all this,
  I thank you, Lord,
  for you are truly faithful.

Amen.

A Benediction
*Draw near to God with a true heart in full assurance of faith,
knowing this: that he who promised is faithful.*

(Hebrews 10: 22 – 23)

On loving God

God is love, and whoever lives in love lives in union
with God and God lives in union with him.

We are ruled by the love of Christ, now that we
recognise that one man died for everyone, which means
that all share in his death. He died for all, so that those
who live should no longer live for themselves, but only
for him. . .

If you love me, you will obey my commandments.

Love the Lord, all his faithful people. What else have
I in heaven but you? Since I have you, what else could
I want on earth? As a deer longs for a stream of cool
water, so I long for you, O God. I thirst for you, the
living God.

You love him, although you have not seen him, and
you believe in him, although you do not now see him.
So you rejoice with a great and glorious joy which words
cannot express.

May the Lord lead you into a greater understanding
of God's love and the endurance that is given by Christ.

(1 John 4: 16b; 2 Corinthians 5: 14-15; John 14: 15; Psalm 31: 23;
Psalm 73: 25; Psalm 42: 1-2a; 1 Peter 1: 8; 2 Thessalonians 3: 5
— all GNB)

Evangelical Christianity invites people to 'accept Christ' (a
term, incidentally, not found in the Bible) but needs more
urgently to encourage them to love Christ. We are ushered
onto church committees, given church jobs, and are rarely
asked 'How are you and God?' The great commandment
is still to love the Lord your God with all your heart,
mind, soul and strength. . . Rather than seeking religion

— even the Christian religion — we should be seeking God.

Believing in God is good, but the devils also believe, and tremble. Being acquainted with God is good, but you can be acquainted with someone without really loving them. When a little girl said, 'God's my best friend!', she was uttering something that is at the heart of true spirituality.

Brother Lawrence was a lame, clumsy man who went to a monastery to atone somehow for his disabilities. He was put to work washing floors and kitchen pots and pans. In the midst of all this he 'practised the presence of God'. When he was dying, his friends asked what he was thinking about. He replied, 'I am doing what I shall do through all eternity — blessing God, praising God, adoring God, giving him the love of my whole heart.'

The Bible suggests about seven tests to measure our love for God.

First, we love God by loving other people. As an old saint put it: you love God just as much as, and no more than you love the person you love least. Second, Jesus said, you prove your love for him by obeying him. Third, if you love someone you'll want to linger in their company. Sheila Cassidy in her *Prayer for Pilgrims* says real prayer is not just *spending* time with God, but *wasting* time with him. And real prayer is listening more than talking.

Fourth, our words are an index of our loves: out of the fullness of our hearts we speak. Fifth, to love someone who's absent is to keenly anticipate their return. Sixth, there's the test of idolatry. An idol is whatever you worship, whatever you've committed your life to achieving, whatever you get excited about, whatever turns you on.

Finally, there's the ultimate test — martyrdom. What are you prepared to die for? Jesus said you can't have any greater love than being willing to die for someone. The martyrs in the Apocalypse did not cherish their own lives even in the face of death (Revelation 12: 11).

Charity, says the anonymous author of *The Cloud of Unknowing*, 'is nought else but love of God for himself above all creatures'.

I love you, Lord
  not doubtingly
  but with absolute certainty.
Your Word beat upon my heart
until I fell in love with you
and now the universe
  and everything in it
tells me to love you. . .

Augustine of Hippo

A century ago, a hymn by John Newton was often sung
in the churches, the first stanza of which ran like this:

> 'Tis a point I long to know,
>   Oft it causes anxious thought:
> Do I love the Lord, or no?
>   Am I his, or am I not?

The gravest question any of us face is whether we do or
do not love the Lord. . . Our Lord told his disciples that
love and obedience were organically united, that the keeping of his sayings would prove that we loved him, and
the failure or refusal to keep them would prove that we
did not. This is the true test of love. . . Not sweet
emotions, not willingness to sacrifice, not zeal, but
obedience to the commandments of Christ. Love for
Christ is a love of willing as well as a love of feeling. . .
  If we would turn from fine-spun theological speculations
about grace and faith, and humbly read the New Testament with a mind to obey what we see there, we would
easily find ourselves, and know for certain the answer to
the question that troubled our fathers and should trouble
us: Do we love the Lord or no?

A. W. Tozer, 'Love's Final Test'

Perceiving, as [others] have not perceived, the burning
love of God, the saint gives God love for love. He cannot
help it. Certainly, it is not the fruit of labour. Having
seen the love of God, his own love leaps in response. His
heart is drawn out of him and lost in God's immensity.

No mortal can love as God loves, but the saint loves with all that there is of him. . . It is by love that the saint becomes free — free of that awful self-centredness which is the mark of most mortals. . . It is by love that we come to freedom, and there is no other way.

W.E. Sangster, *The Pure in Heart*

He had always been governed by love, without selfish views; and having resolved to make the love of God the *end* of all his actions, he had found reasons to be well satisfied with his method. He was pleased when he could take up a straw from the ground for the love of God, seeking him only, and nothing else, not even his gifts. . .

'I did not engage in a religious life but for the love of God, and I have endeavoured to act only for him; whatever becomes of me, whether I be lost or saved, I will always continue to act purely for the love of God. I shall have this good at least, that till death I shall have done all that is in me to love him.'

Brother Lawrence, *The Practice of the Presence of God*

O God, I love thee, I love thee —
Not out of hope of heaven for me
Not fearing not to love and be
In the everlasting burning.
Thou, thou, my Jesus, after me
Didst reach thine arms out dying,
For my sake sufferedst nails and lance,
Mocked and marred countenance,
Sorrows passing number,
Sweat and care and cumber,
Yea and death, and this for me.

And thou couldst see me sinning:
Then I, why should not I love thee,
Jesus, so much in love with me?
Not for heaven's sake; not to be
Out of hell by loving thee;
Not for any gains I see;
But just the way that thou didst love me

I do love and I will love thee:
What must I love thee, Lord, for then?
For being my king and God. Amen.

Gerard Manley Hopkins

[A fearful person said, 'I fear lest I should be cast into hell.' Another anxious person said, 'I dread lest I should be deprived of the joy of heaven. . .'] A third was very happy and contented. [He was asked] 'What is the secret of your joy and peace?' He said, 'My constant prayer to God is that he may grant me to love him with heart and soul, and I may serve and worship him by love alone. Should I worship him from fear of hell, may I be cast into it. Should I serve him from desire of gaining heaven, may he keep me out. But should I worship him from love alone, may he reveal himself to me, that my whole heart may be filled with his love and presence.'

Sadhu Sundar Singh, *The Spiritual Life*

'. . .When thoughts come, welcome them; and when they do not flow freely, simply rest back and love, and grant me the shared joy of being loved by you. For I, too, by my very nature, am hungry with an insatiable hunger for the love of all of you, just as your love reaches out at your highest moments to all the people about you.

'So child, I, even I, God, whom people have foolishly feared and flattered for my gifts, I want love and friendship more than I want grovelling subjects. So while we love each other, child, my share is as keen as yours.'

Frank Laubach, *Letters by a Modern Mystic*

Thou knowest not what, saving that thou feelest in thy will a naked intent unto God. . . this darkness and this cloud. . . hindereth thee, so that thou mayest neither see him clearly by light of understanding in thy reason, nor feel him in sweetness of love in thy affection. And therefore shape thee to bide in this darkness as long as thou mayest, evermore crying after him whom thou lovest. For if ever thou shalt see him or feel him as it may be here, it must always be in this cloud and in this darkness. . .

Smite upon that thick cloud of unknowing with a sharp
dart of longing love.

The Cloud of Unknowing

When the next step comes, you do not take the step, you
do not know the transition, you do not fall into anything.
You do not go anywhere, and so you do not know the
way by which you got there or the way by which you
come back afterward. You are certainly not lost. You do
not fly. There is no space, or there is all space: it makes
no difference.

The next step is not a step. . . And here all adjectives
fall to pieces. Words become stupid. Everything you say
is misleading — unless you list every possible experience
and say: 'That is not what it is', 'That is not what I am
talking about.'

What it is, is freedom. It is perfect love. It is pure
renunciation. It is the fruition of God. . . It is freedom
living and circulating in God, who is Freedom. It is love
loving in Love. It is the purity of God rejoicing in his
own liberty.

Thomas Merton, *New Seeds of Contemplation*

To the few who are converted, goodness is pleasant and
needs no sanctions. It needs no authority, for it has been
verified by experience. But when people have to be coerced
into goodness, it is plain that they do not care for it.

Walter Lippmann, *A Preface to Morals*

'Marvellously close, God, help me to keep thinking of you
all day today, as love crowding gently as the ether, warm
as the sunlight, into every nook and cranny of my
thoughts, words, looks, acts — love pressing in, and
oozing out, floating like perfume out to others.

> O Love that wilt not let me go,
> I rest my weary soul in thee;
> I give thee back the life I owe,
> That in thine ocean depths its flow
> May richer, fuller be.

'My child, this makes me happy. Now let love flow out to my world of needy people all about you. Despise not one of the least. Do not see colour or clothes, just souls and my children. Do not hear titles or languages, just hear me speak through them. I call from behind every eye, I float upon every wave of speech and song and sigh. See me in people, for I seek to make them grow in Christlike love.'

Frank Laubach, *Learning the Vocabulary of God*

In Graham Greene's novel, *The Heart of the Matter*, Scobie is torn between love for his wife and his mistress, and decides to commit suicide. Sitting in his car, he holds a very moving conversation with God, acknowledging that he is guilty before God and that he can no longer face the altar. 'You'll be better off when you lose me once and for all. You'll be at peace when I'm out of your reach,' he tells God.

God replies. . . 'You say you love me, yet you'll do this to me — rob me of you for ever. I made you with love. I've wept your tears. . . and now you push me away, put me out of your reach. I am as humble as any other beggar. Can't you trust me as you'd trust a faithful dog? I've been faithful to you for 2000 years. . . Can't you trust me to see that the suffering isn't too great?'

Ivor Bailey, *Live and Let Love*

I no longer want to build empires,
to ascend thrones,
or to be number one in my little kingdom.
I want to love you,
and to respond to your love for me
by communicating such love to others.
This is what I want, O Lord,
but you know my soft spots, my hang-ups.
May the victory be yours today, O Lord.
In Jesus' name. Amen.

Leslie F. Brandt, *A Book of Christian Prayer*

I arise today
Through God's strength to pilot me:
God's might to uphold me,
God's wisdom to guide me,
God's eye to look before me,
God's ear to hear me,
God's word to speak for me,
God's hand to guard me. . .

Christ with me, Christ before me, Christ behind me,
Christ in me, Christ beneath me, Christ above me,
Christ on my right, Christ on my left,
Christ when I lie down, Christ when I sit down,
Christ when I arise.
Christ in the heart of every one who thinks of me,
Christ in the mouth of every one who speaks of me,
Christ in every eye that sees me,
Christ in every ear that hears me.

I arise today
Through a mighty strength, the invocation of the Trinity.

St Patrick

Lord, I am your child. In some mysterious sense, my Father, you are hungry for my love. Your love is mediated through words and the Word, through sunsets and rain and the whispering trees, soft shadows on the water. I was created for friendship with you, my Creator. I was redeemed for friendship with you, my Saviour. I am cared for for friendship with you, my ever-present Friend. Lord, it's not a self-improvement course I want, but you.

> *We taste thee, O thou living Bread,*
> *And long to feast upon thee still.*
> *We drink of thee the fountainhead,*
> *And thirst our souls from thee to fill.*

I have tasted a little of your goodness, Lord, and it has both satisfied me and made me hunger for more. My desire is to desire you more. Give me a gift of love — for you and for

*others.   And to journey towards the final self-forgetfulness —
to revel in your love forever.*

A Benediction
*Keep yourselves in the love of God, as you wait for our Lord
Jesus Christ in his mercy to give you eternal life.   May God's
grace be with all those who love our Lord Jesus Christ with
undying love.*

Praise. . . the business of eternity

Ascribe to the Lord, O mighty ones,
   ascribe to the Lord glory and strength.
Ascribe to the Lord the glory due to his name;
   worship the Lord in the splendour of his holiness.

I will always thank the Lord; I will never stop praising
him. I will praise him for what he has done; may all
who are oppressed listen and be glad! Proclaim with
me the Lord's greatness; let us praise his name together!

I will praise you forever for what you have done; in
your name I will hope, for your name is good. I will
praise you in the presence of your saints.

I will praise you, O Lord, with all my heart; I will
tell of all your wonders.

Then I heard every creature in heaven and on earth
and under the earth and on the sea, and all that is in
them, singing: 'To him who sits on the throne and to
the Lamb be praise and honour and glory and power,
for ever and ever!'

Then a voice came from the throne, saying: 'Praise our
God, all you his servants, you who fear him, both small
and great!' Then I heard what sounded like a great multitude, like the roar of rushing waters and like loud peals of
thunder, shouting: 'Hallelujah! For our Lord God Almighty
reigns. Let us rejoice and be glad and give him glory!'

All the angels were standing around the throne and
around the elders and the four living creatures. They
fell down on their faces before the throne and worshipped God, saying: 'Amen! Praise and glory and
wisdom and thanks and honour and power and strength
be to our God for ever and ever. Amen!'

(Psalm 29: 1-2, NIV; Psalm 34: 1-3, GNB; Psalm 52: 9; Psalm 9: 1; Revelation 5: 13; Revelation 19: 5-7a; Revelation 7: 11-12 — all NIV)

Praise is the business of eternity. Extravagant, demonstrative, passionate praise! Heaven is filled with the noise of our God's praises!

But the earth is strangely quiet. The angels continuously declare Jesus' glory. King David boldly declared the works of God in the midst of God's people. But the church has substituted silence for praise. Worship is sometimes more like a funeral than a festivity.

What is praise? Some ill-timed shout of 'Hallelujah'? Emotions running out of control? The mindless repetition of some catch-phrase like 'Praise the Lord'?

Biblical praise is both vocal and public in nature. It involves the affirmation of who God is as well as what he has done. Silently I may thank God for the specific things he has done in my life this week, but only as I verbalise that to another person can it be said that God has truly been praised.

The church gathered together needs to become a place of celebrating our God's wonder: a word of testimony to answered prayer; an expression of gratitude for the Lord's healing of a loved one; a declaration of God's wisdom, holiness, compassion, grace, love.

Away with trite, routine worship services! Away with songs and prayers that are more human-centred than exaltations of our great God and Redeemer! Let God's people gather in worship that is a joyful adoration of the work and worth of our marvelous God!

❧❦❧

We live in a society where the value of almost everything seems to be estimated in terms of what it is good for. Nothing appears to deserve esteem simply for its own sake; nothing seems to have intrinsic value; and, for many of us, the world can be divided between the useful and the useless. In such a world, those who want to get ahead choose their friends, their goods and their activities on the basis of what these can do for them. Under such circumstances, much of mutuality is simply a kind of shared selfishness; and in such a world, much of religious behaviour can be understood as getting what one can out of God. It is scarce wonder, no wonder at all, that in a society dedicated to consumerism, people ask, 'What can I get out of worship?' As if getting something out of everything expresses an appropriate response to life! The question of worship, when so stated, does not take God seriously. It does not ponder the true worth of God, for to treat God as if God were a means to our ends is to imagine that we ourselves are gods. God is not humanity's servant.

John E. Burkhart, *Worship*

Getting ready early enough on Saturday to arrive on time on Sunday, coming in a *spirit* of praise that springs from a *life* of praise and devotion, and coming with a willingness to pour out your *energy* in praise are all issues that demand something of you. You dare not come unprepared to spill yourself in the work of praise. You simply owe God a tithe of your emotions, your tears, your joy and your intellectual commitment. To save something of yourself for God on Sunday is a volitional act that Satan will labour long and hard to subvert.

James R. Spruce, *Come, Let Us Worship*

We should never forget that God created us to be joyful worshippers, but sin drew us into everything else but worship. Then in God's love and mercy in Christ Jesus, we were restored into the fellowship of the Godhead through the miracle of the new birth.

'You have been forgiven and restored,' God reminds us. 'I am your Creator and Redeemer and Lord, and I delight in your worship.'

I don't know, my friend, how that makes you feel — but I feel that I must give God the full response of my heart. I am happy to be counted as a worshipper.

A.W. Tozer, *Whatever Happened to Worship?*

We may say, 'If only the place of worship were more beautiful, comfortable, with (or without) visual symbolism — *then* we could truly worship.' We may say, 'If there were only more awe, more reverence, more sense of the mystery of God,' or 'If only people were more relational, and possessed a real sense of warmth and community'. . . The real factor in worship is a heart desire for God; the reason it fails to occur in the pew is because it fails to occur in the daily routine of living.

Ronald Allen and Gordon Borror, *Worship: Rediscovering the Missing Jewel*

The bridegroom does not merely give the ring itself to the bride; it is a sign and token of his loyal-love and commitment. In genuine worship, psalms and hymns, prayers and gifts are the signs and tokens of self-oblation. No-one has truly worshipped unless we have given ourselves in work and service, for the Christian liturgy does not end with the benediction. In order that it may be made in life as a whole, it should be made in the context of worship.

Stephen Winward, *Reformation of Our Worship*

Praise is at once the most powerful tonic for a tired soul and the greatest therapy for a heavy spirit. Praise is the church's secret weapon against which the enemy has no defence and before which his ranks fall into confusion and disarray. Praise douses doubts and waters faith at the same time.

Jack Taylor, *The Hallelujah Factor*

The church is the church in her worship. Worship is not an optional extra, but is of the very life and essence of the church. Nor is it a false grovelling in the dust of the religiously minded. We are never more truly human than when we worship God. We rise to all the heights of human dignity when we worship God, and all God's purposes in creation and redemption are fulfilled in us as together in worship we are renewed in and through Christ, and in the name of Christ we glorify God. So by the grace of God we seek to voice for all creatures the praises

of God and realise our God-given destiny to be the priests
of creation under Christ our great High Priest.

James B. Torrence

To worship is to quicken the conscience by the holiness
of God, to feed the mind with the truth of God, to purge
the imagination by the beauty of God, to open the heart
to the love of God, to devote the will to the purpose of
God.

William Temple

There are not three stages in spiritual life — worship,
waiting and work. Some of us go in jumps like spiritual
frogs — we jump from worship to waiting, and from
waiting to work. God's idea is that the three should go
together. They were always together in the life of our
Lord. He was unhasting and unresting. It is a discipline;
we cannot get into it all at once.

Oswald Chambers, *My Utmost for His Highest*

It seems the Christian worshipper has a responsibility to
be selective. We must insist that everything in a given
week prepare us for the great event on Sunday morning,
including the use of time, the way we spend our money,
and, perhaps most importantly, the expenditure of our
priceless emotional energy. If praise is to be worthy, the
sacrifice will be costly. And the greatest sacrifice may be
in what is *not* given indiscriminately, but is reserved only
for the honour of God.

James R. Spruce, *Come, Let Us Worship*

---

*Father, we acknowledge you alone as God: supreme in your
authority, limitless in your power, unswerving in your faithfulness, blazing in your glory, unending in your mercy, dazzling
in your beauty, unfathomable in your love.*

*We confess that we have not praised you as we should have,
for truly you are worthy. Enlarge our hearts and teach us to
be better worshippers. Help us, Lord! Set our spirits free to
adore you richly, to be a sweet, joyful sound in your ear. Fill*

our hearts and mouths with praise and worship every day, O God. Make our lives bastions of your glorious praise. Amen.

A Benediction
Now may the Lord God Almighty, who alone is worthy of all adoration, so fill your actions, your words and your attitudes that in all things at all times your life will be to the praise of his glory.

In his presence

You have made known to me the path of life; you will fill me with joy in your presence, with eternal pleasures at your right hand.

Let us come into his presence with thanksgiving! Let us make a joyful noise to him with songs of praise!

Blessed are those who have learned to acclaim you, who walk in the light of your presence, O Lord.

You have set our iniquities before you, our secret sins in the light of your presence.

Create in me a pure heart, O God, and renew a steadfast spirit within me. Do not cast me from your presence or take your Holy Spirit from me. Restore to me the joy of your salvation and grant me a willing spirit, to sustain me.

Let us not love with words or tongue but with actions and in truth. This then is how we know that we belong to the truth, and how we set our hearts at rest in his presence.

In the shelter of your presence you hide them from the intrigues of men; in your dwelling you keep them safe from the strife of tongues.

The Lord replied, 'My presence will go with you, and I will give you rest.' Then Moses said to him, 'If your presence does not go with us, do not send us up from here. How will anyone know that you are pleased with me and with your people unless you go with us? What else will distinguish me and your people from all the other people on the face of the earth?'

Where can I go from your Spirit? Where can I flee from your presence? If I go up to the heavens, you are there; if I make my bed in the depths, you are there. If

I rise on the wings of the dawn, if I settle on the far side of the sea, even there your hand will guide me, your right hand will hold me fast.

We know that the one who raised the Lord Jesus from the dead will also raise us with Jesus and bring us with you in his presence.

(Psalm 16: 11, NIV; Psalm 95: 2, RSV; Psalm 89: 15; Psalm 90: 8; Psalm 51: 10-12; 1 John 3: 18-19; Psalm 31: 20; Exodus 33: 14-16; Psalm 139: 7-10; 2 Corinthians 4: 14 — all NIV)

On a green hillside on the outskirts of a provincial Australian city sits the small headstone of a recently dug grave. It is a reminder of the life — and now death — of my father. It bears the text: 'In thy presence is fullness of joy' (Psalm 16: 11). It says to whoever might pause to read it that the burial of the bodily remains of an elderly man was not the end of life and happiness for him; it was rather the beginning of a new phase of happiness for him — of life and joy in the presence of the Lord he loved and served.

I cannot do more than begin to ponder what that means for him. Perhaps he is experiencing something like Isaiah did in the presence of the Lord: 'Holy, holy, holy is the Lord Almighty' (Isaiah 6: 3). Maybe he is part of an adoring and praising throng affirming 'to him who sits on the throne and to the Lamb be praise and honour and glory and power, for ever and ever' (Revelation 5: 13). But even the most biblical of imaginings leads me to a mystery that will not be explained or understood until my time comes to join him beyond the grave.

That simple yet profound text also speaks to those of us who knew my dad in his earthly life. It provides the key to the joyful and contented spirit which was obvious to all who crossed his path. He was a man who knew something of what it meant to live in the presence of God.

And none of us has to wait until eternity to experience that dimension of life!

We can experience the presence of God in worship and thanksgiving, as we turn our eyes and hearts to the Creator and Redeemer who reveals himself in his majesty and love. We can open our lives to the scrutiny of his holiness and light and receive his forgiveness and cleansing. We can be motivated by his truth, be protected and guided by his faithful care. We are never beyond the reach of his presence in this life, and can anticipate the certainty of its richer joys in the next.

'In his presence' — this way of living is both a choice and a discipline. In our busy and complex world, neither is easy. The clutter of people, objects and tasks can push the awareness of God's presence to the perimeter rather than the core of our beings, unless we choose to find time and effort for worship and reflection. Even then, we might be fooled into contemplating a mirage of our own making rather than being in touch with the living God. And we wonder why the cleansing, empowering, guidance and joy of his presence are not evident in our lives!

Brother Lawrence, the famous exponent of 'the practice of the presence of God', said: 'I cannot imagine how religious persons can live satisfied without the practice of the presence of God.' If in this area of life alone I were able to follow in the steps of my beloved father, I would have set a most worthy goal.

❧❧

Being in the dazzling presence of God is a wondrous experience; realising God's majestic, just and compassionate action in the world and in our lives urges us to let all thanks break loose!

We come so often to God, if we come at all, as beggars. We ask and beg: give me; bless me; help me; guide me; grant me. And that's one necessary level of our existence.

But in thanksgiving and adoration we come to God not to ask but to give! We come not whimpering but shouting praise; not in guilt but in gratitude. We feel not distant from God but close to God. We are like a traveller who is home again at last, the prodigal at a banquet. Those moments may be seldom, but when they happen we know that we were created *for God*.

Don Postema, *Space for God*

In the act of worship, God communicates his presence to his people.

Oswald Sanders, *Enjoying Intimacy with God*

What is worship? Worship is to feel in your heart and express in some appropriate manner a humbling but delightful sense of admiring awe and astonished wonder and overpowering love in the presence of that most ancient Mystery, that Majesty which philosophers call the First Cause, but which we call Our Father Which Art in Heaven.

A.W. Tozer, *Knowledge of the Holy*

A striking feature of worship in the Bible is that people gathered in what we could call only a 'holy expectancy'. They believed they would actually hear the *Kol Yahweh*, the voice of God. When Moses went into the Tabernacle he knew he was entering the presence of God. The same was true of the early church. It was not surprising to them that the building in which they met shook with the power of God. It had happened before (Acts 2: 2; 4: 31). When some dropped dead and others were raised from the dead by the word of the Lord, the people knew that God was in their midst (Acts 5: 1-11; 9: 36-43, 20: 7-10).

As those early believers gathered, they were keenly aware that the veil had been ripped in two and, like Moses and Aaron, they were entering the Holy of Holies. No intermediaries were needed. They were coming into the awful, glorious, gracious presence of the living God. They gathered with anticipation, knowing that Christ was present among them and would teach them and touch them with his living power.

How do we cultivate this holy expectancy? It begins in us as we enter the *Shekinah* of the heart. While living out the demands of our day we are filled with inward worship and adoration. We work and play and eat and sleep, yet we are listening, ever listening, to our Teacher.

Richard Foster, *The Celebration of Discipline*

As Brother Lawrence had found such an advantage in walking in the presence of God, it is natural for him to recommend it earnestly to others; but his example was a stronger inducement than any arguments he could propose. His very countenance was edifying; such a sweet and calm devotion appearing in it as could not but affect the beholders. And it was observed that, in the greatest hurry of business in the kitchen, he still preserved his recollection and heavenly-mindedness. He was never hasty nor loitering, but did each thing in its season, with an even uninterrupted composure and tranquillity of spirit.

'The time of business,' said he, 'does not with me differ from the time of prayer; and in the noise and clutter of my kitchen, while several persons are at the same time calling for different things, I possess God in as great tranquillity as if I were upon my knees at the Blessed Sacrament.'

Brother Lawrence, The Practice of the Presence of God

Worship the Lord in the beauty of holiness,
bow down before him, his glory proclaim;
gold of obedience and incense of lowliness
bring, and adore him: the Lord is his name.

Low at his feet lay thy burden of carefulness,
high on his heart he will bear it for thee,
comfort thy sorrows, and answer thy prayerfulness,
guiding thy steps as may best for thee be.

John Samuel Bewley Monsell

The beginning of the spiritual life is often difficult not only because the powers which cause us to worry are so strong, but also because the presence of God's Spirit seems barely noticeable. If, however, we are faithful to our disciplines, a new hunger will make itself known. This new hunger is the first sign of God's presence. When we remain attentive to this divine presence, we will be led always deeper into the kingdom. There, to our joyful surprise, we will discover that all things are being made new.

Henry J.M. Nouwen, Making All Things New

Of all today's miracles the greatest is this: to know that I find thee best when I work listening. . . Thank thee, too, that the habit of constant conversation grows easier each day. I really do believe *all* thought can be conversations with thee.

Frank Laubach, *Learning the Vocabulary of God*

The world really doesn't need more busy people, maybe not even more intelligent people. It needs 'deep people', people who know that they need:
   solitude, if they are going to find out who they are;
   silence, if their words are to mean anything;
   reflection, if their actions are to have any significance;
   contemplation, if they are to see the world as it really is;
   prayer, if they are going to be conscious of God, if they
      are to 'know God and enjoy God forever'.

Don Postema, *Space for God*

Jesus, the very thought of thee
with sweetness fills my breast,
but sweeter far thy face to see
and in thy presence rest.

Jesus, our only joy be thou,
as thou our prize wilt be;
in thee be all our glory now
and through eternity.

Bernard of Clairvaux

Christians often say that the most wonderful thing of all will be to see our Lord face to face. I have pondered that much and feel it is surely worded inadequately. To see the Lord is but a lesser thing to one who has had a close spirit-with-Spirit communion with him all along. What matter the colour of his eyes or the shape of his face? That is not what makes him precious. Nothing is so deeply intimate as spirit knit with Spirit, and that we can and should enjoy right now while here on earth.

   I think what is meant is to be with the Lord *with the root of sin gone*. To fellowship with him without the lazy flesh dragging us back, or unwanted thoughts of pride and self constantly staining us. To be finally rid of corruption, to worship and enjoy him with heart purged into his own purity, *that* will be an advance over anything that is possible on earth.

Isobel Kuhn, *In the Arena*

Love divine, all loves excelling,
joy of heaven, to earth come down,
fix in us thy humble dwelling,
all thy faithful mercies crown:
thee we would be always blessing,
serve thee as thy hosts above,
pray, and praise thee, without ceasing,
glory in thy perfect love.

Finish then thy new creation,
pure and spotless let us be,
let us see thy great salvation,
perfectly restored in thee:
changed from glory into glory,
till in heaven we take our place,
till we cast our crowns before thee,
lost in wonder, love and praise.

Charles Wesley

Father God, our creator and sustainer, we do not understand the mystery of your holy and loving presence, but we know that it is a place of joy.

Jesus Christ, our redeemer and friend, we look forward to kneeling in your presence to acknowledge you King of Kings and Lord of Lords.

Holy Spirit, our teacher and guide, we acknowledge that your constant presence with us enlightens and empowers us to walk in your ways.

Triune God, help us, day by day and moment by moment, to make the conscious choice to live in the awareness of your presence, that we may worthily reflect you to others, so that they, too, may be drawn to you, in whose presence alone is fullness of joy. Amen.

A Benediction
May he strengthen your hearts so that you will be blameless and holy in the presence of our God and Father when our Lord Jesus comes with all his holy ones. And now to him who is able to keep you from falling and to present you before his glorious presence without fault and with great joy — to the only God our Saviour be glory, majesty, power and authority, through Jesus Christ our Lord, before all ages, now and for evermore! Amen.

1 Thessalonians 3: 13, Jude 24-25

8

Choosing the better part

Listen, Israel, Yahweh our God is the one Yahweh. You shall love Yahweh your God with all your heart, with all your soul, with all your strength.

One of the Pharisees invited [Jesus] to a meal. When he arrived at the Pharisee's house and took his place at the table, a woman came in who had a bad name in the town. She had heard he was dining with the Pharisee and had brought with her an alabaster jar of ointment. She waited behind him at his feet, weeping, and her tears fell on his feet, and she wiped them away with her hair; then she covered his feet with kisses and anointed them with the ointment.

When the Pharisee who had invited him saw this, he said to himself, 'If this man were a prophet, he would know who this woman is that is touching him and what a bad name she has.' Then Jesus took him up and said, 'Simon, I have something to say to you.' 'Speak, Master,' was the reply. 'There was once a creditor who had two men in his debt; one owed him five hundred denarii, the other fifty. They were unable to pay, so he pardoned them both. Which of them will love him more?' 'The one who was pardoned more, I suppose,' answered Simon. Jesus said, 'You are right.'

In the course of their journey he came to a village, and a woman named Martha welcomed him into her house. She had a sister called Mary, who sat down at the Lord's feet and listened to him speaking. Now Martha who was distracted with all the serving said, 'Lord, do you not care that my sister is leaving me to do the serving all by myself? Please tell her to help me.' But the Lord answered: 'Martha, Martha,' he said, 'you worry and fret about so many things, and yet few are needed, indeed only one. It is Mary who has chosen the better part; it is not to be taken from her.'

(Deuteronomy 6: 4-5; Luke 7: 36-43; Luke 10: 38-42 — all JB)

I have always felt a sneaking sympathy for some of the people involved in situations which wound up getting reported in the Gospel stories. Particularly dangerous, it seems, was to have Jesus around for a dinner party. Simon the Pharisee did. His party was gate-crashed by the woman with the box of ointment and, before he knew it, the whole disastrous thing had gone down in holy writ with millions of people reading about it!

Then there was the Mary/Martha luncheon. Just as famous, and almost as embarrassing! But that's the nature of the gospel. It has to do with the presence of Christ in the ordinary things of life. As such, the ordinary things become more than ordinary. Or their ordinariness is seen, in fact, to have extraordinary depth and meaning.

My sympathy in the first instance lies with poor Martha. After all, she took the responsibility. She was trying to get the lunch ready. But Mary, her sister, was nowhere to be seen; nowhere near the kitchen, anyway. She was in the lounge room sitting at the feet of Jesus. Fine. But what about getting the soup plates onto the table before everything got cold? So Martha complained, innocently thinking she was having a quiet tiff with a lazy sibling. Instead, she tumbled into religious history as the domestic busybody who got her priorities wrong!

But Luke has saved this incident — not to put Martha down, but because of the significance of the word of Jesus. 'You worry and fret about so many things, and yet few are needed, indeed only one.' That's worth pondering. It's a feature of our modern life — and it doesn't seem to matter much what walk of life we are in — that we are busied by a thousand tasks, pulled in a dozen directions, and responsible for too many projects. We know what it is to be anxious and troubled about many things and wonder if they are going anywhere or amounting to anything.

Only one thing is needful, said Jesus. That's not quite so clear. The many things we are caught up in are often unavoidable. True, perhaps we could trim a bit here and cut a bit there. But it's hard to see how we can escape the treadmill altogether. It can't be that Jesus is calling for us to abandon responsibility for keeping food on the table. I don't think he is. Rather, he is asking us in the midst of our busyness not to lose contact with the thing — the one thing — that can give an ultimate meaning to all our various tasks and efforts. It is not an abandoning of complexity so much as finding in complexity a deeper unity of purpose; a value which can give peace and a sense of worthwhileness to it all. It is not just getting the meal, but knowing and aiming at the fact that Christ is partaker of the meal, that gives depth and eternal significance to the Martha story. It's that that gets it into the Gospel.

But what about Mary? She was sitting listening to Jesus talk. That's not something that can simply be taken for granted as a good thing either. Jesus was no supporter of religiosity for its own sake. Indeed, quite the reverse. He was severely critical of much religion. Jesus often took issue with religious people on the grounds that their religion was a screen by which they protected themselves from coming to terms with God; from really hearing what God was saying.

That, essentially, was the debate that went on with Jesus at Simon the Pharisee's dinner party. Simon was very religious. That's what a Pharisee was. But his religion prevented him from seeing the one thing needful. He couldn't see that God was calling him to act in the world with compassion and justice, not just with piety and prayer. He could only turn away from the prostitute that gate-crashed his party in anger and self-righteousness. Jesus claimed that God was calling for Simon's commitment to action to redress her awful situation.

But one thing is needful. Mary has chosen the better part. It shall not be taken from her. What is the one thing needful? The one thing that can give a sense of unity and deep meaning to our troubled and anxious busyness? The one thing that can make our faith genuine and not a pious subterfuge or religious self-deception? What is the 'better part' that Mary chose? The story puts it with great simplicity: she 'sat down at the Lord's feet and listened to him speaking'.

That is it. The final reality, the deep ground upon which our human life stands, if it is to stand at all, is God. God is the one with whom we have ultimately to deal. But for us to face up to God, to reckon with that final human reality, is to face up to Jesus Christ. It is in Christ that we see what God is like and what he offers us of his love and his demand. It is Christ who, at Martha's dinner party, placed before both Mary and Martha the ultimate possibility of their living and their acting. It was Christ who precipitated the decision whether they would live to serve the meaning of God in their human journey; or avoid that meaning altogether. The same Christ faces us with the same possibility and the same decision.

It is no cop-out to sit at Jesus' feet and hear his word. Just before he tells this story, Luke relates Jesus' encounter with the lawyer who wanted to know how to live so that he might inherit eternal life. Jesus replied with the famous parable of the Good Samaritan. Just after this story, Luke tells how Jesus taught his disciples to pray with the famous words we now know as the Lord's Prayer. The Mary/Martha dinner party comes between this call to give ourselves to the alleviation of human suffering on the streets of the world, and learning how properly to pray. 'To do justice and to walk humbly with our God,' as the prophet put it. This is the one thing needful.

Know that, by nature, every creature seeks to become like God. Nature's intent is neither food nor drink nor clothing nor comfort nor anything else in which God is left out. Whether you like it or not, whether you know it or not, secretly nature seeks, hunts, tries to ferret out the track on which God may be found.

Meister Eckhart

Batter my heart, three-personed God; for you
As yet but knock, breathe, shine and seek to mend;
That I may rise and stand, o'erthrow me and bend
Your force to break, blow, burn and make me new.
I, like an usurped town, to another due,
Labour to admit you, but Oh, to no end;
Reason, your viceroy in me, me should defend,
But is captived and proves weak or untrue.
Yet dearly I love you and would be loved fain,
But am betrothed unto your enemy:
Divorce me, untie or break that knot again,
Take me to you, imprison me, for I
Except you enthrall me, never shall be free,
Nor ever chaste, except you ravish me.

John Donne

An Organisation and Methods Unit visited a University
to examine the efficiency and effectiveness of the workings
of the Vice-Chancellor's Office. The visit coincided with
one of the concerts of the Royal Philharmonic Orchestra,
to which the Vice-Chancellor was in the habit of going.

On this occasion he could not go, and with his usual
generosity gave his ticket to the leader of the O and M
Unit, who had never been to a symphony concert before.
The main work that night was Schubert's Unfinished Symphony.

When he asked his visitor the following morning how
he had enjoyed the concert, the Vice-Chancellor was
surprised to be handed a typewritten report:

(1) For considerable periods the four oboe players had
nothing to do. The number should be reduced and their
work should be more conveniently spread over the whole
concert, thus eliminating peaks of activity.

(2) All the twelve violins were playing identical notes.
This seems unnecessary duplication. The staff of this
section should be drastically cut and, if a large volume of
sound is really required, this could be obtained by means
of an electronic amplifier.

(3) Much effort was absorbed in the playing of demi-
semiquavers. This seems to us an excessive refinement

and it is recommended that all notes be rounded up to the nearest semiquaver. If this were done it should be possible to use trainees and lower-grade operators.

(4) There seems to be too much repetition of some musical passages. No useful purpose is served by repeating with horns the passage that has already been handled by the strings. If all such redundant passages were eliminated, the whole concert time of two hours would have been reduced to twenty minutes and there would have been no need for an interval. If the composer had attended to these matters he would probably have been able to finish his symphony.

Loughborough University of Technology

The most conclusive. . . sign of a religious act, as distinct from all other acts of mind or spirit, is an attendant insight into the fact that *of its essence it cannot be fulfilled* by any finite object belonging to, or itself forming, the 'world'. In this sense Augustine of Hippo's dictum, *Inquietum cor nostrum, donec requiescat in te*, is a basic formula for all religious acts. . .

In the religious act we envisage a being which is *different* from any finite being and also from any being which is non-finite or infinite in some specific *way* (such as infinite time, infinite space, infinite number, etc.); we find ourselves directed towards something whose place cannot be taken by any finite good, however worthy of love, since religious love transcends the essential nature of all such goods. In the religious act, we are seeking a felicity concerning which we are perfectly clear that no progress of humanity, no perfection of society and no kind of multiplication of the internal and external causes of human happiness can bring to pass. . . Thus. . . our mind *oversteps* the bounds not only of this or that one finite thing, but of the very sum and substance of all finite things.

Max Scheler, *On the Eternal in Man*

To sit at Jesus' feet and hear his word — that is the *unum necessarium*. Not, of course, to sit there idly and to hear with an otiose and curious interest, as [people] had heard the words of the scribes. The word of Jesus is not a word that can easily be listened to in that way. It is such that we have either to stop our ears to it or else make it the master word of all our hearing. I am quite sure this is the one thing that matters for us all. It is far from being the only thing permitted to anybody, but it is the one thing necessary for everybody. It was a favourite contention of that great man Baron von Hügel, that only by renouncing the claim to be *everything* could religion maintain the claim to be the *chief thing*. But it is the chief thing not only in the sense that it is the best of things, but in the sense that it alone is necessary, that without it all other good things are dust and ashes, and that they must every one, if need should arise, be surrendered for its sake.

John Baillie, *Christian Devotion*

Belatedly I loved thee, O Beauty so ancient and so new, belatedly I loved thee. For see, thou wast within and I was without, and I sought thee out there. Unlovely, I rushed heedlessly among the lovely things thou hast made. Thou wast with me, but I was not with thee. These things kept me far from thee; even though they were not at all unless they were in thee. Thou didst call and cry aloud, and didst force open my deafness. Thou didst gleam and shine, and didst chase away my blindness. Thou didst breathe fragrant odours and I drew in my breath; and now I pant for thee. I tasted, and now I hunger and thirst. Thou didst touch me, and I burned for thy peace.

Augustine of Hippo, *Confessions*

Eternal God and Father, by whose power we are created and by whose love we are redeemed: guide and strengthen us by your Spirit, that we may give ourselves to your service, and live this day in love to one another and to you; through Jesus Christ our Lord. Amen.

An Australian Prayer Book

O Christ, Word of God incarnate, grant us grace to listen to your speaking. Forgive our tendency to be distracted by the demands of life which make us too busy to listen; and our timidity which, when hearing, lacks the courage to obey. Make us, we pray, both hearers and doers of your word; for your name's sake. Amen.

A Benediction
May the God of peace equip us with everything good so that we may do his will; and may he work in us that which is pleasing in his sight; through Jesus Christ, to whom be glory for ever. Amen.

9

Away from anxiety

Anxiety in a person's heart weighs down, but a good word makes glad.

Don't be anxious about living. . . Surely life is more important than food, and the body more important than the clothes you wear. Look at the birds in the sky. . . Can any of you, however anxious, make yourself a centimetre taller? And why do you worry about clothes? Consider how the wild flowers grow. They neither work nor weave, but I tell you that even Solomon in all his glory was never arrayed like one of these!

God. . . is not far from any one of us. Indeed, it is in him that we live and move and have our being.

My dear son, you have been with me all the time and everything I have is yours.

Don't worry over anything whatever; tell God every detail of your needs in an earnest and thankful prayer, and the peace of God, which transcends all human understanding, will keep constant guard over your hearts and minds as they rest in Christ Jesus.

So long as we are clothed in this temporary dwelling we have a painful longing, not because we want just to get rid of these 'clothes', but because we want to know the full cover of the permanent house that will be ours. We want our transitory life to be absorbed into the life that is eternal.

Let Christ's teaching live in your hearts, making you rich in the true wisdom. Teach and help one another with your psalms and hymns and Christian songs, singing God's praises with joyful hearts. And whatever work you may have to do, do everything in the name

of the Lord Jesus, thanking God the Father through him.
(Proverbs 12: 25, RSV; Matthew 6: 25-29; Acts 17: 27-28; Luke 15:
31; Philippians 4: 6-7; 2 Corinthians 5: 4-5, Colossians 3: 16-17 —
all J.B.Phillips)

Anxiety is certainly not an attractive fellow, yet we keep him
as a much used messenger. We send him out with our
children (lest they should come to harm), we take him with
us when we visit the physician, we let him question our
future plans and expectations. He is a very poor servant
and a grudging, gloomy master. Useless in what we send
him out to do, he extracts from us ease of mind and spirit
and puts his dark fingermarks upon even the good things
which finally reach us. We employ him to help structure
life and destiny; we use him as a form of social control.

We observe that in one part of Matthew chapter 6, Jesus
three times refers to 'anxiety' and couples him with people
of dehydrating faith. He tells us not to use him, but
instead, and airily, he calls us to take notice of the birds
in their freedom from restraint, and the wild flowers nod-
ding colourfully without care in the fields.

Jesus asks us to *look at* birds and to *consider* the wild
flowers with the expectation of insight. Solomon in front
of the mirror of his opulence, choosing carefully from a
great wardrobe painstakingly made, has nothing to show
compared with these.

Our transition into the wisdom of 'letting go and letting
God' may begin with considering the lilies, paying attention to everything. The art is also called contemplation.
By looking at everything that we sense is present to us —
and this calls for practice — we honour the Creator and
put ourselves in the way of praise and gratitude.

The single daffodil catching our eyes on a dull winter's
day vibrates with the same intelligence as comes to us in
the creed. We believe in one Lord Jesus Christ, the only
Son of God. . . Through him all things were made. . . For
us men and women and for our salvation he came down
from heaven. . . For our sake he was crucified under Pontius
Pilate. . . the third day he rose again from the dead.

Not every strand of the pattern is reproduced in us at the time of sight and insight. But afterwards, when we come to review the day before God, the movement of felt experience allows us to touch him with a gratitude which takes in the creation and our recreating; the Creator and the Saviour in one greening. The road from anxiety passes by fields of flowers, forests, vineyards, pilgrims and solitudes. Here the Son is always shining.

'Be amazed that God exists and then you will discover that everything is alive.' So contemplation makes us good companions, first of all to ourselves and then to other pilgrims. Because I learn to pay attention, I look at you and I see you. I see you as given to me, in the same way as the sight of the daffodil was, part of the greening of God in us both. This interior work of the Spirit stirs up interest, compassion and wonder. You and I share the givenness of the relationship and can go on to discover that, within it, confidences are exchanged, burdens are lightened and good humour flows, becoming a spiritual solvent of care.

When we look at the Bible together we learn that paying attention comes to us without our choosing; it plucks on the sleeve of interest and says, 'Dear friend, stop here a while.' And we who are forever going on long treks and are forever industrious and long-leggedly anxious (I must reach Jezreel, Patmos and Psalm 150 by Tuesday) hear the Saviour saying, 'You were anxious and troubled about many things. But now you have chosen the good portion, which shall not be taken from you.' So we remain seated, paying attention, and in those small delights of interest, surprise and recognition, we come to love and admire our Friend much for his unique style. 'The style of Jesus is the style of God,' you say and I think how far you have come since we first met.

He is the Truth.
Seek him in the Kingdom of Anxiety:
You will come to a great city that has expected your return for years.

W.H. Auden, Sing Alleluia

Attention animated by desire is the whole foundation of religious practices.

Attention is the only faculty of the soul that gives access to God.

If just once and even in a small way we leave our egos unprotected, as we do when we appreciate something of beauty for itself, God comes and plants a small seed in our souls. If we do not choke the growth of that seed by refusing it, it will grow until a day comes when the soul belongs to God; when it not only consents to love, but when truly and effectively it loves.

Those who are unhappy have no need for anything in this world but people giving them their attention. The capacity to give one's attention to a sufferer is a very rare and difficult thing. It is almost a miracle. It is a miracle.

Simone Weil, *Waiting on God*

We do not really look at things if we do not see their cause, which is God.

Paul Claudel, in *Prayer at the Heart of Life*

Contemplation is capacity for admiration, a reflex of surprise — in other words, a coming out of oneself.

Pierre-Yves Emery, *Prayer at the Heart of Life*

When I began to pray with the heart, everything around me became transformed and I saw it in a new and delightful way. The trees, the grass, the earth, the air, the light and everything seemed to be saying to me that it exists to witness to God's love for us all and that it prays and sings of God's glory. Now I understood what I had read in the Philokalia about the knowledge of the speech of all creation.

Anonymous, *The Way of a Pilgrim*

The town was orient and immortal wheat, which never should be reaped nor was ever sown. I thought it had stood there from everlasting to everlasting. . . The Men! O what venerable and reverend creatures did the aged seem! Immortal cherubims! And young men, glittering and sparkling angels, and maids. . . strange seraphic pieces

of life and beauty! Boys and girls tumbling in the street
and playing were morning jewels. I knew not that they
were born or should die; but all things abided eternally
as they were in their proper places. Eternity was manifest
in the light of day and something infinite behind everything appeared.

Thomas Traherne, *Centuries*

Attention is the sign of sincere repentance. Attention is
the appeal of the soul to itself. . . It is the beginning of
contemplation or rather its necessary condition. . . attention is serenity of the mind. . . its standing firmly planted
and not wandering, through the gift of God's mercy. It
is the abode of remembrance of God. . .

Nicephorus the Solitary, *Writings of the Philokalia*

With regard to the world around one, there should be a
conscious willed period of attentiveness each day. It is
the will that has to be used to raise the consciousness from
the depths of the self to the world outside. It's important
to notice positively the objects in one's environment, the
things in a familiar street, the flowers and trees in the
garden and park and above all the people one passes to
and from one's work. Each is complete in itself, but it
needs our recognition, just as we need the recognition of
others to be fully human. If we do not trouble to recognise
others because of inner preoccupation, no-one will trouble
to recognise us. It's important not only to recognise and
acknowledge the uniqueness of each object and each person, but also to flow out of them in silent gratitude for
being what they are. All life in awareness is a blessing
and we show this by blessing those around us.

Martin Israel, in *Friday Afternoon*

The heart of the contemplative experience [is] to discipline
ourselves to the point where we know something of the
quality of what we witness — we pay attention, we endure
the moments of loneliness and boredom and then, sooner
or later, we receive the gift of seeing our world unified
and transformed.

Contemplation is the way of feeling at home in one's environment, of letting oneself off the need to fight it all the time, and permitting oneself to enjoy it. It is the voice of conservation, relishing what is already known and asking only to be allowed to know it in greater detail and in greater depth. It is concerned with depth, with growth, with meaning on an almost wordless level; it touches upon the deep springs of the individual and of the society.

Monica Furlong, *Contemplation Now*

I think that I shall never see
a billboard lovely as a tree.
Perhaps unless the billboards fall
I'll never see a tree at all.

Ogden Nash, 'Song of the Open Road'

O Holy Spirit,
Fiery Comforter Spirit,
Life of all the creatures,
Holy are you,
  You that give existence
  to all form.

Holy are you,
  You that are balm for the
  mortally wounded.

Holy are you,
  You that cleanse deep hurt.

Fire of love,
Breath of all holiness,
You are so delicious to our hearts,
You infuse our hearts deeply with
the good smell of virtue.

Hildegard of Bingen, *Meditations*

For a long time, dear Lord, I called you in as secretary to my prayers, to record my zeal, my gifts, my success, in hope of rapid promotion. Time passed and I called you out of darkness, the long distance call of failure, anger, depression. Now Lord, I'm told, the Spirit is at prayer and I listen and learn, open and find, heart-wisdom, Christ.

A Benediction
May your hearts and minds know the peace of God which leads away from anxiety, and the wisdom of God which lights the way ahead. Amen.

10

The privileges of trial

I tell you the truth, unless a kernel of wheat falls to the ground and dies, it remains only a single seed. But if it dies, it produces many seeds. The one who loves life will lose it, while the one who hates life in this world will keep it for eternal life.

How foolish! What you sow does not come to life unless it dies.

But we have this treasure in jars of clay to show that this all-surpassing power is from God and not ourselves. We are hard pressed on every side. . . but not abandoned. . . We always carry around in our body the death of Jesus, so that the life of Jesus may also be revealed in our body.

For it has been granted to you on behalf of Christ not only to believe on him, but also to suffer for him.

In this you greatly rejoice, though now for a little while you may have to suffer grief in all kinds of trials. These have come so that your faith — of greater worth than gold, which perishes even though refined by fire — may be proved genuine and may result in praise, glory and honour when Jesus Christ is revealed.

Sow for yourselves righteousness, reap the fruit of unfailing love, and break up your unploughed ground; for it is time to seek the Lord, until he comes and showers righteousness on you.

Now if we are children, then we are heirs — heirs of God and co-heirs with Christ, if indeed we share in his sufferings in order that we may also share in his glory. I consider that our present sufferings are not worth comparing with the glory that will be revealed in us.

(John 12: 24-25; 1 Corinthians 15: 36; 2 Corinthians 4: 7-10; Philippians 1: 29; 1 Peter 1: 6-7; Hosea 10: 12; Romans 8: 17-18 — all NIV)

In our present society we have all the conveniences of life. Pain is a word and symptom to be avoided, at all costs. But you who have ears, listen to what the Spirit says to us: 'The one who wishes to find life must lose it, must give it away, must die to self.' How inconvenient and uncomfortable, and something that, if left up to us, would be avoided.

Dietrich Bonhoeffer states, 'When Christ calls someone, he bids that person come and die.' But death to self is painfully uncomfortable. Many of us instead choose daily to live a life of complacency and self-satisfaction. Amy Carmichael writes, 'I think often we accept the cross in theory, but when it comes to practice, we either do not recognise it for what it is, or we recognise it and try to avoid it. This we can do, for the cross is something that can be taken up or left, just as we choose.' Whatever became of Christ's command, 'All who would come after me must deny themselves, and take up their cross and follow me'?

If we desire a Christ-centred, Christ-like life, a life that will make a difference, our thinking is foolish if we think it can be accomplished without death to self.

Often I was startled by Christ's statement, 'Many are called but few are chosen' (Matthew 22:14). Who are the chosen ones? It's my belief that he gives us the choice of whether or not we'll be chosen, by our daily decision. If we choose to walk the road of self-denial, daily dying to self so that others may live, and to partake with Christ in 'the fellowship of his suffering', picking up our cross daily and following him, we'll be amongst the chosen few.

Although this way at times may be a dark, lonely, silent journey, he promises us he will sustain us according to his word, and his presence will always be with us. And it's when we walk this walk that we experience the power of his resurrected life coming alive in us. Hallelujah!

❧❧

Be still, my soul: the Lord is on your side;
bear patiently the cross of grief and pain;
leave to your God to order and provide;
in every change he faithful will remain.
Be still, my soul: your best, your heavenly friend
through thorny ways leads to a joyful end.

Be still, my soul: your God will undertake
to guide the future as he has the past.
Your hope, your confidence let nothing shake,
all now mysterious shall be clear at last.
Be still, my soul: the tempests still obey
his voice, who ruled them once on Galilee.

Katharina von Schlegel

We have much to learn as the children of God.
The most difficult, perhaps, is to learn
how to regard our trials and tribulations
even the tragedies that beset us as
capable of enhancing and enriching our lives.
Whereas God does not send them, he does permit
them, and he can use them to draw us closer
to him and thereby accomplish his purposes
in and through us.
We desperately need the wisdom to accept these
painful happenings and with graciousness, even
with joy, knowing that whatever they may be,
God can transform them from ugliness into
beauty, from the plots of Satan designed to
destroy into the purposes of God destined to
do us good.
The key is genuine faith in a loving God, a faith
that frees us and strengthens us to endure whatever may come our way.

Leslie F. Brandt, *Epistles Now*

We aren't always responsible for the circumstances in
which we find ourselves. However, we are responsible
for the way we respond to them. We can give up in
depression or suicidal despair. Or we can look to a

sovereign God who has everything under control, who can use the experiences for our ultimate good by transforming us to the image of Christ.

Joni Eareckson

It's no longer either dangerous or costly to become a Christian. Grace has become not free, but cheap. We are busy these days proving to the world that they can have all the benefits of the gospel without any inconvenience to their customary way of life. It's all this and heaven too!

A.W. Tozer, *Keys to the Deeper Life*

Satan does not tempt us to do wrong things; he tempts us in order to make us lose what God has put into us by regeneration, i.e., the possibility of being of value to God. He does not come on the line of tempting us to sin, but on the line of shifting the point of view.

Oswald Chambers, *My Utmost for His Highest*

You will learn most in the times of deprivation, deep meditation and silence of the soul before God. It is here where you will learn to renounce your own selfish spirit and to love humility, obscurity, weakness and submission. These things, so despised by the world, are the accomplished teachers of all truths. Human knowledge can only stand in the way.

Francois Fénélon, *Let Go*

Discipleship means allegiance to the suffering Christ, and it is therefore not at all surprising that Christians should be called to suffer.

Dietrich Bonhoeffer, *The Cost of Discipleship*

'Endure hardship as a good soldier of Jesus Christ,' cries the great apostle. This is no time to think of self, to consult with dignity, to confer with flesh and blood, to think of ease, or to shrink from hardship, grief and loss. This is the time for toil, suffering and self-denial. We must lose all for Christ in order to gain all for Christ.

E.M. Bounds, *The Weapon of Prayer*

O Love that wilt not let me go,
I rest my weary soul in thee:
I give thee back the life I owe,
that in thine ocean depths its flow
may richer, fuller be.

O Light that followest all my way,
I yield my flickering torch to thee:
my heart restores its borrowed ray,
that in thy sunshine's blaze its day
may brighter, fairer be.

O Joy that seekest me through pain,
I cannot close my heart to thee:
I trace the rainbow through the rain,
and feel the promise is not vain,
that morn shall tearless be.

O Cross that liftest up my head,
I dare not ask to fly from thee:
I lay in dust life's glory dead,
and from the ground there blossoms red
life that shall endless be.

George Matheson

---

*O God of peace, who has taught us that in returning and rest
we shall be saved, in quietness and in confidence shall be our
strength: by the might of your Spirit lift us, we pray, to your
presence, where we may be still and know that you are God;
through Jesus Christ our Lord.* Amen.

Book of Common Prayer

*Come, Lord, work upon us, set us on fire and clasp us close,
be fragrant to us, draw us to your loveliness, let us love, let
us run to you.*

Augustine of Hippo

Today I want to live in his name —
in him who is the Lord of Glory.
I want Christ's radiance to brighten my countenance,
that I might bring the light of joy to people
who are living in the shadows of difficulty;
May Christ's light spill over the brim of my life in such a way
that the people capture a sense of your warmth.
Without my having to seem or sound 'religious',
may the weight —
the genuine 'heavy-weight' reality of Christ's
character —
be increased in me.
Let the stamp of his
personality be left where I have been.
In his name. Amen.

Jack Hayford, Living and Praying in Jesus' Name

A Benediction
I ask God to fill you with the knowledge of his will
through all spiritual wisdom and understanding.
I pray this in order that you may live a life worthy
of the Lord and that you may please him in
every way: bearing fruit in every good work,
growing in the knowledge of God, being
strengthened with all power according
to his glorious might so that you may
have great endurance and patience, and
joyfully giving thanks to the Father,
who has qualified you to share in the inheritance
of saints in the kingdom of light.

Colossians 1: 9b-12 (NIV)

11

Jesus — Prince of Peace

For to us a child is born, to us a son is given, and the government will be on his shoulders. And he will be called Wonderful Counsellor, Mighty God, Everlasting Father, Prince of Peace. Of the increase of his government and peace there will be no end. He will reign on David's throne and over his kingdom, establishing and upholding it with justice and righteousness from that time on and forever. The zeal of the Lord Almighty will accomplish this.

He was treated harshly, but endured it humbly; he never said a word. Like a lamb about to be slaughtered, like a sheep about to be sheared, he never said a word. He was arrested and sentenced and led off to die, and no one cared about his fate. He was put to death for the sins of our people. He was placed in a grave with evil men, he was buried with the rich, even though he had never committed a crime or ever told a lie.

I have told you this while I am still with you. The Helper, the Holy Spirit, whom the Father will send in my name, will teach you everything and make you remember all that I have told you. Peace is what I leave with you; it is my own peace that I give you. I do not give it as the world does. Do not be worried and upset; do not be afraid.

On the evening of that first day of the week, when the disciples were together, with the doors locked for fear of the Jews, Jesus came and stood among them and said, 'Peace be with you!' After he said this, he showed them his hands and side. The disciples were overjoyed when they saw the Lord. Again Jesus said, 'Peace be with you! As the Father has sent me, I am sending you.'

Here is my servant, whom I have chosen, the one I love, and with whom I am pleased. I will send my Spirit upon him, and he will announce my judgment to the nations. He will not argue or shout, or make loud speeches in the streets. He will be gentle to those who are weak, and kind to those who are helpless. He will persist until he causes justice to triumph, and on him all peoples will put their hope.

Simon Peter, who had a sword, drew it and struck the High Priest's slave, cutting off his right ear. The name of the slave was Malchus. Jesus said to Peter, 'Put your sword back in its place! Do you think that I will not drink the cup of suffering which my Father has given me?'

Two other men, both of them criminals, were also led out to be put to death with Jesus. When they came to the place called 'The Skull', they crucified Jesus there, and the two criminals, one on his right and the other on his left. Jesus said, 'Forgive them, Father! They don't know what they are doing.'

At that time you were apart from Christ. You were foreigners and did not belong to God's chosen people. You had no part in the covenants, which were based on God's promises to his people, and you lived in this world without hope and without God. But now, in union with Christ Jesus, you who used to be far away have been brought near by the death of Christ. For Christ himself has brought us peace by making Jews and Gentiles one people. With his own body he broke down the wall that separated them and kept them enemies. He abolished the Jewish Law with its commandments and rules, in order to create out of the two races one new people in union with himself, in this way making peace. By his death on the cross Christ destroyed their enmity; by means of the cross he united both races into one body and brought them back to God. So Christ came and preached the Good News of peace to all — to you Gentiles, who were far away from God, and to the Jews, who were near to him. It is through Christ that all of us, Jews and Gentiles, are able to come in the one Spirit into the presence of the Father.

He was humble and walked the path of obedience all the way to death — his death on the cross. For this reason God raised him to the highest place above and gave him the name that is greater than any other name. And so, in honour of the name of Jesus all beings in heaven, on earth, and in the world below will fall on their knees, and all will openly proclaim that Jesus Christ is Lord, to the glory of God the Father.

(Isaiah 9: 6-7, NIV; Isaiah 53: 7-9, GNB; John 14: 25-27, GNB; John 20: 19-21, NIV; Matthew 12: 18-21; John 18: 10-11; Luke 23: 32-34; Ephesians 2: 12-18; Philippians 2: 8-11 — all GNB)

It is altogether incredible that a man called Jesus who lived in Israel 2000 years ago has had such immense and continuing influence. Very few people who have lived on this earth over the centuries are even known by name. A few gain momentary notoriety and disappear. Sometimes the fortuitous presence of an historian or other scribe will ensure a person's name will live on for a time. The great words or deeds of a small number of gifted people and the acts of barbarity and infamy of others assure their memory for posterity. But the words and deeds, in fact the person of Jesus Christ, straddle 2000 years of human history like a mighty colossus. It is this solitary figure who has revised our thinking about good and evil, life and death, war and peace.

The word 'peace' is closely identified with the expected Messiah in the Old Testament — especially in Isaiah's writings. The Hebrew word 'shalom' — 'Prince of Peace' (Isaiah 9: 6) — has been enshrined in our terminology by the composer Handel's usage of the phrase in his memorable chorus from the oratorio, *The Messiah*.

A people as sorely oppressed as the first century Jews were understandably preoccupied with their longing for a deliverer. They had awaited the arrival of the messianic age of peace foreseen and predicted by the prophets of Israel with eager anticipation. There was universal agreement that this long-awaited Messiah would usher in the age of peace. The writer of the book of Daniel prophesied about one who 'was given authority, honour and royal power, so that the people of all nations, races and languages would serve him. His authority would last forever, and his kingdom would never end' (Daniel 7: 14, GNB).

Isaiah reveals a vision of messianic peace and justice as amazing and descriptive as that of any other biblical prophet: 'Wolves and sheep will live together in peace, and leopards will lie down with young goats. Calves and lion cubs will feed together, and little children will take care of them' (Isaiah 11: 6, GNB).

The early Christian church declared Jesus to be the fulfilment of these and other Old Testament prophecies about the one who would come and reign in peace. Matthew quoted Isaiah 9: 'The people who live in darkness will see a great light. On those who live in the dark land of death the light will shine' (Matthew 4: 16, GNB).

Jesus is the Prince of Peace. He brings a sense of peace. He is the 'bright and morning star, the fairest of ten thousand to my soul'. He is the altogether lovely one whose fragrance is sweeter than honey and whose beauty exceeds the most perfect rose. 'All that thrills my soul is Jesus, he is more than life to me. . .'

❧❦

A monastery had fallen on hard times. The few old monks who remained longed to see their once great order revived. They sought advice from a rabbi who regularly prayed in a hermitage in the wood nearby. The only advice he could offer was, 'The Messiah is one of you.'

The monks pondered this strange insight. 'Do you suppose he meant the Abbott? Yes, he probably meant Father Abbott. . . On the other hand, he might have meant Brother Thomas. Certainly Brother Thomas is a holy man. Certainly he could not have meant Brother Elred! Elred gets crotchety at times. But come to think of it, even though he is a thorn in peoples' sides, when you look back on it, Elred is virtually always right. . . But surely not Brother Phillip. Phillip is so passive, a real nobody. But then, almost mysteriously, he has a gift for somehow always being there when you need him. . . Maybe Phillip is the Messiah. Of course the rabbi didn't mean me. . . I'm just an ordinary person. Yet supposing he did? Suppose I am the Messiah. O God, not me. I couldn't be that much for you, could I?'

As they contemplated in this manner, the old monks began to treat each other with extraordinary respect. On the off chance that each monk himself might be the Messiah, they began to treat themselves with extraordinary respect.

M. Scott Peck, *The Different Drum*

No image more powerfully contrasts Jesus' peaceful, messianic conception with violent contemporary expectations than that of the Suffering Servant. Popular Jewish thought hoped for a warlike, Davidic Messiah who would destroy the heathen oppressors. The early church taught that the Jewish messianic hope had been fulfilled in the humble Suffering Servant foreseen in Isaiah 53.

R. Sider and R. Taylor, *Nuclear Holocaust and Christian Hope*

. . .Because the walls of hostility between God and humankind were broken down in the life and death of the true, perfect servant, union and well-being between God and the world were finally fully possible.

R. Sider and R. Taylor, *Nuclear Holocaust and Christian Hope*

Christ is the world's light, he and no other;
born in our darkness, he became our brother.
If we have seen him, we have seen the Father:
    Glory to God on high.
Christ is the world's peace, he and no other;
no one can serve him and despise his brother.
Who else unites us, one in God the Father?
    Glory to God on high.

Frederick Pratt Green

All people, even revolutionaries and warmongers, desire peace; they are always striving for what they imagine would be a more settled condition of life. There is, as Jesus implies, a peace which the world can give. Temporary freedom from distraction, anxiety and strife is often obtainable, enabling people to settle down for a short time at least to do what they want to do, and live their lives in their own way with relatively little interference.

There is also the peace of momentary flight from the unpleasant things of life sought in daydreams, pleasure and amusement, the peace of escapism. And there is the peace of false security, when people cry, 'Peace, peace' where there is no peace, the peace that is so often the prelude to disaster. The peace which Jesus offers his disciples is something very different. It is *his* peace. *My peace*, he tells them, *I give unto you.* He himself enjoyed this peace, for he was never for one moment unmindful of his Father's will and was ready in obedience to it. . .

The disciples had witnessed something of what Jesus calls *my peace* when they had seen him restoring calm to human lives racked by the misery of sin and disease; and they had more than once themselves sheltered in the security of his presence as they heard his reassuring words, 'It is I. Be not afraid.' His return to the Father, he now assures them, would mean, not the lessening, but the heightening of the experience of this peace, because exalted to the right hand of God, he would be able to communicate to them from the original source of divine power and authority. . . the very peace of God himself.

R.V.G. Tasker, *The Gospel According to St John*

Crown him, the Lord of peace,
Whose power a sceptre sways
from pole to pole, that wars may cease
absorbed in prayer and praise:
his reign shall know no end,
and round his pierced feet
fair flowers of paradise extend
their fragrance ever sweet.

Matthew Bridges and Godfrey Thring

. . .Occasional, alien, uncharacteristic: his characteristic was non-violence; the symbol of his ministry is not the whip, but the Cross.

John Stott, 'Calling for Peacemakers in a Nuclear Age'

I will praise thee, oh Lord, with my whole heart (Psalm 9: 1). My whole heart I lay upon the altar of thy praise, a holocaust of praise I offer to thee. . . let the flame of thy love set on fire my whole heart; let nought in me be left to me, nought wherein I may look to myself, but may I wholly burn towards thee, wholly be on fire towards thee, as though set aflame by thee.

Augustine of Hippo

Christ Jesus, our Lord, we refuse to let our hearts be troubled because we believe in God and believe also in you.
   Yet we pray, with tears, for those who are troubled:
   the cancer patient facing pain and death,
   the pregnant girl fearing family condemnation,
   the businessman with crippling debts,
   the social worker swamped by need,
   the unemployed youth.
May our hearts never accept a superficial peace
that exults in our own peace with God
while other hearts are troubled.

Tony Cupit

Christ is our peace.
He has reconciled us to God
in one body by the cross.
We meet in his name
and share his peace.
The peace of the Lord
be always with you.
And also with you.

Terry Falla

A Benediction
Christ be with you, Christ within you,
Christ behind you, Christ before you,

Christ beside you, Christ to win you,
Christ to comfort and restore you,
Christ beneath you, Christ above you,
Christ in quiet, Christ in danger,
Christ in mouth of friend or stranger

St Patrick's Breastplate, adapted

12

Healthy roots produce enduring fruits

A person away from home is like a bird away from its nest.

[The righteous] are like trees that grow beside a stream, that bear fruit at the right time, and whose leaves do not dry up.

Two are better than one, because they have a good return for their work: if you fall down, your friend can help you up. But pity the one who falls and has no one to help! Also, if two lie down together, they will keep warm. But how can one keep warm alone? Though one may be overpowered, two can defend themselves. A cord of three strands is not quickly broken.

When Jesus heard that John had been put in prison, he returned to Galilee. Leaving Nazareth, he went and lived in Capernaum, which was by the lake in the area of Zebulun and Naphtali. . . From that time on Jesus began to preach, 'Repent, for the kingdom of heaven is near.'

After this, Jesus went around in Galilee, purposely staying away from Judea because the Jews there were waiting to take his life. But when the Jewish Feast of Tabernacles was near, Jesus' brothers said to him, 'You ought to leave here and go to Judea, so that your disciples may see the miracles you do. . . Jesus told them, 'The right time for me has not yet come. . .' However, after his brothers had left for the feast, he went also, not publicly, but in secret.

All the believers were together and had everything in common. Selling their possessions and goods, they gave to anyone who had a need. . . All the believers were one in heart and mind. They did not claim any of their possessions as their own, but they shared everything they had.

(Proverbs 27: 8, GNB; Psalm 1: 3, GNB; Ecclesiastes 4: 9-12; Matthew 4: 12, 13–17; John 7: 1-3, 6–10; Acts 2: 44–45; 4: 32 — all NIV)

A Yale University psychologist, Daniel Levinson, reports in his study of Yale graduates, *Seasons of a Man's Life,* that few of them had friends after high school. In a changing corporate environment, they found some companions with common interests, but where were the long-term bonds of friends who really knew and depended on each other?

We might preface any move to a different place or position with a life-sustaining inquiry: will we make friends there? The question occurs for us because we sometimes have to move — as Jesus did.

According to Matthew, Jesus did not begin his public ministry until he had chosen a home. The context of Jesus' 'locating' may provide some answers to questions about the need to have a settled place.

Locating in Capernaum came after two unsettling events. First there was the temptation in the wilderness. That occurred at the only time in Jesus' ministry when he was without human companionship. Is this significant?

Well, consider the other time of temptation in Gethsemane when the sorrow in his heart almost crushed him. What he required then was the prayerful presence of his closest companions. Jesus' advice to his sleepy disciples was 'watch and pray'. Watch for what? They were to be aware of each other and sustained by alert and caring partners. This is what he needed, what they needed — and how about us?

Prayer is nourished in friendship and, in a time of crisis, we want dependable, 'watchful' friends. And how is that possible without tested experiences of reliability and daily or weekly contacts that let us know the needs of another whom we cherish?

In the second 'unsettling' event that precipitated the locating in Capernaum, Matthew explains Jesus' move in terms of security. He wanted to be away from the political territory of the murderous Herod who had just imprisoned John the Baptist. Later, when his brothers goaded him to make a public journey into areas where Judean authorities sought his life, Jesus rejected them and 'stayed on in Galilee' until he knew the time had come for him to head towards Jerusalem.

So what's the right time for a secure place, and when do we know the time has come to venture out from a nurturing location?

For Jesus, there was a secure thirty year period of growth in body and mind among kin in Nazareth before his ministry. But as he began to itinerate throughout Galilee after he found a home in Capernaum, it wasn't long before his ministry brought him into conflict with his home town, Nazareth (Luke 4: 16-30) and his adopted home in Capernaum (Matthew 11: 20-24).

However, after those rejections he still found a home. He carried with him the ability to establish long-term bonds in a new location. For example, after the successful training mission for disciples, Jesus found rest in the home of Mary, Martha and Lazarus (Luke 10: 1-23, 38-42). This was the home to which he returned when a friend died (John 11) and the sanctuary for a symbolic anointing before his death (John 12: 1-8).

It takes time to find a home away from home. But more important than time is vulnerability. We need to know and let others know that companionship is more important than money, and appreciation for kindness than secular success. That's a problem, for modern professional and business life encourages the Judas in us to think about our purse and our piety whenever an understanding friend gets too close to our weaknesses.

Is it worth the effort to find and re-find a place? In the context of Jesus' ministry it would seem so. The choice of disciples (according to Matthew) came after Jesus found his new home in Capernaum and was out walking on the seashore. He observed Simon Peter and Andrew, James and John in the hometown activity, fishing. This was the context for strong and bold discipleship for them and for us. It can begin in one chosen place and should be sustained by the kind of friends we carry from those secure moments throughout life.

❧

No-one would choose to live without friends, even if one had all other goods.

Aristotle

Home is the place where, when you have to go there, they have to take you in.

Robert Frost, 'Death of a Hired Man'

We all want someone who knows us better than anyone else does, and yet accepts us, enjoys us, needs us, holds nothing back from us, keeps our secrets, and is there for us when we want to be near.

Lewis B. Smedes, *Caring and Commitment*

Our society doesn't promote friendship. Activities are promoted, new homes are pushed, materialism is hawked. But there is no structural push for friendship; it's more that you stumble into it.

Interviewee, 'The Friendship Paradox'

Life in contemporary suburbia, you may have noticed, is not conducive to friendship. Many of us live in 'bedroom communities,' sorry imitations of villages with no defined downtown areas and no sense of neighbourhoods. Newer suburbs, even if they possess some sort of downtown, rarely have footpaths more than a few blocks long. So suburbanites glide through their 'community' in automobiles, armoured and glassed off from their 'neighbours'. We work in one suburb (or the city), go to church in another suburb, shop in a third, and join health clubs in a fourth. Our children attend schools in separate neighbourhoods or even separate communities. . .

In short, the social and economic demands of suburbia create space for material attainment and status seeking, but destroy space for the practice of friendship. And it is not simple overinflated rhetoric to say that friendship has become a counter-cultural practice. If such is the case, the church in suburbia may have a surprising new mission: to establish a cultural space for the birth and supported practice of friendship.

Rodney Clapp, 'The Celebration of Friendship'

In the community of faith we can find the climate and the support to sustain and deepen our prayer and we are enabled to constantly look forward beyond our immediate and often narrowing private needs. The community of faith offers the protective boundaries within which we can listen to our deepest longings, not to indulge in morbid introspection, but to find our God to whom they point. In the community of faith we can listen to our feelings of loneliness, to our desires for an embrace or a kiss, to our sexual urges, to our craving for sympathy, compassion or just a good word; also to our search for insight and to our hope for companionship and friendship.

In the community of faith we can listen to all these longings and find the courage, not to avoid them or cover them up, but to confront them in order to discern God's presence in their midst. There we can affirm each other in our waiting and also in the realisation that in the centre of our waiting the first intimacy with God is found. There we can be patiently together and let the suffering of each day convert our illusions into the prayer of a contrite people. The community of faith is indeed the climate and source of all prayer.

Henry Nouwen, *Reaching Out*

Most of us know that feeling of being alone, isolated. It's not the same as choosing to be alone once in a while, or being independent at times. It's the feeling that no-one is near, that no-one remembers, that there is no-one to live for. It's a feeling of deep isolation, of not belonging to anyone. And when we have that feeling, 'To whom?'

becomes our lonely cry of distress and longing.

God hears that question. So what we do at such times is very important for our spiritual as well as for our emotional lives. We can try to escape the loneliness by working harder, even putting in overtime; by reading a book; by going to a bar and joining other lonely people sitting in a row; by playing tennis; by calling someone — anyone. Or we can stay with that loneliness a little while and become aware of life at a deeper level. If we do, we might realise that no amount of work, busyness, food or drink, even of companionship, will completely release us from our lonely condition. Something larger, deeper, more lasting is necessary. . .

Even when events and people say: 'You don't belong', God's gentle voice reassures us: 'You do belong — to me.' 'To whom?' is a cry God can both hear and answer. In fact, God is waiting to answer, as a loving parent waits with open arms for a child who has left home.

The parable of the prodigal son tells us, 'There is a homecoming for us all because there is a home!' [Thielicke, *The Waiting Father*]. Belonging means we have an address, a place where we are 'at home'. We belong to God and God will not let us go as others might. That belonging is more lasting, more constant, more loving than any belonging that job, school, club, church, friends or even family can provide.

Don Postema, *Space for God*

It is important to remember that the Christian community is a waiting community, that is, a community which not only creates a sense of belonging, but also a sense of estrangement. In the Christian community we say to each other, 'We are together, but we cannot fulfil each other. . . we help each other, but we also have to remind each other that our destiny is beyond our togetherness.' The support of the Christian community is a support in common expectation. That requires a constant criticism of anyone who makes the community into a safe shelter or a cosy clique, and a constant encouragement to look forward to what is to come.

Henri J.M. Nouwen, *Reaching Out*

What is an unspeakable gift of God for the lonely individual is easily disregarded and trodden under foot by
those who have the gift every day. It is easily forgotten
that the fellowship of Christian community is a gift of
grace, a gift of the Kingdom of God that any day may be
taken from us, that the time that still separates us from
utter loneliness may be brief indeed. Therefore, let those
who until now have had the privilege of living a common
Christian life with other Christians praise God's grace from
the bottom of their hearts.

Dietrich Bonhoeffer, *Life Together*

In life, no house, no home
my Lord on earth might have;
in death, no friendly tomb
but what a stranger gave.
What may I say?
Heaven was his home;
but mine the tomb wherein he lay.

Samuel Crossman

Holy Spirit, our companion and guide,

*Show us the way home. Construct in our imagination the
heavenly city where we have perfect fellowship and never know
any as strangers. Gather to us the people who share our vision,
that we may be supported and challenged by citizens in the
coming Kingdom of our Father.*

*Use our vision of the future kingdom to find an earthly resting
place. Meet us with faith and love along the way, lest we
become suffocated by ever-present greed and selfish shoving in
the crowded ways of urban existence. Let the eternal city shine
through the darkness of perverse relationships and the blinding
rage of continuous betrayal. May we find a lampstand for our
candle of love while others blindly stumble with curses against
our mutual obstacles.*

*Place us where we may honour the diversity of others without
losing ourselves. Provide for us the daily nourishment of a
morning greeting, a special remembrance, a helping hand. Give
us guarantees of your faithfulness in our return to hospitable*

surroundings at the end of the day and the quietness of a safe rest in the night. Open our eyes each day to fresh beauty in a small space that shows our satisfaction with where we are placed.

Surround us with enough peace and joy in our place today that tomorrow will be worth living for ourselves and others. Amen.

A Benediction

Go out into the world with a determination to live with contentment and hospitality wherever your place may be. May your roots go deep into the lives of others and bring forth the fruit of friendship that will endure to the glory of God. Amen.

13

The voice of God is never silent

The heavens are telling the glory of God;
and the firmament proclaims his handiwork.
Day to day pours forth speech,
and night to night declares knowledge.
There is no speech, nor are there words;
their voice is not heard;
yet their voice goes out through all the earth,
and their words to the end of the world.

Be still before the Lord, and wait patiently for him.

Do not come near; put off your shoes from your feet, for the place on which you are standing is holy ground.

Then the Lord answered Job out of the whirlwind: 'Who is this that darkens counsel by words without knowledge? Gird up your loins like a man, I will question you, and you shall declare to me.'

The Spirit immediately drove him into the wilderness. And he was in the wilderness forty days, tempted by Satan; and he was with the wild beasts; and the angels ministered to him.

Likewise the Spirit helps us in our weakness; for we do not know how to pray as we ought, but the Spirit himself intercedes for us with sighs too deep for words. And he who searches our hearts knows what is in the mind of the Spirit, because the Spirit intercedes for the saints according to the will of God.

Mary. . . sat down at the feet of the Lord and listened to his teaching. Martha was upset over all the work she had to do, so she came and said, 'Lord, don't you care that my sister has left me to do all the work by myself? Tell her to come and help me!'

The Lord answered her, 'Martha, Martha! You are wor-

ried and troubled over so many things, but just one thing
is needed. Mary has chosen the right thing, and it will
not be taken away from her.'
Listen, then, if you have ears!

(Psalm 19: 1-4; Psalm 37: 7; Exodus 3: 5; Job 38: 1-3; Mark 1:
12-13; Romans 8: 26-27 — all RSV; Luke 10: 39-42; Matthew 11:
15 — both GNB)

The voice of God is never silent. In every circumstance
and situation God is speaking. But are we able to hear
and to receive what he is offering?

We have to learn to comprehend the many languages
of the Spirit. And this insight, this ability to perceive the
speech that pours forth without words is itself a gift of
the Spirit. It is given to those who will wait patiently
upon the Lord.

Without speech, without sounds, yet through all the
sound and fury of our stormy beings, and in all the
dullness and emptiness, God speaks.

God speaks without words and in forms we may not
at first recognise as having any meaning at all. But if we
wait patiently on him, we can learn to recognise his
presence and his meaning in such things as the rhythms
of our lives. There he is inviting us to know new dimensions of health, activity and rest. In our relationships, in
the great tapestry of the years, God speaks. God speaks,
and faith learns to listen.

Paul Tillich encouraged us to think of God speaking to
us from 'the darker side'. He knew this from his own
experience, especially his sense of being enveloped by
death while serving as a chaplain in World War I. His
theological work grew out of that lifelong struggle with
the darker side. Tillich spoke of the sacred void and of
an absent God. But this gap is intentional, in the
philosophical sense; that is, the gap has a meaning and
signifies something rather than nothing.

Tillich also spoke of God being present with him at the
'needlepoint' of absolute despair. Later still he gave
thanks for God's presence with him through long periods

of silent unknowing.

We have since learned — or rediscovered — the spiritual disciplines of listening to God, speaking to us from the storm *and* in what someone has called 'the long littleness' of our everyday existence. God is not with us only in our moments of devotion or intense religious feeling. God is always with us. In the storm, or in the humdrum, God is there.

But what can we do when we cannot hear? Then faith takes on a different meaning for us, at least for a time. Faith then is a 'holding on' and an enduring.

When we cannot hear and cannot read the silence or the turmoil, faith persists. Faith persists, when all is perplexity and we do not even know what questions to ask, or to whom. Faith persists, till it learns the language of his silence, and the language of our silence. Faith persists, till we sense his presence and hear his voice in all the activity and all the stillness, in all the world.

Persisting, waiting, listening: these, too, are dimensions of prayer and of theology. In these times, too, we are learning the language of God.

❦

Our spirituality should not only touch our so-called inner life — which in any case is significantly shaped by all that we do and experience in our day-to-day affairs — but emerge through and connect with the complex web of situations, incidents and encounters that make up our lives. It, too, should have an everyday cost to it: we should constantly be meeting God *in* it, not only *apart* from it. Through intimations, parables and dreams as well as through what we hear, read and observe, the voice of God, which as the Psalmist reminds us is never silent, should echo in our minds.

Robert Banks, *All the Business of Life*

The garden of our private worlds is cultivated not only when we draw apart for times of silence and solitude, but also when we begin, in that environment, to deliberately practise the discipline of listening. I have not met many who know how to listen to God. Busy people find it hard to learn how. Most Christians learned at an early age how to talk to God, but they did not learn to listen as well.

Gordon MacDonald, *Ordering your Private World*

It is the work of the Spirit that removes God from our sight, not only for some of us, but sometimes for many in a particular period. We live in an era in which the God we know is an absent God. But in knowing God as the absent God, we *know* of him; we feel his absence as the empty space that is left by something or someone that once belonged to us and has now vanished from our view. God is always infinitely near and infinitely far. We are fully aware of him only if we experience both of these aspects. But sometimes, when our awareness of him has become shallow, habitual — not warm and not cold — when he has become too familiar to be exciting, too near to be felt in his infinite distance, then he becomes the absent God. The Spirit has not ceased to be present. The Spiritual Presence can never end. But the Spirit of God hides God from our sight.

Paul Tillich, 'Spiritual Presence'

Honest doubt is a form of faith; it is faith facing the storm, faith searching for God, even though all we sense are clouds of confusion and threatening questions. If we will not shirk it, but cling to our quest for truth, for integrity, for meaning, that in itself is a sign of faith and of hope. And God honours that. God appears. God embraces the faith of those who in honest doubt accept their plight, who face the issues, who travel right into the heart of the storm.

It is the Spirit who leads us into such a wilderness and, though Satan is there to tempt us, and the wild animals may roar about us, so too the angels are there to minister to us.

Frank Rees

Individuals cry out for God because they remember; that memory serves both to sustain faith and at the same time to throw it into question. A lively recollection of previous mutuality and trust prevents retreat into a view that denies authentic relationship on the vertical dimensions, for humans are reminded that a bond once existed and hence may be restored at some time in the future. Here is the ultimate locus of hope which springs eternal in the human breast that is torn apart by its own agony over an apparent change in God. At the same time, here is also the source of consternation, for something has disturbed a vital relationship and everything seems to point an accusing finger at the deity.

James L. Crenshaw, *A Whirlpool of Torment*

You keep on asking me, 'How can I find fulfilment?'

If only I could lay my hand on your shoulder and go with you along the way. Both of us together, turning towards him who, recognised or not, is your quiet companion, someone who never imposes himself. Will you let him plant a source of refreshment deep within you? Or will you be so filled with shame that you say, 'I am not good enough to have you near me'?

What fascinates about God is his humility. He never punishes, domineers or wounds human dignity. Any authoritarian gesture on our part disfigures his face and repels. As for Christ, 'poor and humble of heart' — he never forces anyone's hand. If he forced himself upon you, I would not be inviting you to follow him.

In the silence of the heart, tirelessly he whispers to each of us, 'Don't be afraid; I am here.'

Wait for him, even when body and spirit are dry and parched. Wait, too, with many others for an event to occur in our present day. An event which is neither marvel nor myth, nor projection of yourself. The fruit of prayerful waiting, it comes concretely in the wake of a miracle from God.

In prayer, prayer that is always poor, like lightning rending the night, you will discover the secret: you can find fulfilment only in the presence of God. . . and also, you will awaken others to God, first and foremost, by the life you live.

With burning patience, don't worry that you can't pray well. Surely you know that any spiritual pretension is death to the soul before you begin. Even when you cannot recognise him, will you stay close to him in long silences when nothing seems to be happening? There, with him, life's most significant decisions take shape. There the recurring 'what's the use?' and the scepticism of the dis-illusioned melt away.

Tell him everything, and let him sing within you the radiant gift of life. Tell him everything, even what cannot be expressed and what is absurd. When you understand so little of his language, talk to him about it.

In your struggles, he brings a few words, an intuition or an image to your mind. . . And within you grows a desert flower, a flower of delight.

Brother Roger, *The Wonder of a Love*

Thine is what we are and have. We consecrate it to thee. Receive our thanks when we say grace, consecrating our food and with it all that we receive in our daily life. Prevent us from using empty words and forms when we give thanks to thee. Save us from routine and mere convention when we dare to speak to thee.

We thank thee when we look back at our life, be it long or short, for all we have met in it. And we thank thee not only for what we have loved and for what gave us pleasure, but also for what brought us disappointment, pain and suffering, because we *now* know that it helped us to fulfil that for which we were born. And if new disappointments and new suffering take hold of us and words of thanks die on our tongues, remind us that day may come when we are ready to give thanks for the dark road on which thou hast led us.

Our words of thanks are poor and often we cannot find words at all. There are days and months and years in which we were or are still unable to speak to thee. Give us the power, at such time, to keep our hearts open to the abundance of life and, in silent gratefulness, to ex-perience thine unchanging, eternal presence. Take the silent sacrifice of a heart when words of thanks become rare in us. Accept our silent gratefulness and keep our hearts and minds open to thee always!

Paul Tillich, 'In Everything Give Thanks'

You wait for us
until we are open to you.
We wait for your word
to make us receptive.
Attune us to your voice,
to your silence,
speak and bring your son to us —
Jesus, the word of your peace.

Your word is near,
O Lord our God,
your grace is near.
Come to us, then,
with mildness and power.
Do not let us be deaf to you,
but make us receptive and open
to Jesus Christ your son,
who will come to look for us and save us
today and every day
for ever and ever.

Huub Oosterhuis, *Your Word is Near*

Lord, make me receptive to your many voices, in all your languages. Teach me to listen, with my whole being and in all the business of my life.

Open my dull heart and frightened spirit to the music of your creation.

Give me the courage to go with your Spirit into the wilderness. Make me prepared to move and feel and think beyond the fringes of the familiar places, to follow you into dark and uninhabited places, to face the Tempter and dwell among the wildest elements, and there to meet with you.

Assure me that no doubt and no despair can separate me from your love. Forgive me that I imagined your presence with me depended on my believing. Help me simply to accept your grace, the gift of your mysterious, healing and transforming presence, wherever I am and whatever I may believe and feel.

Help me to wait upon your presence. In waiting help me to be compassionate with all who share the journey. Grant me the grace to be gentle with myself, and in everything to give thanks. Amen.

A Benediction
May the mystery of his presence light your way, guide your actions and nourish your innermost being, till you find your rest in him. Amen.

Theme: Direction and hope

Rivers through the desert

Stop dwelling on past events
and brooding over days gone by.
I am about to do something new;
this moment it will unfold.
Can you not perceive it?
Even through the wilderness I shall make a way,
and paths in the barren desert.
The wild beast will do me honour,
the wolf and the desert-owl,
for I shall provide water in the wilderness
and rivers in the barren desert,
where my chosen people may drink,
this people I have formed for myself,
and they will proclaim my praises.

                              Isaiah 43: 18-21, REB

14

The heavenly vision. . . for the people of earth

The word of the Lord came to Abram in a vision, 'Fear not, Abram, I am your shield; your reward shall be very great.' But Abram said, 'O Lord God, what wilt thou give me, for I continue childless. . . ?' [The Lord] brought him outside and said, 'Look toward heaven, and number the stars, if you are able to number.' Then he said to him, 'So shall your descendants be.' And he believed the Lord; and he reckoned it to him as righteousness.

God spoke to Israel in visions of the night. '. . . do not be afraid to go down to Egypt, for I will there make of you a great nation.'

The Lord said, '. . .while my glory passes by I will put you in a cleft of the rock, and I will cover you with my hand until I have passed by.' Moses did not know that the skin of his face shone because he had been talking with God.

In those days there was no frequent vision. Where there is no vision the people perish. Her prophets obtain no vision from the Lord.

In accordance with all. . . this vision, Nathan spoke to David. Of old thou didst speak in a vision to thy faithful one.

The vision of Obadiah. The vision of Nahum of Elkosh. The vision of Isaiah the son of Amoz. A stern vision is told to me.

They seek a vision from the prophet. . . they shall eat their bread with fearfulness, and drink water in dismay. . . on account of the violence of all those who dwell in [the land]. The days are at hand, and the fulfilment of every vision.

Daniel had understanding in all visions and dreams. 'Your dream and the visions of your head. . . are these: To you, O King, as you lay in bed came thoughts of what would be hereafter.' 'I saw in the visions of my head. . . a watcher, a holy one, came down from heaven.' 'I saw in the night vision. . . there came one like a son of man, and he came to the Ancient of Days and was presented before him.'

I spoke to the prophets, it was I who multiplied visions.

I will pour out my spirit on all flesh; your sons and daughters shall prophesy, your old men shall dream dreams, and your young men shall see visions. Write the vision; make it plain upon tablets, so he may run who reads it.

They perceived that [Zechariah] had seen a vision in the temple.

As they were coming down the mountain, Jesus commanded them, 'Tell no one the vision, until the Son of man is raised from the dead.'

They came back saying they had even seen a vision of angels, who said he was alive.

The Lord said to him in a vision, 'Ananias'. . . Peter was inwardly perplexed as to what the vision which he had seen might mean. . . A vision appeared to Paul in the night: 'Come over to Macedonia and help us.' The Lord said to Paul one night in a vision, 'Do not be afraid, but speak. . . for I have many people in this city. . .' 'King Agrippa, I was not disobedient to the heavenly vision.'

(Genesis 15: 1–2, 5–6; 46: 2-3; Exodus 33: 22; 34: 29; I Samuel 3: 1 — all RSV; Proverbs 29: 18, AV; Lamentations 2: 9; I Chronicles 17: 15; Psalm 89: 19; Obadiah 1: 1; Nahum 1: 1; Isaiah 1: 1; 21: 2; Ezekiel 7: 26; 12: 19–23b; Daniel 1: 17b; 2: 28b–29; 4: 13; 7: 13; Hosea 12: 10; Joel 2: 28; Habakkuk 2: 2; Luke 1: 22; Matthew 17: 9; Luke 24: 23; Acts 9: 10; 10: 17; 16: 9; 18: 9–10; 26: 19 — all RSV)

We have always wanted to know the future. From the gypsy with her crystal, or tarot cards, or reading the lines in your palm, or the astrologer with his stars, we long to know what will happen to the world in general, and to *our* world in particular. And visions undoubtedly do sometimes relate to the future, as the Bible makes clear. Daniel's explanation of Nebuchadnezzar's vision of a mighty statue with its head of gold, breast and arms of silver, belly and thighs of bronze, legs of iron, and feet a mixture of iron and clay meant it would take centuries before its meaning was outworked. John's vision on the isle of Patmos is taking millennia to reach its fulfilment.

But the scriptures also describe some visions that are for the here and now. Israel needs to know whether it is right to take the promised people into Egypt, away from the promised land. David is told that his idea of a temple is magnificent, but not for him to build. Paul is directed to go to Macedonia, or to stay in Corinth. Clearly not every decision we take is communicated through a vision, but some major turning points in the history of Israel and the church certainly have been.

Whilst other people's visions are urgent and important, they make us realise that we need a vision, too — something that we will follow, give our lives to undertaking, work for with all our heart. Peter Block suggests a vision should be both strategic and lofty. But your vision will be precisely that — *your* vision. The scriptures show only Joseph and Pharaoh, and Daniel and Nebuchadnezzar had the same dreams or visions — and both for the purpose of explanation. Your vision will be unique to you, just as God has made you unique, brought you specially to himself, and commissioned you to labour in his vineyard. Jesus says to his disciples, 'You did not choose me, but I chose you and appointed you that you should go and bear fruit and that your fruit should remain, so that whatever you ask the Father in my name, he may give it to you' (John 15: 16).

Be thou my vision, O Lord of my heart;
Naught be all else to me, save that thou art —
Thou my best thought, by day or by night,
Waking or sleeping, thy presence my Light.
High King of heaven, after victory won,
May I reach heav'n's joys, O bright heaven's Sun!
Heart of my own heart, whatever befall,
Still be my vision, O Ruler of all.

Ancient Irish Hymn

This is no war of domination or imperial aggrandisement
or material gain; no war to shut any country out of the
sunlight and means of progress. It is a war, viewed in its
inherent quality to establish, on impregnable rocks, the
rights of the individual, and it is a war to establish and
revive the stature of man.

Winston Churchill, on the day Britain declared war in 1939

The real problem is in defining reality. In my mind, reality
is the market, the numbers, the comparisons with others.
The first two or three months, I had many, many meetings
— probably fifteen a *day* — where we discussed facts.
Not opinions, just facts. This was a company used to
discussing ideas and opinions. My contribution was to
transform this thinking to our way of behaving, from
concepts to numbers. I am a great believer in the power
of numbers. Of course you have to understand and interpret them. They are a good starting point for any plan,
any action.

Lee Iacocca

If you are planning for one year, plant rice. If you are
planning for ten years, plant trees. If you are planning
for 100 years, plant people.

Indian proverb

The vision was to establish a workshop on the estate
providing employment, help and outreach to the local
community. It became a reality after much prayer and
planning by the committee when a grant was given,

premises became available in the school on the estate, and a workshop manager was appointed. By early February, the workshop began to function in the way that had been foreseen three years earlier, much to the excitement and encouragement of those who had worked for it.

Information Sheet, The Carpenters' Shop

This very remarkable man
Commends a most remarkable plan.
You can do what you want
If you don't think you can't,
So don't think you can't; think you can.

Charles Inge

Let your vision be your commission.

WEC motto

Go ahead and do it; you can always apologise later.

Rear Admiral Grace Hopper

The first ingredient in [renewal] is a powerful vision — a whole new sense of where a company [church, society or organisation] is going and how to get there. It is important to understand trends. . . but it is not enough. You must also discover the special way that your company fits into the business environment. The company's vision becomes a catalytic force, an organising principle for everything that the people in the corporation do.

John Naisbitt, *Re-inventing the Corporation*

One minister pointed out that there were no more jobs left for his people. Apparently some churches only need a third of the membership to keep the church ticking over. We are back again to the vision of the leadership. What are we here for? Visions that stop at the church door offer little challenge. Perhaps we should stop berating the 'less committed' and begin to ask the more committed what they are committed to.

Peter Neilson, 'Life and Work'

The creation of humankind crowns the work [of God in Genesis 1 and 2], but the sabbath is its supreme goal. Now, what is the meaning of the sabbath that was given to Israel? It relativises the works of humankind, the contents of the six working days. It protects us from total absorption by the task of subduing the earth. It anticipates the distortion which makes work the sum and purpose of human life. And it informs us that we will not fulfil our humanity in our relation to the world which we are transforming [unless] we raise our eyes above, in the blessed holy hour of communion with the Creator. With this meaning it would be no exaggeration to state that the sabbath sums up the difference between the biblical and the Marxist visions. The essence of humankind is not work!

Henri Blocher, In the Beginning

Lewis Carroll in *Through the Looking Glass* tackles the problem of attempting the impossible. The White Queen is speaking to Alice.

'I can't believe that,' said Alice.

'Can't you?' the Queen said, in a pitying tone. 'Try again: draw a long breath and shut your eyes.'

Alice laughed: 'There's no use trying,' she said. 'One *can't* believe impossible things.'

' I daresay you haven't had much practice,' said the Queen. 'When I was your age, I always did it for half-an-hour a day. Why, sometimes I've believed as many as six impossible things before breakfast.'

Most of us follow Alice — we don't believe in the impossible. The disciples felt that it was impossible for Jesus to have risen from the dead on the third day. No-one had ever done that before. Who would believe in blue snow? But that's what the scientists found on Jupiter's moon Io as Voyager, the spacecraft, took coloured photographs as it swept past — a kind of volcanic precipitate.

The seven last words of the church are said to be. 'We have always done it this way.' Change? Impossible! But we follow an impossible God who can give us a vision to do the impossible.

Peter Brierley, Vision Building

I am what I am becoming.

Anonymous

You see things as they are and ask 'Why?' But I dream things that never were and ask, 'Why not?'

George Bernard Shaw

Vision is imaginative insight, statesmanlike foresight, sagacity in planning.

Concise Oxford Dictionary

Vision is not a fragile thing. It is the heart of corporate strategy and purpose; an integrating force; it helps overcome barriers to change; it channels energies by enabling everyone to point in the same direction.

Lyndon Bowring

The Alpine climber who is trying to reach a summit can, on the upward path, scarcely see his goal except at certain fortunate moments. What he *does* see is the strong path that must be trodden, the rocks and precipices to be avoided, the unbending slopes that become even steeper. He feels the growing weakness, the solitude and the burden. And yet, the inspiration of the climber is the sight of the goal. Because of it, all the hardships of the journey count for naught.

Samuel Zwemer, *Call to Prayer*

Lead me, Heavenly Father, into your creative purpose for my gifts, skills and knowledge of your ways, limited though they are. Give direction not just for today but for the next five years, or ten years, or my lifetime. Then I will see more clearly what I must do more of this week in order to begin to fulfil your long-term desires for me.

Oh, Lord Jesus, help me to be willing to go where I am led. Forgive my fears at being given a task that seems too long. Forgive my reluctance to move from my security. Forgive my complacency with the needs of a sinful world all round me. Help me to be conscious of your presence, grateful for your power, guided by your peace.

Holy Spirit, thank you for making me what I have been becoming. Take me as I am, and continue to break me and mould me into becoming what you would have me to be. I do not ask for my sake, but for the glory of him who died for me, chose me and appointed me, that my life might bear fruit, even Jesus Christ my Lord. Amen.

Almighty God,
whose chosen servant Abraham
faithfully obeyed your call
and rejoiced in your promise
that, in him, all the families of the earth should be blessed;
give us a faith like his,
that, in us, your promises may be fulfilled;
through Jesus Christ our Lord.

Almighty and everlasting God,
increase this gift of faith;
that, forsaking what lies behind
and reaching out to that which is before,
we may run the way of your commandments
and win the crown of everlasting joy,
through Jesus Christ our Lord.

Alternative Service Book

A Benediction
May God give us light to guide us, courage to support us and love to unite us, now and evermore. Amen.

15

The hazardous journey

In due time their foot will slip. Their day of disaster is near and their doom rushes upon them. The Lord will judge his people and have compassion on his servants when he sees their strength is gone.

But as for me, my feet had almost slipped; I had nearly lost my foothold. For I envied the arrogant when I saw the prosperity of the wicked.

I know that nothing good lives in me, that is, in my sinful nature. For I have the desire to do what is good, but I cannot carry it out. For what I do is not the good I want to do; no, the evil I do not want to do — this I keep on doing.

I will sprinkle clean water on you, and you will be clean; I will cleanse you from all your impurities and from all your idols. I will give you a new heart and put a new spirit in you; I will remove from you your heart of stone and give you a heart of flesh.

My eyes are ever on the Lord, for only he will release my feet from the snare.

How long must I wrestle with my thoughts and every day have sorrow in my heart? How long will my enemy triumph over me? Look on me and answer, O Lord my God. Give light to my eyes, or I will sleep in death. . . But I trust in your unfailing love; my heart rejoices in your salvation.

Some of the wise will stumble, so that they may be refined, purified and made spotless until the time of the end, for it will still come at the appointed time.

The Lord will be your confidence and will keep your foot from being snared.

Create in me a pure heart, O God, and renew a steadfast spirit within me. Do not cast me from your presence or take your Holy Spirit from me. . . Restore to me the joy of your salvation and grant me a willing spirit, to sustain me.

For we are God's workmanship, created in Christ Jesus to do good works, which God prepared in advance for us to do.

Now the Lord is the Spirit, and where the Spirit of the Lord is, there is freedom.

O God, you are my God, earnestly I seek you; my soul thirsts for you, my body longs for you, in a dry and weary land where there is no water. On my bed I remember you; I think of you through the watches of the night. Because you are my help, I sing in the shadow of your wings. I stay close to you; your right hand upholds me.

How precious to me are your thoughts, O God! How vast is the sum of them! Were I to count them, they would outnumber the grains of sand. When I awake, I am still with you.

Test me, O Lord, and try me, examine my heart and my mind; for your love is ever before me, and I walk continually in your truth. My feet stand on level ground; in the great assembly I will praise the Lord.

I will instruct you and teach you in the way you should go; I will counsel you and watch over you.

Delight yourself in the Lord and he will give you the desires of your heart.

(Deuteronomy 32: 35–36a; Psalm 73: 2–3; Romans 7: 18–19; Ezekiel 36: 25–26; Psalm 25: 15; Psalm 13: 2, 3 and 5; Daniel 11: 35; Proverbs 3: 26; Psalm 51: 10-12; Ephesians 2: 10; 2 Corinthians 3: 17; Psalm 63: 1, 6-8; Psalm 139: 17–18; Psalm 26: 2-3 and12; Psalm 32: 8; Psalm 37: 4 — all NIV)

There is a view of Christian guidance that I learnt in youth group that God is in control — commend the day to God, sit back and see God's hand at work. This optimistic view is expressed by Alexander Pope in a poem which concludes, 'Whatever is, is right.'

So I wove my way through life — thankful for God's goodness, trying to be loving, avoiding the nasty things and knowing God is achieving his purposes. I look back now and feel God would not have been impressed by this 'loyalty' which avoided taking my responsibilities and sinfulness more seriously. But it was a case of 'Give as much of yourself that you know, to as much of God that you know.'

The innocence of this approach vanished when I could no longer weave around problems and 'crashed' into little pieces, and others were involved in my accident — wounded, hurt and wondering about 'my' God and 'my' faith. Was this a God achieving his 'good plan' or was he just a monster? I had betrayed him badly to myself and others and needed to reorientate my life, discovering again his forgiveness, his unconditional love and care in putting the pieces back together in his good time.

For me this involved taking responsibility, little by little, for myself — my actions and decisions. That was tough when I wanted everyone to like me. This involved finding new paths to follow and learning to live with tensions — finding a balance between extremes of dependence and independence; acting and reflecting; death and life. The simplicity of the past had been replaced by a creative tension in the present which is reflected in the sign on my bathroom mirror:

You are looking at the face of the person who is responsible for your happiness today. Good morning, Jesus; thank you for loving me; what have you got going today?

Yes, on some mornings this has been tough to face as I have felt lonely, not knowing who I really was; concerned as to what others thought, as making choices was tough and living with the consequences somewhat frightening. So what way to go often involved scary paths as Robert Frost suggests in his poem, 'The Road Not Taken':

Two roads diverged in a wood, and I —
I took the one less travelled by,
And that has made all the difference.

Obviously there will be surprises, particularly in who you may find on this road. In expressing this journey I wrote the following:

As I look up and down this tortured path
there are climbers labouring hard and long.
There is a joy and peace that lights up their faces
both fresh and veined,
their voices are music to me.
Can you hear?
Yes, of course, for you hum the tunes,
those travellers' songs.

It all takes a lot of getting used to, reorientating attitudes while trying to be open. Choices just had to be made day by day in ways that often led to new paths while I was also facing old hurts, questions and consequences of decisions. Gordon MacDonald speaks of this pain:

It was not a one-time choice. We made it again and again as time passed. A score of ways could be found to bring back the pain. And each time the choice had to be made again. Would we fight the pain or permit it to be the environment in which God speaks? Usually, we chose the latter. And when for a moment we strayed toward the former, something seemed to happen to soon remind us that there was a better way.

That better way involved picking up the pieces with God's support and this is how I saw it while meditating on Psalm 34:

I need your helping hand again, O Lord,
for I feel thrown down, not able to rise. . .
Lead on, my Lord!

A guilt complex is not another name for a sense of sin. Indeed, a guilt complex can sometimes obscure the reality of our sinfulness. It causes us to look within ourselves or at those around us, and it tempts us to seek excuses for our sinful behaviour ('I can't help it: I'm made that way'). A sense of sin, on the other hand, points us to God and leaves us with nothing to say about ourselves except that we are sinners.

John Gunstone, *Free in Christ*

Because I am human, I will fall; because I have been redeemed, I am able to rise again. To listen with my mind already made up is an empty gesture. Only when I allow the voice of God to release my inner freedom from the bonds of pride and wilfulness that enslave me can I discover the purpose for which I alone was made. My role in the world: to be his servant, inspiring others by my relaxed and joyful incarnation of Christ within the limits of my abilities.

Adrian Van Kaam & Susan Muto, *Am I Living a Spiritual Life*

And then he allows some of us to fall more severely and distressingly than before — at least that is how we see it. And then it seems to us, who are not always wise, that all we set our hands to is lost. But it is not so. We need to fall, and we need to see that we have done so. For if we never fell we should not know how weak and pitiable we are in ourselves. Nor should we fully know the wonderful love of our Maker.

In heaven we shall see truly and everlastingly that we have grievously sinned in this life; notwithstanding, we shall see that this in no way diminished his love, nor made us less precious in his sight.

The testing experience of falling will lead us to a deep and wonderful knowledge of the constancy of God's love, which neither can nor will be broken because of sin. To understand this is of great profit.

Julian of Norwich

So we are called to wholeness and simultaneously to recognise our incompleteness; called to power and to acknowledge our weakness; called to both individuation and interdependence. Thus the problem — indeed, the total failure — of the 'ethic' of rugged individualism is that it runs with only one side of this paradox, incorporates only one half of our humanity. It recognises that we are called to individuation, power and wholeness. But it denies entirely the other part of the human story: that we can never fully get there and that we are, of necessity in our uniqueness, weak and imperfect creatures who need each other.

M. Scott Peck, The Different Drum

'There are only two ways out of chaos,' I will explain to a group after it has spent a sufficient period of time squabbling and getting nowhere. 'One is into organisation — but organisation is never community. The only other way is into and through emptiness.'

M. Scott Peck, The Different Drum

We can never escape from obedience to God. . . When we have the feeling that on some occasion we have disobeyed God, it simply means that for a time we have ceased to desire obedience. Of course it must be understood that, where everything else is equal, we do not perform the same actions if we give our consent to obedience as if we do not; just as a plant, where everything else is equal, does not grow in the same way if it is in the light as if it is in the dark. The plant does not have any control or choice in the matter of its own growth. As for us, we are like plants which have the one choice of being in or out of the light.

Simone Weil, Waiting On God

Lead, kindly Light, amid the encircling gloom,
Lead thou me on!
The night is dark, and I am far from home —
Lead thou me on!
Keep thou my feet; I do not ask to see
The distant scene — one step enough for me.

John H. Newman, 'The Pillar of the Cloud'

The way we see, interpret and react to whatever happens to us is the important thing. Sometimes the very worst thing that may happen *to* us can bring about the best thing that could ever happen *in* us. And we must assume this responsibility for what happens in us. We must assume responsibility for our attitudes. Only if we accept this responsibility can we grow through the various circumstances of life.

John Powell, *The Christian Vision*

There are men and women who reach their twenties with a strong sense of dependence motivating their life. They are afraid to take charge of their own being and consciously or unconsciously find themselves in a relationship or situation of continuing dependence. . . The dependent person may remain so throughout life. A significant proportion, however, begin to emerge from their dependence in the mid-thirties to the fifties. Gradually they find the confidence to take increasing charge of their own life. They seek greater control over their destiny and they challenge authority. . . The challenge can be defiant or quietly assertive, but a new life is certainly born whose resolution is implacable.

Gerald O'Collins, *The Second Journey*

Self-knowledge, the beginning of wisdom, is ruled out for most people by the increasingly effective self-deception they practise as they grow older. By middle age, most of us are accomplished fugitives from ourselves. Yet there's a surprising usefulness in learning not to lie to yourself.

John Gardner, *Self Renewal*

We grow in self-awareness not only by introspection but by tackling the jobs that lie to hand, by measuring our strength and skill against taxing work and difficult people. In middle and later life after the heat of the struggle to succeed is over and such measure of success as we have attained has lost all its novelty and most of its charm, then especially we are ready to devote energy to the task of gaining deeper self-awareness. Until we know ourselves, we cannot really possess ourselves. And until we possess ourselves and have the inner peace that comes from self-possession, we shall find it impossible to relate to other people except either by trying to possess and dominate them or by letting them possess or dominate us.

Christopher Bryant, *The River Within*

C.S. Lewis wrote, 'To love at all is to be vulnerable. Love anything and your heart will certainly be wrung and possibly broken.' He goes on to say that if you keep your heart intact, it will become 'unbreakable, impenetrable, irredeemable'. Because the more I commit myself to a person, the greater the pain I shall feel when he lets me down or hurts or rejects or avoids me.

Also, it is only when I am close to another that I see the 'speck' in her eye and then learn the painful truth that the speck in her eye is simply a reflection of the log that is in mine. I haven't yet met a Christian anywhere in the world with a deep mature love who hasn't gone through considerable suffering in the area of relationships. So, the pressures and pains in our relationships can, if we learn to forgive and be forgiven, produce this rare and fragrant love.

David Watson, *Through the Year with David Watson*

But in life, wherever else we are, we are always also on the Delectable Mountains from which we can catch a glimpse of the Celestial City. . . The necessary conflicts of our life are for the time being resolved. And we experience a foretaste of their final and permanent resolution.

God, we believe, accepts us, accepts all persons, unconditionally, warts and all. Laughter is the purest form of our response to God's acceptance of us. For when I laugh at myself I accept myself and when I laugh at other people in genuine mirth I accept them. Self-acceptance in laughter is the very opposite of self-satisfaction or pride . . . In laughing at my own claims of importance or regard I receive myself in a sort of loving forgiveness which is an echo of God's forgiveness of me.

Altogether, I suggest that laughter is the best and clearest reflection we ever get in this world of God's love for his creation. In laughter we see the Celestial City in what is more than a passing glimpse.

Harry Williams, *Tensions*

O Lord, journeying is fun sometimes, but at other times I'm exhausted and discouraged. I come to you for strength: physical, emotional and spiritual. I need to sort out a few things first. The way you do things is often so mysterious; why do you allow me to stumble along and fall down? At other times your protection is breathtaking. I find you have saved me yet again — Thanks! I am slow to learn that your ways are different to my limited ways of thinking and acting. Thanks for being patient, merciful and forgiving! I am not sure I am honest with you and others. Lord, help me to deal with anything I'm resenting in others that I haven't honestly faced.

Lord, I don't want just a surface change, so please reach into the depths of my being — to cleanse, reorientate and transform with your healing hand. I don't want to wander around in circles and get nowhere. Lord, unless you give me light, I will never know who I am. So please help to find more unity between my conscious and unconscious that will help me find wholeness and direction for the journey ahead.

Lord, take your knife and cut away at the tendency towards dishonesty and self deception. Thank you for the assurance of your forgiveness. Please take my hand and lead on through the 'valley of the shadow' as well as the treacherous hillside. Guide my feet across the rocky terrain and around the many traps. Thank you for journeying with me. I don't want to leave your side for the rest of my life, so Lord, please lead on. Amen.

A Benediction
For thus says the Lord God: Behold, I, I myself will search for my sheep, and will seek them out. As a shepherd seeks out his flock when some of his sheep have been scattered abroad, so I will seek out my sheep; and I will rescue them. . . And I will bring them out. . . and gather them. . . and I will feed them. . . I myself will be the shepherd of my sheep. . . I will seek the

lost and I will bring back the strayed, and I will bind up the crippled, and I will strengthen the weak, and the fat and strong I will watch over; I will feed them in justice.

Ezekiel 34: 11-16, RSV

16

2/2/97

This holy whisper

(Thomas Kelly)

Hear, O heavens! Listen, O earth! For the Lord has Is.1:2 spoken.

The Lord would speak to Moses face to face, as a person speaks with a friend.

Eli realised that it was the Lord who was calling the boy, so he said to him, 'Go back to bed; and if he calls you again, say, 'Speak, Lord, your servant is listening.' 1 Sam 3 So Samuel went back to bed.

The Lord came and stood there, and called as he had before, 'Samuel! Samuel!'

Samuel answered, 'Speak; your servant is listening.'

The Lord said, 'Go out and stand on the mountain in the presence of the Lord, for the Lord is about to pass by.' Then a great and powerful wind tore the mountains apart 1 kings 19 and shattered the rocks before the Lord, but the Lord was not in the wind. After the wind there was an earthquake, but the Lord was not in the earthquake. After the earthquake came a fire, but the Lord was not in the fire. And after the fire came a gentle whisper. . . Then a voice said to him, 'What are you doing here, Elijah?'

Ears that hear and eyes that see — the Lord has made them both.

The Sovereign Lord has given me an instructed tongue, to know the word that sustains the weary. He wakens me morning by morning, wakens my ear to listen like one being taught. The Sovereign Lord has opened my ears, and I have not been rebellious; I have not drawn back.

The word of the Lord came to me, saying, 'Before I formed you in the womb I knew you; before you were

127

born I set you apart; I appointed you as a prophet to
the nations.'

Abraham said, 'If they do not listen to Moses and the
prophets, they will not be convinced even if someone
rises from the dead.'

But blessed are your eyes because they see and your
ears because they hear. For I tell you the truth, many
prophets. . . longed to see what you see but did not see
it and to hear what you hear but did not hear it.

If you have ears, then hear.

I tell you the truth, whoever hears my word and
believes him who sent me has eternal life and will not
be condemned.

Faith comes from hearing the message, and the message is heard through the word of Christ.

That which was from the beginning, which we have
heard, which we have seen with our own eyes, which
we have looked at and our hands have touched — this
we proclaim concerning the Word of life. . . We proclaim
to you what we have seen and heard.

(Isaiah 1: 2; Exodus 33: 11 — both NIV; 1 Samuel 3: 8-10, GNB;
1 Kings 19: 11-13; Proverbs 20: 12; Isaiah 50: 4-5; Jeremiah 1: 4
-5; Luke 16: 31; Matthew 13: 16-17, 43; John 5: 24; Romans 10:
17; 1 John 1: 1, 3 — all NIV)

When I play
my records
(at full volume,
in stereo)
I have to
close all
the windows.

I can't stand
the noise
of the birds
outside
in the trees.

Steve Turner

This satirical comment on our noisy society suggests why so many of us have difficulty praying. We become uneasy when the noise stops and fear something must be wrong. This sad reality means we are losing our ability to listen. Without the art of listening we not only lack meaningful relationships, but forget something basic about prayer. True prayer always includes a careful listening for God.

The Bible is filled with stories of God speaking to people. Prophets heard and then declared 'the word of the Lord'. That hearing came in many ways, sometimes through dramatic experiences, but often through the events of everyday life. The story of Elijah on Mount Horeb (1 Kings 19) offers a striking example of the need to strain in order to hear the quiet whisper of God. In our sin we are very deaf.

Without listening there can be no true love or even companionship. Marriages fail because one or both forget to listen. It is a peculiar and superficial friendship if one constantly chatters and never listens to the other. A great test of friendship is when we can keep silence with our friends with complete enjoyment and without embarrassment of any kind. Prayer is being with God. It is commonly a higher form of fellowship simply to be quiet and to enjoy God's presence rather than that 'shopping-list' kind of speaking we often call prayer.

Learning to listen and to love God is the best preparation for listening to and loving others. Conversely, true listening to others is essential if we are to discover God speaking to us.

Our existence is meant to be dialogue. Prayer is dialogue. Life with others is designed to be dialogue, not monologue. As we hear the whisper of God coming to us from silence, we know we are loved. That whisper prompts us to 'lend our ears' to others struggling with confusion, loneliness, pain and failure. In that listening we again hear the whisper of God.

❧

When we speak of 'listening' to God we are talking about a listening of the spirit, a tuning of our inmost being to 'hear' the word of God. By 'the word of God' I mean not only the actual written words of the scriptures, but God's message in all its manifestations. God 'speaks' to us through the scriptures, through the events in our lives, through the people we meet, through history, through nature — through everything. But, as in ordinary physical listening, we must keep silence if we are to hear what God is saying to us.

Sheila Cassidy, *Prayer for Pilgrims*

Who is a prophet? Someone who is searching — someone who is being sought. Someone who listens — and who is listened to. Someone who sees people as they are, and as they ought to be. Someone who reflects his or her time, yet lives outside time.

A prophet is forever awake, forever alert — never indifferent, least of all to injustice, be it human or divine, whenever or wherever it may be found. God's messenger to us, the prophet, somehow becomes our messenger to God.

Restless, disquieting, prophets are forever waiting for a signal, a summons. Asleep they hear voices and follow visions; their dreams do not belong to them.

Elie Wiesel, *Five Biblical Portraits*

The awful and inspiring thing about the Bible is that it enables us to hear the word which God addresses to us, and it gives us the high position of those whom God treats as responsible persons, as friends to whom he makes known his counsels. We take our place by the side of the people of the Bible with whom the living God held converse; we stand alert, responsible, listening to the word which he commits to our keeping: 'Son/daughter, stand upon your feet and I will speak with you' (Ezekiel 2: 1).

Alan Richardson, *Preface to Bible Study*

When God speaks, he likes no other voice to break the stillness but his own. . . When God speaks, he speaks so loud that all the voices of the world seem dumb. And yet when God speaks, he speaks so softly that no-one hears the whisper but yourself.

Henry Drummond, *The Ideal Life*

Samuel's prayer was, 'Speak, Lord, for thy servant heareth', but it has been said that our prayer is often, 'Hear, Lord, for thy servant speaketh.'

Denis Lant, *First Steps in Prayer*

There is a divine abyss within us all, a holy infinite centre, a heart, a Life who speaks in us and through us to the world. We have all heard this holy whisper at times. At times we have followed the whisper. . . But too many of us have heeded the Voice only at times. Only at times have we submitted to his holy guidance. We have not counted this holy thing within us to be the most precious thing in the world. We have not surrendered *all else*, to attend to it alone. Let me repeat. Most of us, I fear, have not surrendered all else, in order to attend to the Holy Within.

Thomas Kelly, *A Testament of Devotion*

I don't know who — or what — put the question, I don't know when it was put. I don't even remember answering. But at some moment I did answer Yes to Someone — or Something — and from that hour I was certain that existence is meaningful and that, therefore, my life in self-surrender had a goal. From that moment I have known what it means 'not to look back', and 'to take no thought for the morrow'.

Dag Hammarskjöld, *Markings*

Most importantly, through my interviewing, I came to realise there was a great value in listening to people, a value for them, for me — and for the audience. I knew somehow it was important for us as a community to hear of the lives and ideas of others, and I developed my gift for listening. . . Often I had a sense of being a listening instrument, through which people might hear something of value for them, but I did not interpret this in any religious way. Now I think the gift of listening is one of

several keys to the awakening in me of conscious awareness of a religious dimension to life — an awareness that
would first plunge me into blackness and then bring me
safely into the light. . .
There followed a number of conversations over many
months with two priests separately who seemed able to
discern the yearning child within the public figure. I knew
that the wisdom, acceptance, gentleness and generous *ac-
cessibility*, the *listening* of these men were signs of God,
were human portrayals of a loving Creator who is waiting
for his children to come home to him. . .
I try to be mindful in my work, monitoring to see if it
is building community, tapping insight, revealing inspiration. This is an act of my will and a determination to use
my talents but I also listen, like a witness, to hear if it
rings true to my understanding of divine will, revealed
through scripture and my conscience.

Caroline Jones, *The Search for Meaning*

There is a real act of self-denial in every authentic experience of hearing. I am called to turn down the record
that is forever playing in my head so there is silence
enough for me to hear a word from beyond. It is so easy
for me to project upon another a shadow out of my own
past experience rather than letting that person be what he
or she is in this moment, and receive in that moment a
new and fresh experience.

John Claypool, *The Preaching Event*

If you wish to enter the world of those
who are broken or closed in upon themselves,
it is important to learn their language.

Learning a language
is not just learning French or Spanish or German.
It is learning to understand what people are really
saying,
the non-verbal as well as the verbal language.
The verbal, exterior language is the beginning
and is absolutely necessary,

but you must go deeper
and discern what it means to listen:
to listen deeply to another,
    to the cry flowing from the heart,
    in order to understand people,
    both in their pain and in their gift;
to understand what they are truly asking
    so that you can hold their wound, their pain
    and all that flows from it:
    violence, anger or depression,
    self-centredness and limitless demands;
    the suffocating urge to possess,
    the refusal to let go;
to accept these with compassion,
    without judging, without condemning. . .

If you come in this way,
open, listening humbly, without judging,
then gradually you will discover
that you are trusted.
Your heart will be touched.
You will begin to discover the secret of communion.

          Jean Vanier, *The Broken Body*

Lord let me hear, hear more and more,
Hear the sounds of great rejoicing, hear a person
barely sigh,
Hear the ring of truth and hollowness of those who
live a lie,
Hear the wail of starving people who will die,
Hear the voice of our Lord in the cry,
Lord let me hear.

          Ross Langmead, *On the Road*

---

*Lord, in this noisy world, I sometimes feel as though I am deaf.
Help me to turn down that record playing in my head and
again to discover silence. I remember that lovely hymn which
tells me that Jesus knelt to share with you 'the silence of eternity,
interpreted by love'. Help me, when earthquake, wind and fire*

threaten to overwhelm my senses, to hear your 'still, small voice of calm'. . .

Today as I pray, I want not so much to speak, but to listen. . . listen to you in scripture, in my loved ones, in this world, in my experiences.

And yet I know I must go out to people deafened by unceasing clamour. Help me to find space for others. Give me ears to hear what others really are crying out to me. I want to listen, not so that I can inject an answer when there is a lull in conversation, but to offer understanding and acceptance. Help me not to feel I must always speak, to know there are times when nothing has to be said but my presence is itself a needed gift.

Speak, Lord, your servant is listening.

A Benediction
May you have ears to hear what the Lord is saying and eyes to see what the Lord is doing. May you have a mind to learn what the Lord is teaching and a heart to love the Lord and your neighbour as yourself. Amen.

17

Real questions

I will not keep silent; I will speak out in the anguish of my spirit, I will complain in the bitterness of my soul. . . Who are we that you make so much of us, that you give us so much attention, that you examine us every morning and test us every moment?. . . Does it please you to oppress me, to spurn the work of your hands. . . Your hands shaped and made me — will you now destroy me?

Jonah was greatly displeased and became angry. He prayed to the Lord, 'O Lord, is this not what I said when I was still at home?'. . . But God said to Jonah, 'Do you have a right to be angry. . .?' 'I do', he said, 'I am angry enough to die.'

He has turned his hand against me again and again, all day long; he has walled me in so that I cannot escape . . . Like a bear lying in wait, like a lion in hiding, he dragged me from the path and mangled me. . . he has filled me with bitter herbs and sated me with gall. He has broken my teeth with gravel; he has trampled me in the dust.

You have covered yourself with anger and pursued us; you have slain without pity. You have covered yourself with a cloud so that no prayer can get through. You have made us scum and refuse among the nations. . . My eyes will flow unceasingly, without relief, until the Lord looks down from heaven and sees.

Though he slay me, yet will I hope in him; I will surely defend my ways to his face.

Then Abraham approached him and said: 'Will you sweep away the righteous with the wicked? What if there are fifty righteous people in the city?. . . Far be it from you to do such a thing.'

'It is not right to take the children's bread and toss it to the dogs.' 'Yes Lord,' she said, 'but even the dogs eat the crumbs that fall from the master's table.' Then Jesus answered, 'Woman, you have great faith!'

'My soul is overwhelmed with sorrow to the point of death. . . Father, everything is possible for you. Take this cup from me.'

At the ninth hour Jesus cried out in a loud voice. . . 'My God, My God, why have you forsaken me?'

During the days of Jesus' life on earth, he offered up prayers and petitions with loud cries and tears to the one who could save him from death, and he was heard.

(Job 7: 11, NIV; 17-18, free translation; 10: 3, 8; Jonah 4: 1, 2, 9; Lamentations 3: 3, 7, 10-11, 15-16, 43-45 and 49-50; Job 13: 15; Genesis 18: 23-24a, 25a; Matthew 15: 26-28; Mark 14: 34a, 36; Mark 15: 34; Hebrews 5: 7 — all NIV)

The trouble with some Christian testimonies is that they leave too many questions answered. Yes, you did read me right — there's no 'un' before the last word. The book of Job is there in the Bible as a constant reminder that if there are easy answers, we're probably asking the wrong questions. Job's friends are full of suitably pious answers to his inexplicable sufferings, while Job rages on and on — yet it is Job who, God says, has 'spoken of me what is right'.

Some years ago, it was fashionable to display posters and stickers bearing the legend 'Jesus is the answer'. Not surprisingly, enterprising graffiti artists added, 'What's the question?' Discovery begins, not with hunting answers, but with asking the right questions. If we don't know what the questions are, answers will mean nothing.

We must also learn to hear 'the question behind the question'. Most cries of perplexity, anger, despair, though they may take the form of questions, are not actually requests for an answer — they are simply requests to be truly heard. Job asks 'why?', but he is answered with 'who' and that is enough. Jesus, in Gethsemane and on the cross, questions God's actions, but his real need is to know that God is still there. Abraham's central concern is not so much to save Sodom, as to be reassured of God's justice: 'Will not the Judge of all the earth do right?' Even the sulky Jonah is not really looking for an explanation, but for God to show that he is on Jonah's side.

What is refreshing about these biblical cross-questioners of God is their lack of inhibition about putting God on the spot, saying exactly what they feel and expecting God to respond in kind. Jesus' apparent rebuff cannot keep the spunky Syro-Phoenician woman from capping his argument — and he concedes the point. So we see that humility is not necessarily about silent, unquestioning submission to events. The writer of Hebrews tells us Jesus was heard because of his 'reverent submission' — but what did this consist of? 'Loud cries and tears'! Humility can mean being careless enough of our own dignity to speak up boldly and risk looking an 'unspiritual fool'.

Are we too mealy-mouthed about laying it on the line to God? He's taken a lot worse on the cross.

Gentile question: Why does a Jew always answer a question with another question?
Jewish answer: Why not?

The basic question of the book of Job is not, Why does suffering come? What is its origin? What is its meaning? Why me? — but, What am I to do about it? Not, *Why* I am suffering, but *How* can I suffer? The answer of the book of Job is clear: the undeserving sufferer must protest to God, must hold him responsible, and must never desist from demanding satisfaction from God. Job speaks directly to God almost every time he opens his mouth. . . His instinct is right; it is God with whom he has to do, it is God who is responsible. He is single-minded in insisting that God answer him.

David Clines, 'Beyond all Proportion'

Anna was standing on the bed, her eyes wide and wild, tears streaming down her cheeks, both hands pressed over her mouth as if to stifle a scream. . . I cried; I don't know if I cried for her or for myself. . . Suddenly out of my tear-filled void I heard Anna's voice. 'Please, please, Mister God, teach me how to ask real questions. Oh please, Mister God, help me to ask real questions.'

Fynn, *Mister God, this is Anna*

People is always telling us
You is the answer
But we didn't ask them
Any questions.
You may be the answer, Jesus,
But I hope you know how we all feel.

Carl Burke, *Treat me cool, Lord*

Pray as you can and do not try to pray as you can't.

Abbot John Chapman

Talk to him in prayer of all your wants, your troubles, even of the weariness you feel in serving him. . . If God bores you, tell him that he bores you, that you prefer the vilest amusements to his presence, that you only feel at your ease when you are far from him. . . You cannot speak too freely, too trustfully to him.

Francois Fénélon

Put a name to my sorrows
and I shall let them pass
loose my angry grip upon
these precious shards of glass

but the name must be grand and great
the name must be true
spoken on a hill's side
cold in the dew

O I see the name printed
printed on the page

and tears come running in a stream
releasing my rage

I let go the fragments
my palm begins to bleed
the name of my sorrows
who climbs a hill may read

Veronica Zundel, Put a Name

To conceal your grief is to find no remedy for it.

Turkish proverb

Do you know what 'le vice Anglais' — the English vice
— really is?. . .
  It's our refusal to admit our emotions.

Terence Rattigan, In Praise of Love

I was angry with my friend;
I told my wrath, my wrath did end.
I was angry with my foe;
I told it not, my wrath did grow.

William Blake, 'A Poison Tree'

The tigers of wrath are wiser than the horses of instruction.

William Blake, 'Proverbs of Hell'

Anger is one of the sinews of the soul. Who lacks it hath
a maimed mind.

Thomas Fuller

Anger — no peevish fit of temper, but just, generous,
scalding indignation — passes (not necessarily at once)
into embracing, exultant, re-welcoming love. That is how
friends and lovers are truly reconciled. Hot wrath, hot
love. Such anger is the fluid that love bleeds when you
cut it. The *angers*, not the measured remonstrances, of
lovers are love's renewal.

C.S. Lewis, Prayer: Letters to Malcolm

Ah my dear angry Lord,
Since thou dost love, yet strike;
Cast down, yet help afford;
Sure I will do the like.

I will complain, yet praise;
I will bewail, approve;
And all my sour-sweet days
I will lament, and love.

George Herbert, *Bitter-sweet*

'Read your complaint,' said the judge. . . 'Enough', said the judge. And now for the first time I knew what I had been doing. While I was reading, it had, once and again, seemed strange to me that the reading took so long; for the book was a small one. Now I knew that I had been reading it over and over; perhaps a dozen times. I would have read it for ever, quick as I could. . . if the judge had not stopped me. . . At last the judge spoke. 'Are you answered?' he said. 'Yes,' said I. The complaint was the answer. To have heard myself making it was to be answered. . .

I ended my first book with the words *No answer*. I know now, Lord, why you utter no answer. You are yourself the answer. Before your face, questions die away. What other answer would suffice?

Queen Orual in C.S. Lewis, *Till We Have Faces*

'Surely our wrath shall praise thee; the remainder of wrath shalt thou restrain.' Lord God, I find this a mystery; that it is not in thanking you for your goodness that I draw closest to you, but in complaining to you, shouting at you, even accusing you. It frightens me, exposing to you the naked truth of my frequent antagonism to you; yet somehow I know that 'What on earth do you think you're up to, Lord?' is often a more honest prayer than a meek 'Your will be done'. For I still call you, Lord, even when I question you.

It's just like human relationships; it's the friend you trust with whom you dare to quarrel. Politeness is for mere acquain-

tances. The first row — if it leads to the first making-up, and a greater depth of understanding — is a major step in the growth of love.

Give me the courage, then, Lord, to speak my mind to you without fear; for only when I have confessed what my own will is, can I come truly to the conclusion: 'Your will be done.'

Give your people the integrity to turn to you with our real questions, when you hand us over to suffering or allow us to wander in the maze of our own sinfulness. Keep us seeking you, in anger, frustration or confusion — for when we stop seeking you, then we are really lost.

When we are too weak to summon the joy to praise you, let our anger praise you; and restrain us from the overwhelming wrath which destroys, rather than heals. Free us to show you our real feelings; then free us to let go of them and let them be transformed by you.

A Benediction

And now unto him who is able to keep us from falling and lift us from the dark valley of despair to the bright mountain of hope, from the midnight of desperation to the daybreak of joy; to him be power and authority, for ever and ever. Amen.

Martin Luther King

18

On vocation

The angel of the Lord appeared to him in flames of fire from within a bush. . . When the Lord saw that he had gone over to look, God called to him from within the bush, 'Moses! Moses!' And Moses said, 'Here I am.' . . .the Lord said. . . 'So now, go. I am sending you to Pharoah to bring my people the Israelites out of Egypt.'

'When Israel was a child, I loved him, and out of Egypt I called my son.'

The Lord came and stood there, calling as at the other times, 'Samuel! Samuel!' Then Samuel said, 'Speak, for your servant is listening.'

In the year that King Uzziah died, I saw the Lord seated on a throne, high and exalted, and the train of his robe filled the temple. . . Then I heard the voice of the Lord saying, 'Whom shall I send? And who will go for us?' And I said, 'Here am I. Send me!'

As Jesus walked beside the Sea of Galilee, he saw Simon and his brother Andrew casting a net into the lake, for they were fishermen. 'Come, follow me,' Jesus said, 'and I will make you fish for people.' At once they left their nets and followed him.

Jesus looked at him and said, 'You are Simon son of John. You will be called Cephas. . .'

But when God, who set me apart from birth and called me by his grace, was pleased to reveal his Son in me so that I might preach him among the Gentiles, I did not consult any one. . .

Paul, called to be an apostle of Christ Jesus by the will of God. . . To the church of God in Corinth, to those sanctified in Christ Jesus and called to be holy, together with those everywhere who call on the name of our Lord Jesus Christ. . .

Each one should remain in the situation which they were in when the Lord called them.

As a prisoner for the Lord, then, I urge you to lead a life worthy of the calling you have received. Be completely humble and gentle; be patient, bearing with one another in love. Make every effort to keep the unity of the Spirit through the bond of peace. There is one body and one Spirit — just as you were called to one hope when you were called — one Lord, one faith, one baptism; one God and Father of all, who is over all and through all and in all. But to each one of us, grace has been given as Christ apportioned it. . . It was he who gave some to be apostles, some to be prophets, some to be evangelists, and some to be pastors and teachers, to prepare God's people for works of service, so that the body of Christ may be built up. . . attaining to the whole measure of the fullness of Christ.

(Exodus 3: 2,4,10; Hosea 11: 1; 1 Samuel 3: 10; Isaiah 6: 1,8 — all NIV; Mark 1: 17-18, NIV/NRSV; John 1: 42; Galatians 1: 15-16; 1 Corinthians 1: 1-2; 1 Corinthians 7: 20; Ephesians 4: 1-7,11-13 — all NIV)

The notion of vocation or calling is one that has almost dropped out of our vocabulary. And we are all the poorer for its absence. Its biblical and Reformation roots hold together our sense of identity, history and community. Without a providential sense of vocation for the church and the individual, identity becomes individualistic, history becomes atomistic, and community becomes conformity.

The biblical view of vocation exclaims *vive la difference* to our created diversity, enables us to breathe the fresh air of Christian freedom without fear of others' judgment because our calling is different to theirs, and exhorts us to find and develop our character and biography based on the prominent lines of God's providence in our lives, personally and corporately.

In a day when managerial and therapeutic models of ministry are dominant (and they have many useful things to say), we must still ask ourselves what our distinctive calling or vocation in ministry is. In a schizophrenic world, the distinction between the real or whole self and the role (or work) self has become axiomatic.

As a prescription to counter burnout, we are often rightly counselled to distinguish ourselves from our ministry, but we need to remember that we cannot completely separate real self and role self without losing our integrity and even our sanity. The notion of vocation enables us to see ourselves as more than just our ministry and the current preacher's popularity rating, and yet integrate ministry and identity.

The nervous modern pursuit of personal identity, the search for one's self, is in considerable contrast to the situation of someone like Paul. Like Peter, even his name was changed because of his call. In fact, on countless occasions in scripture what you were named or called was directly related to your calling by God. In Galatians 1, it is clear that Paul found his person in the light of the purpose God had called him to as apostle to the Gentiles. Indeed, the sin he regularly refers to is his opposition to that purpose in his persecution of the church.

In the call narratives of figures like Moses, Samuel, Isaiah and Paul, there is a rough pattern of vision — of God in his glory; of admission — of human unworthiness; of passion — a singlemindedness that is not easily separated from who you are as a person; and mission — that gets you going and keeps you going into the world.

Many of us today want the vision and experience of God without the mission or passion, and we cannot have it. God demands all our attention to the point of what many moderns would regard as obsession. To distinguish whether we have a divine or personal obsession is a difficult task. It is the distinction between being driven or called, the difference between being a Saul or a David.

God's call, as distinct from a personal obsession, has a number of characteristics: it is a gift that frees us to be who we were made to be; it calls us out into Christian community, the *ekklesia*, the gathered people of God; and it calls us into the world as part of the scattered people of God; it calls us appropriately at different ages and stages of life, with partner and children or in singleness with friends; and above all it calls us to Christlike character where we find our role and real self in his story and are led in the direction of the kingdom.

With such a sense of calling(s), discerned in direct relationship to God, and indirectly through his people, we find a balance that saves us from the imperialism of an individualistic, subjective sense of call that carries everyone else along with us, and yet enables us to maintain a critical sense of distance from those we serve, so that we and they know that God and not they are our master.

☙❧

The great social and cultural maladies of the modern age all have this common characteristic: that they deny personal vocation.

Denis de Rougemont, *The Christian Opportunity*

Here lies the body of Thomas Jones, born a man, died a grocer.

Alleged Scottish gravestone

What is he?
– A man, of course.
Yes, but what does he do?
– He lives and is a man.
Oh quite! but he must work. He must have a job of some
    sort.
– Why?
Because obviously he's not one of the leisured classes.
– I don't know. He has a lot of leisure. And he makes
    quite beautiful chairs.
There you are then! He's a cabinetmaker.
– No, no!
Anyhow a carpenter and joiner.
– Not at all.

But you said so.
– What did I say?
That he made chairs, and was a joiner and carpenter.
– I said he made chairs, but I did not say he was a
  carpenter.
All right then, he's an amateur.
– Perhaps! Would you say that a thrush was a professional
  flautist, or just an amateur?
I'd say it was just a bird.
– And I say he is just a man.
All right! You always did quibble.

D.H. Lawrence, 'What is he?'

No elaborate argument is required to justify the Christian
doctrine of vocation. It follows indisputably from two
propositions. The first, that God is everywhere active in
human affairs and his will operative at all times. The
second, that he is a rational God, fully aware that the
world needs farmers and miners as well as priests and
nuns. . . The doctrine of Providence stresses the ceaseless
and ubiquitous intrusion of God into human affairs. The
doctrine of Vocation defines a prime mode of that intrusion.

Henry Blamires, *The Will and the Way*

For [God] knows with what great restlessness human nature flames, with what fickleness it is borne hither and
thither, how its ambition longs to embrace various things
at once. Therefore, lest through our stupidity and rashness
everything be turned topsy-turvy, he has appointed duties
for everyone. . . and has named these various kinds of
living 'callings'. . . Accordingly, your life will be best
ordered to this goal. . . each. . . will bear and swallow
discomforts, vexations, weariness and anxieties. . . From
this will arise a singular consolation; that no task will be
so sordid and base, provided you obey your calling in it,
that it will not shine and be reckoned precious in God's
sight.

John Calvin, *Institutes of the Christian Religion*

If we are rightly disposed, like Samuel, to respond to all legitimate calls from the Lord, whether they come directly or indirectly, even if we repeatedly seem to make mistakes or actually do make them in the process of discernment and turn even repeatedly in the wrong directions, an untiring God will keep calling until we find our way. God called Samuel four times! This passage also highlights the importance of the role of the spiritual father. Even such an obtuse and poor man of God as the priest Eli was, in the end, by God's grace given in response to the humble faith of his disciple, able to help Samuel to discern and respond to his call.

Basil Pennington, *Called*

Who of us knows ourselves. . . as God knows us and therefore as we really are? Who can say with absolute certainty. . . that we are this or that, that our nature is thus, that these are the limits which even God must observe if he wishes to call us? An authoritative and reliable light is shed. . . only by the calling in which we are authentically addressed and claimed by our Creator and Lord. . . And in the light of this calling we will not merely find ourselves summoned to be what we are; we will also find ourselves summoned as the one we are to new existence and action.

Saul as the one he is and has been is to become Paul. This means that the previous state of his vocation has to undergo an expansion. He must not become hopelessly enamoured of what he was. He must let himself be wrested from any passion for his previous existence. He is invited to a journey to new harbours in which he will again be himself. . . in a new form, perhaps becoming a source of astonishment not only to others but even to himself. . .

Karl Barth, *Church Dogmatics*

The external limitation of every human vocation has a corresponding internal limit. This consists in the personal aptitude. . . we must not wish to jump out of our own skin. It is just as we are that we may come, when the command of God calls us to meet the new thing which we are to be in the strength of this call. . . we must not ask why this is the point of departure. We must not compare it with that of others. We must not envy or despise others because theirs is different. We must not waste time considering how fine it would be if ours were like theirs. If it is good enough for God to begin dealings with us at this point, then it ought to be good enough for us to begin dealings with God at this point.

Karl Barth, *Church Dogmatics*

Christ appears to have begun with the distinction between the *called* and the *driven*. Somehow he separated people out on the basis of their tendency to be driven or their willingness to be called. He dealt with their motives, the basis of their spiritual energy, and the sorts of gratification in which they were interested. He called those who were drawn to him and avoided those who were driven and wanted to use him.

Gordon MacDonald, *Ordering Your Private World*

Can driven people be spotted? Yes, of course. There are many symptoms that suggest a person is driven. . .

1. A driven person is most often gratified only by accomplishment. . .
2. A driven person is preoccupied with the symbols of accomplishment. . .
3. A driven person is usually caught in the uncontrolled pursuit of expansion. . .
4. Driven people tend to have a limited regard for integrity. . .
5. Driven people often possess limited or undeveloped people skills.
6. Driven people tend to be highly competitive. . .
7. A driven person often possesses a volcanic force of anger. . .
8. Driven people are usually abnormally busy. . .

Gordon MacDonald, *Ordering Your Private World*

Any of us can look within and suddenly discover that *drivenness is our way of life.* We can be driven toward a superior Christian reputation, toward a desire for some dramatic spiritual experience, or toward a form of leadership that is really more a quest for domination of people than servanthood. A homemaker can be a driven person; so can a student. A driven person can be any of us. . .

Can the driven person be changed? Most certainly. It begins when such a person faces up to operating according to drives and not calls. That discovery is usually made in the blinding, searching light of an encounter with Christ. As the twelve disciples discovered, an audience with Jesus over a period of time exposes all the roots and expressions of drivenness.

To deal with drivenness, one must begin to ruthlessly appraise one's motives and values just as Peter was forced to do in his periodic confrontations with Jesus. The person seeking relief from drivenness will find it wise to listen to mentors and critics who speak Christ's words to us today. We may have some humbling acts of renunciation, some disciplined gestures of surrender of things — things that are not necessarily bad, but that have been important for all the wrong reasons. . .

Paul the apostle in his pre-Christian days was driven. As a driven man he studied, he joined, he attained, he defended, and he was applauded. The pace at which he was operating shortly before his conversion was almost manic. He was driven toward some illusive goal and, later, when he could look back at that lifestyle with all of its compulsions, he would say, 'It was all worthless.'

Paul was driven until Christ called him. One gets the feeling that when Paul fell to his knees before the Lord while on the road to Damascus, there was an explosion of relief within his private world. What a change from the drivenness that had pushed him toward Damascus in an attempt to stamp out Christianity to that dramatic moment when, in complete submission, he asked Jesus Christ, 'What shall I do, Lord?' A driven man was converted into a called one.

Gordon MacDonald, *Ordering Your Private World*

> Be thou my vision, O Lord of my heart;
> Naught be all else to me, save that thou art;
> Thou my best thought, by day or by night,
> Waking or sleeping, thy presence my light.

God of the burning bush, grant me a vision of your throne filling this earthly temple, meet me in the midst of my daily routine as you met the disciples mending their nets, encounter me on the Damascus roads running through my life, call me and woo me away from my own desperate drivenness.

Lord, I admit that so often my desires and drives become demands, compulsions that can never be met. And yet I hunger, I crave for Christ, I have a passion that burns in my bones, to be your person, to find myself and my ministry in your purpose, to go out today caught up in your mission to the world. Take my passion up within your passionate concern, my person within your purpose, and my ministry within your mission for the world.

God who calls irresistibly in earthquake, wind and fire, and in the still, small voice: sensitise my hearing to the tone of your voice through your word. Give me discernment to hear your call in the midst of a myriad of calls and demands. Telephone calls, pastoral calls, call committees or nominators, job advertisements, my needs and the needs of my family and my church. Never ending needs! And yet I know, Lord, the need isn't necessarily the call. In the midst of all my activity like Martha, help me to take time for the luxury, the necessity to sit at your feet like Mary, and discover the one thing needful.

Lord of my history and personality, give me wisdom to discern between my desire for change, my search for stability, my wanting recognition and fulfilment, and my longing to be my best for you, myself, my loved ones, your people, your world. Through these diverse demands and desires, plant in me, Lord, those deeper, enduring desires that delight in you and are promised fulfilment in your kingdom.

I was all hot for honours, money, marriage: and you made mock of my hotness. In my pursuit of these, I suffered most bitter disappointment, but in this you were good to me since I was thus prevented from taking delight in anything not yourself.

ACENTA

EFES MÜZESİ
EPHESUS MUSEUM

TARİHE AÇILAN KAPI

T.C.
KÜLTÜR VE TURİZM BAKANLIĞI
Republic of Turkey Ministry of Culture and Tourism

EFES MÜZESİ
EPHESUS MUSEUM

www.muze.gov.tr

MUZE

000147008

AD/NAME:

SOYAD/SURNAME:

ÜLKE/COUNTRY:

D.TARİHİ/D. OF BIRTH:

E-POSTA/E-MAIL:

Sizi bilgilendirmemiz için lütfen formu doldurunuz. For more information we would like to get in touch with you.

000147008

EFES MÜZESİ
EPHESUS MUSEUM

Bu bilet yalnızca Efes Müzesi için geçerlidir.
This ticket is valid only at Ephesus Museum.

Satılan biletler geri alınmaz.
Tickets are non-refundable.

Biletinizi gezi süresince saklayınız.
Please keep your ticket during the visit.

Bu bilet yalnızca bir kişi ve bir giriş için geçerlidir.
This ticket is valid only for one person and only for a single entry.

K.D.V. ve kurum payları dahildir. V.U.K. hükümlerine tabi değildir.
VAT included.

Look now into my heart, Lord, by whose will I remember all this and confess it to you. Let my soul cleave to you now that you have freed it from the tenacious hold of death.

Augustine of Hippo

Forth in thy name, O Lord, I go,
My daily labour to pursue;
Thee, only thee, resolved to know,
In all I think, or speak, or do.
The task thy wisdom hath assigned,
O let me cheerfully fulfil;
In all my works thy presence find,
And prove thine acceptable will.

Charles Wesley

God has called [name];
he will not fail [him/her].
God has called [name];
he will not fail [him/her].
God has called [name];
he will not fail [him/her].
So trust in God and obey him.
God has called you, he will not fail you.
So trust in God and obey him.
God has called us, we will not fail him.
So trust in God and obey him.

Diane Davis

A Benediction
May the God of Abraham, Moses and Paul,
the God who irresistibly calls,
give you an assured sense of purpose,
a quiet confidence about who you are,
sensitive discernment of his will,
and decisiveness in following his direction for your life,
as you step out faithfully in the footsteps of Christ and with
the Spirit at your side. Amen.

19

Seeing more

Lift up your eyes from where you are and look north
and south, east and west.

O Lord our Lord, how majestic is your name in all the
earth!. . . When I consider your heavens, the work of your
fingers, the moon and the stars which you have set in
place, what are human beings that you are mindful of them. . .?

For God so loved the world that he gave his one and
only Son, that whoever believes in him shall not perish
but have everlasting life.

We would like to see Jesus.

When they looked up, they saw no one except Jesus.

Let us fix our eyes on Jesus, the author and perfecter
of our faith, who for the joy set before him endured the
cross, scorning its shame, and sat down at the right hand
of the throne of God. Consider him who endured such
opposition from sinners, so that you will not grow weary
and lose heart.

Then I saw a lamb, looking as if it had been slain. . .
You are worthy. . . because you were slain, and with
your blood you purchased for God's saints from every
tribe and language and people and nation. You have
made them to be a kingdom and priests to serve our
God, and they will reign on the earth.

'Worthy is the Lamb, who was slain, to receive power
and wealth and wisdom and strength and honour and
glory and praise!'

The Lamb will be in the city and his servants will
serve him. They will see his face.

Do not be afraid; God has heard. . . Then God opened
her eyes. . .

(Genesis 13: 14, NIV; Psalm 8: 1, 3-4, NIV/NRSV; John 3: 16; John
12: 21; Matthew 17: 8; Hebrews 12: 2-3 — all NIV; Revelation 5:
6, 9-10, NIV/NRSV; Revelation 5: 12; Revelation 22: 3-4; Genesis
21: 17,19 — all NIV)

28/6/98

Lift up your eyes from where you are and look. . .
What do you see?
'What do you see?' the master asked, as the students
gathered round. 'I see lilium chalcedonicum, I think,' said
Thomas, with a frown. And all the students were puzzled
too, for neither were we sure of the answer that the master
sought in the field of red and green and blue.
'What do you see?' he asked again, and our Matthew,
counting slowly, said, 'Three scarlet petals and four leaves
of green — but I cannot count them all.' And all together
we nodded as we looked around that day, for thousands
upon thousands of the blooms were on display.
'What do you see?' the master pressed, and Judas spoke
out next. 'A fallow field which, ploughed and sown, could
a goodly profit yield.' And we all marvelled at our fellow
who could see gain in every place, but there, that day,
material wealth seemed strangely out of place.
'What do you see?' The master's challenge had still not
yet been met. 'A symbol of our freedom. The emblem of
our land!' And we, the students, looked confused at the
sword in Simon's hand, embarrassed by our Zealot's image
of struggle for freedom in an occupied land.
Then Mary rose and picked a bloom — a stillness filled
the crowd — 'I love you, Master,' was all she said, and
laid the flower down as a tribute to her gentle Lord. Then,
with the love gift at his feet, she asked the only question
left. 'What should we see?' our Mary asked, and we all
leaned close to hear. 'A caring God,' our master said, 'who
clothes the common flower with beauty, excelling that of
kings, and cares for all his world — here, and in every
place, and of all the wonders he has made, you, yes you,
are the objects of his grace.'
And then our eyes were opened, and we saw the field
anew. Beyond the leaves, beyond the colours, our Creator
stood on view, and never again did we see the world _ _ _

through the limits of physical sight, for the master had helped us see, helped us to see deeper, helped us to see further, helped us to see aright — helped us to see the God who lies behind every field, every flower, every face.

❧

To say. . . that Jesus taught in 'parables' is not in itself to say that he did something mysterious or very innovative; any good speaker or writer uses 'parables' from time to time.

What made Jesus' teaching different from much other teaching then and now was the centrality for him of parabolic speech. Many preachers pop the occasional illustration or story into their sermons in order to add interest and to illuminate the idea that they have been trying to explain. Someone like Paul does this in his letters (e.g. Romans 11: 16-24), but Jesus, especially when speaking to the crowds, spoke almost entirely pictorially, explaining his ideas in and through stories, and not just using stories as an aid to illustrate his points. Whereas much preaching is like a monochrome carpet with a little pattern round the edge to relieve the monotony, Jesus' teaching is like a carpet with bold and distinctive patterns woven throughout. Jesus taught profound theology, yet he did so not in long and complex discourses, but through down-to-earth, real-life stories. . .

The fact that Jesus taught so graphically through stories and sayings which reflect first-century Palestinian life tells us much about the sort of person Jesus was. He was no ivory-tower theologian expounding abstract and abstruse theories; he was someone with his feet very much on the ground, able to talk to ordinary people in ordinary terms. The Christian doctrine of the incarnation is that in Jesus God became man; it is evident from Jesus' parabolic teaching that he was not simply human, but that he was a man who felt with, and identified with, the world and situation of his contemporaries in a way that is not always characteristic of religious leaders.

David Wenham,
The Parables of Jesus: Pictures of Revolution

All the evidence of human experience, the evidence of the greatest of the poets, the artists, the scientists and the saints, goes to suggest that knowledge is accessible to those who are ready to keep the door open, to venture beyond what is clear and unquestionable, even if it involves the risk of being mistaken or talking nonsense. . . the active principle is the willingness to go out beyond what is certain, to listen to what is not yet clear, to search for what is hardly visible, to venture the affirmation which may prove to be wrong, but which may also prove to be the starting point for new conquests of the mind.   In the traditional language of Christianity the name for that active principle is faith.

Lesslie Newbigin, *Honest Religion for Secular Man*

God is to be found and seen, not through an illimitable vacancy between himself and our spirits, but in and through all things that stir us to love.   He is to be seen in the light of a cottage window as well as in the sun or the stars. . . God is revealed to us in the known, not hidden in the unknown; and we have to find him where we are.

Arthur Clutton-Brock

'In a short time you will no longer see me, and then a short time later you will see me again.'   We are living in this short time.   We can live in it creatively when we live it out of solitude — that is, detached from the results of our work.   And when we live it with care — that is, crying with those who weep and wail.   But it is the expectation of his return which moulds our solitude and care into a preparation for the day of great joy.

This is what we express when we take bread and wine in thanksgiving.   We do not eat bread to still our hunger or drink wine to quench our thirst.   We just eat a little bit of bread and drink a little bit of wine in the realisation that God's presence is the presence of the One who came, but is still to come; who touched our hearts, but has yet to take all our sadness away.

And so when we share some bread and some wine

together, we do this not as a people who have arrived, but as men and women who can support each other in patient expectation until we see him again. And then our hearts will be full of joy that no one can take away from us.

Henri J.M. Nouwen

Then a woman said, Speak to us of Joy and Sorrow.

And he answered;

Your joy is your sorrow unmasked.

And the selfsame well from which your laughter rises was oftimes filled with your tears.

And how else can it be?

The deeper that sorrow carves into your being, the more joy you can contain.

Is not the cup that holds your wine the very cup that was burned in the potter's oven?

And is not the lute that soothes your spirit the very wood that was hollowed with knives?

When you are joyous, look deep into your heart and you shall find it is only that which has given you sorrow that is giving you joy.

When you are sorrowful, look again in your heart, and you shall see that in truth you are weeping for that which has been your delight.

Kahlil Gibran

. . .*Imagination* must come before the *implementation*. Our culture is competent to implement almost anything and to imagine almost nothing. The same royal consciousness that makes it possible to implement anything and everything is the one that shrinks imagination because imagination is a danger. Thus every totalitarian regime is frightened of the artist. It is the vocation of the prophet to keep alive the ministry of imagination, to keep on conjuring and proposing alternative futures to the single one the king wants to urge as the only thinkable one.

In the language of R.D. Laing, people must simply practise the proper *behaviour* because they are no longer able to experience their own *experience*. Clearly the

[dominant] regime is interested not in what people experience but in their behaviour, which can be managed. . .
   It is the business of kings to attach the word 'forever'
to everything we treasure.   The great dilemma is that
religious functionaries are expected to use the same
forever, to attach it to things and make it sound theologically legitimated.   But 'forever' is always the word of
Pharaoh, and as such it is the very word against which
Yahweh and Moses did their liberating thing.

Walter Brueggemann, *The Prophetic Imagination*

Then Job answered the Lord:
   I know that thou canst do all things
   and that no purpose is beyond thee.
   But I have spoken of great things which
   I have not understood,
   things too wonderful for me to know.
   I knew of thee then only by report,
   but now I see thee with my own eyes.
   Therefore I melt away;
   I repent in dust and ashes.

(Job 42: 1-6, NEB)

   Job's closing comments are terse and cryptic.   How does
Job 'see' God?   In what sense does he repent?   Apparently
Job experienced the full impact of God's mysterious other-
ness as he confronted the majestic power and wisdom of
the Creator.   He 'saw' God by returning to the primordial
world with his Maker and there reliving God's dramatic
creative labours.   God had honoured Job by entering into
dialogue with him about these ancient wonders.   He had
left most of Job's questions unanswered, but he had arranged a face-to-face encounter in his sovereign presence.
   Job, addressed as first man, had been led back to the
beginnings, the archetypal realities governing the universe.
Before the ultimate mastermind of all things, Job is acutely
aware of his own finitude.   He is an ignorant creature
whose end is to return to dust and ashes.   To that lot he
resigns himself, humble and penitent, but with his integrity as a human being affirmed by the very coming of

the Creator. He is the God of all beginnings. With him a new birth, a new creation from the dust, is a real possibility. By affirming he is nothing, Job is in a condition to be recreated out of nothing.

Norman C. Habel, *The Book of Job*

Father who sees all, help me to see more of you.
Father who knows all, help me to know more of you.
Father who is in all, help me to live more in you.

My God, forgive my wilful blindness, for I have chosen not to see your presence in your world. Father, forgive my wilful ignorance, for I have chosen not to acknowledge your wisdom — always available to me. Father, forgive my resentment, for at times I feel alone and unsupported. It is then that I have chosen not to receive your ever-present ministry of love.

Father, help me see, know and become more in you.

A Benediction
Go now, and go in peace, and go with your eyes open. Be not afraid. God has heard. Amen.

The still small voice

And he arose, and did eat and drink and went in the strength of that meat forty days and forty nights unto Horeb the mount of God. And he came thither unto a cave, and lodged there; and, behold, the word of the Lord came to him, 'What doest thou here, Elijah?' And he said, 'I have been very jealous for the Lord, the God of hosts; for the children of Israel have forsaken thy covenant, thrown down thine altars, and slain thy prophets with the sword: and I, even I only, am left; and they seek my life, to take it away.'

And he said, 'Go forth, and stand upon the mount before the Lord.' And, behold, the Lord passed by, and a great and strong wind rent the mountains, and brake in pieces the rocks before the Lord; but the Lord was not in the wind; and after the wind an earthquake; and after the earthquake a fire; but the Lord was not in the fire; and after the fire a still small voice.

And it was so, when Elijah heard it, that he wrapped his face in his mantle, and went out, and stood in the entering in of the cave. And behold, there came a voice unto him and said, 'What doest thou here, Elijah?'

(I Kings 19: 8-13, AV)

This is such a familiar story that many of us, including most modern translators — for instance, of the New English Bible, the Good News Bible, or the Jerusalem Bible — have been unwilling to face the sheer *peculiarity* of what is going on here. The most literal English translation of the Hebrew words for what the prophet hears after the noisy exhibitionism of the earthquake, the wind and the fire would be 'a voice of thin silence'. Given that in Elizabethan English 'small' could still mean 'thin' (as in Wyatt's description of his beloved's arms as 'long and small'), the Authorised Version's 'still small voice' is a remarkably accurate rendering of the original. Something very odd, boundary-breaking, and *new* was happening to Elijah.

Ancient Hebrew had no word for (and therefore no concept of) 'nature'. The normal progression of the seasons was seen as being as divinely instigated as the whirlwind that whisked Elijah to heaven. As a result, there could be no concept of the miraculous either. The whole relationship between humanity and the environment was experienced in a way fundamentally different from ours.

What is struggling to inarticulate and painful birth in this strange story of the prophet's failure is nothing less than the long revolution in ideas that was eventually to allow us to distinguish 'wind' from 'spirit', natural fire from Pentecostal, and the shaking of the earth from the shaking of the foundations. Here we see the primitive world of primal participation — in which neither the concept of the 'natural', nor, consequently, the concept of the 'divine' could exist — in the act of giving way to a world where for the first time science and religion were possible.

The story is given a very specific setting. After the rout of the prophets of Baal, Jezebel the Queen threatened Elijah's life. Believing himself to be the sole survivor of the faithful, he has fled to Horeb. The full force of what follows depends on our recognising Horeb as Sinai, the traditional 'mountain of the Lord' where Moses himself had encountered God before the burning bush.

Elijah has now come with certain expectations precisely because of that sense of history that was, in Israel, distinctively the product of the insights of the prophets. Before the assembled prophets of Baal, he had already vindicated Yahweh — the God who had traditionally manifested his power in fire — by the most spectacular pyrotechnics yet. Now he awaits some further revelation or instruction.

The disconfirmation that follows is the more unexpected. He is indeed treated to a more spectacular display of natural violence than ever, but Yahweh is *not* a fire god. His presence, when at last it is revealed, is experienced as something mysteriously apart from the world of natural phenomena that had been in such convulsions. Instead, Elijah's own categories are challenged. What comes is a simple question: 'What doest thou here, Elijah?'

He had come with certain confident assumptions — which are now systematically overthrown. To begin with, his own report turns out to be incorrect: there are, apparently, still seven thousand in Israel who have not bowed the knee to Baal (verse 18). He is told to return and help to organise what amounts to nothing less than two separate *coups d'état*. Hazael is to be anointed king of Syria, and Jehu king of Israel (v. 15-16). History is yet again to be shaped by revelation, just as, long before, Moses had been sent back from Horeb to lead his people out of Egypt. Finally — and ominously — Elijah is ordered to appoint his own successor.

At every level the ambiguous discontinuity persists. Any attempt at 'explaining' the contrast between the natural phenomena and the mysterious 'voice of thin silence' is in danger of losing that sense of connection between the two that is emphasised even by the very act of dissociation. Yahweh is not a fire god, nor one of winds and earthquakes, although wind had always been the traditional symbol of the spirit. Yet from whom, if not from him, did these things come?

Moreover, how are we to interpret this story? Is what is being described a 'miracle' (in our modern sense of an apparent suspension of the laws of nature) as we are encouraged to think of Moses' encounter with the burning bush, or is it rather a 'vision' — in the same category perhaps as Isaiah's vision of the Lord in the temple when he, too, is purged by fire?

The whole effect of Elijah's experience seems to be to deny, *and* yet simultaneously affirm, certain connections. Thus Yahweh *is*, and *is not*, a god of nature (a paradox

more familiar to us under the much later theological notions of immanence and transcendence); revelation is both
'natural' and 'miraculous'; God is concerned both with the
fate of the individual and with the shaping of history. The
story seems to insist that at each level of understanding,
these modes are at once completely discontinuous and yet
inseparable. Something utterly new and beyond human
experience is being called into being for the first time in
language.

It is enough. Now, O Lord, take away
my life, for I am not better than
my fathers. I only am left, and they
are seeking my life, to take it. Then,
why do you make me eat? I have seen
enough of killing, enough of power,
of acts of God — a hand gathering the rain,
wind, earthquake and your all-consuming fire.
What am I doing here? Lord, in these acts
you speak, and what you speak is history,
but my life lies, there are so many inert facts.
And now I have come, searching this mystery,
wondering, 'What are you doing here, Elijah?'
Is silence still to be my only answer?

Nicholas Bielby

The raging fire, the roaring wind,
Thy boundless power display;
But in the gentler breeze we find
Thy spirit's viewless way.

John Keble

Surgi: che fai? [What doest thou here?]

Beatrice to Dante

Oh delicate touch of the word, delicate, yea wondrously
delicate, to me, which, having overthrown the mountains
and broken the stones in Mount Horeb with the shadow
of thy power and strength that went before thee, didst

reveal thyself to the prophet with the whisper of gentle
air.

John of the Cross

Breathe through the heats of our desire
Thy coolness and thy balm;
Let sense be dumb, let flesh retire;
Speak through the earthquake, wind and fire,
O still small voice of calm!

John Greenleaf Whittier

. . .the experience of disconfirmation is a common biblical event. . . such a language of disconfirmation and
ambiguity is not merely a concomitant of religious experience, but is actually characteristic of, and historically
central to, our experience of God. Elijah on Horeb,
Moses and the burning bush, the Incarnation itself
present events so baffling as to imply quite new ways
of seeing the world. . .

Stephen Prickett

The ancient stoics used to say, 'Know thyself'. They
presented it as a modest alternative to the hubris of trying
to understand the universe. They did not realise that
theirs was the ultimate hubris — the ultimate folly — for
trying to understand the universe is child's play compared
with trying to unravel the mystery of ourselves.

Stephen Prickett

Not, I'll not, carrion comfort, Despair, not feast on thee;
Not untwist — slack they may be — these last strands of
    man
In me, ór, most weary, cry *I can no more.* I can;
Can something, hope, wish day come, not choose not to be.
But ah, but O thou terrible, why wouldst thou rude on me
Thy wring world right foot rock? lay a lion limb against me?
    scan
With darksome devouring eyes my bruiséd bones? and fan,
O in turns of tempest, me heaped there; me frantic to avoid
    thee and flee?

Why? That my chaff might fly; my grain lie, sheer and clear.
Nay in all that toil, that coil, since (seems) I kissed the rod,
Hand rather, my heart lo! lapped strength, stole joy, would
    laugh, chéer.

Cheer whom though? The hero whose heaven-handling flung
    me, fóot tród
Me? or me that fought him? O which one? is it each one?
    That night, that year
Of now done darkness I wretch lay wrestling with (my God!)
    my God.

Gerard Manley Hopkins

If the spectator could enter into these images in his imagination, approaching them on the fiery chariot of his
contemplative thought. . . then he would arise from his
grave. . .

William Blake

Would to God that all the Lord's people were prophets.

Numbers 11: 29

Our little systems have their day;
They have their day and cease to be:
They are but broken lights of thee,
And thou, O Lord, art more than they.

Tennyson

---

*Lord, our minds are cluttered with assumptions whose origins
we have never thought to examine, beliefs of whose limitations
we have taught ourselves to be proud, convictions which have
become walls rather than gateways. In a world of ceaseless and
inexorable change, we have tried to turn our religion into a cave
of refuge.*

*Let your word be to us an earthquake to break down our
defences; a wind to blow away the staleness of our enclosed
atmospheres; a fire to blast, smelt and refine our low-grade ores
into what you alone can shape as part of a plan we can never
fully comprehend. Open us to the unexpectedness of your word.*

Disconfirm our complacencies; challenge our certainties. May we learn to face, even with fear and trembling, the shock of the new. Give us grace not to translate the word into our terms, but always to allow ourselves to be translated by it.

A Benediction
Almighty God, the fountain of all wisdom, who knows our necessities before we ask, and our ignorance in asking; have compassion upon our infirmities; and those things which for our unworthiness we dare not, and for our blindness we cannot ask, vouchsafe to give us, for the worthiness of your Son Jesus Christ our Lord. Amen.

21

In praise of work

We command you in the name of our Lord Jesus Christ to keep away from all who are living a lazy life and who do not follow the instructions that we gave them. You yourselves know very well that you should do just what we did. We were not lazy when we were with you. We did not accept anyone's support without paying for it. Instead, we worked and toiled; we kept working day and night so as not to be an expense to any of you.

We did this, not because we have no right to demand your support; we did it to be an example for you to follow. While we were with you, we used to say to you, 'Whoever refuses to work is not allowed to eat.' We say this because we hear that there are some people among you who live lazy lives and who do nothing except meddle in other people's business. In the name of the Lord Jesus Christ we command these people and warn them to lead orderly lives and work to earn their own living.

Whatever you do, work at it with all your heart, as though you were working for the Lord and not for your masters. Remember that the Lord will give you as a reward what he has kept for his people. For Christ is the real Master you serve.

Love must be completely sincere. Hate what is evil, hold on to what is good. Love one another with mutual affection and be eager to show respect for one another. Work hard and do not be lazy. Serve the Lord with a heart full of devotion. Let your hope keep you joyful, be patient in your troubles, and pray at all times. Share your belongings with your needy fellow-Christians, and open your homes to strangers.

Everything leads to weariness — a weariness too great for words. Our eyes can never see enough to be satisfied; our ears can never hear enough.

Stay in that same house, eating and drinking whatever they offer you, for a worker should be given his pay.

As long as it is day, we must keep on doing the work of him who sent me; night is coming when no-one can work.

While we were with you, we used to say to you, 'Whoever refuses to work is not allowed to eat.'

You will have to work hard and sweat to make the soil produce anything, until you go back to the soil from which you were formed. You were made from soil, and you will become soil again.

You have six days in which to do your work, but do not work on the seventh day, not even during ploughing time or harvest. Lord our God, may your blessings be with us. Give us success in all we do!

Then people go out to do their work and keep working until evening.

So then, my dear brothers, stand firm and steady. Keep busy always in your work for the Lord, since you know that nothing you do in the Lord's service is ever useless.

(2 Thessalonians 3: 6-12; Colossians 3: 23-24; Romans 12: 9-13; Ecclesiastes 1: 8; Luke 10: 7; John 9: 4; 2 Thessalonians 3: 10; Genesis 3: 19; Exodus 34: 21; Psalm 90: 17; Psalm 104: 23; 1 Corinthians 15: 58 — all GNB)

Work, said a cynic, is whatever you're doing when you'd rather be doing something else.

So why work? A Western businessman asked a sleeping African, 'Why aren't you working?' The African: 'I just enjoy doing nothing: why should I work?' The Westerner replied, 'To make money.' 'And, sir, what should I do with the money?' 'Oh, you can buy a house, and a car and a boat and other things.' 'And,' the African asked, 'what do you do when you've got all that?' 'Oh. . .' said the Westerner, 'I'd sit around and do nothing!'

Work, for a Christian, is essentially service to God. It's a form of worship. We are created in the image of a working God.

The scriptures are full of praise for the work of human hands, hearts and minds. Even God makes, forms, builds and plants (Genesis 2: 4,7-8,19,23). Work skills are described as gifts of God: the Lord 'called' Bezalel, filled him with his Spirit, with ability, intelligence, knowledge and craftsmanship (Exodus 35: 30-32). Jesus was immersed in the life and problems of working people. The apostles sometimes returned to the jobs they left to follow Jesus. . . and Jesus was a carpenter for most of his adult life. His parables refer to sowers, vineyard labourers, harvesters, house-building, tending pigs and women sweeping their home.

We were created to find fulfilment in our working. Paul criticised idleness and exhorted Christians to work (2 Thessalonians 3: 6). For Marx, 'the shortening of the workday' and never the elimination of good work itself is portrayed as the entrance to the 'realm of freedom'. Simone Weil writes about the holiness of the poor — the peasant, the labourer, the worker. She talks about the person who at the end of the day drops on the bed from exhaustion.

There's an integrity about doing one's daily work to the best of one's abilities and energies. Work must not be regarded as the antithesis of human fulfilment. We are not creatures destined for freedom who are now trapped in an alienated realm of necessity. We are called to manifest the image of God and, hence, to be free precisely *in and through* our work.

All human activities are equally God-given. No one type of human activity can claim religious priority over another. So we echo Tyndale's declaration that 'to wash dishes and to preach is all one, as touching the deed, to please God'. We are not apprentice angels, better suited to and waiting for an existence on another spiritual plane. We have been created to tend the earth and serve one another through work. Paul made no distinction between physical and spiritual work and used the same terms to refer to both the manual labour by which he earned a living and also his apostolic service.

And part of our calling is to rest. God rested after creating the universe. The commandment not to labour on the Sabbath carries as much weight as those not to kill or steal. The sabbath idea is written deep into the life and laws of the people of Israel, and into the life of God's creatures. We do more and better work in six days than in seven.

Resting is more than recuperation and preparation for work. Indeed, rest and work may involve similar activities, but activities done in a different spirit. Resting is tied to faith — which is one reason most of us avoid rest. The scriptures frequently relate lack of rest to unbelief (eg. Psalm 95: 8-11; Hebrews 3: 7 – 4:10). Note William Lamb's interesting phrase about 'sabbathless Satan'.

A distortion of the 'Protestant work ethic' encourages us to define who we are by what we do. 'I work, therefore I am.' You can spot workaholics by asking them to say who they are without reference to their jobs: they find that very hard. But the welfare state mentality says: 'I am, therefore I am owed food, health, clothing, shelter and happiness.' It's the clash of the ethic of achievement vs. the ethic of entitlement. Both are dehumanising, demeaning and unbiblical. Paul said, 'If anyone doesn't work he shouldn't eat.' But he took up collections on behalf of the poor. In Romans 12: 11 we read, 'Work hard and don't be lazy,' but just two verses later, 'Share your belongings with your needy fellow-Christians, and open your homes to strangers.'

So let us plan, use our energies, and serve the Lord as if we were going to live on earth for ever; and let us live day by day as if we were going to meet the Lord tomorrow.

❧

I went to see the doctor in Ballarat about the rheumatism in my right arm. He attributes it to working too hard when I was young, and when I got up each Saturday morning at 3.00 am to thresh loose barley in order to provide straw for thirty-eight head of cattle on the Sunday. Of course I continue to work hard, but this is no longer a hardship because it has now become second nature. . .

I work hard and for long hours, for I feel it is my duty, and I am happy doing it. . . A heap of gold could slip out of my hand in a few hours. Health and work are our greatest assets, and provide for contentment and happiness. . .

I was at work at 6.30 am. I can turn up as early as I like because I am on contract-work, otherwise they would mob me in this Colony if I turned up too early to do salaried work.

Diary of a Welsh Swagman, 1869-1894

We are living in a society where 'average' is enough. Workers punch in at nine o'clock and begin their countdown to five. For managers and employees alike, the job is seen as an interruption between weekends. . .

There is no such thing as a born winner. Success is not in the stars. It's in persistent, hard, daily effort. Success takes preparation, self-discipline, hard work, courage, perseverance and faith. Remember the third servant in our Lord's parable: he was condemned not because he used his talent for evil or because he tried and failed, but because he didn't do anything with it at all.

Denis Waitley, The Joy of Working

One lesson, Nature, let me learn of thee,
One lesson which in every wind is blown,
One lesson of two duties kept at one
Though the loud world proclaim their enmity —
Of toil unsever'd from tranquillity!

Matthew Arnold, 'Quiet Work'

When God wanted sponges and oysters, he made them, and put one on a rock, and the other in the mud. When he made humans, he did not make them to be sponges or oysters; he made them with feet and hands, and head and heart, and vital blood, and a place to use them, and said 'Go, work!'

Frank S. Mead

Work saves us from three great evils: boredom, vice and need.

Voltaire, Candide

Work is not the curse, but drudgery is.

Henry Ward Beecher

When hard work
soaks the shirts of humble folk,
look about you and you'll see
angels gathering
drops of sweat
as though gathering diamonds.

Dom Helder Camara, A Thousand Reasons for Living

Labour without joy is base. Labour without sorrow is base. Sorrow without labour is base. Joy without labour is base.

John Ruskin, Time and Tide

No race can prosper until it learns there is as much dignity in tilling a field as in writing a poem.

Booker T. Washington

The ant is knowing and wise but doesn't know enough to take a vacation.

Clarence Day, This Simian World

It's true hard work never killed anybody, but I figure why take a risk!

Ronald Reagan

When we rest, we acknowledge that all our striving will, of itself, do nothing. It means letting the world pass us by for a time.

Genuine rest requires acknowledgment that God, and our brothers and sisters, can survive without us. . . . a recognition of our own insufficiency and a handing over of responsibility. It is a real surrender to the ways of God. It is a moment of celebration when we acknowledge that blessing comes only from the hand of God. This is why rest requires faith. It is also why salvation can be pictured as rest. When we rest we accept God's grace: we do not seek to earn, we receive; we do not justify, we are justified.

Paul Marshall, 'Work and Rest'

Teach me, my God and King,
In all things thee to see,
And what I do in anything
To do it as for thee.
A servant with this clause
Makes drudgery divine;
Who sweeps a room as for thy laws
Makes that and the action fine.

George Herbert

Thou O God dost sell us all good things at the price of labour.

Leonardo da Vinci, Notebooks

Lord, cure me of laziness, an inordinate dislike of work, and workaholism, an inordinate love of work. Rather, help me to work and play and rest, all for your glory. I'd like to live for you, not for either work or leisure. May I integrate labour and relaxation, work and prayer, activity and contemplation, and so become more like the creating and redeeming and providential God I worship.

And teach me that the Christian life is not all fun and games. There are responsibilities to be carried out, jobs to be done, battles to be fought, sins to be overcome. Help me to be content with enough, to be grateful to be neither richer nor poorer, and to be generous. May I never take your good gifts for granted.

Thank you, Lord, for all who serve me in any way, for the skill of those who make life more beautiful, and the faithfulness of those who work in mundane jobs.

You, Lord, are still labouring to make us lovable. Help us to cooperate with you in that endeavour. Amen.

A Benediction

And so whatever your ordained calling, may you put your whole heart into it, for the glory of the Lord, not merely for the glory of self or others. May the blessing of God the Creator, Jesus the carpenter and the Spirit our helper be on you and your work, now and always. Amen.

Peace and prayer

First of all, then, I urge that petitions, prayers, requests and thanksgivings be offered to God for all people; for kings and all others who are in authority, that we may live a quiet and peaceful life. . .

And seek the peace of the city whither I have caused you to be carried away captives, and pray unto the Lord for it: for in the peace thereof shall ye have peace.

Pray for the peace of Jerusalem: 'May those who love you be secure. May there be peace within your walls and security within your citadels.'

Therefore put on the full armour of God, so that when the day of evil comes, you may be able to stand your ground and, after you have done everything, to stand. Stand firm then, with the belt of truth buckled round your waist, with the breastplate of righteousness in place and with your feet fitted with the readiness that comes from the gospel of peace.

In addition to all this, take up the shield of faith, with which you can extinguish all the flaming arrows of the evil one. Take the helmet of salvation and the sword of the Spirit, which is the word of God. And pray in the Spirit on all occasions with all kinds of prayers and requests. With this in mind, be alert and always keep on praying for all the saints.

Pray also for me, that whenever I open my mouth, words may be given me so that I will fearlessly make known the mystery of the gospel, for which I am an ambassador in chains. Pray that I may declare it fearlessly, as I should.

(1 Timothy 2: 1-2, GNB; Jeremiah 29: 7, KJV; Psalm 122: 6-7, NIV; Ephesians 6: 13-20, NIV)

Peace will not just evolve. It is both a divine gift and a human work. We must work at it and for it. Christians are called to be peacemakers, called to be bearers of peace. Jesus said, 'Happy are those who work for peace. . .' (Matthew 5: 9, GNB). Because we are activists, we immediately ask what we can do to bring about peace. We begin to believe it all depends on us, on our activity, on our zeal. And so we neglect to pray.

Prayer is not a last resort. Prayer is not a substitute for action. It is the one supreme central action that gives purpose and impetus to what we do. By praying, we indicate our conviction that without God, we can do nothing. To believe in the power of prayer is to believe that the God of history is involved in the affairs of human beings.

It is in prayer, both corporate and private, that we encounter Jesus, the source of our peace. We are renewed in our faith and our Christian hope is affirmed as we pray. Prayer can calm the troubled spirit, but its effect need not stop there. The prayer of faith, we are told, can move mountains (Matthew 21: 1-22).

The history of the Christian church is studded with incidents of amazing answers to prayer. Miracles did not cease centuries ago. They happen today. It stretches our credulity to argue that it is just the threat of the other side's nuclear armoury that has prevented a massive global holocaust for nearly half a century. That ignores the millions of God's people in dozens of nations who constantly cry out to our heavenly Father for peace in our world. It overlooks God's loving nature, his desire that people should live at peace. It denies the power of prayer.

But it is not only at the international global level that prayer for peace is important. How many mothers cry out to God for peace in their homes (when all else has failed)? Prayer in relationships can be the unifying agent that brings harmony and joy to individuals and families. The popular maxim, 'The family that prays together, stays together', is so relevant. People who pray that others find peace often themselves discover the 'peace that passes all understanding'.

A Christian doctor wrote the following words a few days before his death in a tragic boating accident: 'Unhealthy life-styles and negative thought-patterns are potent causes of distress. The subconscious mind responds to the negative or positive messages we keep pouring into it. Prolonged anxiety may bring physical or emotional illness — or breakdown. Life is out of balance; harmony and the rhythm of life is lost.

'Jesus the Prince of Peace, the night before his death, was able to offer his disciples a quality of peace the world cannot know or give. It is available to us. The greatest power of prayer consists not in asking, but in knowing how to receive.'

As we pray, we are God's agents for peace. Where there is conflict, it can be addressed by prayer. And as we pray for others, we find we cannot maintain hostile feelings towards them!

Jesus put his finger on one of our most basic human problems: namely, *we do not know the things that make for our peace.* Now to be sure, here is a reality we all say we want in the depths of our hearts. As it is used in the Bible, the word 'peace' catches up all the positive aspirations of the human quest. It is an inclusive term, standing for wholeness, completeness, fulfilment, well-being, satisfaction, joy. It represents what every human being in his or her right mind basically and urgently wants. There is little debate about the desire for peace in our heart.

The difficulty lies in knowing how to achieve it. As the end for which we strive, the question of peace poses no problem. It is in terms of the means we utilise that we humans run into trouble. . .

The only way peace can come, I think, [is] when one first refuses to be drawn into destructive polarisation and then calls to all others involved to embrace a higher way. This is precisely how Jesus went about peacemaking and someone like Simon Peter never got over marvelling that 'when reviled, he reviled not in return. . .'

The One who is more committed to our peace and whole-ness than we are has neither turned his back on us nor turned on us in rage. Look — listen — he weeps and continues to say: 'Jerusalem! Jerusalem! How I would have gathered you as a hen gathers her chicks!' He still wants to do that. He wants even yet to teach us the ways of peace.

John Claypool, 'The Things That Make for Peace'

What, then, is the contemporary mood of the world of nations to which biblical faith must speak and testify of God's rule? I would describe it as apocalyptic utopianism. The title of one of Peter Sellers' films put it much better and less pretentiously — *How I Learned to Stop Worrying and Love the Bomb*. Our post-war world has quickly learned to transmute its fear of atomic extinction into a strange hope.

Because the unthinkable has not happened, hope grows of a world community flourishing in the shadow of the H-bomb's mushroom cloud, its unity assured by a balance of terror, its optimism vested in a gigantic paradox — the possibility of the instrument of our destruction becoming the guarantee of our security. Over the imposing entran-ces to our multiplying international institutions might be graven those words of Winston Churchill: 'Peace shall be the sturdy child of terror!'

Certainly there is little of the old liberal Utopianism about. Two wars have purged the world of any expecta-tion that universal brotherhood or sisterhood can issue from the conquest of the darker side of our nature and the expression of our innate selflessness and goodwill. Ours is truly an apocalyptic utopianism because it is based upon the blinding perception that in the Nuclear Age the whole world is the smallest possible unit of survival.

The appropriate image of our time is not the Greek one of the human being as Apollo, the charioteer of the sun, rising ever higher, untrammelled in achievement, but an African one of humankind welded into one tribe by the fear of a common enemy, huddled round the fire, friend and foe alike, driven together by terror of the nameless things in the dark beyond the flickering light.

Colin Morris, *Mankind My Church*

Peace, n., In international affairs, a period of cheating between two periods of fighting.

Desk calendar quote

No wonder we crave for calm in the midst of the storm! In Robert Louis Stevenson's novel, *Kidnapped*, a man says to Jim Hawkins: 'Keep the boat steady.' And Jim replies: 'How can I keep it steady when I'm not steady inside?'

John Gladstone, 'The Christ who Brings a Great Calm'

Because peace, like the kingdom of God itself, is both a divine gift and a human work, the church should continually pray for the gift and share in the work.

U.S. Bishops' Pastoral Letter, 'The Challenge of Peace: God's
Promise and our Response'

Please do not reject this exhortation as a piece of pietistic irrelevance. . . we have been commanded to do it. Jesus our Lord specifically told us to pray for our enemies.

John Stott, *Issues Facing Christians Today*

And we who delighted in war, in the slaughter of one another and in every other type of iniquity, have in every part of the world converted our weapons into instruments of peace — our swords into ploughshares, our spears into farmers' tools — and we cultivate piety, justice, brotherly charity, faith and hope which we derive from the Father through the crucified Saviour.

St Justin

Prayer for peace and prayer for people who do not know peace are areas where the church must minister. God's word in Jeremiah 29 to his people was, 'Seek the peace of the city whither I have caused you to be carried away captives, for in the peace thereof shall ye have peace' (Jeremiah 29: 7). Paul's example to the church at Corinth was, 'I will pray with my spirit, but I will pray also with my mind' (1 Corinthians 14: 15, GNB). Intelligent prayer must be based on information, so a part of the educational process should include reading daily news and interpreting events in the light of intercessory prayer, corporate prayer, prayer groups, prayer partners, and individual praying should focus on people affected by war.

Carolyn Weatherford, 'Missions and Peace'

Drop thy still dews of quietness,
Till all our strivings cease;
Take from our souls the strain and stress,
And let our ordered lives confess
The beauty of thy peace.

John Greenleaf Whittier

Dear God, if we pray, 'lift up your countenance upon us and give us peace', it is because we know that we will not find peace anywhere else but in you. We realise just how little we deserve your grace and favour. Why should we whose attitudes often prevent others being at peace, expect that your peace should flood our lives? Yet strangely, we keep on asking because you keep on listening. . .

Tony Cupit

When peace like a river attendeth my way,
When sorrows like sea billows roll,
Whatever my lot thou hast taught me to say,
It is well, it is well, with my soul.

Horatio G. Stafford

A Benediction

Go into the world acutely conscious that Christ is there, even as Christ is in you. Go into the world with a song on your lips, with a spring in your step and with a prayer in your mind. Greet adversity with faith, challenges with resolve, friends with warmth, enemies with love, the mundane with creativity and the commonplace with expectancy. Thank God for the privilege of sharing life with him as you share it with others. Embrace the lonely, comfort the sick, befriend the social misfit, encourage the doleful, welcome the stranger and accept and affirm all. Do this today. . . and tomorrow. . . and until limbs are tired and breath spent, and so enhance the work of the Kingdom. Amen.

23

To will one thing

(Soren Kierkegaard)

For the eyes of the Lord range throughout the earth to strengthen those whose hearts are fully committed to him.

Not that I have already obtained all this, or have already been made perfect, but I press on to take hold of that for which Christ Jesus took hold of me. Beloved, I do not consider myself yet to have taken hold of it. But one thing I do: forgetting what is behind and straining towards what is ahead, I press on towards the goal to win the prize for which God has called me heavenwards, in Christ Jesus.

If we confess our sins, he is faithful and just and will forgive us our sins and purify us from all unrighteousness.

And we know that in all things God works for the good of those who love him, who have been called according to his purpose. For those God foreknew he also predestined to be conformed to the likeness of his Son, that he might be the firstborn within a large family.

When they had finished eating, Jesus said to Simon Peter, 'Simon son of John, do you truly love me more than these?'

'Yes, Lord,' he said, 'you know that I love you.' Jesus said, 'Feed my lambs.'

Again Jesus said, 'Simon son of John, do you truly love me?' He answered, 'Yes, Lord, you know that I love you.' Jesus said, 'Take care of my sheep.'

The third time he said to him, 'Simon son of John, do you love me?'. . . He said, 'Lord, you know all things; you know that I love you.'

Jesus said, 'Feed my sheep. I tell you the truth, when you were younger you dressed yourself and went where you wanted; but when you are old you will stretch out your hands, and someone else will dress you and lead you where you do not want to go.' Jesus said this to indicate the kind of death by which Peter would glorify God. Then he said to him, 'Follow me!'

(2 Chronicles 16: 9; Philippians 3: 12-14; 1 John 1: 9 — all NIV; Romans 8: 28-29, NIV/NRSV; John 21: 15-19, NIV)

In *Hamlet*, Shakespeare has Polonius give this advice to his son, as he leaves home in pursuit of an academic career:

To thine own self be true
And it must follow as the night
the day,
Thou canst not then be false to
any man.

But what is 'self'? Elizabeth O'Connor in *Our Many Selves* describes the inner complexity of a person. The kind of self-love which tries to get the best place in the synagogue, or to be seen praying on the streets is pathological. This is self-love at the expense of the interests of others. But self-love which moves from self-acceptance to love of neighbour is surely biblical. So our 'self' needs both a change of master and direction. How can Christ be Lord of the inner self?

First, we must reckon with the past. Forgiveness is not simply theoretical. When Jesus healed the Gadarene demoniac, a complete change took place: the man had a new self-identity.

Then, in the present, we are in the process of 'becoming' the self God intended us to be. Our changing circumstances are less in control than is our heavenly Master.

The future security a Christian anticipates is a function of trust in a trustworthy God.

John Sanford (*The Kingdom Within*) writes: 'For the sake

of our own relationship to the Kingdom, as well as our relationships with other people, our attitude towards ourself must be one of self-acceptance. This comes as a shock to people who have often been trained to reject themselves.'

So there is a forgetfulness.
You cannot turn the past into a blank:
the Bible does not encourage this.
In reality, this is not possible.

There can be selective forgetfulness.
Let the failures of the past *teach* you.
Let them *not terrorise* you. . .
Not despair but development.

You must learn to forget successes.
Their remembrance must make us grateful and humble.
Conceit and self-sufficiency are hindrances to growth in faith.
There is also a forwardness in faith.
The goal is 'Christlikeness'.

When a child is born, the family looks for 'resemblance' in the physical appearance of the baby to the ancestors — present and past. One day, when the wheels of time stop spinning — and we 'move on' — then, God looks for the recognisable resemblance with the 'Elder Brother', Jesus Christ.

Refusing to surrender to God does not mean that we have not surrendered to any other. All of us surrender to something. Most of us surrender to ourselves as 'god'. But we dislike this 'god'. We do as we like and by now we do not like what we do. We express ourselves, but dislike the self we express. We do not like ourself as it is and others also do not like it.

❧

So may thou give to the intellect, wisdom to comprehend that one thing; to the heart, sincerity to receive this understanding; to the will, purity that wills one thing. In prosperity may thou grant perseverance to will one thing; amid distraction, collectedness to will one thing;

in suffering, patience to will one thing.

Soren Kierkegaard, *Purity of Heart is to Will One Thing*

Our perfection, therefore, is not to be flawless, but to be in tune with our redeemed destiny in Christ.

P.T. Forsyth, *Christian Perfection*

Faith is the condition of spiritual maturity in the sense of adultness, of entering on the real heritage of the soul. It is the soul coming to itself, coming of age, feeling its feet, entering on its native powers. Faith is perfection in this sense. It is not ceasing to grow, but entering on the normal region of growth.

P.T. Forsyth, *Christian Perfection*

Setting up a saving relationship with Christ is not essentially different from setting up a warm human friendship. In the latter the steps are five: (1) The stage of drawing near. This is a tentative, explorative stage. You are not certain whether you want to give yourself inwardly to the other person. It is the stage of yes and no. (2) The stage when there is the inward decision to give yourself to the other person — the stage of decision. (3) You implement the decision — you actually make the inward surrender to the other person. (4) Having given to the other person, you are now free to take from that person. There is an exchange of selves — you belong to that person, and that person belongs to you. You are one. (5) There is a continuous mutual adjustment of mind to mind, will to will, and being to being down through the years. The friendship unfolds.

E. Stanley Jones, *Conversion*

What happens to the self when surrendered to God? Does he wipe it out or wipe it clean? He wipes it clean of selfishness. The very act of self-surrender gives him the opportunity to cleanse us from our central selfishness. He gives the self back to itself. When we obey the deepest law of the universe it works: 'If you would save your life you will lose it' — centre yourself on yourself and the self will disintegrate. Every self-centred person is a disintegrating person. Centre yourself on your self and you won't like yourself — and no one else will like you. But the rest of that verse is just as true: 'Whoever loses his life for my sake, he will save it' — lose yourself in the will of God by self-surrender and you will find your self again. It is a paradox, but you are never so much your own as when you are most his.

Bound to him you walk the earth free. Low at his feet you stand straight before everything else. You suddenly realise that you have aligned yourself with the creative forces of the universe so you are free — free to create, free to love, free to live at your maximum, free to be, to be all he wills you to be.

E. Stanley Jones, *Victory Through Surrender*

Read John 21: 15-19 again and reflect upon your own life calling.

1. If you were asked the same question that Jesus asked Peter, how would you respond?
    a. Yes — all of the time.
    b. Yes — most of the time.
    c. Yes — some of the time.
    d. Huh?
    e. Ask me tomorrow.

2. 'Take care of my sheep.' If Jesus said this to you three times, what would this mean to you now?
    a. Get going.
    b. I'm counting on you.
    c. Get your eyes off yourself.
    d. Consider the whole world.
    e. Seek first the kingdom of God.

3. In the past three months, where have you seen the most progress in your life?
    a. Personal discipline
    b. Spiritual development
    c. Self-confidence
    d. Concern for others
    e. Family relations
    f. Moral courage
    g. Bible understanding

h. Openness to God's will
i. Change in priorities
j. Attitude about work/school
k. Ability to relax/unwind

L. Coleman, D. Rydberg, R. Pearce, G. Christopherson
(eds), *Serendipity New Testament for Groups*

In the eleventh century, King Henry III of Bavaria grew tired of court life and the pressures of being a monarch. He made application to Prior Richard at a local monastery, asking to be accepted as a contemplative and spend the rest of his life in the monastery.

'Your Majesty,' said Prior Richard, 'do you understand that the pledge here is one of obedience? That will be hard because you have been a king.'

'I understand,' said Henry. 'The rest of my life I will be obedient to you, as Christ leads you.'

'Then I will tell you what to do,' said Prior Richard. 'Go back to your throne and serve faithfully in the place where God has put you.'

When King Henry died, a statement was written: 'The king learned to rule by being obedient.'

When we tire of our roles and responsibilities, it helps to remember God has planted us in a certain place and told us to be a good accountant or teacher or mother or father. Christ expects us to be faithful where he puts us, and when he returns, we'll rule together with him.

Steve Brown, *Leadership*

Loved with everlasting love, led by grace that love to know;
Spirit breathing from above, thou hast taught me it is so!
Oh, this full and perfect peace! Oh, this transport all divine!
In a love which cannot cease, I am his and he is mine.

His forever, only his: who the Lord and me shall part?
Ah, with what a rest of bliss, Christ can fill the loving heart!
Heav'n and earth may fade and flee, first-born light in
  gloom decline,
But while God and I shall be, I am his and he is mine.

George W. Robinson

Long my imprisoned spirit lay
Fast bound in sin and nature's night;
Thine eye diffused a quick'ning ray,
I woke, the dungeon flamed with light;
My chains fell off, my heart was free,
I rose, went forth and followed thee.

Charles Wesley

Almighty God, Father of all mercies,
we your unworthy servants give humble and hearty thanks
for all your goodness and loving kindness to us. . .
we bless you for our creation, preservation and all the blessings
    of this life;
but above all for your amazing love
in the redemption of the world by our Lord Jesus Christ;
for the means of grace;
and for the hope of glory.
And, we pray, give us that due sense of all your mercies,
that our hearts may be truly thankful and that we may declare
    your praise
not only with our lips, but in our lives,
by giving up ourselves to your service,
and by walking before you in holiness and righteousness all our
    days;
through Jesus Christ our Lord,
to whom, with you and the Holy Spirit, be all honour and glory
    now and for ever. Amen.

An Australian Prayer Book

A Benediction
And now may the God of peace who brought again from the
dead our Lord Jesus, the great Shepherd of the sheep, equip you
with all you need for doing his will, through the blood of the
everlasting agreement between God and you.   And may he
produce in you through the power of Christ all that is pleasing
to him, to whom be glory forever and ever.   Amen.

Hebrews 13: 20-21, LB

24

Idolatry and the image of God

Do not make for yourselves images of anything in heaven or on earth or in the water under the earth. Do not bow down to any idol or worship it, because I am the Lord your God and I tolerate no rivals.

Be certain that you do not forget the covenant that the Lord your God made with you. Obey his command not to make yourselves any kind of idol, because the Lord your God is like a flaming fire; he tolerates no rivals.

Our ancestors refused to obey him; they pushed him aside and wished that they could go back to Egypt. So they said to Aaron, 'Make us some gods who will lead us. We do not know what has happened to the man Moses, who brought us out of Egypt.' It was then that they made an idol in the shape of a bull, offered sacrifice to it, and had a feast in honour of what they themselves had made.

You know that while you were still heathen, you were led astray in many ways to the worship of lifeless idols.

'It is my opinion,' James went on, 'that we should not trouble the Gentiles who are turning to God. Instead, we should write a letter telling them not to eat any food that is ritually unclean because it has been offered to idols. . .'

So then, about eating the food offered to idols: we know that an idol stands for something that does not really exist; we know that there is only the one God. Even if there are so-called 'gods', whether in heaven or on earth, and even though there are many of these 'gods' or 'lords', yet there is for us only one God, the Father, who is the Creator of all things and for whom we live; and there is only one Lord, Jesus Christ, through whom all things were created and through whom we live.

(Exodus 20: 4-5; Deuteronomy 4: 23-24; Acts 7: 39-41; 1 Corinthians 12: 2; Acts 15: 19-20a; 1 Corinthians 8: 4-6 — all GNB)

The belief that God is not to be depicted in the form of an image is integral to the biblical worship of God. Its basis is in the Mosaic Law. The idea of the jealous nature of God is usually mentioned in connection with idol worship.

God is not to be conceived of as essentially remote from the world and therefore in need of material representation. Rather he is a God that we cannot master or control, least of all in visible form. Imagination is not permitted free rein when it comes to describing God, for all things have been created by him, are subject to him and cannot, therefore, be compared with him.

In the New Testament, idols are not merely alternative gods, but unreal gods and therefore false as distinct from real gods. Paul believed there was not truth or reality in the gods represented by idols. He believed demons were behind idol worship. Offerings to idols are in fact offerings to demons. Demons are not the same as the gods the idolatrous worshipper worships; rather demons deceive worshippers into acknowledging them to be gods. John in his apocalyptic vision sees the whole of humankind worshipping demons and idols (Revelation 9: 20). Satan is behind all paganism — sophisticated or primitive, materialistic or magical.

Humans are not free to choose whether or not they will worship gods. In this sense there are no atheists. We are all committed to someone or something within or outside ourselves. The choice we make is between the true and living God, and one or more from a pantheon of false gods. Some 'gods that are not God' are noble. They may include service of our fellow-humans, or attainment in the arts, or the advancement of knowledge. But when these — or anything — become ends in themselves, we are worshipping idols.

The most common, and most insidious, idol is the self, the ego. When we are enslaved to ourselves, we may become famous or rich or influential, but decrease in stature in the process.

Idolatry, then, is the worship of anything *created*, instead of worshipping the Creator. In our culture, modern rivals to God include the 'five p's' — popularity, power, prestige, prominence and patriotism — together with wealth, physical beauty and bodily pleasure. Idols are objects of extreme devotion, whether they be the 'almighty' dollar, sport, drugs, sex, science, or whatever.

Idols detract from God, and distract us from worship of him alone. Idols do not point us to him: none yet have extolled his greatness and power and glory. God is jealous, not because he has some personality defect that requires our adulation, but jealous for our good. Right here is the most important single issue for any human person or group: to let God, not gods rule us; to worship and enjoy him — not them — forever.

❧

The Christian faith does not argue there is nothing good in other religious traditions or teaching. Christians do not say there are no points of common understanding between various religions. The followers of Christ do not say Christianity is all light and all other ways are, in fact, systems that are entirely in the dark. What Christians claim is that God has revealed his plan of salvation in and through the Christian faith and that the locus of that salvation is to be found in Jesus Christ.

God is immediately near in his created world. There is a mystic immanence which touches all. The Holy Spirit of God is near to all. He is touching us at every moment. And, in response, some may be touching him. Even so, there may be touch but no truthful perception, no vital fellowship and no living relationship. The Divine may be near but not apprehended. There may be contact but no communion. Pregnant events may be near to birth but nothing is born.

Graham Houghton, 'Idolatry and the Image of God'

Now, what if that which you are worshipping as a god — that is, looking up to and relying upon in an ultimate sense — is not in fact God — that is, does not have the power to sustain and satisfy and fulfil your life? This is at the bottom of all human tragedy — people set their ultimate hopes on that which does not have the power to save or fulfil. And when this happens, just as Jesus said, that which is 'built on sand' collapses and goes to pieces and ends up in disintegration.

I once saw a bumper sticker that said: 'Let God be God.' On first glance, a phrase like that sounds like so much religious doubletalk and 'gobbledegook'. But on deeper reflection, I realised it stated the most important imperative of life. What could be more important, really, than letting one's god be the true God — letting the One who is God by nature function as one's god, in fact?

John Claypool, 'God for Each of Us'

Idolatry is the practice of ascribing absolute value to things of relative worth. . . Idolatry is always popular among religious people, but idols made out of things like the Denomination, the Bible, the Liturgy, the Holy Images, are apt to seem so limited in real power even to their idolaters that there is always the hope that in time they will over-throw themselves.

It is among the unreligious that idolatry is a particular menace. Having ushered God out once and for all through the front door, the unbeliever is under constant temptation to replace him with something spirited in through the service entrance. From the moment the eighteenth-century French revolutionaries set up the God-dess of Reason on the high altar of Notre Dame, there wasn't a head in all Paris that was safe.

Frederich Buechner, *Wishful Thinking*

What about people who say 'I believe in God' when their mental orientation, overall purposes and conversational obsessions reveal that in fact they believe primarily and earnestly in the ladder of promotion, the achievement of the maximum number of personal comforts and the promiscuous pursuit of the opposite sex? Conversely, what about those who say 'No, I don't believe in any God', then their mental orientation, daily activity and daily chatter reveal that they believe passionately and profoundly in money, cars and betting on horses? Surely they, too, are guilty of lying. Their gods are money, cars and gambling. To call one a believer (a theist) and the other an unbeliever (an atheist) would be most misleading. . . For practical purposes they are both polytheists.

Harry Blamires, 'Where Do We Stand Against
Current Idolatries?'

It is painfully apparent that radical Christians have not always been true to the whole counsel of God's judgment. An ideological selectivity intrudes, a political bias which undermines the credibility and power of prophetic witness. The idolatries of the establishment are attacked while the idols of the anti-establishment receive less critical treatment. The evils of the majority culture are assailed, but the sins of the counterculture are often passed over. The political prisoners of right-wing dictatorships seem to generate more interest than those languishing in the gaols of leftist regimes. . . Prophecy is, in fact, profoundly anti-ideological.

Jim Wallis, 'Idols Closer to Home'

In Latin America, the doctrine of *Seguridad Nacional* [means that] every trend toward change is interpreted as a threat to 'national security', every proposal to extend food and shelter and education to those now denied it is seen as a communist plot. Consequently, in the interests of national security, any measures are legitimate to thwart the proponents of change, from persuasion to arrest to exile to torture to execution. It is carefully concealed from the people that such 'security' is only for the few who have power and want to keep it, and that it really means insecurity for the rest. . .

The doctrine of national security is what the Bible calls 'idolatry', which is a fancy name for worshipping a false god. It says that in this case, the nation has become a false god, and that won't work. Whenever we say 'anything goes. . .' in defending a nation, we have made the nation into a supreme object of our allegiance, and that is what we call a god. Our national temptation, in other words, is never atheism, but always to polytheism, to the creation of other gods in addition to the true God.

Robert McAfee Brown, *Creative Dislocation*

Idols [such as] work, alcohol, consumerism, pornography [and such like] mottle so many of our lives. The one God who is the maker of heaven and earth is not in competition with our decent, proper use of any creatures. Both we and all other creatures come from this one God, so in God's eyes there is no strife among us. . . The problem of idolatry is that we easily lose perspective, lose our sense of God's overriding presence and so fixate on something less than God. This something less can be our selves, with their so many virtues and anxieties, or it can be something external that we think will make us happy. . .

We are not what we eat, what we wear, what we earn, what others think of us. We are possibility, the potential, the humble yet wonderful creature of God brought into focus and warmed from the core by a force, a most gentle power, that we cannot see or grasp or name or deny, a force that has given us the best moments of our lives, the times we knew why Genesis says that God looked on our creation and called it very good.

John Carmody, *Towards a Male Spirituality*

A poor French sculptor had just completed a very beautiful clay model. That night it became bitterly cold and wet, and he was afraid that the model might be damaged by the frost. At length he took his blankets and, wrapping them around the model, lay down again. In the morning he was found dead, but the model was intact. . .

Sadhu Sundar Singh, *The Spiritual Life*

We are made in the image of God. And while sin has marred that image to a greater or lesser degree, it means that, despite where and how we might worship God, there remains something of that image in us, calling us, attracting us to reaches higher than ourselves. . . to higher plains of moral integrity and being than that of the gods we worship.

Graham Houghton, 'Idolatry and the Image of God'

To reach satisfaction in all
desire its possession in nothing.
To come to the knowledge of all
desire the knowledge of nothing.
To come to possess all
desire the possession of nothing.
To arrive at being all
desire to be nothing.

St John of the Cross

The English *Cloud of Unknowing* develops the picture of the soul suspended in prayer between two 'clouds': below is the cloud of forgetting, the veil which hides created concerns and lesser loves; above, the cloud of unknowing, the darkness of God which can be passed through only by the 'dart of longing love' answering the obscure ray of grace which kindles it like a 'sparkle from the coal'.

Rowan Williams, *A Dictionary of Christian Spirituality*

Lord, help me to understand that an awesome war is going on inside me all the time, as the God who made me does battle with the gods I have made.

Lord, you are the divine surgeon, who is horrified by that which is destroying me, who desires my wholeness and fulfilment, and who labours unceasingly to get rid of any spiritually cancerous growth which is taking over my mind or spirit.

Only you, my Creator, can fully satisfy and genuinely fulfil me, the creature. You have made us for yourself — not for other gods — and our hearts are restless until they rest in you.

Rescue me from depending for my salvation on anything which does not have the power to save, or relying ultimately on something that is ultimately unreliable.

You, Lord, are my God. Help me to love you with all my

heart and soul and mind and strength. May you be my heart's desire, the object of my greatest devotion, now and always. Amen.

A Benediction
Now may God who is the living God, the Creator who made all things, who redeems us from all idolatries, who gives us peace, make us holy in every way and keep our whole being — spirit, soul and body — free from every idolatry at the coming of our Lord Jesus Christ. He who calls us will do it, because he is faithful. Alleluia. Amen.

1 Thessalonians 5: 23-24 (adapted)

Short cuts are risky

Now when Pharaoh let the people go, God did not lead them by the road towards the Philistines, although that was the shortest; for he said, 'the people may change their minds when they see war before them, and turn back to Egypt.' So God made them go round by way of the wilderness towards the Red Sea.

For the moment all discipline seems to be painful rather than pleasant. Later it yields the peaceful fruit of righteousness to those who have been trained by it.

Do not ignore this one fact, beloved, that with the Lord one day is as a thousand years, and a thousand years as one day. The Lord is not slow about his promise as some count slowness, but is forbearing towards you, not wishing that any should perish.

I do not claim that I have already succeeded or have already become perfect. I keep striving to win the prize for which Christ Jesus has already won me to himself. Of course, beloved, I really do not think I have already won it; the one thing I do, however, is to forget what is behind me and do my best to reach what is ahead. So I run straight towards the goal in order to win the prize, which is God's call through Christ Jesus to the life above.

Although he was a son, he learned obedience through what he suffered.

'All this I will give you,' the devil said, 'if you will kneel down and worship me.'

My brothers, whenever you have to face trials of many kinds, count yourselves supremely happy, in the knowledge that such testing of your faith breeds fortitude, and if you give fortitude full play you will go on to complete a balanced character that will fall short in nothing.

You should try your hardest to supplement your faith with virtue, virtue with knowledge, knowledge with self-control, self-control with fortitude, fortitude with piety, piety with brotherly kindness and brotherly kindness with love. These are gifts which, if you possess and foster them, will keep you from being either useless or barren in the knowledge of our Lord Jesus Christ.

(Exodus 13: 17-18, NEB; Hebrews 12: 11, RSV; 2 Peter 3: 8-9, RSV; Philippians 3: 12-14, GNB; Hebrews 5: 8, RSV; Matthew 4: 9, GNB; James 1: 2-4, NEB; 2 Peter 1: 5-8, NEB)

In these days of instant cash, it is well to remind ourselves that there is no such thing as instant Christian character and maturity, and that attempts to find short cuts in these matters can lead to a good deal of disillusionment and frustration. It takes a lifetime to grow to what Paul calls 'the measure of the stature of the fullness of Christ'. We are still 'being saved', and the whole process is attended by growing pains and obstacles which may not be dispensed with without stultifying the whole thing. There are no short cuts.

We fall into this trap in many ways. For example, there are some among us who think that all the problems which beset our world would be solved overnight if everybody suddenly became Christians. It is not as simple as that: they would still need to be worked at and thought out by consecrated minds. And many of what we see now as problems, God surely sees as opportunities.

Even Jesus was tempted to try short cuts to his goals: 'All these I will give you if. . .' But he deliberately took the long way round, past Galilee and Judea, past the high priest's palace, past Gethsemane, past Pilate's court, by way of the cross to the tomb in Joseph's garden. 'It became him, in bringing many sons to glory, to make the captain of their salvation perfect through suffering' — not 'in spite of it', but 'by means of it'.

God does an infinitely bigger thing for us than giving us a short cut through our difficulties and instant solutions to our problems when he makes us wise enough and strong enough to find our own way through these things. Which of us, in our better moments, would rather stand without sweating on some mountain peak which God had reduced for us to the size of a molehill, than climb to the peak of some mountain of achievement, with torn hands and bleeding feet, but thanking God for the strength he gave us to get there? To people facing the problems of that age, Jesus apparently gave no specific directions, no easy solutions, but he did tell them how to become the kind of people who would know in their hearts what had to be done. And there are no short cuts to that condition of mind and heart.

Think now of some of the ways in which we tend to become victims of this very human failing; when we become a little impatient with bereaved people passing through the long and painful process of working through deep grief, and try to cheer them up, thinking that it is 'time they pulled themselves together'; when we hang labels on people and put them in categories, without the prior arduous attempt to understand them in depth; our giving glib advice on important matters without really listening to the questions; our inadequate ideas and practice of evangelism; our wrong expectations of prayer and guidance, imagining that these are to save us from the often painful task of thinking through our problems, and acting on our own God-given insight; our craving for quick 'results' in God's work — all that comes into Bonhoeffer's concept of 'cheap grace'. In all these ways we try to find easy short cuts through our difficulties. (An imaginative reading between the lines of the fragment of the story of Paul's second missionary journey in Acts 16: 6-9 is to be recommended.)

If the way to the goal of our dreams sometimes seems to be unnecessarily long and devious, and we think that we can find a more direct route, may we have the faith and courage to obey him, believing that when God is leading, the longest way round is indeed the shortest way home.

Short cuts are as risky in religion as in hiking, but not nearly as harmless. I have just spent three hours with a young man who was 'soundly converted' at an evangelistic rally some months ago. Now that the emotional excitement has died down, he is back where he started, indeed further back. The glow has faded, and he is distressed because he has fallen down on his conversion, broken his vows and dishonoured Christ. . .

As we talked, it became obvious to me that here was a young man accepting a premature solution to a problem that had not been sufficiently explored. . . he had come to terms with Christ on too narrow a front. . . It was not the whole person who was committed to Christ, but that part which stood in obvious and pressing need.

W.B.J. Martin, *Five Minutes to Twelve*

> There is no expeditious road
> to pack and label men for God,
> And save them by the barrel load.

Francis Thompson, *A Judgment in Heaven*

The trouble is that the modern world is so dynamic and explosive that we cannot continue for long without becoming conscious of our need for answers to ultimate questions. When we do, our chief danger is that, in our desperation and inexperience, we try to take religious short cuts, like the idolaters of the ancient world. There is already plenty of evidence that this is just as much one of the dangers of the modern world as so-called 'irreligion'.

Daniel Jenkins, *The Christian Belief in God*

In the language of psychoanalysis, we are in conflict with ourselves, in the grip of neurotic patterns. How wonderful it would be if we could be saved from the pain of such conflicts! Well, there is help at hand. . . fanaticism, drugs, religion, sex, power: all of these will help relieve the pain of inner conflict, and save us the trouble of striving for a mature way of being in the world. They will also enable us to elude love, and will prevent us from finding our way 'home'.

Alan Jones, *Soul Making*

There are no supersonic flights to the Celestial City or even to the Palace Beautiful. Increased awareness can only be obtained by a journey on foot by way of the Slough of Despond, the Hill Difficulty, Doubting Castle and the rest.

H.A. Williams, 'Theology and Self-Awareness'

Nothing is too early or late for me which is due time for thee.

John Baillie, *A Diary of Private Prayer*

. . .the devil urges upon [Jesus] the well-tried methods of all human reformers. They had failed only because they were not able to back their programs with the power to carry them out. But link the irresistibility of the divine omnipotence to the politician's dream of universal plenty, or to the known ability of sheer display to dazzle the human mind. . . or to the 'realism' of skilful diplomacy — and with any such program how could he fail to win the world? But Jesus rejects in turn each of these suggestions. . . There could be no short cuts to the kingdom of God.

John A.T. Robinson, *Twelve New Testament Studies*

One of the most important factors in the Gesell studies is their working hypothesis that the stages of growth [in children] are not evenly related to each other. There is a jagged rhythm of growth. There will be a spurt of growth and activity, a time of breaking out and vigorous expansion, a time of. . . troubled and confused behaviour, and a time of rounded, balanced, smooth and consolidated behaviour. . .

Parents tend to interpret the behaviour of children as being good or bad in terms of the spurts of growth and the periods of quiescent consolidation. Growth is considered to be times of difficulty, badness and unmanageableness. . . On the other hand, the times of quiescence and consolidation are likely to be identified with goodness, virtue and perfection in behaviour.

Wayne E. Oates, *The Psychology of Religion*

It is not for you to turn the buds into blossoms.
Your touch spoils them,
You tear the petals and scatter them in the dust.
He who can open the bud
Does it so simply.

D.T. Niles, *The Preacher's Task and the Stone of Stumbling*

What all life does say to us is that God does not conduct his rivers, like arrows, to the sea. The ruler and compass are only for finite mortals who labour, by taking thought, to overcome their limitations, and are not. . . infinite. . . The expedition demanded by humanity's small power produces the canal, but nature, with a beneficent and picturesque circumambulancy, the work of a more spacious and less precipitate mind, produces the river. Why should we assume that, in all the rest of his ways, he rejoices in the river, but in religion, can use no more adequate method save the canal?

John Oman, *Grace and Personality*

The day returns and brings us the petty round of irritating concerns and duties. . . Help us to perform them with laughter and kind faces; let cheerfulness abound with industry. [Enable] us to go blithely on our business all this day; bring us to our resting beds weary and content and undishonoured, and grant us in the end the gift of sleep.

R.L. Stevenson

O God, in whose strong hands are the threads of every person's life, I thank you that you have a purpose for the world, and that in that purpose my little life has its place and a part to play. Forgive me that so often I want life on other terms than you have granted, and that so often I seek the easiest way through the obstacles that beset me, thus robbing myself of the real fruit of pain and frustration. For often I forget that these experiences are the means by which we grow into the likeness of our Lord, who learned obedience by the things he suffered. Keep me from seeking easy short cuts, and from the snare of cheap, quick results from the service I try to render. Let me never forget the way Jesus deliberately set himself. Let my life fulfil your gracious design, and increasingly display the qualities of the life he seeks to live in me. Amen.

Book of Prayers for Students

A Benediction
Be thou within me, Lord, to purify me; above me, to draw me higher; beneath me, to sustain me; before me, to lead me; behind me, to restrain me; round about me, to protect me. Amen.

Book of Prayers for Students

26

To the beat of a different drum

Whatever was to my profit I now consider loss for the sake of Christ. What is more, I consider everything a loss compared to the surpassing greatness of knowing Christ Jesus my Lord, for whose sake I have lost all things. I consider them rubbish, that I may gain Christ and be found in him, not having a righteousness of my own that comes from the law, but that which is through faith in Christ — the righteousness that comes from God and is by faith.

I want to know Christ and the power of his resurrection and the fellowship of sharing in his sufferings, becoming like him in his death, and so, somehow, to attain to the resurrection of the dead. Not that I have already obtained all this, or have already been made perfect, but I press on to take hold of that for which Christ Jesus took hold of me.

I do not have time to tell about Gideon, Barak, Samson, Jephthah, David, Samuel and the prophets, who through faith conquered kingdoms, administered justice, and gained what was promised; who shut the mouths of lions, quenched the fury of the flames, and escaped the edge of the sword; whose weakness was turned to strength; and who became powerful in battle and routed foreign armies. Women received back their dead, raised to life again. Others were tortured and refused to be released, so that they might gain a better resurrection.

Some faced jeers and flogging, while still others were chained and put in prison. They were stoned; they were sawn in two; they were put to death by the sword. They went about in sheepskins and goatskins, destitute, persecuted and ill-treated — the world was not worthy of them. They wandered in deserts and mountains, and in caves and holes in the ground. These were all commended for their faith, yet none of them received what had been promised.

We have this treasure in jars of clay to show that this all-surpassing power is from God and not from us. We are hard pressed on every side, but not crushed; perplexed, but not in despair; persecuted, but not abandoned; struck down, but not destroyed. We always carry around in our body the death of Jesus, so that the life of Jesus may also be revealed in our body. For we who are alive are always being given over to death for Jesus' sake, so that his life may be revealed in our mortal body.

Your attitude should be the same as that of Christ Jesus:
Who, being in very nature God,
    did not consider equality with God something to be
    grasped,
but made himself nothing,
    taking the very nature of a servant,
    being made in human likeness.
And being found in appearance as a man,
    he humbled himself
    and became obedient to death — even death on a cross!
Don't let the world around you squeeze you into its own mould, but let God re-mould your minds from within, so that you may prove in practice that the plan of God for you is good, meets all his demands and moves towards the goal of true maturity.

(Philippians 3: 7-12; Hebrews 11: 32-39; 2 Corinthians 4: 7-11; Philippians 2: 5-8 — all NIV; Romans 12: 2, Phillips)

History is sprinkled with such people. So is the Bible. People who stand out from the crowd, who don't quite fit the expected model. The dreamers, the high achievers, the entrepreneurs, the eccentrics, the loners, the misfits. Sometimes we admire them, sometimes we demean them.

Often we misunderstand them.

Perhaps more conventional people sometimes wonder why such people choose to be different, or at least remain different. It may be for the challenge of being the 'first', or the thrill of being noticed. It may be because that is just the way they are, and to change would be impossible or too painful. This statement by Thoreau provides an alternative perspective (applicable to both genders!):

If a man does not keep pace with his companions,
perhaps it is because he hears a different drummer.
Let him step to the music he hears,
however measured or far away.

Such imagery of course reminds of the precision of a military drill — there is great pressure on one to keep in step with the rest of the marching team! But the same pressure to conform appears in other contexts: in the peer group we are urged to 'be like us'; in society we are often reminded that 'this is the way we've always done it'.

God's economy is different — he creates and calls unique individuals, trains us according to his timetable and curriculum, asks that we be willing to be servants and perhaps martyrs. The beat we must listen to does not come from the drummer of external circumstances, but from the inner music of the Holy Spirit. Sometimes that may seem indistinct and out-of-step with our immediate surroundings. For the life of faith, while grounded in history and reality, beckons us towards the unseen and the unknown.

In Christ, we are all called to a journey on which we march to the beat of a different drum. Our challenge is to pick up the beat and make the choice to follow it. When the road seems strange or lonely, we can trust in God whose beat is never devious or 'out of sync' with his purposes. And we can be encouraged by the determination and faithfulness of those who have been ahead of us on the way.

⋘⋙

Stories about Abraham or Moses, Joshua or Josiah, Daniel or Esther, Stephen or Paul, were preserved partly to offer examples for other believers called to live by faith, to exercise leadership, to withstand the pressures of life in a foreign land, to witness boldly before Jews and Gentiles. It is this function of stories which is taken up by a passage such as Hebrews 11. Stories illustrate *the commitments which the faith entails.*

John Goldingay, 'Preaching on the stories in Scripture'

As we grow up, our minds develop in a score of different ways. Our experience and our insight into people, ideas and problems grows deeper. At the same time, unless we have allowed ourselves to become bogged down by some rigidity in our religious thinking, our ideas of God expand greatly, and there come times when we realise with an awe-struck humility that what we once worshipped as God was only, so to speak, the shimmering hem of his garment.

If we are foolish, we cling with desperate loyalty to the limited conception of God that we have at present, but if we are wise, we 'launch out into the deep' (Luke 5: 4), and allow every true experience of life, every touch or sight of goodness, truth and beauty, to open fresh windows upon the illimitable magnificence of God.

We cannot hold too big a conception of God, but the more our hearts and minds and imaginations are used, the more astounding becomes the central fact of our faith — that so infinite a God allowed himself to be, so to speak, scaled down to fit the narrow limits of humanity. For all his vastness and mystery, he has made himself known in an unforgettable character by which all can see what sort of a person it is 'with whom we have to do' (Hebrews 4: 13). It is as though, having once accepted this tremendous fact, we view all that we can see or discover of the complex wisdom of God through a Christ-shaped aperture.

J.B. Phillips, *Making Men Whole*

What were we made for? To know God. What aim should we set ourselves in life? To know God. What is the 'eternal life' that Jesus gives? Knowledge of God. 'This is life eternal, that they might know thee, the only true God, and Jesus Christ, whom thou has sent' (John 17:

3). What is the best thing in life, bringing more joy, delight and contentment, than anything else? Knowledge of God.

'Thus says the Lord, "Let not the wise man glory in his wisdom, neither let the mighty man glory in his might, let not the rich man glory in his riches; but let him that glories, glory in this, that he understands and knows me."' (Jeremiah 9: 23f). What, of all the states God ever sees human beings in, gives him most pleasure? Knowledge of himself.

J.I. Packer, Knowing God

The rich variety of differences between us is fully recognised in the Bible. In many things we are encouraged to be different from each other. Yet our differences need to be expressed in a spirit of tolerance and harmony. An appreciation of the factors which make us what we are should not only show us the possibilities and limits of our own freedom to change, but make us understanding towards others who are in the same position. Then, while we seek to live responsibly within the limits of our background, temperament, religious awareness and sexual disposition, we shall do so in the context of living responsibly before God and others.

But perhaps above all, we ought to regard our differences as a challenge and an opportunity — a challenge to become conformed to Jesus Christ rather than to the world, and an opportunity to contribute uniquely to God's purposes. For we are not automata, able to do nothing but react mechanically to our genes, our environment or even God's grace. We are personal beings created by God for himself. And just as we have a set of genes possessed by nobody else (unless we have an identical twin), so we have the possibility of serving God in a way that nobody else can. What is true of us is equally true of others. We rejoice in our variety. We affirm with enthusiasm the unique temperaments and gifts which God has given to others as well as to ourselves, all to be used in his service.

John Stott, Free to be Different

Can you become anything you want to be? Unfortunately not. Your genes, for one, will place some limits on your potential. God will have some limits also — though I find some Christians don't readily accept this. When scripture speaks of the 'body of Christ' (for example, in 1 Corinthians 12: 12-31) it is clear that some of us must be content to be a toe, while others get to be the more glamorous hands or fingers.

Whatever your potential is in the precious life God has given you, it will only be glorious and radiant if it fulfils what God wants you to be. Believe this. Trust this. Follow it with all your heart.

But your problem may be of a different sort. God may want you to be an arm or a head. If so, don't be content to remain a toe. Rise up and claim your potential.

What blocks most men and women from fully developing their gifts and achieving adequate self-esteem is not their lack of talent or their inborn genetic or other limitations. It is their failure to develop and use the talents they have to the fullest. They don't respond to the call of God.

Archibald D. Hart, *The Success Factor*

In every major city of the world, Christians are being called to moral and spiritual compromise by those people who would easily deny faith. They may dress up their proposals to sound reasonable and modern, but the new moralities are just the old immoralities in a new dress. But the church is not called to be well-adjusted to a society that is going to hell. The church is not called to conform to the standards of this world. Christians today are called to march to the beat of a different drum. We are called not be trendy, but to be transformed into the image of Christ.

Gordon Moyes, *Discovering the Young Church*

We're pilgrims on the journey of the narrow road,
And those who've gone before us line the way.
Cheering on the faithful,
encouraging the weary,
Their lives a stirring testament to God's sustaining grace.

Surrounded by so great a cloud of witnesses,

Let us run the race not only for the prize;
But as those who've gone before us,
let us leave to those behind us
The heritage of faithfulness passed on through godly lives.

After all our hopes and dreams have come and gone,
And our children sift through all we've left behind,
May the clues that they discover
and the memories they uncover
Become the light that leads them to the road we each must find.

Oh, may all who come behind us find us faithful;
May the fire of our devotion light their way.
May the footprints that we leave lead them to believe,
And the lives we live inspire them to obey.
Oh, may all who come behind us find us faithful.

Jon Mohr

Life on the road may well be difficult for some of us, especially if we have been brought up on a privatised Christianity which has avoided the hard socio-economic decisions that are inevitably part of a responsible Christian lifestyle. However, it will never be boring. With each new challenge that comes to us in the community of God's new people also comes a new opportunity to follow Jesus and with that opportunity comes the promise of grace. The Jesus who graciously calls us to a new lifestyle on the road is the same one who accompanies us as we journey into the future.

This life of discipleship is essentially a pilgrimage in the company of all others who are being led by the one who first set his face to Jerusalem. The road to Jerusalem leads to the cross and travels on to the resurrection. The crucified and risen one calls and empowers his followers as they journey towards that day when his kingdom will be revealed in all its glory as his will is accomplished on earth as in heaven, and all his people live together in justice and peace.

Athol Gill, *Life on the Road*

One of the things a calling to be an individual of integrity means is a calling to speak out, to be outspoken. We are called to overcome the psychology of helplessness, of reticence. If we see a lie, we are called to name it a lie. If we see insanity, we are called to name it as such. If you are a preacher, you are called to preach the gospel, no matter how unpalatable it may be to your congregations. . . There are others who will respond to your outspokenness with gratitude for that leadership that gives them the courage to speak out in turn.

Remember that you are marching into this battle to the beat of a different drum. It is a battle to change the rules of human communication. We cannot change the rules through playing by the old ones.

M. Scott Peck, *The Different Drum*

O Jesus, I have promised to serve you to the end;
Lord, be for ever near me,
my master and my friend;
I shall not fear the battle
if you are by my side,
nor wander from the pathway
if you will be my guide.

Lord, let me see your footmarks
and in them plant my own;
that I may follow boldly
and in your strength alone:
O guide me, call me, draw me,
uphold me to the end;
and then in heaven receive me,
my Saviour and my friend.

John Ernest Bode

A Benediction

May your ears ever be open to the voice of God, may your heart be obedient to his will, and may your feet ever be strong as you walk in his ways, even if it be to the beat of a different drum. Amen.

Theme: Barrenness and despair

Rivers into desert

When I came, why was there no-one?
   When I called, why was there no-one to answer?
Was my arm too short to ransom you?
   Do I lack the strength to rescue you?
By a mere rebuke I dry up the sea,
   I turn rivers into a desert;
their fish rot for lack of water
   and die of thirst.
I clothe the sky with darkness
   and make sackcloth its covering. . .
Who among you fears the LORD
   and obeys the word of his servant?
Let him who walks in the dark,
   who has no light,
trust in the name of the Lord
   and rely on his God.

Isaiah 50: 2,3,10, NIV

27

Trials and palm trees in the desert
(Origen)

Some wandered in desert wastes,
finding no way to a city to dwell in;
hungry and thirsty,
their soul fainted within them.
Then they cried to the Lord in their trouble,
and he delivered them from their distress.
The wilderness and the dry land shall be glad,
the desert shall rejoice and blossom;
like the crocus it shall blossom abundantly,
and rejoice with joy and singing. . .
For waters shall break forth in the wilderness,
and streams in the desert. . .
And a highway shall be there,
and it shall be called the Holy Way.
　　Seek the Lord while he may be found,
call upon him while he is near;
let the wicked forsake their way,
and the unrighteous their thoughts;
let them return to the Lord, that he may have mercy on them,
and to our God, for he will abundantly pardon.
　　They thirsted not when he led them through the deserts;
he made water flow for them from the rock;
he cleft the rock and the water gushed out.
　　[John the Baptist said] 'I am the voice of one crying
in the wilderness, "Make straight the way of the Lord".'
　　Our fathers ate the manna in the wilderness; as it is
written, 'He gave them bread from heaven to eat.' . .
Jesus said to them, 'I am the bread of life; whoever
comes to me shall not hunger, and whoever believes in
me shall never thirst.'

Filled with the Holy Spirit, Jesus left the Jordan and was led by the Spirit through the wilderness. . .

. . .the woman fled into the wilderness, where she has a place prepared by God, in which to be nourished. . .

First seek the counsel of the Lord.

You guide me with your counsel, and afterwards you will take me into glory.

Plans fail for lack of counsel. . .

And I will ask the Father, and he will give you another Counsellor to be with you forever — the Spirit of truth. . . the Holy Spirit, whom the Father will send in my name, will teach you all things and will remind you of everything I have said to you. Peace I leave with you; my peace I give you. . . do not let your hearts be troubled and do not be afraid.

Oh, the depth of the riches of the wisdom and knowledge of God! How unsearchable his judgments, and his paths beyond tracing out!. . . For from him and through him and to him are all things. To him be the glory forever! Amen.

(Psalm 107: 4-6, RSV; Isaiah 35: 1-2,6b,8a, RSV; Isaiah 55: 6-7, NRSV; Isaiah 48: 21, RSV; John 1: 23, RSV; John 6: 31, 35, RSV; Luke 4: 1, JB; Revelation 12: 6, RSV; 1 Kings 22: 5, NIV; Psalm 73: 24, NIV; Proverbs 15: 22, NIV; John 14: 16-17a, 26-27, NIV; Romans 11: 33, 36, NIV)

The desert is a place of confrontation with the physical elements, but also with oneself. It is not by accident that the 'desert experience' has been recognised as a deeply spiritual one, whether by the Desert Fathers and Mothers of reclusive or monastic spirituality from the third century, by the sixteenth century reformed Carmelites, or by 'desert fathers' of our own century like Charles de Foucauld, Thomas Merton, or Carlo Carretto.

Aspects of the 'desert vocation' belong to all Christians who hear Paul's dictum: 'Do not model yourselves on the behaviour of the world around you, but let your behaviour change, modelled by your new mind. This is the only way to discover the will of God and know what is good, what it is that God wants, what is the perfect thing to do' (Romans 12: 2, JB). The desert, literal or metaphorical, is a place of refuge, renewal and purification; an opportunity for return to the sources of one's faith; a time for the stripping away of distraction and corruption; a place for discernment between authentic and inauthentic religious experiences.

From the ancient *Apophthegmata patrum*, the Sayings of the Desert Fathers, and other writings from the third to the fifth centuries, we need to learn again to cultivate the positive, joyful fear of God, and to purify the heart; and the desire to interrelate the life of the spirit and the life of work. Origen (AD 185-254) interpreted the desert wanderings of Israel as a type of the Christian spiritual life — the outward journey in correlation with the inward journey seeking God. Antony of Egypt (251-356) withdrew to his 'inner desert' in the 280s to confront the deepest human tensions and fragilities in solitude, and established a new and powerful Christian practice of spirituality.

Evagrios the Solitary (345-399) learnt from Origen, and from the Copts of the desert of Kella, to link the speculative and practical dimensions of the Christian life. Basil (330-379), a Cappadocian Father, founded a monastery at Annesi on the Black Sea, and sought to link work and prayer, charity and obedience. The Latin Father Ambrose (330-397) learnt from Origen, the Cappadocians, Alexandria and Jerusalem, and popularised Greek sources of spirituality in the West: we need his reminder that 'we have *everything* in Christ'.

The spiritual commentaries and counsel, even the concrete ascetical practices, of the Desert Fathers and Mothers of the past have much to teach and enlighten the inward journeys of modern Christians. Carlo Carretto, Thomas Merton, Henri Nouwen and others have sought in their own spiritual disciplines and their writings to interpret the creative solitude of the desert experience as containing the very essence of the Christian vocation. May we, too, learn to come aside, be silent and pray, that our living may better reflect our loving, our life, *the* Life.

Seek aloneness. When you are with someone else you are
not alone. When you are 'with God' you are not alone.
The only way to really be with God is to be utterly alone.
Then, hopefully, God will be and you will not.

Anthony de Mello, *One Minute Wisdom*

An exile in a weary land,
My soul sighs for release,
It wanders in war's wilderness,
And cries for Peace — for Peace.

G.A. Studdart Kennedy, 'A song of the desert'

The lean man of the desert speaks:
Your hearts are stale from greed and care.
O come out in the desert air
And wash your hearts in desert creeks
For love comes when the heart is bare.
We piped to you, but you did not dance;
We sang you dirges, you did not weep.

David Campbell, 'A song and a dance'

Yet there are some like me turn gladly home
From the lush jungle of modern thought, to find
The Arabian desert of the human mind,
Hoping, if still from the deserts the prophets come,
Such savage and scarlet as no green hills dare
Springs in that waste, some spirit which escapes
The learned doubt, the chatter of cultured apes
Which is called civilisation over there.

A.D. Hope, 'Australia'

First pray for the gift of tears, so that through sorrowing
you may tame what is savage in your soul. And having
confessed your transgressions to the Lord, you will obtain
forgiveness from him. Pray with tears and all you ask will
be heard. For the Lord rejoices greatly when you pray with
tears. . . Prayer is the flower of gentleness and of freedom
from anger. Prayer is the fruit of joy and thankfulness.

Evagrios, 'On Prayer'

Drink Christ, for he is the vine. Drink Christ, for he is the rock from which water gushed. Drink Christ, for he is the fountain of life. Drink Christ, for he is the river whose current brings joy to the city of God. Drink Christ, for he is peace. Drink Christ, for streams of living water flow from his body. Drink Christ, and drink the blood by which you were redeemed. Drink Christ and drink his words.

Ambrose, *Explan. Psalm*

Thus we have everything in Christ. Let every soul go to him, whether it be sick from the sin of the body, or pierced with the nails of some desire of this age; or still imperfect — provided that it goes forward in persevering meditation, or is already perfect in many virtues: everything is within Christ's power, and Christ is everything to us.

If you wish to be healed of your wound, he is the healer; if you burn with fevers, he is the fountain; if you are laden with iniquity, he is justice; if you have need of help, he is strength; if you fear death, he is life; if you desire heaven, he is the way to it; if you flee from darkness, he is the light; if you seek food, he is nourishment. 'Taste, then, and see how good is the Lord: happy are those who hope in him.'

Ambrose, *De virginitate*

'They departed from the bitter waters and camped at Helim. Helim is a place where there are twelve springs of water and seventy-two palm trees.' See, after the bitterness and difficulties of temptations, what delightful places welcome you. You would not have arrived at the palm-trees if you had not endured the bitter trials; you would not have arrived at the sweetness of the springs if you had not overcome sadness and difficulties. Not that this is the end of the journey and the achievement of everything, but God, who rules the economy of souls, places along the very course of the journey, in the intervals of work, refreshment, thanks to which the soul, reanimated and refreshed, comes back ready to confront the rest of the work.

Origen

Our fastings, our vigils, meditation on scripture, poverty and privation of all things are not perfection, but the instruments for acquiring it.

Cassian, *Conferences*

Once, as I rode by train through a great desert, I saw a cow lying out in the blistering sun, and nestled close to her in the shade of her body was a newborn calf. That cow stayed in the intolerable heat to lend comfort to the calf until it would be strong enough to seek shelter in a barn. . . Now you too can be a 'hiding place' for others! When others come to you for help, first make sure that you are not trying to win praise or admiration. . . to mix love with any alloy renders you useless to others. . . Just get so close to God that his Presence manifests through you in peace and love.

Glenn Clark, *Windows of Heaven*

O loving God,
the beyond who is among us,
the thirst and the quenching,
the hunger and the satisfaction,
help us to live out our own prayers,
trusting you more lovingly,
listening more carefully,
and obeying more faithfully.
Then will our thirsty desert
blossom like a rose;
in our wilderness
we will eat manna;
in our seeking
we shall be surely found.
The glory of the Lord shall possess us,
the splendour of our God revealed,
and we shall truly rest.

Bruce Prewer, 'Hunger and thirst'

God, how we need your help!
Without you, life is like the Stony Desert;
with you, life is like the Channel Country

after abundant rains.
If we have become bare and unfruitful,
like a neglected paddock,
be to us as a plough in hard ground.
If we have wandered in waste places,
becoming lost and blinded in sandstorms,
lead us to some quiet, verdant gully,
where there is living water to refresh us,
soft ferns to caress our tiredness away,
and sweet rest on the mossy bank
of your grace, mercy and peace.

Bruce Prewer, 'Without you, life is desert'

For what is it to die but to stand naked in the wind and
to melt into the sun? And what is it to cease breathing
but to free the breath from its restless tides, that it may
rise and expand and seek God unencumbered?

Only when you drink from the river of silence shall you
indeed sing. And when you have reached the mountain
top, then you shall begin to climb. And when the earth
shall claim your limbs, then shall you truly dance.

Kahlil Gibran, *The Prophet*

Society. . . was regarded [by the Desert Fathers and Mothers]
as a shipwreck from which we must swim for our lives. . .
They believed that to let oneself drift along, passively
accepting the tenets and values of what they knew as
society, was purely and simply a disaster.

Thomas Merton, *The Wisdom of the Desert*

And if you cannot go into the desert, you must nonetheless
'make some desert' in your life. Every now and then
leave others and look for solitude to restore, in prolonged
silence and prayer, the stuff of your soul. This is the
meaning of 'desert' in your spiritual life. One hour a day,
one day a month, eight days a year, for longer if necessary,
you must leave everything and everybody and retire, alone
with God. . . If you. . . do not withdraw in order to enjoy
intimacy with God, the fundamental element of the

relationship with the All-Powerful is lacking: love. And without love, no revelation is possible.

Carlo Carretto, *Letters from the Desert*

Solitude [of the desert] is not a private therapeutic place. Rather, it is the place of conversion, the place where the old self dies and the new self is born, the place where the emergence of the new man and the new woman occurs. . . The wisdom of the desert is that the confrontation with our own frightening nothingness forces us to surrender ourselves totally and unconditionally to the Lord Jesus Christ. . .

Precisely because our secular milieu offers us so few spiritual disciplines, we have to develop our own. We have, indeed, to fashion our own desert where we can withdraw every day, shake off our compulsions, and dwell in the gently healing presence of our Lord. Without such a desert, we will lose our own soul while preaching the gospel to others. But with such a spiritual abode, we will become increasingly conformed to him in whose Name we minister. . .

If you would ask the Desert Fathers why solitude gives birth to compassion, they would say, 'Because it makes us die to our neighbour.' At first this answer seems quite disturbing to a modern mind. But when we give it a closer look, we can see that in order to be of service to others we have to die to them; that is, we have to give up measuring our meaning and value with the yardstick of others. To die to our neighbours means to stop judging them, to stop evaluating them, and thus to become free to be compassionate.

Henri J.M. Nouwen, *The Way of the Heart*

Grant, O Father, that I may seek you; and keep me from error: that in my search nothing but you yourself will be presented to me. If it is true that I desire nothing other than you, grant, I pray, O Father, that I might find you. And if there is still in me any superfluous desire, be pleased

to strip me of it yourself, and make me capable of seeing you.
Augustine of Hippo, *Soliloquies*

A Benediction
May the Lord keep you from the heat and demons of the desert; may he watch over your wanderings in the wilderness of your own and others' making; may he strengthen and counsel you in the trials of your inward and outward journeys; and through his Holy Spirit, may he bring you the refreshment of the palm-tree oases of his love. Rise from solitude and go in his service, and may his desert peace go with you. Amen.

28

A desolate place

Early the next morning, Abraham took some food and a skin of water and gave them to Hagar. He set them on her shoulders and then sent her off with the boy. She went on her way and wandered in the desert of Beersheba.

When the water in the skin was gone, she put the boy under one of the bushes. Then she went off and sat down nearby, about a bow-shot away, for she thought, 'I cannot watch the boy die.' And as she sat there nearby, she began to sob.

God heard the boy crying, and the angel of God called to Hagar from heaven and said to her, 'What is the matter, Hagar? Do not be afraid; God has heard the boy crying as he lies there. Lift the boy up and take him by the hand, for I will make him into a great nation.'

Then God opened her eyes and she saw a well of water. So she went and filled the skin with water and gave the boy a drink.

Elijah was afraid and ran for his life. When he came to Beersheba in Judah, he left his servant there, while he himself went a day's journey into the desert. He came to a broom tree, sat down under it and prayed that he might die. 'I have had enough, Lord,' he said. 'Take my life. . .' Then he lay down under the tree and fell asleep.

All at once an angel touched him and said, 'Get up and eat.' He looked around, and there by his head was a cake of bread baked over hot coals, and a jar of water. He ate and drank and then lay down again.

The angel of the Lord came back a second time and touched him and said, 'Get up and eat, for the journey is too much for you.' So he got up and ate and drank. Strengthened by that food, he travelled for forty days and forty nights until he reached Horeb, the mountain of God.

This is what the Lord says: 'You say about this place, "It is a desolate waste, without people or animals." Yet in the towns of Judah and the streets of Jerusalem that are deserted, inhabited by neither people nor animals, there will be heard once more the sounds of joy and gladness, the voices of the bride and bridegroom, and the voices of those who bring thank-offerings to the house of the Lord. . .'

In all their affliction he was afflicted,
and the angel of his presence saved them. . .

The people. . . found grace in the wilderness.

At that time, Jesus came from Nazareth in Galilee and was baptised by John in the Jordan. As Jesus was coming up out of the water, he saw heaven being torn open and the Spirit descending like a dove. And a voice came from heaven: 'You are my Son, whom I love; with you I am well pleased.'

At once the Spirit sent him out into the desert, and he was in the desert forty days, being tempted by Satan. He was with the wild animals, and angels attended him.

My God, my God, why have you forsaken me?

The angel said to the women, 'Do not be afraid, for I know that you are looking for Jesus, who was crucified. He is not here; he has risen, just as he said. . .'

He who was seated on the throne said, 'I am making everything new!' Then he said, 'Write this down, for these words are trustworthy and true.'

He said to me: 'It is done. I am the Alpha and the Omega, the Beginning and the End. To him who is thirsty I will give to drink without cost from the spring of the water of life.'

(Genesis 21: 14-19, NIV; I Kings 19: 3-8, NIV; Jeremiah 33: 10-11, NIV; Isaiah 63: 9, RSV; Jeremiah 31: 2, RSV; Mark 1: 9-11, NIV; Matthew 27: 46b; 28: 5-6, NIV; Revelation 21: 5-6, NIV)

The desert is a wasteland, harsh and inhospitable, largely abandoned by people, animals and vegetation. It is full of extremes — heat which by the day can kill, and cold which by night is equally deadly. Food is scarce and adequate shelter hard to find. It is a disturbing place, where a person is vulnerable.

The desert pervades the Bible. Its desolate spaces form the arena for many of the most significant encounters between God and his people. There Hagar and Ishmael found deliverance, Moses encountered the burning bush, and the Hebrew slaves escaping from Egypt were miraculously sustained. In this inhospitable country the Hebrews were protected, guided and brought into a covenant relationship with God. Elijah found refuge in the desert, and hope in his despair. Jesus faced fierce temptation and found strength, help and a renewed understanding of his relationship with his Father. It is not surprising that the desert experience has become one of the most significant images of the life of faith.

Life in the desert is stripped to its bare essentials. There are no luxuries, no props, no artificial disguises to hide harsh reality. For this reason, it is in the desert that things are often seen more clearly and truly. The normal supports and distractions of life are absent and we are forced to face things. The realisation of our essential helplessness, our lack of adequate resources for survival, our appalling fragility, confronts us starkly. Our brokenness, loneliness and sinfulness cannot easily be covered up.

The desert is a very human place to be.

It takes courage to stay in the desert and not try and escape it or to take refuge in the fantasies and mirages it tempts us with. The desert is the desert, and must be treated with the respect it demands. To be there is a hard, lonely experience and often the spirit faints and longs to be elsewhere. But if we will wait with honesty and integrity, we will find that the moment of truth which comes to us is double-edged. There is the knowledge that all hope seems lost, that there is no life there, that it has overwhelmed us and we are doomed. But precisely then, mysteriously and miraculously, grace confronts us.

To our amazement, in some way or other we will discover the hidden well of God's presence with its life-giving waters. We will even stumble across delicate but beautiful desert flowers. Then we see that life not only becomes possible; it positively beckons us with vibrancy and hope. The God of the desert has declared himself.

❧❦

The essential fact to grasp is that in the desert we live by trust and naked faith. All props, all non-essentials, all luxuries are taken away. The desert road is one of solitude and emptiness and it exhausts the soul. It is the place of sterility and of the divine presence, of demons and of the encounter with God.

Kenneth Leech, *True Prayer*

The desert was created simple, to be itself, not to be transformed into something else. . . The desert therefore is the logical place for those who seek to be nothing but themselves — that is to say, creatures solitary and poor and dependent upon no one but God, with no project standing between them and their Creator.

Thomas Merton, *Thoughts in Solitude*

And the wilderness belongs to us. It is always lurking somewhere as part of our experience, and there are times when it seems pretty near the whole of it. . . Most people's wilderness is inside them. . . an inner isolation. It's an absence of contact. It's a sense of being alone — boringly alone, or saddeningly alone, or terrifyingly alone. . .

This sense of being isolated and therefore unequipped, is a necessary part, or a necessary stage, of our experience as human beings. It therefore found a place in the life of Jesus: he too did time in the wilderness. And what happened to him there shows us what is happening to ourselves. Here, as always, we see in his life the meaning of our own.

H.A. Williams, *The True Wilderness*

To live a spiritual life we must first find courage to enter into the desert of our loneliness and to change it by gentle and persistent efforts into a garden of solitude. This requires not only courage but also a strong faith. As hard as it is to believe that the dry desolate desert can yield endless varieties of flowers, it is equally hard to imagine our loneliness is hiding unknown beauty. . .

The real spiritual guide is the one who, instead of advising us what to do or to whom to go, offers us a chance to stay alone and take the risk of entering into our own experience. He makes us see that pouring little bits of water onto our dry land does not help, but that we will find a living well if we reach deep enough under the surface of our complaints. . .

Henri J.M. Nouwen, *Reaching Out*

The law of the Cross is not that evil has been eliminated, but that it has been transformed into possibility. . . The Cross of Christ is the penetration of God into that unholy area where we would least expect him. . .

John Shea, *Stories of God*

A life within. Poetry of the Spirit of God. Fulfilment of your longing.

In every person there is a spiritual strength which does not come from [within]. It can be refused or rejected but it is always there. It is never taken away. It is a wellspring of confident trust planted by the Spirit of the living God. Everything flows from this.

Brother Roger of Taizé, *Letter from the Desert*

The flower I held in my hands withered in my hands. . .
At the turn of the lane the wall rose up before me. . .
Suddenly between the trees I saw the end of the forest which I thought had no end. . .
The testing time had come. . .

But it did not bring me unalleviated sorrow. On the contrary, a glorious, unsuspected joy invaded my soul: because, in the collapse of those immediate supports I had risked giving to my life, I knew with a unique experiential certainty that I would never again rely for support on anything save your own divine stability.

Teilhard de Chardin, *Hymn of the Universe*

It seemed to me I was wandering in a desert with no end, with empty horizons and unattainable mirages which melted into nothing. . . a place where I could not find any real water.

And then something came out of the silence. . . something stirred with the chants. . . nothing tangible, nothing I could see — no, nothing like that. . . just something which moved out of the darkness, to enter into my soul and touch it with a kind of healing.

It was a presence in my desert. . . like dew silently filling the air and melting the cracked earth. . . I heard no voice — but that was of no importance. . . I was not suddenly overjoyed — no — but that was not important either. It only mattered that God has been in my desert, unbeknown to me. . . this is all that matters because with God are the hidden wells of water.

Karen Manton, *Journal*

Thou sweet well for the one who thirsteth in the desert! It is closed to the one who speaks, but it is open to the silent. When the one who is silent comes, lo, the well is found.

Egyptian, thirteenth century B.C.

When desertions, doubts, discouragements and the silences of God seem to cover everything, will you discern the desert flower?. . .

Didn't you know? In the desert of the heart there were unfailing resources welling up, a life within, an inner light.

Brother Roger of Taizé, *And Your Deserts Shall Flower*

'The desert is beautiful,' the little prince added. And that was true. I have always loved the desert. One sits down on a desert sand dune, sees nothing, hears nothing. Yet through the silence something throbs and gleams. . .

'What makes the desert beautiful,' said the little prince, 'is that somewhere it hides a well. . .'

Antoine de Saint-Exupery, *The Little Prince*

Lord God, when I am in the desert, give me the courage to wait there for you. For it is a surprising fact that you do make the desert beautiful. Somewhere it hides the well of your life and always you open my eyes to see it just when I had thought all was lost.

Remind me that Jesus, too, had his time in the desert. He struggled there to be true to his faith and in that desolate place found the inner resources he needed to continue his pilgrimage.

I thank you that no desert is too vast or too dangerous for your presence, that no peril is beyond your power to save and deliver.

Only give me the steadfastness to remain here with integrity, knowing that in the very place of my aridity you will cause a spring of water to bubble upwards with vibrant new life. Amen.

[I am] waiting for you, O Christ. . ., when all is immersed in the silence of God, waiting for you and discovering at any age, in the hollow of the heart, a source of freshness: your confidence, and the spirit of simplicity.

To each of us, you speak the same language: 'Look, I am here, at the heart of your solitude as well as in your times of joy and serenity. You are waiting for me and searching for me, so look: here I am. Why do you doubt? I have already met you.'

Brother Roger of Taizé, *And Your Deserts Shall Flower*

A Benediction
May the Lord, the God of your ancestors. . . bless you as he has promised you!

Deuteronomy 1: 11, RSV

29

When through the deep waters

He was despised and rejected, a man of sorrows, and familiar with suffering. . . He was oppressed and afflicted, yet he did not open his mouth; he was led like a lamb to the slaughter, and as a sheep before her shearers is silent, so he did not open his mouth. . . After the suffering of his soul, he will see the light of life and be satisfied.

If they persecuted me, they will persecute you too. . . The time will come when anyone who kills you will think that by doing this they are serving God.

Although he was a son, he learned obedience from what he suffered. . . If we share Christ's sufferings, we will also share his glory. . . We rejoice in our sufferings, because we know that suffering produces perseverance; perseverance, character; and character, hope. . . You have been given the privilege of serving Christ, not only by believing in him, but also by suffering for him.

Dear friends, do not be surprised at the painful trial you are suffering, as though something strange were happening to you. But rejoice that you participate in the sufferings of Christ.

I reckon that the sufferings we now endure bear no comparison with the splendour, as yet unrevealed, which is in store for us. . . In everything, as we know, [the Spirit] co-operates for good with those who love God and are called according to his purpose.

Even if I go through the deepest darkness, I will not be afraid, Lord, for you are with me.

(Isaiah 53: 3,7,11, NIV; John 15: 20; 16: 2, GNB; Hebrews 5: 8, NIV; Romans 8: 17b, GNB; Romans 5: 3-4, NIV; Philippians 1: 29, GNB; 1 Peter 4: 12-13, NIV; Romans 8: 18, 28, NEB; Psalm 23: 4, GNB)

'I know that God will not let anything bad happen to me. I fully believe he has thrown a wall of protection around me.' It was the confident assertion of a new Christian. What she had not yet learned is that there have been those in every age who have claimed exemption from suffering and disaster, but have finally had to realise that these experiences are part of the fabric of life for every person — the righteous, the wicked, the Christian, the non-Christian, the deserving, the undeserving.

The book of Job is a very ancient drama that tells of a very good man who was struck by disaster. We are led to envisage a conference taking place between God and heavenly beings, including the adversary, Satan. 'Of course Job worships you,' says Satan. 'You protect him and everything he owns. Take away everything he has and he will curse you.'

The idea persists in many circles. 'It pays to serve Jesus,' sings one. 'Do all the right things and God will give you prosperity,' says another. 'If people would only believe in God, bad things would not happen.'

People who have such expectations do not understand a basic teaching of Jesus and the New Testament. Those who respond to Christ's call to follow him, to be his disciples, learn that, not only are they not exempt from the difficulties and calamities that come to all humankind; they have the added prospect of persecution and suffering that come from being a follower.

Malcolm O. Tolbert says: 'A disciple is not a person who memorises vast amounts of religious tradition so that orthodox answers can be given to theological questions. The disciple is a person who follows after Jesus, gladly sharing in his redemptive suffering.'

'Rabbi, who sinned, this man or his parents that he was born blind?' (John 9: 2). The question of the disciples expressed an old accepted view that all suffering came as the result of sin and that blame could be assigned. The friends of Job had the same idea. Said Eliphaz: 'Who, being innocent, has ever perished? Where were the upright ever destroyed?' (Job 4: 7).

But the lives of people such as Job and Jeremiah could not be explained in such a way. Their suffering needed a more adequate explanation.

The English historian Herbert Butterfield writes: 'The period associated with the Jewish Exile provides us with a remarkable example of the way in which the human spirit can ride disaster and wring victory out of the very extremity of defeat. . . Through a long period of other vicissitudes, the Old Testament people vindicated human freedom and the power of personality. They showed that using resources inside themselves, they might turn their catastrophe into a springboard for human achievement, even when the catastrophe was of that irresistible kind which breaks people's backs.'

Peter, writing to first century Christians, accepts that some of his readers were reacting with surprise that their Christian lives involved 'fiery ordeals'. He exhorted them to react positively, not in retaliation, but with acceptance in the name of Christ, making sure that the testimony of their lives did not give cause for reproach. His words must have challenged Christians in later centuries as churches increased in number and persecutions continued.

Tertullian, the early church apologist, said, 'The blood of the martyrs is the seed of the church.' Many men and women through the centuries were content to suffer patiently for Christ's sake. Some even courted persecution, thinking that thereby their testimony would be more real.

There is enough disaster and calamity in today's world without the need to look for it. Such trouble will not necessarily come in the form of persecution — though that is not an impossibility in some countries. In a world where the popular belief is that life is meant to be easy, and the chief aims are affluence and ease, the Christian needs to be aware that no person is exempt from sorrow. As the writer O. Henry expressed it, 'Life is made up of sobs, sniffles and sighs, with sniffles predominating.'

So: what to do when sorrow, pain or suffering strike? Some people allow themselves to become peevish and bitter, while others are sweetened and refined by adverse circumstances. The latter result will come when people let God use their experiences to become the means to a closer relationship with him. C.S. Lewis has said, 'God whispers to us in our pleasures, speaks in our conscience, but shouts in our pains. It is his megaphone to rouse a deaf world.'

Brian Hession, suffering from cancer, wrote: 'In our anguish we love that cry of Christ, "My God, my God, why hast thou forsaken me?" We are glad he said it; we are glad that he was tempted in all points just as we are. In the midst of our dark tunnel of difficulties, depression or suffering, Christ is there. "My God, my God!" If he could cry that, so can we. If he could go through the barriers, the sound effects of suffering, and come out on the other side with God, so can we. It may not be in the wisdom of these things for us always to live. We have to learn to die gracefully or to live gracefully.'

The Christian can express faith in the words of the eighteenth century hymn:

When through the deep water he calls thee to go,
The rivers of grief shall not thee overflow;
For he will be with thee in trouble to bless,
And sanctify to thee thy deepest distress.

❧❦❧

The disciples wanted [Jesus] to save their lives. He said, 'Those who lose their lives for my sake shall find them.' This is a hard saying. It was hard for the disciples; they didn't want a suffering, dying, crucified God; they wanted a God alive and victorious, with priests and kings and Roman governors kneeling at his feet. It was hard for the martyrs; they didn't want a painful death; they wanted to be happy, ordinary citizens with wives and children and a small business.

And it is hard for us. We don't want a Christianity that demands we give up our lives; we'd prefer a Christianity that would show us an easy way of keeping them. Though we often couple death and resurrection in one phrase, we are seldom quite as sure of our promised resurrection as we are of our inevitable death. And we hesitate to gamble our lives on Jesus' promise.

Joy Davidman, *Smoke on the Mountain*

We speak of martyrs in the past tense; the tyrannies of our own time have seen the folly of making martyrs. What, indeed, could be more self-defeating than the measures of the old Roman government? To pick the most distinguished, or the most stubborn of the Christians, and do them to death in amphitheatres, before ten thousand eyes, with all the circumstance and drama of a Spanish bullfight — was it surprising that the blood of the martyrs proved to be the seed of the church? No anti-Christian regime is likely to repeat the error.

Christians will be condemned for fiddling the currency, or leaguing with the national enemy; for economic sabotage or political subversion; not for loyalty to Christ. They will not be given the opportunity of attesting the faith they profess; they will be given the opportunity of confessing the crimes they have not committed; and they will do it; for they will be subjected to a technique of suspended torture and psychological persuasion capable of breaking any mind.

So there are to be no more martyrs, only involuntary apostates; and this depressing fact seems to some of us the greatest obstacle in the way of faith.

Austin Farrer, *Love Almighty and Ills Unlimited*

The problem of pain is always with us. And he (Jesus) chose pain. He never said that pain is a good thing; he cured it. But he chose it. The ancient world stumbled on that very thing. God and a Godlike person, their philosophers said, are not susceptible to pain, to suffering. . . Then if Jesus suffered, he was not God; if he was God, he did not suffer. The church denied that. . . he chose pain, and he knew what he was choosing. Then let us be in no hurry about refusing it, but let us look into it. He chose it — that is the greatest fact known to us about pain.

T.R. Glover, *The Jesus of History*

The Christian doctrine of suffering explains, I believe, a very curious fact about the world we live in. The settled happiness and security which we all desire, God withholds from us by the very nature of the world; but joy, pleasure and merriment he has broadcast. We are never safe, but we have plenty of fun and some ecstasy.

It is not hard to see why. The security we crave would teach us to rest our hearts in this world and oppose an obstacle to our return to God; a few moments of happy love, a landscape, a symphony, a merry meeting with our friends, a bath or a football match, have no such tendency. Our Father refreshes us on the journey with some pleasant inns, but will not encourage us to mistake them for home.

C.S. Lewis, *The Problem of Pain*

Pain, considered in isolation, is, no doubt, an evil. But we easily misconceive the problem of pain as it presents itself to a Christian mind. The world, starting from a crude notion of justice as consisting in a correlation of pain and guilt, as though so much pain could be regarded as wiping out so much guilt, is bewildered by the suffering of the innocent. The Christian has no interest in solving the problem as thus stated; we must begin by formulating it afresh. For the evil of sin is so great that no amount of pain could ever be regarded as a counter-weight. . .

Sin is the setting by us of our wills against God's — consciously (when guilt is also involved) or unconsciously. This is the essential evil; no pain is comparable to it. . . Pain is in fact evil only in a secondary sense; it is something which, other things being equal, it is right to avoid. . . it is harder to see the justification in the eyes of the righteous God of pain which degrades the sufferer, however guilty he may be, than of pain which ennobles the sufferer, however innocent she may be.

William Temple, *Readings in John's Gospel*

Amid my list of blessings infinite,
Stands this the foremost,
'That my heart has bled.'

Edward Young

Thou needest not to worry about me. I live my day through and it is never too long for me; and though on the surface it may be rough weather or a storm, at a depth of twenty fathoms it is quite calm. God has taken us thoroughly in hand and has cast us into his furnace, but telling us again and again, and proving to us, that he has our own good in mind. He will stop his bellows in good time, and we must let him carry on until he completes to his liking, in his wonderful wisdom, the whole of the work that has been such a care to thee.

Anonymous German pastor in prison, 1939

In the cross of Christ, God confronts the successful person with the sanctification of pain, sorrow, humility, failure, poverty, loneliness and despair. That does not mean that all this has a value in itself, but it receives its sanctification from the love of God, the love which takes all this upon itself as its just reward.

Dietrich Bonhoeffer, *Ethics*

Take away out of our hearts, O Lord God, all self-confidence and boasting, all high and vain thoughts, all desire to excuse ourselves for our sins or to compare ourselves proudly with others; and grant us rather to take as Master and King him who chose to be crowned with thorns and to die in shame for others and for us all, thy Son our Saviour, Jesus Christ.

Dean Vaughan

Oh thou whose strength sustains us without cease,
Bestow us patience all our load to bear
In lonely days, oppressed with gloom and fear;
Oh, fill our hearts for ever with thy peace.
Oh, make us free from our self-centred will
And ready thine own holy will to serve,
Then may we near thy goal, and never swerve,
Till thou dost rise before us great and still.

Anonymous German pastor in prison, 1939

We bring before you, O Lord, the troubles and perils of people and nations; the sighing of prisoners and captives; the sorrows of the bereaved; the necessities of strangers; the helplessness of the weak; the despondency of the weary; the failing powers of the aged. O Lord, teach them, in their hour of need, to draw near to you, and may they be conscious of your presence with them.

O God, our Father, We thank you for those who take up their cross and follow you; for those who tread the way of sorrow in the calm of faith; for those who battle for the right in your strength; for those who bear pain with grace and patience; for those who are enabled to teach the way of true life; for those who love unselfishly in you.

Enlarge our soul, O God, with a divine love, that we may hope all things and endure all things: and may we become a messengers of your healing mercy to the sorrows and sufferings of men and women. Through Jesus Christ our Lord. Amen.

Benediction

O Lord our God, teach us, we beseech thee, to ask thee aright for the right blessings. Steer thou the vessel of our life towards thyself, thou tranquil haven of all storm-tossed souls. Show us the course wherein we should go. Renew a willing spirit within us. Let thy spirit curb our wayward senses, and guide us into that which is our true good, to keep thy laws, and in all our works evermore to rejoice in thy glorious and gladdening presence. For thine is the glory and praise from all thy saints, for ever and ever.

Basil (329-379)

May the grace of love, courage, gaiety and the quiet mind, which is the grace of the Lord Jesus, be with us now and always.

Robert Louis Stevenson (adapted)

The desert in the heart

As a hart longs for flowing streams, so longs my soul
for thee, O God. My soul thirsts for God, for the living
God. When shall I come and behold the face of God?

O God, thou art my God, I seek thee, my soul thirsts
for thee; my flesh faints for thee, as in a dry and weary
land where no water is. So I have looked upon thee in
the sanctuary, beholding thy power and glory.

I stretch out my hands to thee; my soul thirsts for
thee like a parched land.

'All my springs are in you.'

With joy you will draw water from the wells of salvation.

I will open rivers on the bare heights, and fountains
in the midst of the valleys; I will make the wilderness
a pool of water, and the dry land springs of water.

Ho, every one who thirsts, come to the waters; and
you that have no money, come, buy and eat! Come,
buy wine and milk without money and without price.

For waters shall break forth in the wilderness, and
streams in the desert; the burning sand shall become a
pool, and the thirsty ground springs of water.

And on the banks, on both sides of the river, there
will grow all kinds of trees for food. Their leaves will
not wither nor their fruit fail, but they will bear fresh
fruit every month, because the water for them flows
from the sanctuary. Their fruit will be for food, and
their leaves for healing.

Then he showed me the river of the water of life,
bright as crystal, flowing from the throne of God and
of the Lamb through the middle of the street of the city;

also, on either side of the river, the tree of life with its
twelve kinds of fruit, yielding its fruit each month; and
the leaves of the tree were for the healing of the nations.
(Psalm 42: 1-2; Psalm 63: 1-2; Psalm 143: 6; Psalm 87: 7; Isaiah
12: 3; Isaiah 41: 18 — all RSV; Isaiah 55: 1, NRSV; Isaiah 35: 6b-7a;
Ezekiel 47: 12; Revelation 22: 1-2 — all RSV)

The full text for this chapter heading comes from the
English poet W.H. Auden:

In the desert of the heart
Let the healing fountains start,
In the prison of his days
Teach the free man how to praise.

The first and third lines express complementary inter-
pretations of the human predicament. The second and
fourth lines tell of the solution.

There is more than one desert in the heart, and the poet
of Psalm 84 speaks (probably from his own experience) of
a vale of misery which the God-blessed person finds to
be a well, with pools of water to refresh the journey.

The most famous well in Palestine is Jacob's well near
Nablus, several miles from biblical Samaria. The well is
deep: a coin dropped into it takes several seconds before
one hears the splash. The water is cold and clear, and
visitors are invited to drink a small glassful by the guar-
dian monk. The well is associated with the world's
loveliest love story, that of Jacob and Rachel (Genesis 29),
and even earlier with that of Abraham's steward sent to
find a bride for Isaac (Genesis 24).

For Christians there is the more heart-touching account
of Jesus sitting tired by the well, and his request to the
Samaritan woman to draw water for him to drink, followed by the conversation about the water of life which
Christ supplies: 'Whoever drinks of the water that I shall
give will never thirst. . . it will become a spring of water,
welling up to eternal life', a spring from which others may
drink (John 4).

C.H. Dodd, one of the greatest New Testament scholars of the twentieth century, quotes a poem from Longfellow's *Songs of King Olaf*, the meaning of which I have witnessed in my own visits to the Abrahamic country of the Negev:

> As torrents in summer,
> Half-dried in their channels,
> Suddenly rise, tho' the
> Sky is still cloudless,
> For rain has been falling
> Far off at their fountains —
> So hearts that are fainting
> Grow full to o'erflowing,
> And they that behold it
> Marvel, and know not
> That God at their fountains
> Far off has been raining.

Where there is water, trees will ultimately grow, and a passage from Isaiah gives a list of them drawing their nourishment from open rivers on the heights, previously rocky — cedar, acacia, myrtle, olive, cypress, plane and pine. This may refer to God's control of national history: Israel may be as weak as a worm, but God will make it strong and great, so that all its people will rejoice in the Lord, the Holy One of Israel (Isaiah 41: 16-20).

The poet who wrote the first psalm in the psalter makes this insight personal. The Jerusalem Bible makes verse 1 clear: 'How blessed is anyone who rejects the advice of the wicked and does not take a stand in the path that sinners tread, nor a seat in company with cynics, but who delights in the Law of Yahweh and murmurs — reads meditatively — his law day and night.' The godly person is like a tree growing near a stream, putting its roots down into the moist earth, so that the life-giving sap rises to every part of the tree — branches, twigs, leaves and fruit.

Ezekiel's vision and that of the seer in Revelation may have relevance to the task of restoring the decay of our inner cities, where towering office blocks and rejected beehives of slum flats, the lack of social amenities and inadequate family homes breed poverty, despair and greed for quick profits, as well as un-neighbourly relationships. We who care for the good life can thank God that we are becoming aware of our failure and the crying need of so many of our fellow humans.

As we go further in our social and moral audit, there are other kinds of deserts in the heart. There is a desert of loneliness, with so many old people living alone and often spending a whole day without a visit or even a word from another human. The dialled telephone would seem a God-given gift for such a desert.

There is the desert of language in our prayer life, trying to find a word to describe the Indescribable, the Inexpressible. That need not be too difficult practically, for God knows the silent feeling of the heart, and to him all hearts are open, all desires known and from that Eternal Wisdom and Love no secrets are hidden.

And there is the desert of suffering that comes to disabled people or to those troubled by the diminishments and irritations of old age. When ill or in pain, or through failing eyesight or increasing deafness, it is difficult to pray. I often wish that our Lord had lived on into old age, so that he could have shown us a pattern for accepting such limitations.

Two thoughts have helped me in my desert. The first is to make an immediate act of trust in God, shooting up an arrow of prayer to him. The second is to remember Paul's words, when his unspecified and unhealed 'thorn in the flesh' was hurting him — 'I can do (or bear) all things through Christ, who strengthens me' (Philippians 4: 13).

So in conclusion, I come back to Auden's verse from which I began, with a slight amendment to cheer the occasional stretches of depression in my own old age:

In the deserts of the heart
Let the healing fountains start;
In any prison of my days
Teach me freedom how to praise.

Many people as they grow older fear the coming of old age. They regret the failing of physical and mental powers, the withdrawal from active life, posts of leadership and the satisfaction of being used creatively. These increasing diminishments can be seen as a hollowing-out of the material and the temporal, in order to be ready to be filled with the spiritual and the eternal.

George Appleton, *Journey for a Soul*

There are credits as well as debits in the aging process — but the debits gain greater prominence. Each stage of life brings its own rewards, and old age is no exception. The happy people are those who accept their age and major on the credits rather than the debits.

Blind optimism is not warranted, however, for growing old is not all fun! The handicaps and limitations are not easy to take. Declining health, decreasing mobility, the waning of one's powers are, for many, too painfully real to be ignored.

With his accustomed realism, Paul recognised this when he wrote, 'Outwardly we are wasting away' (2 Corinthians 4: 16). His own sufferings — see 2 Corinthians 11: 23-28 — must have taken a heavy toll of his physical frame, so he is speaking from painful experience. But he did not stop there; instead, he added the secret of his staying power: 'Yet inwardly we are being renewed day by day.'

Indeed, he shared something else he had learned over the years: 'I have learned the secret of being content in any and every circumstance. . . I can do everything through him who gives me strength' (Philippians 4: 12-13). His secret? A daily appropriation of Christ's strength to meet his weakness.

J.O. Sanders, 'Age is in Attitudes — not Arteries'

Nobody grows old merely by living a number of years. People grow old by deserting their ideals. Years may wrinkle the skin, but to give up interest wrinkles the soul. In the central place of every heart, there is a recording chamber; so long as it receives messages of beauty, hope, cheer and courage, so long are you young. When the wires are all down and your heart is covered with the snows of pessimism and the ice of cynicism, then, and then only, are you grown old.

Douglas MacArthur

The wisdom of the heart is its growing old in experience, recollected in tranquillity, and digested in grace, humility and love. What other wisdom is worth seeking and having? If people are rightly aging, they are showing in that wisdom and, as their years increase, so does this wisdom.

Carroll E. Simcox, 'The Gift of Aging'

I love looking at you,
hundred-year-old tree,
loaded with shoots and boughs
as though you were a stripling.
Teach me the secret
of growing old like you,
open to life, to youth, to dreams,
as somebody aware
that youth and age
are merely steps
towards eternity.

Dom Helder Camara, *A Thousand Reasons for Living*

Old people are approaching a new frontier. Some will have a quiet faith in the God and Father of Jesus and will live each day as it comes, taking the crossing into the new dimension in their stride. Others will want to explore, experiencing the spiritual dimension within their own being, learning from those who left insights before they crossed, living now in the values of the beyond, recognising that the only currency they can take with them is love.

George Appleton, *Journey for a Soul*

Through all the changing scenes of life,
in trouble and in joy,
the praises of my God shall still
my heart and tongue employ.

Of his deliverance I will boast,
till all that are distressed,
when learning this, will comfort take
and calm their griefs to rest.

O make but trial of his love;
experience will decide
how blest are they, and only they,
who in his truth confide.

Nahum Tate and Nicholas Brady

When the signs of age begin to mark my body (and still more when they touch my mind); when the ill that is to diminish me or carry me off strikes from without or is born within me; when the painful moment comes in which I suddenly awaken to the fact that I am ill or growing old; and above all at that last moment when I feel I am losing hold of myself and am absolutely passive within the hands of the great unknown forces that have formed me; in all those dark moments, O God, grant that I may understand that it is you (provided only my faith is strong enough) who are painfully parting the fibres of my being in order to penetrate to the very marrow of my substance and bear me away within yourself.

Teilhard de Chardin

Thank you, Lord!
When trees are stripped, bent, bowed and torn
In howling gale, torrential rain;
For every wind which leaves forlorn,
Produces stronger growth through pain;
Though rain's sharp needles wound perchance,
They bring life-giving sustenance.

Thank you, Lord!
For flames which purify life's dross,
Shifting all sediment and dross,
Till clear, bright purity can hold
Sure image of the Master's cross:
Praise for the fire; the icy blast;

Thank you, Lord, that your hold is fast.

Thank you, Lord!
When powerful forces wrench a soul;
When sore heart's praise comes haltingly,
That shattered lives can be made whole
If handed to you willingly.
Then every stumbling 'Thank you, Lord!'
Will lift, expand, proclaim your word.

Betty Stevens

Grant, O Lord, that the years that are left may be the holiest, the most loving, the most mature. I thank you for the past and especially that you have kept the good wine until now. Help me to accept diminishing powers as the opportunity to prepare my soul for the full and free life to come in the state prepared by your Son, Jesus Christ, our Lord. Amen.

George Appleton, *Journey for a Soul*

A Benediction
May the ever-present God, the source of living water, open rivers and streams before you in the deserts of your heart. May he be your life in times of spiritual barrenness, your companion in times of loneliness, your strength in times of weakness, and your provider of fruitfulness in your years of old age. Amen.

31

The last enemy to be overcome

Lo! I tell you a mystery. We shall not all sleep, but we shall all be changed, in a moment, in the twinkling of an eye, at the last trumpet. For the trumpet will sound, and the dead will be raised imperishable, and we shall be changed. For this perishable nature must put on the imperishable, and this mortal nature must put on immortality. When the perishable puts on the imperishable, and the mortal puts on immortality, then shall come to pass the saying that is written:

Death is swallowed up in victory.
O death, where is thy victory?
O death, where is thy sting?

The sting of death is sin, and the power of sin is the law. But thanks be to God, who gives us the victory through our Lord Jesus Christ.

(1 Corinthians 15: 51-56, RSV)

Paul's great triumphant shout of joy, well-known enough, is better known still because of the bass solo version in Handel's *Messiah* — so well-known perhaps that we overlook the depth of meaning.

For what can it be, this victory over death given to us? Not that since Jesus died and rose again we do not die. Of course we will die, all of us. Nor that we simply disregard death, pretend it does not happen, call it by another name. True, some may be able to welcome it:

245

Come lovely and soothing death,
Undulate around the world serenely arriving, arriving,
In the day, in the night, to all, to each
Sooner or later, delicate death.
Prais'd be the fathomless universe,
For life and joy, and for objects and knowledge curious,
And for love, sweet love — but praise! praise! praise!
For the sure-enwinding arms of cool-enfolding death.

Walt Whitman, *When lilacs last in the dooryard bloom'd*

That is appropriate enough for someone who has lived a long and fruitful life, or for someone whose suffering has become unbearable. But what about the violent death of an accident victim, the despairing death of a suicide, the slow starvation of a child who never had a chance in life?

Not for nothing did Paul write of death as the enemy, the last enemy to be overcome, an enemy not just in itself but because of the way it can threaten us. It has the power to distort our relation to God, the source of life itself.

The very fact of death — its arbitrary nature, to whom it comes and when — can threaten faith in God. So the cry is heard when a loved one dies, 'Why him, why her, where's the justice in that?' Or the cry when one does not die soon enough, lingering on in agony, 'How can there be a loving and caring God?'

And the fear of death can threaten faithfulness to God. 'Life's so short,' we hear it said. 'Why make it miserable by having to be obedient to God? You only live once; live it up while you can.'

So death is an enemy, not just because it stands at the end of life, but because it has this capacity to invade life, diminishing life's possibilities in the present. Death is the last enemy to be overcome.

But, Paul is now affirming, *death has been overcome.* Not that we do not die, but that death does not have the last word. Not that death has been eliminated, but that its power to destroy us has been destroyed. Not that death is no longer real, but it is no longer to be feared.

For people fear death because they do not know what is in store on the other side of death, or know only too well that if they are judged, then they will be found wanting. Our wrongdoing in this world will cut us off from life in the next. The sting of death *is* sin; sinners are afraid to die.

But as *forgiven* sinners we need have no such fear, for the great good news of the gospel is that God does not desert us or cut us adrift. He came to us in Jesus Christ, who shares our grief, our sorrow, our suffering, our temptation and our death. He died, as Paul said, even for the ungodly. He died for us. And God who raised Jesus from the dead will raise us to new life in him.

So if we trust God with our life, we can surely trust him with our death, for the one who meets us at the end is none other than the Good Shepherd who gave his life for the sheep and would not rest until all were gathered into the fold.

[The Bible's position is] that God is the creator of death as a natural event. But an untimely death is a form of suffering which has intervened between the Creator and the universe he sustains. During the age of this world, which is the age not of God's creation but only of his preservation, it is in Adam and not simply in God that all live; and it is in Adam that all die. . .

The New Testament is candidly silent about the conditions that will obtain following our [death]. But it is unequivocal about the truth which is of major importance: the God who does not intend our untimely death will have the last word about death. . . For this purpose Jesus Christ took death upon himself, 'that through death he might destroy him who has the power of death, that is, the devil, and deliver all those who through fear of death were subject to lifelong bondage.'

Carl Michalson, *Faith for Personal Crises*

Who is there who can be ready for the future which God gives? Are we so free from anxiety that we cease to cling to the transitory and perishable? Are we free from our own past, from ourselves? There is only one power which can free us from the bondage of self, and take away from us both our fear and our self-despair. It is the power of love. . .

This love of God is not a goal toward which we strive — who could ever obtain it by striving? But it is the power which already enclasps us and enfolds us, and to which our eyes have only to be opened; and we are to turn our gaze and our meditation on him in whom it has appeared incarnate, Jesus Christ. To know oneself to be sustained by this love means to be free from the bondage of the past, from the fetters of oneself, free for the future which God will bestow and for the glory which will be revealed to us.

Rudolf Bultmann, This World and Beyond

All my hope on God is founded;
He doth still my trust renew,
Me through change and chance he guideth,
Only good and only true.
God unknown,
He alone
Calls my heart to be his own.

Joachim Neander

Father in Heaven! When the thought of thee wakes in our hearts, let it not awaken like a frightened bird that flies about in dismay, but like a child waking from its sleep with a heavenly smile.

Soren Kierkegaard, The Prayers of Kierkegaard

A famous tennis player used to spend a great deal of time on the court, not with racquet and balls but just walking around, or standing and looking at the lines. 'Why?' he was asked.

'How can you play your best game if you haven't got a feel for the boundaries?' he replied.

If we do not consider that we shall die; if we do not press on from this truth to the required openness and resolution; if we do not let it forbid us to lose time and command us to make time for ourselves, then we are not genuinely and properly what we could be. We must consider that we shall die; otherwise we cannot be wise. And without wisdom, the true and proper life for which we are destined is quite impossible.

Karl Barth, Church Dogmatics

Treat the living as though they were dying.

Anonymous

The unsuppressed knowledge about death unveils the deepest and most crucial possibilities in life. Philip of Macedon turned this realisation into a kind of one-a-day brand elixir. His slave had a standing order. Every morning he was to enter the quarters of his king and shout, 'Philip, remember that thou must die!'

Carl Michalson, Faith for Personal Crises

> Lord, in the strength of grace,
> With a glad heart and free,
> Myself, my residue of days,
> I consecrate to thee.

Charles Wesley

Give me, O Lord,
A steadfast heart, which no unworthy affection may drag downwards;
An unconquered heart, which no tribulation can wear out;
An upright heart, which no unworthy purpose may tempt aside.

Thomas Aquinas

To number our days, to remember that we must die means in the first place. . . to acknowledge and endure our predicament. . . The wise heart belongs to one who knows that in the hour of death we have nothing to rely upon except God's mercy.

But there is another thing to be remembered. What happened in the death of Jesus did not happen *against* us, but *for* us. What took place was not an act of God's wrath against us. Quite the opposite holds true. Because in

Jesus, God so loved us from all eternity — truly all of us — because he has elected himself to be our dear Father and has elected us to become his dear children whom he wants to save and to draw unto him.

Therefore he has in the one Jesus written off, rejected, nailed to a cross and killed our old self who, as impressively as it may dwell and spook about in us, is not our true self. God so acted for our own sake.

Karl Barth, *Deliverance for the Captives*

It is precisely in the face of death that God's power hidden in the world is revealed. We cannot work out for ourselves the resurrection from the dead. But we *may* in any case rely on this God who can be defined as a God of the living and not of the dead; we may absolutely trust in his superior power even in the face of inevitable death; [we] may approach our death with confidence. The Creator and Conserver of the universe and of humankind can be trusted, even at death and as we are dying, beyond the limits of all that has hitherto been experienced, to have still one more word to say: to have the last word as he had the first.

Hans Küng, *On Being a Christian*

So we do not lose heart. Though our outer nature is wasting away, our inner nature is being renewed every day. For this slight momentary affliction is preparing us for an eternal weight of glory beyond all comparison, because we look not to the things that are seen, but to the things that are unseen; for the things that are seen are transient, but the things that are unseen are eternal.

2 Corinthians 4, 16-18, RSV

Fixed on this ground will I remain,
Though my heart fail and flesh decay;
This anchor shall my soul sustain,
When earth's foundations melt away;
Mercy's full power I then shall prove,
Loved with an everlasting love.

Johann Andreas Roth

*Help me, O Lord, not to make too much of my own death, nor
too little. Save me from coasting through the rest of my life,
thinking that the best is behind me,
not believing in creative possibilities yet to come,
disappointed by hopes unfulfilled, longings unanswered.
Strengthen me in prayer and action for those who find life a
living death:*

* *accident victims and others paralysed, trapped in a body
that seems like a tomb; tortured by minds that mislead,
confuse and terrify them;*

* *sons and daughters caring for aging parents, resentful that
they have to do so much, yet guilty when they cannot do
more;*

* *men and women stuck in jobs they long to change,
or overcome with work demands they cannot meet,
obsessed by work that dominates them,
distraught at work they cannot find.*

*I am so thankful that my life has been free of that living
death. Most of my time has been given to study and work that
I find worthwhile and rewarding; I've had time for family and
friends; my body and mind have enabled me to know and to
share the joy of your creation.*

*Help me to show my gratitude in a life lived more fully to
your glory, more committed to the needs of others, more open
to the future, more accepting of what is yet to be, echoing in
my life what I affirm with my lips:*

'The best of all is, God is with us.' Amen.

A Benediction

*And now to God who was in the beginning and will be at our
end; who in Jesus Christ died and rose again to overcome the
last enemy; whose Spirit breathed life into us and will give us
life anew; to Father, Son and Holy Spirit we commit ourselves
and those we love, trusting you with our death as we trust you
in life, world without end. Amen.*

If any want to become my followers, let them deny themselves and take up their cross and follow me. For those who want to save their life will lose it. . .

He said to them, 'Follow me, and I will make you fish for people.' Immediately they left their nets and followed him.

Sell all that you have and distribute to the poor. . . and come, follow me.

No one who puts a hand to the plough and looks back is fit for the kingdom of God.

Servants are not greater than their master.

Five times I have received. . . forty lashes less one. Three times I have been beaten with rods; once I was stoned. Three times I have been shipwrecked. . .

But whatever gain I had, I counted as loss for the sake of Christ. . . For his sake I have suffered the loss of all things, and count them as refuse, in order that I may gain Christ and be found in him.

Take your share of suffering as a good soldier of Christ Jesus.

So Jesus also suffered outside the gate in order to sanctify the people through his own blood. Therefore let us go forth to him outside the camp, bearing abuse for him.

We know love by this, that he laid down his life for us — and we ought to lay down our lives for one another.

Blessed is anyone who endures temptation. Such a one has stood the test and will receive the crown of life that the Lord has promised to those who love him.

(Mark 8: 34-35; Matthew 4: 19-20; Luke 18: 22; Luke 9: 62; John 13: 16; 2 Corinthians 11: 24-25; Philippians 3: 7-9; 2 Timothy 2: 3; Hebrews 13: 12-13; 1 John 3: 16; James 1: 12 — all NRSV)

Cross-less Christianity is 'the go' in some quarters of Christendom today. We are seduced by many gods. The god of *ease* woos us in the form of shorter working hours, long weekends and holidays, electronic and mechanised technology in the workplace, numerous household appliances, and countless aids to leisure. These are but some of its attractions. The god of *comfort* likewise makes its appeal to middle class Westerners, through air conditioned homes and cars, soothing stereo music, spa baths, elegant furniture and home decor. Consider, too, the god of *convenience*, clamouring individual rights, set daily routines, priority times for self and so on.

It's not that the 'good life' doesn't have virtue and legitimacy. Rather, it has become an idol to many Christians, so that when the call for availability, personal sacrifice, commitment, reliability and service goes out, the gods of comfort, ease and convenience are under threat.

Wait a minute! Didn't Jesus say something about taking up a cross? Wasn't discipleship meant to be a daily death to self and resurrection newness of life in him? Isn't the nub of salvation deliverance from the claims of self and its tyranny? Or is a cushion, rather than a cross, the central symbol of the gospel?

Could it be that we have stressed too much the good news of what God has done, still does, and is yet to do for me, and too little about the 'bad news' of what I am required to do for him? The unwelcome tidings of confession of and repentance from sin, and the surrender of my life to Christ's new management as Lord are just the beginning of authentic discipleship.

In one of his works, Soren Kierkegaard likens many Christians to train passengers travelling through a threatening terrain of hostile people and wild life. There is a tendency to dip into the Bible to enjoy its 'scenery', comforts and novelties, in order to console or titillate our lives, but an unwillingness to step out of the security of being biblical passengers and spectators with the comfortable 'carriages' of cross-less Christianity, to become involved in the dangers and challenges of the 'countryside' around. Cynical perhaps, but uncomfortably close to the truth as well!

Growing, maturing Christians are those who will dare, by contrast, to pay any price, tackle any task, check out any challenge, and attempt any availability in the service of him who has grasped and called them for his own. To parody the words of the late John F. Kennedy, they ask not what Christ and his church can do for them; rather, they ask what they can do for him, his church and his world.

When such a counter culture becomes established in every community, people will be impressed by the difference in the lives of Christians, and then begin to ask from where that difference comes. Until that uniqueness is evident, non-Christians will feel like the philosopher who once observed: 'I cannot believe in the Christians' saviour until the Christians look more saved.'

If the cross was the way the Master went, should not his servants tread it still?

The story of Zinzendorf's conversion is worth recounting. The proud and wealthy nobleman once strode into an art gallery where, after perusing a number of paintings, he came upon a scene of the crucifixion. He stood transfixed before its pathos and challenge. The words of the caption beneath the scene shook him to the core. . . 'All this I did for you. What have you done for me?' From that moment, Zinzendorf resolved to live solely for Christ, and to use his wealth and power to found the great Moravian missionary movement of the eighteenth century.

How do I respond to that challenge? What call of Christ have I left unanswered? What must I now do or become in order to die to self and rise to newness of life in Christ?

It is high time we rejected our comfortable religion, where all the words are comfortable and where nothing to disquiet us is ever said. It is high time we stopped trying to bribe people to come to church by a variety of entertainments and social recreations. That is to say, it is high time we told them quite frankly what Christian discipleship entails, so that for whatever reason they first come, they are not left in the dark. They should realise beyond all doubt that there is no Christianity apart from a cross.

Joost De Blank, *Uncomfortable Words*

Focus upon the kingdom [of God] produces the inward reality, and without the inward reality we degenerate into legalistic trivia. Nothing else can be central. The desire to get out of the rat race cannot be central, the redistribution of the world's wealth cannot be central, the concern for ecology cannot be central. The only thing that can be central in the spiritual discipline of simplicity is to seek *first* God's kingdom and the righteousness, both personal and social, of that kingdom. Worthy as all other concerns may be, the moment *they* become the focus of our efforts, they become idolatry.

Richard J. Foster, *Celebration of Discipline*

The call of Jesus is not to say 'No' to petty vanities and indulgences, but to say 'No' to our *selves* — to say 'No' to the self-government of our lives and to hand the authority over to him.

Joost De Blank, *Uncomfortable Words*

An insidious characteristic of narcissism is that it causes the loss of a sense of the past and of the future. In the extreme, there is no history to draw from and no concern for future generations. There is only me and now. My satisfaction today is the only important thing. So it is with narcissistic conversion. The richness of the history of the people of God is lost, as is the future of the kingdom. The central faith experience becomes focussed on how God is meeting our needs here and now. Our prayers are not for peace but for parking spaces. . . When conversion is devoid of past and future, it is also emptied of any gospel meaning in the present.

Jim Wallis, *The Call to Conversion*

Those with *faint heart and feeble hands* may *go in two ways*, one after the other. But they cannot walk in two ways at the same time: they cannot, at one and the same time, follow their own will, and follow the will of God: they must choose the one or the other; denying God's will to follow their own; or denying themselves to follow the will of God.

John Wesley, *Sermons on Several Occasions*

People of faith, without being driven, willingly and gladly seek to do good to everyone, serve everyone, suffer all kinds of hardships, for the sake of the love and glory of the God who has shown them such grace.

Martin Luther, *Martin Luther: Selections from his Writings*

Eleven Christians had already been thrown to the lions. One of these, Germanicus by name, had even dragged himself toward the sated wild beast that showed reluctance to attack him. This carnage whetted the cruel appetite of the crowd, and the dread cry went up: 'Away with the atheists: let search be made for Polycarp.'

The bishop was seized and brought to the arena by an officer. . . named Herod. . . The governor mercifully sought to save the aged father in God. He urged him to have pity on his own white hairs. Let him but swear by the genius of Caesar, let him but curse Christ, and at once he would be freed. Then came the never-to-be-forgotten answer; 'Eighty and six years have I served him, and he has never done me wrong. How then can I blaspheme him now, my King who saved me?' The lion-baiting being over, the crowd took the law into its own hands and burned Polycarp alive.

J. Aulay Steele and A.J. Campbell, *The Story of the Church*

Lord, in the strength of grace with a glad heart and true, Myself, my residue of days I consecrate to you.

Charles Wesley

A BBC radio program about women terrorists showed they were loyal to the uttermost, they would never betray a colleague, they were totally ruthless, and they were willing to go to any lengths to achieve their objective. Bernadette Devlin said, 'Before, there came a time when one said, "This I can't do!" Now there comes a time when one says, "This I must do!"'

An extremist leader of a violent revolutionary group in North America said they were cutting down their numbers by two-thirds until they had an utterly dedicated group of trained disciples who could bring about a revolution.

Should we expect anything less if we are to see Christ's revolution of love changing the world scene today? But until we respond to this unconditional call to obey. . . we shall never see the light of Christ scattering the darkness of this present gloomy world.

David Watson, *Discipleship*

I am no longer my own, but thine. Put me to what thou wilt, rank me with whom thou wilt; put me to doing, put me to suffering; let me be employed for thee or laid aside for thee, exalted for thee or brought low for thee; let me be full, let me be empty; let me have all things, let me have nothing; I freely and heartily yield all things to thy pleasure and disposal. And now, O glorious and blessed God, Father, Son and Holy Spirit, thou art mine and I am thine. So be it. And the covenant which I have made on earth, let it be ratified in heaven.

Renewal of the Covenant with God, *The Book of Offices*

I am afraid of saying 'Yes', Lord. Where will you take me? I am afraid of drawing the longer straw, I am afraid of signing my name to an unread agreement, I am afraid of the 'Yes' that entails other 'yeses'. . . Son, I want more for you and for your world. Until now you have planned your actions, but I have no need for them. . . Say 'Yes', son. I need your 'Yes' as I needed Mary's 'Yes' to come to earth, for it is I who must do your work, it is I who must live in your family, it is I who must be in your neighbourhood, and not you.

Michel Quoist, *Prayers of Life*

Lord, sometimes I have been a wimp. The claims and call of the cross have been too much. . . too much cost, too much pain, too much insecurity, too much intrusion into my life. And now, with sorrow, I see that I have left you to go it alone.

Forgive my reluctance to surrender totally to you the only life I shall ever possess, so that you can fill up your sufferings in and through me. Extend again the ever-new gospel of the second chance, so that with joy and confidence my remaining years, whether few or many, may honour you with the obedience you deserve. Count me in from now on. 'Here I stand, I can do no other. So help me, God.'

Lord, let me not live to be useless. Amen.

A Benediction
May you be a threat to the powers of darkness. Forgive and love yourself and others, even as God forgives you, for life is too short and too precious to be otherwise. Fling wide the door of your life to those who need you, for in so doing Christ will also enter, and remain with you for ever. In the name of the Father, and of the Son, and of the Holy Spirit. Amen.

33

The suffering of God

The Lord was grieved that he had made humanity on the earth, and his heart was filled with pain.

We despised him and rejected him; he endured suffering and pain.

Was it not necessary for the Messiah to suffer these things and then to enter his glory?

Our High Priest is not one who cannot feel sympathy for our weaknesses. On the contrary, we have a High Priest who was tempted in every way that we are, but did not sin.

In his life on earth Jesus made his prayers and requests with loud cries and tears to God, who could save him from death.

Jesus wept.

(Genesis 6: 6, NIV; Isaiah 53: 3; Luke 24: 26; Hebrews 4: 15; 5: 7; John 11: 35 — all GNB)

Does God care? Does God feel for me when I hurt? Is God touched by my pain?

There are no glib answers to questions like these. Cold academic or doctrinal formulations won't do.

Some early Christians believed in God's 'impassibility' (from the Latin *impassibilis*, incapable of suffering). He was transcendent, beyond humiliation and suffering. Plato thought the gods were beyond pleasure and pain; Aristotle had his notion of an 'Unmoved Mover'. These all believed that if a god felt pain this would contradict his omnipotence.

The Christian God is one who, through Jesus' death on the cross, enters into the experience of our God-forsakenness.

The Easter-event doesn't only have to do with redemption from sin and the gift of eternal life. It's about my suffering, today. As Dietrich Bonhoeffer puts it somewhere: 'Christ helps us, not by virtue of his omnipotence, but by virtue of his weakness and suffering.'

No pain that we bear,
But he has felt its smart;
All forms of human grief and care
Have pierced that tender heart.

Father Damien, living among his lepers, stood up one day to address them and began, 'We lepers'. He, too, had become a leper.

But let us be careful: we must neither glorify suffering on the one hand, nor stoicism on the other. God is both immanent, he is with us in our struggles, and transcendent, beyond and 'above' us. God feels pain and conquers pain. His heart beats in tune with our griefs and sufferings. Jesus wept, more than once.

He understands and cares. We can know a God who knows us. He suffers with the sufferer.

See from his head, his hands, his feet
Sorrow and love flow mingled down.
Did e'er such love and sorrow meet
Or thorns compose so rich a crown?

We are under the Mercy. Amen.

❧

One of the most powerful sermons I know was preached on Sunday 23 January 1983, by the senior minister of Riverside Church, New York, the Reverend Dr William Sloane Coffin. The sermon began thus:

As almost all of you know, a week ago last Monday night, driving in a terrible storm, my son Alexander — who to his friends was a real day-brightener, and to his family 'fair as a star when only one is shining in the sky' — my twenty-four-year-old Alexander, who enjoyed beating his old man at every game and every race, beat his father to the grave. . .

My consolation lies in knowing. . . that when the waves closed over Alex's car, God's heart was the first of all our hearts to break. . . And I know that when Alex beat me to the grave, the finish line was not Boston Harbour in the middle of the night. If a week ago last Monday a lamp went out, it was because, for him at least, the dawn had come. So I shall seek — so let us all seek — consolation in that love which never dies, and find peace in the dazzling grace that always is.

John Williams

It is a mystery [why my daughter was born with a genetic disease]. I gradually began to reflect more and more on the Incarnation and the tenets of the creed which I knew perfectly well by heart, but perhaps had not thought very much about. Gradually the fact that we worship a God who entered into his creation and became helpless in it started to mean a lot to me: the vulnerability of God. . . who not only died in torture but — what is very important — came to bits. . .

Pain is not redeeming. Pain is evil. To think otherwise is one of the most common and nasty Christian heresies. People have got it into their heads — I can't think how — that pain is in some way good for you. In fact it twists and contorts, makes people bitter, sad, lonely, isolated, despondent. The question is whether the evil can be transformed or transmuted or made use of in any way. I believe that our Lord on the cross was attempting at least to share in an experience which in its essence is thoroughly bad, which is totally evil, and yet he shared that totally.

Margaret Spufford, 'Journey through Pain'

The writers of the Bible clearly believed that God acts in the world. Indeed, the Bible has been called the recital of the acts of God, and a God who did not act would be a somewhat redundant deity. But how does he act?. . .

Thinking Israelites [did not believe] that disasters come upon the people through the operation of an inflexible destiny. The Book of Job challenged the correlation of suffering and sin. . . The idea that God was a kind of *deus ex machina* who intervened sporadically when something needed putting right. . . [also] came to be abandoned.

The great act of God was his presence in Jesus Christ. In Christ he came not as Supreme Disposer, but as the one of whom human beings disposed. . . not as compulsive power, but as what people take for weakness, though it is more truly called creative love. [In times when we feel] the sense of helplessness in the face of forces that seem to have got beyond human control. . . we must remember God himself coming apparently helpless in Jesus Christ.

John Macquarrie, *The Humility of God*

William Temple once put it like this: "'There cannot be a God of love,' people say, 'because if there was, and he looked upon the world, his heart would break.' The church points to the cross and says, 'It did break.' 'It is God who made the world,' people say. 'It is he who should bear the load.' The church points to the cross and says, 'He did bear it.'" Although Christ has suffered once-for-all on the cross for our sins, he still today weeps with those who weep, he feels our pain and enters into our sorrows with his compassionate love.

David Watson, *Fear No Evil*

If it wasn't for Jesus Christ I would *believe* in God but I wouldn't trust him.

God is so identified with, and such a participant in, Christ's suffering that we can now see God as the suffering God. To see God as the one who suffers in, with and for his creation, not as one who is aloof and distanced from suffering, helps us to name him 'righteous', even though intellectually there remain many unanswered questions about why any suffering should exist or why it is distributed so unjustly. . . St. Paul says it is because of the suffering that God endured in not sparing his own Son that we can be confident that no kind of suffering can ever separate us from the love (suffering) of God (Romans 8: 31-39). [So] the question shifts from 'Why does God allow his creatures to suffer?' to 'Why does God allow himself and his creatures to suffer?'

Bruce Wilson, 'The God who Suffers'

Richard Rubenstein, in *After Auschwitz*, says that after one learns about Hitler's death camps, to continue to believe in a God of love who acts for the good of God's people is ridiculous. A few years ago, Rabbi Harold Kushner's book *When Bad Things Happen to Good People* was a best seller among those wondering how God can be good and still allow afflictions.

They asked Jesus about life's fairness; he forced them to examine their own relationship with God. We don't want God, we want answers. And God's answers had better not be too confusing or frightening or we'll look for answers elsewhere. We'll look for a god who demands less than repentance.

The notion that only good things happen to good people was put to rest when we hanged Jesus on the cross. This same Jesus takes our question about why bad things happen to good me, and makes it cruciform: Can you trust God, in joy and in pain, to be your God? Can you let go of your demand that God be God on your terms? Can you love God without linking your love to the cards life deals you? God's love carries no promises about good or bad, save the promise that God will not allow anything worse to happen to us than what happened to his own Son.

William H. Willimon, 'When Bad Things Happen'

I am the love
the slayers first slew in their own hearts
before they killed their human kin.
I am the love
that mantled the barrenness of the slain
in the mercy of their common grief.
I am the love that lit their lamp of faith
with assurance their suffering was not in vain.
I am the love

that weeps in the pity of your tears,
and wakes to action in your question.
I am the love
that waits for you, my sons and daughters,
to stand in faith and claim the world to be.
I am in you;
in your transforming faith, your mighty love,
the doomed of Auschwitz live again;
reborn in your new joy as you with them
die in the blackened ashes of their grievous pain.

Mag Oleson

Anyone acquainted with Frederick Buechner's life story knows how from the age of eight he was forced to stare into the nightmare of much of existence. He and his brother, early one morning, heard the self-inflicted gunshot that took his beloved father's life. Things would never be quite the same for him, though he ended up being novelist, poet and theologian. Always the 'unanswerables' will be there. How does he face them? Listen to novelist Buechner's words: 'God doesn't give us answers. . . he gives us himself.'

Pulpit Resource

Lord God Almighty, Father of your well-beloved Son Jesus through whom we learn more about you; God of angels and powers and of the whole creation and of all the righteous and unrighteous who have ever lived; I bless you that you deem me worthy this day and hour to take a part among the martyrs in the cup of suffering from which Jesus also drank.

I pray for strength to endure the horrors of this time and faith to trust in your everlasting mercy. You do not provide answers but the wounds of Jesus for my consolation, and your unseen but ever-real presence to comfort and to guide me through the darkness and the pain.

A Benediction
To you, Father, Son and Holy Spirit, be glory and dominion and power and majesty, for ever and ever. Amen.

34

His cross and ours

And he called to him the multitude with his disciples and said to them, 'If any want to become my followers, let them deny themselves and take up their cross and follow me. For those who save their life will lose it; and those who lose their life for my sake and the gospel's will save it. For what will it profit them to gain the whole world and forfeit their life? Indeed, what can they give in return for their life? Those who are ashamed of me and of my words in this adulterous and sinful generation, of them the Son of man will also be ashamed, when he comes in the glory of his Father with the holy angels.'

[He] cancelled the bond which stood against us with its legal demands; this he set aside, nailing it to the cross. He disarmed the principalities and powers and made a public example of them, triumphing over them in him.

Now I rejoice in my sufferings for your sake, and in my flesh I complete what is lacking in Christ's afflictions for the sake of his body, that is the church.

(Mark 8: 34-38, NRSV; Colossians 2: 14-15; Colossians 1: 24 — both RSV)

What does it mean to take up our cross and follow Jesus? Let us relate the classic views of the cross to our cross bearing. For Jesus, the cross was a demonstration of love. The cross is a neon light heralding the love of God for us. We take up the cross whenever we enter into costly acts of love. For Jesus, the cross was a demonstration of justice. On it Jesus cancelled the bond that stood against us with its legal demands. So, too, we bear the cross whenever we work for justice and reconciliation, standing with the marginalised and the poor.

For Jesus, the cross was a glorious act of worship. For the first time in history a perfect worshipper offered the perfect sacrifice of worship, and thereby turned the cross into an altar. We, too, bear the cross whenever we present ourselves to God in worship. For Jesus, the cross was a demonstration of victory. On the cross, Jesus disarmed the principalities and powers and made a public example of them, triumphing over them.

What is the victory that overcomes the world? Our faith, says John (1 John 5: 4). As we live out our life not according to the present rulers of this age but according to the principles of the kingdom of God, we are bearing the cross of Jesus.

The cross of Jesus was an historic event. It also effects personal salvation. We cannot, however, reduce the cross to history and our own salvation. The cross is the disciples' pattern of ministry. Love, justice, worship and victorious faith are the marks of kingdom ministry, of cross bearing.

With Peter we, too, may reject the cross (Mark 8: 32-34), but this is not the way of Jesus. If we are to identify with Jesus, we must take up our cross. This is not a counsel to be morbid or to martyrdom. Rather it is a call to choose life in love, justice, worship and victory.

❦

Much is said about the 'cross' and 'cross-bearing' that has nothing to do with the uniqueness of Jesus' cross. Both for the reflection on the faith and for the experience of the faith and pastoral care, that creates only a harmful misunderstanding.

Hendrikus Berkhof, Christian Faith

For many years I had the impression that the cross was symbolic of suffering. Thus, any kind of personal suffering which I endured was a personal cross which I needed to bear as Jesus did. In other words, I thought of tragedy, misfortune, accident or physical disease as a cross. It was something I couldn't avoid, something which in his divine providence God allowed to happen to me. As a disciple of Jesus, bearing my cross meant accepting the suffering without complaint and bitterness. This is a gross misunderstanding of the cross.

A cross is never something which God puts upon us. It is not an accident or tragedy beyond our control. A cross is something we deliberately choose. We determine if we want to accept a cross. We make a voluntary decision to embrace the cross. Jesus' use of the words 'If anyone' implies a free, deliberate choice. The cross for Jesus was not something which God forced on him. The cross was the natural, legal and political consequence of his basic ministry. Long before Gethsemane, he was aware that the cross was the inevitable outcome of his aggressive love for others which frequently violated social norms.

Donald B. Kraybill, The Upside-Down Kingdom

To endure the cross is not a tragedy; it is the suffering which is the fruit of an exclusive allegiance to Jesus Christ. When it comes, it is not an accident, but a necessity. It is not the sort of suffering which is inseparable from this mortal life, but the suffering which is an essential part of the specifically Christian life. It is not suffering *per se*, but suffering-and-rejection, and not rejection for any cause or conviction of our own, but rejection for the sake of Christ.

If our Christianity has ceased to be serious about discipleship, if we have watered down the gospel into emotional uplift which makes no costly demands and which fails to distinguish between natural and Christian existence, then we cannot help regarding the cross as an ordinary everyday calamity, as one of the trials and tribulations of life. We have then forgotten that the cross means rejection and shame as well as suffering.

The Psalmist was lamenting that he was despised and rejected, and that is an essential quality of the suffering of the cross. But this notion has ceased to be intelligible to a Christianity which can no longer see any difference between ordinary human life and a life committed to Christ.

The cross means sharing the suffering of Christ to the last and to the fullest. Only one thus totally committed in discipleship can experience the meaning of the cross. The cross is there, right from the beginning; one has only got to pick it up; there is no need to go out and look for a cross, no need to deliberately run after suffering. Jesus says that all Christians have a cross waiting for them, a cross destined and appointed by God.

Dietrich Bonhoeffer, *The Cost of Discipleship*

But it was not only
then that Jesus began to carry his cross.
A cross is not just a piece of wood.
It is everything that makes life difficult:
the 'crosses' we have to bear in life.
It is everything that causes us suffering,
particularly in our efforts to be just
and to create more fraternal social relationships.
That is carrying our cross day by day.
Jesus uncomplainingly carried the crosses of his life
as a poor person and an itinerant prophet.
He accepted not only the tormenting limitations of a
    spirit in the flesh
but also the contradictions of a God made flesh in a
    sinful world.
In a calm and courageous way
he put up with the machinations of the scribes,
the opposition of the Pharisees,
and the lack of understanding among his own disciples.
He endured the great temptation in the garden of
    Gethsemane with sweat and blood.
Now he does not simply accept the cross that is
    imposed on him by the Jews and the Romans.
He embraces it freely out of love.
He transforms the cross
from a symbol of condemnation
into a sacrament of liberation.

Leonardo Boff, *The Way of the Cross — Way of Justice*

Christ's call to discipleship is not primarily for the benefit of the disciple.

David Watson, *Discipleship*

Take up thy cross, the Saviour said,
If thou wouldst my disciple be;
Take up thy cross, with willing heart,
And humbly follow after me.

Take up thy cross; let not its weight
Fill thy weak soul with vain alarm;
His strength shall bear thy spirit up,
And brace thy heart, and nerve thine arm.

Take up thy cross, nor heed the shame,
And let thy foolish pride be still:
Thy Lord refused not e'en to die
Upon a cross, on Calvary's hill.

Take up the cross, then, in his strength,
And calmly every danger brave;
'Twill guide thee to a better home,
And lead to victory o'er the grave.

Take up thy cross, and follow Christ,
Nor think till death to lay it down;
For only one who bears the cross
May hope to wear the glorious crown.

C.W. Everest

'Do you not know that all of us who have been baptised into Christ Jesus were baptised into his death? We were buried therefore with him by baptism into death, so that as Christ was raised from the dead by the glory of the Father, we too might walk in newness of life' (Paul, Romans 6: 3-4).

At our baptism we celebrate the truth that God has reached into the heart of our being, transformed us and empowered us to live a life of grace. Through our baptism we die and are reborn, we receive the gift of God's sanctifying Spirit, we are made saints, we are called to ministry, we are incorporated into the body of Christ. So radically altered are we that we can never again think of ourselves as merely natural persons. A permanent change has been announced and re-enacted. Our vocation is to live into our baptism, to become fully the community who we already are.

John H. Westerhoff, *Building God's People in a Materialistic Society*

Eternal God, holy Father,
our origin, our destiny, depth of our being,
breath of our life, who ever delights
in the worship and service of your children,
be pleased to pour your Holy Spirit upon us.
As your Spirit came upon your prophets
and sages of old, grant us your Spirit
of truth and understanding that we may
know your ways and walk in them.
As your Spirit came upon Jesus at the Jordan,
grant us your Spirit of power and consecration
that we may enter into the ministry
and victory of your Son.
As your Spirit came upon your church in Jerusalem,
grant us your Spirit of grace and love, that our lives
may more fully reflect your glory and that the world
might believe, to the honour of your name.
Through Jesus Christ our Lord.
Amen.

Terry Falla, *Be Our Freedom Lord*

Lord Jesus,
You demonstrated to us that we shall not find life in any other way than by losing it. You left us in no doubt that only a life with the cross at its centre can be radiantly and vitally Christian. Help us, O Lord, to live a life of sacrificial love; to seek justice for all humankind; to present ourselves to you as living sacrifices, holy and acceptable to God, for this is our spiritual worship. Enable us, O Lord, so to live by faith that

your victory becomes the reality of our life and ministry. Should any suffering come as a result of following you, may we bear it in grace. Should any joy or triumph come our way, may we share it in humility — for yours is the kingdom, the power and the glory. Amen.

A Benediction

*God be with you. May the
Spirit of God in Christ go
where you go; guide where
you must make choices;
comfort where you hurt;
and surprise you by the constancy
of love for what you are
and what you do.*

Robert G. Kemper, *The New Shape of Ministry*

35

Tapdancing on the *Titanic*

I will put my laws in their minds and write them on their hearts. I will be their God and they shall be my people. And they shall not teach one another, or say to each other 'Know the Lord', for they shall all know me, from the least of them to the greatest.

In Christ we who are many form one body, and each member belongs to all the others. We have different gifts, according to the grace given us.

But God has combined the members of the body and has given greater honour to the parts that lacked it, so that there should be no division in the body, but that its parts should have equal concern for each other.

When you come together, everyone has a hymn, or a word of instruction, a revelation, a tongue or interpretation. All of these must be done for the strengthening of the church.

The greatest among you will be your servant. All who exalt themselves will be humbled, and all who humble themselves will be exalted.

It was he who gave some to be apostles, some to be prophets, some to be evangelists, and some to be pastors and teachers, to prepare God's people for works of service, so that the body of Christ may be built up. . .

(Hebrews 8: 10-11, NRSV; Romans 12: 5-6; 1 Corinthians 12: 24-25; 1 Corinthians 14: 26 — all NIV; Matthew 23: 11-12, NRSV; Ephesians 4: 11-12, NIV)

Dear God, I keep having this dream, or is it a nightmare? I'm on a large luxury liner; where we are going I'm not quite sure, though most of the time we are surrounded by fog. I wonder what is out there beyond the mist?

While we seem to spend a lot of time playing games, the highlight of the week is the concert on Sunday. We are all encouraged to practise our large party pieces as support acts to the main event or to look after the lighting, sound or to help rearrange the deckchairs. However, we all know our places and the real entertainment is provided by the professional tapdancer and his female partner. Even she seems to be there to make him look good and doesn't get much of a chance to show what she can do.

Why do I feel so restless and uninspired by this floorshow? What are the options? I could go to tapdancing school, study hard and become a professional tapdancer. I could lead a mutiny and take over the ship and do my own tapdance with a new supporting cast. Perhaps I should abandon ship like many others have already done. Or should I remain as I have done for so long, hanging over the rail feeling sick and wondering what I am doing here? But I've paid my money and I'm going to enjoy myself.

However, perhaps on my way to the next performance I could familiarise myself with where the lifeboats are. I wonder if they have a rowing machine in the recreation room: it wouldn't hurt to get into shape, just in case. . .?

Lord, is this some sort of a parable? Why do I remain here in church, year after year, watching the same tired old act? When we have burnt out one tapda. . ., sorry pastor, after three or four years we start the search for a new, more energetic one who can get us going again.

Why is it like this? What has happened to the priesthood of all believers? It seems to me that this idea is not really taken seriously by the clergy or understood by the so-called 'laity'. So the 'professional' Christians are trapped into attempting to be all things to all people and still feel the need to mediate between God and the 'part-time Christian' laity. The laity, on the other hand, often seem to feel that they have fulfilled their obligations by attendance, giving and being part of the 'supporting cast'. They appear to have no vision of their status and calling with God.

Lord, what is to be the role of us non-clergy leaders in releasing the people of God? Is it a little easier for us as perhaps we have 'less to lose'?

Somehow we must communicate to God's people a vision of his purpose and potential for them. We are not the supporting act to a head tapdancer, but the unique channels by which God wishes to reveal himself to the world.

We need to come to a better understanding of what true servant leadership of the body of Christ really means. Then we need to model it to those around about us.

We must enable the people of God to become servants of one another and the world. The structures of our churches, fellowship groups and base communities must allow us to get close to each other and the world in order to learn, to give and to receive.

We must seek to make and train disciples as Jesus did, rather than looking just for church members. Let's use more of the 'hands on', apprenticeship model and less of the lecture style.

We must help Christians to learn how to hear the voice of God and respond to his leading. Let's encourage them to see visions and dream dreams; without them we will perish.

We must provide examples of ministry as well as opportunities and training so the members of the body can be more effective in their service.

❧❦❧

If Christianity is primarily a matter of attendance at a performance, it is not different in kind from a host of other experiences.

E. Trueblood, *The Company of the Committed*

Because some pastors love the limelight and prestige, which is in such contrast to the very meaning of servant or minister, they fear the emergence of the lay ministry. Some pastors see gifted lay leaders as threats to their own eminence.

E. Trueblood, *The Company of the Committed*

'Clergy' is not so much a matter of position or being paid or having a title or receiving a certain status in a community. It is a whole mentality, a mentality of feeling responsible to provide the vision for the church, of leading the church, even running it. It is this feeling of indispensability that drives us to assume a responsibility for the church which rightfully belongs only to the Head, to Christ.

R. Stevens, *Liberating the Laity*

We are so enamoured of those qualifications which we have added to the apostolic that we deny the qualifications of anyone who possesses only the apostolic, whilst we think someone fully qualified who possesses only ours. A young student fresh from a theological college lacks many of those qualifications which the apostle deemed necessary for a leader in the house of God. . . The one who possesses all the apostolic qualifications is said to be unqualified, because he cannot go back to school and pass an examination.

D. Paton and C. Long, *The Compulsion of the Spirit*

What clericalism always does, by concentrating power and privilege in the hands of the clergy, is at least to obscure and at worst annul the essential oneness of the people of God. Extreme forms of clericalism dare to reintroduce the notion of privilege into the only human community in which it has been abolished. Where Christ has made out of two one, the clerical mind makes two again, the one higher and the other lower, the one active and the other passive, the one really important because vital to the life of the church, the other not vital and therefore less important.

I do not hesitate to say that to interpret the church in terms of a privileged clerical caste or hierarchical structure is to destroy the New Testament doctrine of the church.

John R. Stott, *One People*

In our time, it may well be that the greatest single bottleneck to the renewal and outreach of the church is the division of roles between clergy and laity that results in a hesitancy of the clergy to trust the laity with significant responsibility, and in turn to a reluctance on the part of the laity to trust themselves as authentic ministers of Christ, either in the church or outside the church.

Robert B. Munger, in L. Richards and G.Martin,
Lay Ministry Empowering the People of God

The function of professional ministers is to make themselves dispensable by equipping others for ministry. . . The saints are to be equipped *for their own ministry*. . . Equipping happens best where the church has servant leaders and not leading servants.

R. Stevens, *Liberating the Laity*

The churches which are succeeding best are those in which the involvement of the rank and file of the members is most nearly complete. This means a general acceptance on the part of the total membership of the responsibility of being official representatives of Jesus Christ in daily life. It means a fundamental denial of that kind of division of labour in which the majority have a secular responsibility and a minority have a Christian responsibility.

Since commitment is strengthened by public involvement, the more involvement the better. Therefore the Christian ideal must always be the complete elimination of the concept of the laity in favour of the exciting concept of the universal ministry. . .

The only kind of lay ministry which is worth encouraging is that which makes a radical difference in the entire Christian enterprise. To be truly effective it must erase any difference in kind between the lay and clerical Christian. The way to erase the distinction, which is almost wholly harmful, is not by the exclusion of professionals from the ministry as anticlerical movements have tended to do, but rather by the *inclusion* of all in the ministry.

E. Trueblood, *The Company of the Committed*

The voluntary cleric carries the priesthood into the marketplace and the office. It is his or her work not only to minister at the altar or to preach, but to show others how the common work of daily life can be done in the spirit of a priest.

Instead of being ruled by one clergyperson, every church would be led by a college of priests who between them would be responsible for the due conduct of the services and the proper direction of the church.

D. Paton and C. Long, *The Compulsion of the Spirit*

When we deny a clergy/laity distinction, we are affirming the *equality* of all believers! To some this seems a threatening doctrine. It appears to drag the clergy down to the level of the laity. In fact, equality in the church must be understood as lifting all believers up to realise their full potential as the *Laos* of God! The basic reality on which this commitment is based is simply that each believer is equal: no distinction can be made between 'first-class' Christians (the clergy) and 'second-class' Christians (the laity). . .

Every believer, as a member of the *Laos* of God, is a minister. Leaders in the church, as servants of the servants of God, are to guide others into the exercise of their gifts so that the whole body might grow. The 'superstar' approach to ministry is clearly rejected, for each member's function is vital to the growth of the body.

L. Richards and G. Martin, *Lay Ministry: Empowering the People of God*

Yes, I am personally the victim of deferred dreams, of blasted hopes, but in spite of that I. . . still have a dream, because you know, you can't give up in life. If you lose hope, somehow you lose that vitality that keeps life moving, you lose courage to be, that quality that helps you go on in spite of all. And so today I still have a dream.

Martin Luther King, *The Trumpet of Conscience*

Lord, you know that I don't want to go on tapdancing on the Titanic or even to be a supporting act. Give me the grace to hear your still small voice in the wilderness of my confusion. Like Elijah, let me see the many saints around me who have refused to enter into the dance and to realise that you still have something special for me to do, even though it is not as yet clear what it is.

A Benediction
May the Lord of the church grant to all its ministers — clerical and lay — the security to empower one another, and thereby keep discovering their reasons for still being on the earth, and not yet in heaven! Amen.

36

So, you want an eight day week!

But Martha was distracted by all the preparations that had to be made. She came to [Jesus] and asked, 'Lord, don't you care that my sister has left me to do the work by myself? Tell her to help me!'

'Martha, Martha,' the Lord answered, 'you are worried and upset about many things, but only one thing is needed. Mary has chosen what is better, and it will not be taken away from her.'

One thing I ask of the Lord, this is what I seek: that I may dwell in the house of the Lord all the days of my life, to gaze upon the beauty of the Lord and to seek him in his temple.

Be still, and know that I am God; I will be exalted among the nations, I will be exalted in the earth.

But as for me, my feet had almost slipped; I had nearly lost my foothold. For I envied the arrogant when I saw the prosperity of the wicked. . . Surely in vain have I kept my heart pure; in vain have I washed my hands in innocence. . . When I tried to understand all this it was oppressive to me until I entered the sanctuary of God; then I understood. . .

Very early in the morning, while it was still dark, Jesus got up, left the house and went off to a solitary place, where he prayed. Simon and his companions went to look for him, and when they found him, they exclaimed: 'Everyone is looking for you!' Jesus replied, 'Let us go somewhere else. . . '

Yet the news about him spread all the more, so that crowds of people came to hear him and to be healed of their sicknesses. But Jesus often withdrew to lonely places and prayed.

Then, because so many people were coming and going that they did not even have a chance to eat, he said to them, 'Come with me by yourselves to a quiet place and get some rest.'

I have brought you glory on earth by completing the work you gave me to do.

I have fought the good fight, I have finished the race, I have kept the faith.

(Luke 10: 40-42; Psalm 27: 4; Psalm 46: 10; Psalm 73: 2-3, 13, 16, 17; Mark 1: 35-38a; Luke 5: 15-16; Mark 6: 31; John 17: 4; 2 Timothy 4: 7 — all NIV)

Luke 10: 38-42 is an address in Bethany that I have often visited when I have sensed my perspective was becoming blurred and my priorities confused.

The scenario there holds a strange fascination for me because I feel I am seeing myself reflected in the dynamics of that simple domestic scene so long ago. Somehow my values and attitudes seem to be exposed and evaluated each time I visit that story.

There is nothing complicated about the events and words that day. It is the kind of interaction that is almost commonplace. One could hardly compare it to the power of the events on the Mount of Transfiguration or the drama of the disciples in a storm-tossed boat on Galilee! Yet in such an ordinary setting, I find my values and priorities re-examined as I seek to know, love and serve the Lord Jesus.

It may be a domestic scene, but it is not a happy one. Relations rapidly deteriorated as tensions developed between Martha and Mary and then between Martha and Jesus.

Martha so much wanted to serve her Lord and do the very best for him. She seemed possessed by a sense of urgency that appears to have entirely escaped Mary. Jesus was such a special guest. Here was such a unique opportunity to serve him. Can you sense something of that urgency in Martha's perspective as you read the words, '. . .all the preparations that *had* to be made'?

And what of Mary? Somehow she is content to sit and listen to Jesus. Is she insensitive? Is she thoughtless? Is she lazy? How can one sister be so aware of the need to serve and the other sister be seemingly so oblivious to that need?

I identify with Martha. Like so many of my fellow Christian workers, I want to serve the Lord with everything that is within me. There is so much that needs to be done. I want every talent, ability and gift I have to be used in the service of the king and the kingdom. Yes, Martha certainly gets my vote and affirmation.

And Mary? I must confess that I have ambivalent feelings. I am both critical of her and envious of her.

I can't help but feel that she is selfish. I feel something of Martha's indignation when I hear her say, '. . .my sister has left me to do the work by myself. . .' I confess to feeling like that at times towards those in the Body of Christ who seem content to let the few do most of the work while they take everything and give little if anything in return.

Yet I find myself strangely envious of Mary. For whatever reason, I suspect that she possesses a quiet strength that enables her to resist the demands and expectations of others; to graciously say 'No' and not feel guilty about that decision. As I watch her at the feet of Jesus and see the way she listens to his teaching, I sense I am in the presence of someone who is not under obligation to serve the urgent, but who is committed to that which she knows to be important.

If I am to be entirely honest, I must confess that Martha is the kind of person I am and Mary is the kind of person I want to be.

On one of my imaginary visits to Bethany, I suddenly realised that Martha was more committed to programs than to people. Her service to Jesus became more important than her relationship with her sister. Her own negative, critical attitude became so inflamed that she not only criticised her sister, but presumed to give instructions to Jesus concerning what she thought Mary ought to do and, in so doing, cast Jesus in the role of an umpire or referee!

Well, the umpire's evaluation and decision are most instructive. Three words describe Martha's emotional condition — distracted, worried and upset. That's not uncommon among many of us.

The umpire comes down on the side of Mary. He commends her for her choice. And make no mistake about it; it is a *choice*. 'Mary has chosen what is better. . .' Martha had the same choice (even though she may have denied it) and she chose differently from her sister. Martha opened her home and that's good. Mary opened her heart and that, according to Jesus, is better.

Mind you, what we face here is not one person being right and the other being wrong. The issue is one of balance between 'being' and 'doing'. Both are needful, but maintaining the balance is an ever-present tension of priorities.

As has been observed by someone, many things are legitimate, but only one thing is needed. In the everyday responsibilities, Mary seemed to have found the balance and was able to make the right choice, even though it earned her the criticism of Martha.

At a time when words like 'stress', 'burnout' and 'tension' describe many of us, perhaps some resolution could be found if we spent a bit more time in the lounge room before we go out to the kitchen.

❧

Some of the most active church leaders, well-known for their executive efficiency, people we have always admired, are shown, in the X-ray light of eternity, to be agitated, half-committed, wistful, self-placating seekers, to whom the poise and serenity of the Everlasting have never come. . . In some we regret a well-intentioned, but feverish over-busyness, not completely grounded in the depths of peace, and we wish they would not blur the beauty of their souls by fast motion.

Thomas Kelly, *A Testament of Devotion*

The last fruit of holy obedience is the simplicity of the trusting child. . . it is the beginning of spiritual maturity, which comes after the awkward age of religious busyness for the kingdom of God — yet how many are caught and arrested in development within this adolescent development of the soul's growth!

I have in mind something deeper than the simplification of our external programs, our absurdly crowded calendars of appointments through which so many pantingly and frantically gasp. . . It is the Eternal Goodness calling you to return Home, to feed upon the green pastures and walk beside the still waters and live in the peace of the Shepherd's presence. It is the life beyond fevered strain.

Thomas Kelly, *A Testament of Devotion*

Somewhere in those early days we equated the principle of being silent with listening. We wished to be listeners to the deep sources where certain kinds of heavenly truth are tapped only by those who have a heart to be attentive. . .

And what were we learning personally? How insignificant in God's eyes is the applause that comes with organisational leadership and public recognition. How relatively empty the overly busy life no matter how good the goals and objectives. How cheap the mountains of words we pile up in public talk after public talk. Not that these are bad or inconsequential things. But they are fruitless if one operates from a spiritual baseline that is not richly fed and nourished in communion with the deep where God speaks.

Gordon MacDonald, *Re-Building Your Broken World*

The servant is accepted and appreciated on the basis of what he does, the child on the basis of who she is. The servant starts the day anxious and worried, wondering if his work will really please his master. The child rests in the secure love of her family.

The servant is accepted because of his workmanship, the son or daughter because of relationship. The servant is accepted because of his productivity and performance. The child belongs because of her position as a person.

At the end of the day, the servant has peace of mind only if he is sure he has proven his worth by his work. The next morning, his anxiety begins again. The child can be secure all day and know that tomorrow won't change her status.

When a servant fails, his whole position is at stake; he might lose his job. When a child fails, she will be grieved because she has hurt her parents, and she will be corrected and disciplined. But she is not afraid of being thrown out. Her basic confidence is in belonging and being loved, and her performance does not change the stability of her position.

David Seamands, *Healing Grace*

The winds of other people's demands have driven us onto the reef of frustration. . . the urgent tasks call for instant action — endless demands pressure every hour and day. . . Is there any escape from this pattern of living?

The answer lies in the life of our Lord. On the night before he died, Jesus made an astonishing claim. In the great prayer of John 17, he said, 'I have finished the work you gave me to do' (v.4). How could Jesus use the word 'finished'? His three year ministry seemed all too short. A prostitute at Simon's banquet had found forgiveness and new life, but many others still walked the streets without forgiveness and new life. For every ten withered muscles that had flexed into health, a hundred remained impotent. Yet on that last night, with many useful tasks undone and human needs unmet, the Lord had peace; he knew he had finished God's work.

He [had] prayerfully waited for his Father's instructions and for strength to follow them. Jesus had no divinely drawn blueprint. He discerned the Father's will day by day in a life of prayer. By this means he warded off the urgent and accomplished the important.

Charles Hummel, *Tyranny of the Urgent*

The term [burnout] vividly characterises what can happen to individuals most commonly identified until recently in the 'helping' professions who begin with high, perhaps unrealistic aspirations, and who strive long and hard with few or no results. Underlying such burnout is this basic dichotomy between expectation and actuality.

D.G. Kehl, *Burnout: The Risk of Reaching Too High*

You are here and I behold your beauty.
Your glory fills this place.
Call my heart to hear you,
Cause my eyes to see you,
Your presence here is the answer
To the longing of my heart.
I lift my voice to worship and exalt you,
For you alone are worthy.
A captive now set free,
Your kingdom's come to me:
Glory in the highest
My heart cries unto you.

Patty Kennedy

Lord Jesus, I am enfolded by the warm truth that you are my shepherd. With quiet trust I submit myself to your loving authority as you lead me today to lie down in green pastures and to walk beside still waters.

My heart anticipates with joy that you are renewing, restoring and reviving my soul. As you come to me now, surprise me with the strength of your embrace. Release me from those demands and concepts and patterns of thinking and acting that blur the nature of my relationship to you and that create within me an insensitivity to your presence.

I long to see as you see. The beautiful balance of heart and soul and mind and strength that marked your life and ministry is the desire of my heart, too. In the midst of the noisy demands of the urgent, tune my heart to hear the gentle whisper that calls me to the one thing that is needed — the place where I find and embrace the priorities of your heart. Amen.

A Benediction

May the grace of God free you,
May the mercy of God enrich you,
May the peace of God possess you. Amen.

37

In defence of the honest doubter

My God, my God, why have you forsaken me?

I do have faith, but not enough. Help me to have more.

Out of the depths I cry to you, O Lord; O Lord, hear my voice.

I have prayed for you, Simon, that your faith may not fail. And when you have returned to me, strengthen your brothers.

Now Thomas (called Didymus), one of the Twelve, was not with the disciples when Jesus came. When the other disciples told him they had seen the Lord, he declared, 'Unless I see the nail marks in his hands and put my finger where the nails were, and put my hand into his side, I will not believe it.' Though the doors were locked, Jesus came and stood among them and said, 'Peace be with you!' Then he said to Thomas, 'Put your finger here; see my hands. Reach out your hand and put it into my side. Stop doubting and believe.'

Thomas answered, 'My Lord and my God!'

Then Jesus told him, 'Because you have seen me, you have believed; blessed are those who have not seen and yet have believed.'

(Matthew 27: 46; Mark 9: 24 — both GNB; Psalm 130: 1; Luke 22: 32; John 20: 24-29 — all NIV)

Dostoevsky, in his *Crime and Punishment*, tells of a poignant conversation between Raskolnikov the murderer and the girl who had befriended him, Sonia. Faced with the near-impossible task of supporting her impoverished family, the devout girl had become a prostitute. Her greatest fear was that her younger sister, Polenka, would follow her example. The guilt-ridden Raskolnikov mocks Sonia and breaks her heart. Here is the conversation:

> 'It will be the same with Polenka, no doubt,' he said suddenly.
> 'No, no! It can't be, no!' Sonia cried aloud in desperation, as though she had been stabbed. 'God would not allow anything so awful!'
> 'He lets others come to it.'
> 'No, no! God will protect her, God!' she repeated, beside herself.
> 'But perhaps there is no God at all,' Raskolnikov answered with a sort of malignance, laughed and looked at her.
> Sonia's face suddenly changed; a tremor passed over it. She looked at him with unutterable reproach, tried to say something, but could not speak and broke into bitter, bitter sobs, hiding her face in her hands.

'Perhaps there is no God at all.' For some, the possibility that there is no God never crosses their minds. For others it is a very real possibility — and try as they might to convince themselves otherwise, the thought remains — 'Perhaps there is no God.' And with Sonia they know the pain and dismay of doubt.

The author of the conversation just quoted said of his own Christian belief: 'My faith was formed in the crucible of doubt.'

Thomas is the most maligned of the apostles. We've dubbed him Doubting Thomas. But there's something very up-to-date about him. He strikes me as a suitable patron saint for contemporary Westerners. He was not prepared to believe because someone said so. He was no woolly-headed mystic. He wanted a genuine faith or none at all. Besides, why should he believe the other disciples when they told him Jesus had returned from the grave? They'd been wrong before. Like the time when Jesus came walking on the water and they thought he was a ghost.

Maybe this time they really had seen an apparition. Thomas wanted to test their claims on the basis of the evidence.

Thomas may not have displayed great faith at first. But he certainly evidenced intellectual integrity. He was not like the Queen of Hearts who was able and willing to 'believe six impossible things before breakfast'. He was not going to be content with second-hand testimony. If the others had really met the risen Christ, so must he.

Thomas is often seen asking questions. 'Where are you going and how can we know the way?' was his response when Jesus told the disciples he was going to prepare a place for them. Like a lot of people before and since, Thomas was a born questioner. These are the opposite of those who never have a doubt in their entire life. If Jonah is said to have been swallowed by a whale, or if the whale is said to have been swallowed by Jonah — if the Bible says it, that's all there is to it. They don't question anything their Sunday school teachers told them — either in the classroom or in later adult life. At the same time, such people are often the kind who never do any serious thinking about their faith.

People with strong convictions and few questions tend to come down hard on the doubters. They scold them and sometimes excommunicate them. Happily, Jesus didn't expel Thomas or any of the others when they asked questions or expressed doubt. He allowed them time to work through their questions. He continued to love them. He anticipated the day when they would come to a mature and settled faith.

The Bible distinguishes between the questioning of the honest mind and what it calls 'the evil heart of unbelief'. Unbelief has to do with rejecting truth. Honest doubt is the sort of thing Thomas displayed. He wanted to believe. He was not able to. And Jesus accepted him and loved him, doubts and all. I have a feeling he would agree with the one who observed that 'there's more faith in honest doubt, believe me, than in half the creeds'.

Jesus accepted Thomas the doubter and gently led him to the place of faith. Unlike emotional, clinging affectionate Mary who needed to hear the risen Christ say 'Don't touch me', Thomas needed to hear him say 'Reach out your hand and touch me'. His cerebral relationship with the Master needed the personal touch. Many of the church's greatest saints and mystics have been like Thomas. The beatific vision came after years of questioning.

The point is that the Lord accepted Thomas just as he was — doubts and all — and he accepts us the same way.

He wants to lead us into a firm faith. But first he wants us. He is not interested in some fake piety which purports to believe everything the church teaches just because that's the right thing to do. Nor, I suspect, is he overly impressed with the people who believe everything they're told simply because they lack the capacity to ask questions. Jesus loved Thomas. He recognised that Thomas may have had strong doubts and inadequate doctrines, but he had a sincere and teachable heart. And Jesus could work with that kind of raw material. In fact he's been doing the same thing ever since with struggling, questioning people like Augustine, Luther, Wesley and you and me.

Thomas was the last of the disciples to affirm that Jesus was risen from the dead. But after his encounter with the risen Christ, he became the first to say, 'My Lord and my God!'

Thomas had finally got it right. His faith was now doctrinally sound and experientially satisfying. By the grace of God he moved from the shaky soil of doubt to the solid ground of true faith. Certainly he was a slow learner, but some of the slowest believers become the strongest believers. There's good reason to believe that Thomas made his way to India where he preached the gospel, founded a church and died as a martyr. Doctrine and devotion combined make Doubting Thomas a man with a believing mind and burning heart.

There's a place in the church for the person with honest intellectual doubts. Jesus accepted Thomas and led him to faith by a revelation of himself. Questioning is not a sin. The sin is in pretending to possess or believe certain things in order to appear orthodox.

The gospel writers don't try to whitewash the facts by

pretending that the apostles were people of consistent and unshakable faith. Rather they are portrayed for what they are — persons who sometimes believed, sometimes doubted, sometimes were ardent in their devotion to Christ and at other times just the opposite.

In other words, they were pretty much like us. And that's what the Lord used — and is using — to build his church.

Visit then this soul of mine,
Pierce the gloom of sin and grief;
Fill me, Radiance divine,
Scatter all my unbelief;
More and more thyself display,
Shining to the perfect day.

Charles Wesley

There are times when the awakened soul, craving for a revelation which will make sense in the riddle of the universe, of the apparent futility of life and of its own inadequacy, may feel that there is no answer. Sick with longing, it can only cry *De profundis, Domine.* But the desire is everything; for the prayer of desire is not seldom the prelude of the revelation. Suddenly the 'timeless moment' is there, the morning stars sing together, a sense of utter joy, utter certainty and utter unworthiness mingle, and in awe and wonder it murmurs: 'I know.'

F.C. Happold, *Mysticism*

If we desire to enter into our supernatural inheritance, the deep tranquillity of faith, coming unto God, we must be completely absorbed by the thought that he is; and rewards, in such ways as we can endure, them — and them only — that diligently seek him for his own sake alone.

Evelyn Underhill, *The Spiritual Life*

The perfection at which the awakened soul gazes is a magnet, drawing one towards itself. It means effort, faithfulness, courage and sometimes grim encounters if one is to respond to that attraction, and move towards it along the narrow track which leads up and out from the dark valleys of the mind.

Evelyn Underhill, *The Spiritual Life*

My heart to thee I bring,
The heart I cannot read;
A faithless, wandering thing,
An evil heart indeed.
I bring it, Saviour, now to thee,
That fixed and faithful it may be.

Frances Ridley Havergal

O gracious and holy Father,
Give us wisdom to perceive thee,
Diligence to seek thee,
Patience to wait for thee,
Eyes to behold thee,
A heart to meditate upon thee,
And a life to proclaim thee;
Through the power of the Spirit of Jesus Christ our Lord.
Amen.

Benedict

For the saint, heaven in all its blessedness and glory would be void and stale without God; and when the saint lives in communion with God, he or she cares for nothing on earth, for the love of God transcends all other goods. . .

To know God does not consist of knowing a great deal about him, but of this, rather, that we have seen him in the person Christ, that we have encountered him on our life's way, and that in the experience of our soul we have come to know his virtues, his righteousness and holiness, his compassion and grace. . .

If the knowledge of visible things can enrich life, how much more will the knowledge of God make for life? For God is not a God of death and the dead, but for life and the living. . . Knowing God in Christ brings with it eternal life, imperturbable joy and heavenly blessedness. These are not merely effects, but the knowing of God is itself immediately a new, eternal and blessed life.

Herman Bavinck, *Our Reasonable Faith*

True belief is always belief that is *under the constraint of the Object* — which is therefore the subject. And if today I can say that I believe, it is not at all that the so-called 'will to believe' has induced the belief, but that which I believe has itself compelled my belief and because he in whom I believe has himself wrought his own work in me. It no longer seems that it is I who am diligently wooing the divine Lover, but rather that, do what I will, the divine Lover will not let me be.

John Baillie, *Invitation to Pilgrimage*

Give me, O Lord, a steadfast heart, which no unworthy affection may drag downwards; give me an unconquered heart, which no tribulation can wear out; give me an upright heart, which no unworthy purpose may tempt aside. Bestow on me also, O Lord my God, understanding to know thee, diligence to seek thee, wisdom to find thee, and a faithfulness that may finally embrace thee. Amen.

Thomas Aquinas

And grant me also, Good Lord, a believing heart which, responding to the revelation of your presence is able to cry, 'My Lord and my God.' Amen.

A Benediction
*May the God of all grace give to you a faith-filled heart
to believe his promises,
a loving heart to embrace his presence,
an open heart to receive his blessing,
an upward-looking heart to reflect his radiance,
and a heart that sees with the eyes of God-given faith the
glory of the living Christ and thus can say, in true faith
and overflowing with love: my Lord and my God.* Amen.

38

When we're feeling up against it

Israel, the Lord who created you says, 'Do not be afraid — I will save you. I have called you by name — you are mine. When you pass through deep waters, I will be with you: your troubles will not overwhelm you. When you pass through fire, you will not be burnt; the hard trials that come will not hurt you. For I am the Lord your God, the holy God of Israel, who saves you.'

In all these things we have complete victory through him who loved us! For I am certain that nothing can separate us from his love; neither death nor life, neither angels nor other heavenly rulers or powers, neither the present nor the future, neither the world above nor the world below — there is nothing in all creation that will ever be able to separate us from the love of God which is ours through Christ Jesus our Lord.

(Isaiah 43: 1-3; Romans 8: 37-39 — both GNB)

All of us have certain needs which we feel intensely. Sometimes we need assurance in the face of a deep loss, or affirmation because of a sense of self-condemnation or an answer to the problem of meaninglessness. Is it possible for us to find strength to cope when we're feeling up against it?

When we seem to be at the mercy of fate and death, when life appears to be fickle, when it's a battle to survive, what can we say? When we feel like that, the good news of the Bible is that 'there is nothing in all creation that will ever be able to separate us from the love of God which is ours through Christ Jesus our Lord'. We need to recognise the anxiety expressed in our insecurity and powerlessness. The apostle Paul said that the believer can face up to these attacks: 'In all these things we have complete victory through him who loved us!'

When we feel threatened by guilt and condemnation, when life seems to be too demanding, when we struggle to justify ourselves, what can we do? Some people may throw caution to the winds and dispense with any moral standards. Others may cling to rules and regulations legalistically. When we are tempted to go to either extreme, the good news of the Bible is that 'Christ Jesus. . . is at the right-hand side of God, pleading with him for us!' We can confront the threats of lawlessness and legalism in the manner of Paul the apostle: 'There is no condemnation now for those who live in union with Christ Jesus.'

When we feel ruled by purposelessness and emptiness, when life appears to be going nowhere, when we wonder what living is all about, is there any other option? When we feel like that, the good news of the Bible is that 'the Spirit. . . comes to help us, weak as we are.' We can meet the challenge of non-meaning and non-being with the answer of the apostle Paul: 'In all things God works for good with those who love him.'

Believing in God opens up exciting possibilities. It can bring us everlasting life, affirming forgiveness and meaningful purpose. Believing in Jesus Christ puts us in contact with the one by whom, through whom and for whom all things exist. Paul put it well when he wrote: 'The gospel. . . is God's power to save all who believe.' It is possible to find strength to cope when we're feeling up against it.

❧

I suggest that we distinguish three types of anxiety according to the three directions in which non-being threatens being. . . The awareness of this threefold threat is anxiety appearing in three forms, that of fate and death (briefly, the anxiety of death), that of emptiness and loss of meaning (briefly, the anxiety of meaninglessness), that of guilt and condemnation (briefly, the anxiety of condemnation).

Paul Tillich, *The Courage To Be*

Every preacher ought never to forget. . . that one preaches to people who are initially and finally solitary animals with their own fears and courage, grief and guilt, joy and sorrow, anxiety and anger and with deep age-old hunger which the bread of this world cannot satisfy and a thirst which the waters of this life cannot quench.

Gardner C. Taylor, *How Shall They Preach*

During World War II, just after word had arrived that an only son had been killed in battle, a minister was called to the home of his parents. The father, half in grief and half in rage, blurted out as soon as the minister arrived: 'I want to know, where was God when my son was being killed?' The minister thought a long time and then replied softly: 'I guess where he was while his boy was being killed.' This word had a revolutionary impact on the distraught man, for it brought God out of remoteness into that circle as a grieving companion.

John R. Claypool, *Tracks of a Fellow Struggler*

> They whipped and they stripped and they hung me high,
> and they left me there on a cross to die.
> They cut me down and I leapt up on high,
> I am the life that'll never, never die.
> Dance then wherever you may be;
> I am the Lord of the Dance, said he;
> and I'll lead you all wherever you may be,
> and I'll lead you all in the dance, said he.

Sydney Carter

The words bowled me over, for they succinctly articulated the things that mattered most to me. A million bells were set ringing inside me. Those words emphasised so beautifully what I think Christianity is all about: the unavoidable presence of the cross transformed by the certainty and joy of the resurrection.

Mary O'Hara, discovering 'Lord of the Dance', in
The Scent of the Roses

The resurrection will not set us free for the future unless the cross also sets us free from the past. The rock must be smitten before the living water of the Spirit can flow.

John V. Taylor, *The Go-Between God*

The resurrection is God's 'Yes' to the words and deeds, the suffering and death of Jesus from Nazareth.

Terry C. Falla, *Be Our Freedom, Lord*

When through the deep waters he calls you to go,
the rivers of grief shall not you o'erflow;
the Lord will be with you in trouble to bless,
and sanctify to you your deepest distress.
When through fiery trials your pathway shall lie,
his grace all-sufficient shall be your supply;
the flame shall not hurt you, his only design
your dross to consume and your gold to refine.

Richard Keen

It is the fact that Christ shared these 'thousand natural shocks' to their final expression and overcame the last enemy, death, in glorious resurrection, which provides believers again and again with the base point of their confidence, the one firm ground when all else trembles and quakes and collapses in ruin.

James D.G. Dunn

Though we pass through tribulation,
All will be well:
Ours is such a full salvation,
All, all is well.
Happy, still in God confiding;
Fruitful, if in Christ abiding;
Holy, through the Spirit's guiding;
All must be well.

Mary Peters

Lord, I will not be afraid — you will save me. You have called me by name — I am yours. When I pass through deep waters, you will be with me. When I pass through fire, I will not be burnt. For you are the holy God of Israel who saves me. And you are also the God and Father of our Lord Jesus Christ. So I am certain that nothing can separate me from your love which is mine through Christ. In dying or living, in the face of unseen or seen powers, in present or future, in places far or near, I trust you for complete victory through the dying and living Saviour. Thank you, Lord, for being with me, and others like me. I pray in the name of Jesus. Amen.

A Benediction
Depart now in the fellowship of God the Father and, as you go, remember: in the goodness of God you were born into this world; by the grace of God you have been kept all the day long, even unto this hour; and by the love of God, fully revealed in the face of Jesus, you are being redeemed. Amen.

John R. Claypool

39

From conflict to conquest

Listen to my cry, for I am in desperate need.

How long must I wrestle with my thoughts and every day have sorrow in my heart?

My soul is in anguish. How long, O Lord, how long?

Has God forgotten to be merciful? Has he in anger withheld his compassion?

Why, O Lord, do you stand far off?

I said, 'Oh, that I had the wings of a dove! I would fly away and be at rest.'

'Because he loves me,' says the Lord, 'I will rescue him; I will protect him, for he acknowledges my name. He will call upon me, and I will answer him; I will be with him in trouble, I will deliver him and honour him.'

'Do not be afraid. I am the First and the Last. I am the Living One; I was dead, and behold I am alive for ever and ever! And I hold the keys of death and Hades.'

'Be still, and know that I am God.'

'For a brief moment I abandoned you, but with deep compassion I will bring you back.'

The Lord is close to the brokenhearted and saves those who are crushed in spirit.

A bruised reed he will not break, and a smouldering wick he will not snuff out.

The Lord upholds all those who fall and lifts up all those who are bowed down.

'I will not abandon you or leave you as orphans in the storm; I will come to you.'

'Don't be anxious about tomorrow. God will take care of your tomorrow, too. Live one day at a time.'

'Come to me, all you who are weary and burdened,

and I will give you rest.'

Be at rest once more, O my soul, for the Lord has been good to you.

Weeping may remain for a night, but rejoicing comes in the morning.

Wait for the Lord; be strong and take heart and wait for the Lord.

Yet this I call to mind and therefore I have hope: because of the Lord's great love we are not consumed, for his compassions never fail. They are new every morning; great is your faithfulness. . . The Lord is good to those whose hope is in him, to the one who seeks him.

I will take refuge in the shadow of your wings until the disaster has passed.

Though the fig-tree does not bud and there are no grapes on the vines. . . though there are no sheep in the pen and no cattle in the stalls, yet I will rejoice in the Lord, I will be joyful in God my Saviour.

Though he slay me, yet will I hope in him.

I will always have hope; I will praise you more and more.

(Psalms 142: 6; 13: 2; 6: 3; 77: 9; 10: 1; 55: 6; 91: 14-15; Revelation 1: 17-18; Psalm 46: 10; Isaiah 54: 7; Psalm 34: 18; Isaiah 42: 3; Psalm 145: 14 — all NIV; John 14: 18, Matthew 6: 34 — both LB; Matthew 11: 28; Psalms 116: 7; 30: 5; 27: 14; Lamentations 3: 21-23, 25; Psalm 57: 1; Habakkuk 3: 17-18; Job 13: 15; Psalm 71: 14 — all NIV)

Spiritual barrenness is often charged with emotional desperation, especially whenever God seems so far removed or strangely silent, in spite of our most earnest entreaties. Like birds suddenly trapped, we frantically beat against bars which are sometimes of our own making. Serenity is shattered by our clamorous shouts or lonely sobs of 'Why, Lord? Why me?'

This experience is not new. Nor should we feel guilty in expressing our doubts and frustrations. The Psalmist did the same. Yet unlike us, regardless of the beginnings, the Psalms usually end in hope and praise to God. At the end of the day he seemed to live over rather than under the circumstances.

How come?

Experience had taught the Psalmist not to persist with the unanswerable 'Why?', but rather to reaffirm 'Who' is sovereign. We may not choose our circumstances or environment, but we are always responsible for our reactions to them. Hope or despair is always a choice. Hope centres on God's faithfulness, despair on our weakness.

In spite of external disaster, Job could affirm, 'I know that my Redeemer lives, and that in the end he will stand upon the earth' (Job 19: 25-26).

The darker the night, the brighter the stars seem to shine. 'Tears are often the telescope by which we see far into heaven,' said Henry Ward Beecher.

❧❦

If we insist on pursuing the question 'Why?', we shall only increase our sense of frustration and perhaps bitterness. We only add to our injury and block the way for God's love to reach us.

David Watson, *Fear No Evil*

I lay my 'whys'
before your Cross
in worship kneeling,
my mind too numb
for thought,
my heart beyond
all feeling:
And worshipping
realise that I
in knowing you
don't need a 'why.'

Ruth Bell Graham, *It's My Turn*

There are only two joys. One is having God answer all our prayers; the other is not receiving the answer to all our prayers. I believe this because I have found that God knows my needs infinitely better than I know them. And he is utterly dependable, no matter which direction our circumstances take us.

Joni Eareckson, *Joni*

It is not what we *do*, but who we *are* that matters most in life; and it is not *what* we endure, but the *way* we endure it that counts.

David Watson, *Fear No Evil*

Son, I am here.
I haven't left you.
How weak is your faith!
You are too proud.
You still rely on yourself. . .
You must surrender yourself to me.
You must realise that you are neither big enough
    nor strong enough,
You must let yourself be guided like a child,
My little child.
Come, give me your hand, and do not fear.
If there is mud, I will carry you in my arms.
But you must be very, very little,
For the Father carries only little children.

Michel Quoist, *Prayers of Life*

It is this quiet, restful, childlike trust in the Father of Love that will enable us to experience his peace, even in the very worst of storms.

David Watson, *Fear No Evil*

No matter how deep our darkness,
He is deeper still.

Corrie ten Boom

[The critical nervous breakdown suffered in my youth] was the most terrifying wilderness I ever travelled through. I dreadfully wanted to commit suicide, but instead I made some of the most vital discoveries of my life. . . I found God in a desert.

Why is it that some of life's most revealing insights come to us not from life's loveliness but from life's difficulties? As a small boy said, 'Why are all the vitamins in spinach and not in ice cream, where they ought to be?' I don't know. You will have to ask God that, but vitamins are in spinach and God is in every wilderness.

Harry Emerson Fosdick

One of the Hebrew words for pain, *parpar*, expresses the idea of 'moving convulsively, struggling, twitching, jerking' such as is found in Job's description of his pain: 'All was well with me, but he *shattered* me' (Job 16: 12). In modern Hebrew, however, the same word is transformed into a noun to denote a butterfly.

The reason: the beautiful butterfly with its multicoloured appearance was first an ugly grub. Then came the time for its transformation and, by extreme convulsions, pain and struggle, the ugly grub became a golden butterfly. Hence the same word in Hebrew for convulsions and butterfly.

Susan Perlman, *If You Want Life, Expect Pain*

It is doubtful if God can bless anyone greatly without hurting them deeply.

A.W. Tozer

The reason God permitted me to lose both sight and hearing seems clear now — that through me he might cleave a rock unbroken before and let quickening streams flow through other lives desolate as my own once was. I am content.

Helen Keller, *The Faith of Helen Keller*

Eternal God, the light of the minds that know you, the joy of the hearts that love you, and the strength of the wills that serve you; grant that I may know you, that I may truly love you and, so to love you that I may fully serve you, whom to serve is perfect freedom, in Jesus Christ our Lord. Amen.

Augustine of Hippo

Give me the love that leads the way,
The faith that nothing can dismay,
The hope no disappointments tire,
The passion that will burn like fire,
Let me not sink to be a clod;
Make me thy fuel, Flame of God.

Amy Carmichael

Heavenly Father,
giver of life and health:
comfort and restore those who are sick,
that they may be strengthened in their weakness
and have confidence in your unfailing love;
through Jesus Christ our Lord.

The Alternative Service Book for the Church of England

Lord God, the God of security and the enemy of security too; I
come to you, confused, needing the reassurance of your gracious
acceptance; broken, needing your healing — or else the promise
of your presence; thirsting for reality, to the fountain of life;
desolate, yearning for a loving touch as from a parent.

A Benediction
Do not be afraid or terrified. . . for the Lord your God goes
with you; he will never leave you nor forsake you.

Deuteronomy 31: 6, NIV

Theme: Transformation and life

Rivers from the desert

Let the desert and the wasteland rejoice,
Let the wilderness blossom with flowers of spring!
Let them exult and sing for joy. . .
Then shall the eyes of the blind be opened
And the ears of the deaf be unstopped;
Then shall the lame leap like a stag
And the dumb sing for joy!
For waters shall break out in the wilderness
And streams shall flow in the desert;
The burning sand shall become a lake
And the thirsty land bubble with water.
The lairs of jackals shall become rich meadows,
Fields of grass with reeds and rushes.
And there shall be in it a highway
Which shall be called the Holy Way.

Isaiah 35: 1-21, 5-8a, J.B. Phillips

Metamorphosis: Caterpillars into butterflies

There he went into a cave to spend the night. Suddenly the Lord spoke to him. . . Then the Lord passed by and sent a furious wind that split the hills and shattered the rocks — but the Lord was not in the wind. The wind stopped blowing, and then there was an earthquake — but the Lord was not in the earthquake. . . After the earthquake, there was a fire — but the Lord was not in the fire. And after the fire there was the soft whisper of a voice. When Elijah heard it, he covered his face with his cloak. . .

When the day of Pentecost came, all the believers were gathered together in one place. Suddenly there was a noise from the sky which sounded like a strong wind blowing, and it filled the whole house where they were sitting. . . they were all filled with the Holy Spirit and began to talk in other languages. . .

The kingdom of God is like this. A man scatters seed in his paddock. He sleeps at night, is up and about during the day, and all the while the seeds are sprouting and growing. Yet he does not know how it happens. The soil itself makes the plants grow and bear fruit; first the tender stalk appears, then the head and finally the head full of grain. When the grain is ripe, the man starts cutting it with his sickle, because the harvest time has come.

Jesus asked, 'What is the kingdom of God like? What shall I compare it with? It is like this. A man takes a mustard seed and plants it in the ground. The plant grows and becomes a tree.'

Those who are joined to Christ have become new beings; the old is gone, the new has come. All this is done by God, who through Christ changed us from enemies into his friends and gave us the task of making others his friends also.

And so we shall all come together to that oneness in our faith and in our knowledge of the Son of God; we shall become mature people, reaching to the very height of Christ's full stature. Then we shall no longer be children. . .

They took him the water, which now had turned into wine, and he tasted it.

(1 Kings 19: 9, 11-13; Acts 2: 1-4; Mark 4: 26-29; Luke 13: 18-19 — all GNB; 2 Corinthians 5: 17-18, NRSV; Ephesians 4: 13-14; John 2: 8-9 — both GNB)

'In retrospect, my life has been marked by a series of transformations.' So wrote Dr David Suzuki in his book *Metamorphosis — Stages in a Life*. Every Christian can echo those words, for in essence that is what it means to be a Christian.

Whether our point of entry into the faith is through nurture or a sudden conversion experience, Jesus indicates in the Gospels that the life of the disciple is one of transformation and ongoing growth and development.

The parables of the mustard seed and the growing seed have the concept of growing as their central theme. It is growth which involves a metamorphosis: stages through which a living organism passes, from simply possessing the potential of life as a seed, to reaching the fullness of life.

Dr Suzuki is a geneticist and, after three decades of studying the fruit fly, he saw a correlation between the stages of growth in the fruit fly and the growing human being.

In both child and immature fly, each is impressively larger than the preceding one, but still incomplete!

The story of Jesus at the wedding in Cana is a story about transformation, changing water into wine, transforming an everyday essential element into something that enabled celebration to occur.

This story is symbolic of the thrust of the fourth gospel — that in the midst of the ordinary events of life, metamorphosis is occurring. We are reminded that in the ordinary and extraordinary events of life, we can often be brought to the place of metamorphosis — where we move from one stage of our Christian experience to another.

James Loder of Princeton tells us, in his book *The Transforming Moment*, of a road accident in which he was seriously injured, and how this experience led him to the ministry of the church, something he had been considering for some time, but had not been prepared to resolve.

Judith Guest in *Ordinary People* writes about Conrad Jarret, a young man who watches his brother drown after their boat capsizes on a lake during a bad storm. From this traumatic experience his life underwent a metamorphosis — his values and faith came under scrutiny as he tried to re-enter everyday life again.

Many of the people who survived the terrifying British Airways flight in 1982 when the four engines of the aircraft cut out as the plane flew through an invisible cloud of volcanic dust over Indonesia, testify to the changes and transformations that occurred in their lives as a result. Values were reassessed, relationships became more important and the ordinary things of life became precious.

Perhaps we can all point to a significant event which became a turning point; a moment of metamorphosis, a change that has had a lasting effect on our lives.

There is another way in which we can think about metamorphosis: not only as a sudden change, but as a gradual development from one stage to another.

Carl Jung in a number of his books talks about the concept of the 'stages of life'. The first half of our lives he compares to the morning, and the second half to the afternoon of life. During the first stage, the morning, our energies are concerned with establishing ourselves; whereas in the second half of life we are more concerned to find meaning and purpose in living. The stages of life can be moments of metamorphosis.

In Jesus' parable of the growing seed, metamorphosis occurs a number of times from tiny seed to mature plant. The mature plant does not develop without struggle and conflict with its environment.

Can it be any different for those who are called to new life in Christ? Growing into the likeness of our Lord will involve us in many metamorphoses. The new life every Christian receives through the Holy Spirit leads us stage by stage towards 'our faith and knowledge of the Son of God', so that we may 'become mature people reaching the very height of Christ's full stature'.

> *And so from hour to hour we ripe and ripe.*
> *And then from hour to hour we rot and rot.*
> *And thereby hangs a tale.*

Shakespeare, like Jung, is indicating the stages of life: a story of ripening, then decline.

Perhaps the lesson for Christians here is that unless 'we ripe and ripe', we shall surely 'rot and rot'. Unless metamorphosis is occurring in our lives we will remain stagnant, and we will not achieve our potential to become what we can under God's grace.

❧❀❧

My life has been marked by a series of transformations. It's interesting to note that in the rest of the biological world, profound change in the lives of many organisms is a natural and necessary part of their development. Often these changes involve dramatic transitions in physical makeup, behaviour and habitat. This process is called metamorphosis.

David Suzuki, Metamorphosis

Many people remain maggots, growing larger, richer and more powerful without an accompanying evolution in wisdom, sensitivity or compassion.

David Suzuki, Metamorphosis

A typical case of transformation is the change in form that occurs when a caterpillar turns into a butterfly.

James E. Loder, *The Transforming Moment*

A great moment in my life was when I found myself or, rather, was found by God, to be a sinner. For years, my supreme effort was to make myself pure and holy before him. Another great moment was when I found my righteousness, not in me, but in him who was crucified for my sins. For years, I tried to realise in myself and others the gospel of Jesus Christ and him crucified.

A third, and perhaps the last great moment in my life, was when I was shown that my salvation is not yet, and that when Christ shall appear again, then, and not till then, shall I be like him. Conviction of sins, salvation by faith, and hope of his coming — these were three steps by which my soul was lifted to the joy and freedom of the heavenly vision.

Kanzo Uchimura, *The Complete Works*

For forty years I had not thought much about God, religion or the meaning of life. I just got on with it as best I could, puzzled, challenged, excited, defeated, battling on. As an almost accidental visitor to a Mass in the Catholic church, I stumbled on a new reality: as Jesus Christ was, so am I; grapes crushed to become wine; wheat ground to become bread. In changing my form as I do constantly, and as I will in death, I am not annihilated. I am transmuted. I live anew.

Caroline Jones, *What Australians Believe About God*

Solitude is the furnace in which this transformation takes place. . . it is from this transformed or converted self that real ministry flows.

Henri J.M. Nouwen, *The Way of the Heart*

Long my imprisoned spirit lay
fast bound in sin and nature's night:
thine eye diffused a quickening ray —
I woke; the dungeon flamed with light!

My chains fell off, my heart was free,
I rose, went forth, and followed thee.

John Wesley

If we could see beneath the surface of many a life, we would see thousands of people within the church are suffering spiritually from 'arrested development': they never reach spiritual maturity; they never do all the good they were intended to do: and this is due to the fact that at some point in their lives they refused to go further. . . they refused to take the one step which would have opened up for them a new and vital development. They are 'stunted souls'.

Olive Wyon, *The School of Prayer*

It is perhaps difficult for the Western mind to appreciate that we humans develop by growth rather than self-improvement, and that neither the body nor the mind grows by stretching itself. . . It is not a question of improvement, for a tree is not an improved seed. . . Seeds lead to plants, and plants lead to seeds. There is no question of higher or lower, better or worse, for the process is fulfilled in each moment of its activity.

Alan Watts, *The Way of Liberation*

I don't know who — or what — put the question. I don't know when it was put. I don't even remember answering. But at some moment I did answer Yes to someone — or Something — and from that hour I was certain that existence is meaningful and that, therefore, my life, in self-surrender, had a goal.

Dag Hammarskjöld, *Markings*

Follow thou me: I am the Way, the Truth, and the Life. Without the Way, there is no going; without the Truth, there is no knowing; without the Life, there is no living. I am the Way, which thou oughtest to follow; the Truth, which thou oughtest to believe; the Life, which thou oughtest to hope for.

Thomas à Kempis, *The Imitation of Christ*

He did something. . . . It was instead a warm life, like electricity, that started at the bottom of my feet and rushed through my entire body, filling me with such strength and vitality that it almost threw me out of bed. I leaped up singing. . . 'Blessed assurance, Jesus is mine!' In my excitement I picked up Emil Brunner's little book, *The Scandal of Christianity*, and I think I must have read it in ten minutes. It was as if I had suddenly entered into the central intuition out of which the book had been written. So I recognised, more than I read, everything that was being said.

James E. Loder, *The Transforming Moment*

I wanted to read no further, nor did I need to. For instantly, as the sentence ended, there was infused in my heart something like the light of full certainty and all the gloom of doubt vanished away.

Augustine of Hippo, after reading from Romans 13

To be converted, to be regenerated, to receive grace, to experience religion, to gain an assurance, are so many phrases which denote the process, gradual or sudden, by which a self hitherto divided and consciously wrong, inferior and unhappy, becomes unified and consciously right, superior and happy, in consequence of its firmer hold upon religious realities.

William James, *The Varieties of Religious Experience*

The longest way to God,
the indirect,
lies through the intellect.
The shortest way lies through the heart.
Here is my journey's end
and here its start.

Angelus Silesius

Only recently has modern psychology, after a century or more of concentration on mental abnormalities, started to study healthy integrated human beings.

And soon it discovered in the history of these quite

normal people what became known as 'peak experiences' that had never been forgotten, moments in which these ordinary mortals had felt Reality break through, and when, in a flash, life in its inexpressible fullness had opened up and they were overwhelmed with an ineffable, unforgettable bliss.

Frederick Franck, *The Book of Angelus Silesius*

Am I willing to give up what I have in order to be what I am not yet?. . . Am I able to follow the spirit of love into the desert?. . . It is a frightening and sacred moment. There is no return. One's life is changed forever.

Mary Caroline Richards

Are you willing to be sponged out, erased, cancelled, made nothing?
Are you willing to be made nothing?
Dipped into oblivion?
If not, you will never really change.

The phoenix renews her youth
only when she is burnt, burnt alive, burnt down
to hot and flocculent ash.
Then the small stirring of a new bub in the nest
with strands of down like floating ash
Shows that she is renewing her youth like the eagle,
Immortal bird.

D. H. Lawrence

Personal growth is not optional for us. . . God's will that we must grow sums up our human duty.

Pope Paul VI

O Lord, I look around in nature and see the stages of life, the metamorphosis that occurs in other creatures of your creation. Why am I so afraid of change and growth in my life? Why do I hang on to cherished and old beliefs that are not appropriate to the development of faith that ought to be happening within me? Help me to remember the growing seed, the struggle it has to establish and make present its life in a hostile environment.

I affirm that your Spirit can transform me and, through the struggle of change and growth, bring me to a place of maturity in Jesus.   Help me not to resist the movement of my life in you, from the morning stage into the afternoon stage.   Enable me to see that your grace is sufficient for my every need, and for every metamorphosis I experience.   Through Jesus Christ my Lord. Amen.

O most blessed Grace, that makest the poor in spirit rich in virtues, and renderest those who are rich in many goods humble in heart!   Come thou down unto me, come and in the morning fill me with thy comfort, lest my soul faint for weariness and dryness of mind.

Thomas à Kempis

O gracious and holy Father,
give us wisdom to perceive you,
intelligence to understand you,
diligence to seek you,
patience to wait for you,
eyes to behold you,
a heart to meditate upon you,
and a life to proclaim you,
through the power of the Spirit
of Jesus Christ our Lord.

Benedict

O Eternal Trinity! O Godhead! which Godhead gave value to the blood of thy Son, thou O Eternal Trinity art a deep sea, into which the deeper I enter the more I find, and the more I find the more I seek; the soul cannot be satiated in thy abyss, for she continually hungers after thee, the Eternal Trinity, desiring to see thee with light in thy light.   As the hart desires the spring of living water, so my soul desires to leave the prison of this dark body and see thee in truth.

Catherine of Siena

A Benediction

May you walk in the beauty of God's
grace today, because his grace is:
Before you
Behind you
Around you
Above you and
Within you.

Navajo Indian

Know thyself

By the grace of God I am what I am.

He who began a good work in you will carry it on to completion until the day of Christ Jesus.

Not that I have already obtained all this, or have already been made perfect, but I press on to take hold of that for which Christ Jesus took hold of me.

Since we are surrounded by such a great cloud of witnesses, let us throw off everything that hinders and the sin that so easily entangles, and let us run with perseverance the race marked out for us. Let us fix our eyes on Jesus, the author and perfecter of our faith, who for the joy set before him endured the cross, scorning its shame, and sat down at the right hand of the throne of God. Consider him who endured such opposition from sinners, so that you will not grow weary and lose heart.

Consider it pure joy whenever you face trials of many kinds, because you know that the testing of your faith develops perseverance. Perseverance must finish its work so that you may be mature and complete, not lacking anything. If any of you lacks wisdom, ask God, who gives generously to all without finding fault, and it will be given you.

For if those who are nothing think they are something, they deceive themselves. All must test their own work; then that work, rather than their neighbour's work, will become a cause for pride.

Do not think of yourself more highly than you ought, but rather think of yourself with sober judgment, in accordance with the measure of faith God has given you. Just as each of us has one body with many members, and these members do not all have the same function, so in

Christ we who are many form one body, and each member belongs to all the others. We have differing gifts, according to the grace given us.

Those who find their life will lose it, and those who lose their life for my sake will find it.

(I Corinthians 15: 10, RSV; Philippians 1: 6; Philippians 3: 12; Hebrews 12: 1-3 — all NIV; James 1: 2-5; Galatians 6: 3-4 — both NRSV; Romans 12: 3-6, NIV; Matthew 10: 39, NRSV)

'Life begins at forty!' they say. Presumably this is meant to encourage us to believe that the best is yet to come, without too obviously reminding us that the journey is probably halfway through. Perhaps we are supposed to have gained adequate experience and maturity in the first forty years of life to face the future with buoyant confidence and freedom. Or perhaps this is just a device to see us through the threat of a mid-life crisis! Perhaps it is true!

For me, turning forty several years ago coincided with a period of reflection and analysis of where I had been, who I was and where I was going. Although my physical life obviously did not begin at forty, some new and significant understandings of myself and my life began to form around that time.

To that point I had lived life quite happily and successfully, but mostly intuitively. I had taken as 'normal experience' the love and acceptance of my family and friends. I had mostly been able to almost 'grow into' opportunities for work and service. And I had absorbed, at least intellectually, many of the traditional Christian doctrines about who I am:

* I am a unique creation of God, having value to him and others. He has known me and cared for me since my conception and birth, and has gifted me with genetic characteristics, emotions, mental capacities and moral awareness to enable me to live a responsive and responsible life;
* I am a part of the human race which long ago chose to

assert its independence from the creator, and my human nature shares the common struggles between right and wrong, the greater and lesser good, and especially the lesser of two evils;

* I am a child of God, a citizen of the kingdom of God because Jesus Christ acted on my behalf to remove the blockage between me and God and restore a relationship of harmony and obedience; and

* I am now empowered and gifted by the Holy Spirit to live as a member of the kingdom, representing the King to those outside the kingdom and being part of the process by which the people of God are brought to maturity.

Over recent years, my reading and work have encouraged me to ask questions that were before perhaps unconscious, but were now made conscious, and attempt answers that were before mostly intuitive or theoretical, but were now grounded in practical realities:

* How am I specifically unique in personality and potential?

* In what concrete areas am I fallen and especially prone to sinfulness?

* What are the implications of redemption for me in these 'shadow' areas?

* What spiritual gifts are present in me, or available to me, in order that I may live out my unique calling to the full?

My specific personal answers and direction are not important here, but a testimony to the value of the process is. This journey of personal discovery is by no means complete, but it is exciting and enlightening, sometimes threatening and challenging. And it has been important for me to make a start, for the sake of whatever time I have left beyond forty.

But life doesn't *have* to begin at forty! We can discover our true selves and the life that begins afresh every day at *any* stage of life, if we will only open our eyes and hearts to the profound purposes and the sustaining power of God.

❧❧

Know thyself.

Saying inscribed in the temple at Delphi

Thomas Merton, the Trappist monk who probed so much of the meaning of the Christian journey, sought to establish dialogue between monks of the Christian tradition and those of the Buddhist East. In a remarkable encounter with the Dalai Lama, spiritual leader of the Tibetan Buddhists, the Dalai Lama asked Merton this probing question: 'What do your vows oblige you to do? Do they simply constitute an agreement to stick around for life in the monastery? Or do they imply a commitment to a life of progress up certain mystical steps?'

After a long hesitation, Merton shared his understanding of his vows. 'I believe they [my vows] can be interpreted as a commitment to a total inner transformation of one sort or another, a commitment to become a completely new man. No matter where one attempts to do this, that remains the essential thing.'

In that word, Merton described not only the meaning of his monastic vows, but the meaning of all Christian commitment. We become Christian not for the purpose of 'sticking around' the church, but to begin a journey — a journey to become new persons in Christ Jesus.

Maxie Dunman, Alive in Christ

As each man, woman or child emerges into consciousness and then self-consciousness, we feel around inside and outside ourselves for meaning. Our search should lead us in due time to the simplicity of God. But on the way we face or run away from the apparent complexity of ourselves.

Michael Hollings, in Preface to Reaching Out

There is more to me than meets the eye, and more to you than meets yours. You have not even begun to unravel the mystery of your self and your mind; you are deep, unfathomably deep. You cannot be a shallow person; God does not make shallow people. You can, if you choose, close your own mind to the depths within you. But you cannot be shallow. . . When you look in the mirror, you should get your eyes off your midriff and look into your own soul and see yourself as a deep, wonderful mystery of God-likeness.

Lewis B. Smedes, *How Can It Be All Right When Everything Is All Wrong?*

To look honestly at oneself takes tremendous courage. It requires that we strip away all the facade and make-believe we've developed over the years to give us a false feeling of self-esteem, and then accept what is left, even if it is not pretty!

To look honestly at oneself requires that we have some ability to 'step outside'. God has given us, as humans, this capacity for self-reflection. The children of God have always been called to review who they are and what they want to be. In Jeremiah's Lamentations over the misery of Jerusalem, he invited the people thus: 'Let us search and try our ways, and turn again to the Lord' (Lamentations 3: 40). Paul also tells us, 'Examine yourselves, whether you be in the faith: prove your own selves. . .' (2 Corinthians 13: 5).

Archibald Hart, *The Success Factor*

It seems that the emphasis on inter-personal sensitivity has at times made us forget to develop the sensitivity that helps us to listen to our own inner voices. Sometimes one wonders if the fact that so many people ask support, advice and counsel from so many other people is not, in large part, due to their having lost contact with their innermost self. They ask: Should I go to school or look for a job, should I become a doctor or a lawyer, should I marry or remain single, should I leave my position or stay where I am, should I go into the military or refuse to go to war, should I obey my superior or follow my own inclination, should I live a poor life or gain more money for the costly education of my children? There are not enough counsellors in the world to help with all these hard questions, and sometimes one feels as if one half of the world is asking advice of the other half while both sides are sitting in the same darkness.

Henri Nouwen, *Reaching Out*

Life is an obstacle course, it seems, and living is like running an obstacle course. . . there are internal obstacles, such as your shy personality, quick temper or lack of courage, and there are external obstacles, such as the bad economy, uncooperative people or bad timing. There are *always* obstacles — this is the given.

I see reality thinking as a way of being creative whenever we are confronted by obstacles. Reality thinking deals with obstacles by responding to them as challenges to be overcome, not as handicaps to which one must surrender or as reasons for depression. . . After a while, obstacles are welcomed. They represent a test of your creative abilities, so you don't resent them. You receive them gladly. They are the challenges that add zest to life. They send your mind forth in all directions to search for creative ideas and solutions; they expand your experience, causing you to keep an open mind, always observing, analysing, considering and questioning, until you find the hidden key that unlocks the problem.

Archibald Hart, *The Success Factor*

Do you know why you never stop?
You think, perhaps,
it's a sense of responsibility,
a lack of time to waste,
distaste and scorn
for everything preventing you
from making the best use
of life's brief span.
The simple fact is this:
you are deceiving yourself
and trying to avoid a self-to-self encounter.

Dom Helder Camara, *A Thousand Reasons for Living*

One way to express the spiritual crisis of our time is to say that most of us have an address but cannot be found there. We know where we belong, but we keep being pulled away in many directions, as if we were still home- less. 'All these other things' keep demanding our attention. They lead us so far from home that we even- tually forget our true address, that is, the place where we can be addressed.

Henri Nouwen, *Making All Things New*

Self-image is the image that each one of us has of oursel- ves. It is 'a complicated and intricate mental production' which we create for ourselves by a process of self-defini- tion. . . Many people are unaware of what they think of their own worth. It is often only through conscious at- tempts at reflection, or through spiritual direction, counselling or psychotherapy, that they become aware that they are carrying round with them a poor self-image which affects almost all that they say and do.

A habitual poor self-image, which involves a distorted sense of one's true worth in relation to other people and to the world at large, can affect the exercise of authority in a Christian community in several ways and easily lead to abuse. If I habitually have a poor image of my own value, I am likely to try to find a recognised place in a community or group by attempting to please as many people as possible. . . [This] is an abuse of myself as the person in authority because I risk neglecting my own genuine needs and even submerging my own identity and integrity. . . It is a characteristic of a person with a low self-evaluation to be unhappy about allowing others the scope and freedom to exercise their own gifts.

David Lonsdale, 'Authority: the Sources of Abuse'

What God has given us is not to be regarded as a static endowment. Our character can be refined. Our be- haviour can change. Our convictions can mature. Our gifts can be cultivated. Scripture and Christian history are full of examples of the transforming grace of God. Grace gives us the personal moral resources both to push back some of the limits of nature and nurture, and to come to terms with what cannot be changed. In both cases our personal freedom is thereby expanded. We are indeed free to be different, by God's grace and for his glory.

John Stott, *Free to Be Different*

We all long to know who we are — to become full, complete persons who are *real* to ourselves and to others. We often hide from our true feelings and depend on our relationships with others for our sense of reality.

Authenticity is best developed under conditions of acceptance, understanding and genuineness. We can achieve this through our encounters with others with courage and openness.

Christians who accept the basic tenets of God's love and forgiveness are better able to come to terms with themselves and are better equipped to cope with the feelings of isolation which are so prevalent today. Authenticity, integrity and adaptability are developed as we let God release us from our emotional prisons. Life in Christ frees and transforms us and provides the strength to overcome the barriers to becoming real, as we learn to set realistic goals and deal with unsatisfactory conditions in everyday life. Paradoxically, as we abandon ourselves to God, we become more free to realise our full potential.

Arch Hart, *Unlocking the Mystery of your Emotions*

The folly of that impossible precept, 'Know thyself'; till it be translated into this partially possible one, 'Know what thou canst work at.'

Thomas Carlyle, *Past and Present*

O God, you know me inside and out,
    through and through.
Everything I do,
    every thought that flits through my mind,
    every step I take,
    every plan I make,
    every word I speak,

you know, even before these things happen.
You know my past;
   you know my future.
Your circumventing presence covers my every move.
Your knowledge of me sometimes comforts me,
   sometimes frightens me;
   but always it is far beyond my comprehension.

There is no way to escape you, no place to hide.
If I ascend to the heights of joy,
   you are there before me.
If I am plunged into the depths of despair,
   you are there to meet me.
I could fly to the other side of our world
   and find you there to lead the way.
I could walk into the darkest of nights,
   only to find you there
   to lighten its dismal hours.

You were present at my very conception.
You guided the moulding of my unformed members
   within the body of my mother.
Nothing about me, from beginning to end
   was hid from your eyes.
How frightfully, fantastically wonderful it all is!

May your all-knowing, everywhere-present Spirit
   continue to search out my feelings and thoughts.
Deliver me
   from that which may hurt or destroy me,
   and guide me along the paths of love and truth.

   Leslie F. Brandt, 'Psalm 139'

A Benediction:

May you seek to know yourself, with all your complexities, as
only God knows you. May you come to accept yourself, with
all your strengths and weaknesses, as only God accepts you.
And may the wisdom and peace of God be yours, as you live
out your unique identity and calling for his glory. Amen.

The 'Aha!' sign

Now that same day two of them were going to a village called Emmaus, about seven miles from Jerusalem. They were talking with each other about everything that had happened. As they talked and discussed these things with each other, Jesus himself came up and walked along with them; but they were kept from recognising him.

He asked them, 'What are you discussing together as you walk along?'

They stood still, their faces downcast. One of them, named Cleopas, asked him, 'Are you the only one living in Jerusalem who doesn't know the things that have happened there in these days?'

'What things?' he asked.

'About Jesus of Nazareth,' they replied. . .

He said to them, 'How foolish you are, and how slow of heart to believe all that the prophets have spoken! Did not the Christ have to suffer these things and then enter his glory?' And beginning with Moses and all the prophets, he explained to them what was said in all the scriptures concerning himself.

As they approached the village to which they were going, Jesus acted as if he were going further. But they urged him strongly, 'Stay with us, for it is nearly evening; the day is almost over.' So he went in to stay with them.

When he was at the table with them, he took bread, gave thanks, broke it and began to give it to them. Then their eyes were opened and they recognised him, and he disappeared from their sight. They asked each other,

'Were not our hearts burning within us while he talked with us on the road and opened the scriptures to us?'
(Luke 24: 13-19; 25-32, NIV)

Have you ever noticed the power of a familiar sign to awaken consciousness of something? You saw or heard the familiar and exclaimed, 'Aha!', for all of a sudden a light flashed on and you grasped the whole truth or situation. Something was happening all the while, but you didn't notice until the 'sign' clanged a bell that woke you up.

That's what the breaking of bread did for these two disciples. It was an 'Aha!' sign, experienced so many times it stripped away the blinders covering their eyes. Suddenly the unseen was seen, the unheard heard, the unrecognised recognised.

We need such a sign. Aren't we often like these two disciples? We travel down the road with unseeing eyes, unhearing ears, incognizant minds. We talk *about* him. We may even talk *to* him. But we don't know it is him. Our eyes are glazed. Our ears are deaf. Our minds are dull. He's there, but he's an unknown companion travelling the same road. But then comes the 'Aha!'

I've often wondered why these two disciples took so long to recognise Jesus. Cleopas and the unnamed disciple weren't among the Twelve, but surely they had seen and heard Jesus often enough to recognise who he was during an all day trip from Jerusalem to Emmaus, perhaps forty kilometres! Had he changed so radically in the resurrection?

Luke, you notice, didn't note any difficulty in Jesus' appearance. He posited the problem, rather, in the disciples: 'they were kept from recognising him' (24: 16). From what transpired during the journey, we'd have to say they suffered from more than visual limitations, for they missed all kinds of signals.

It didn't seem to help that they had Jesus on their minds. Yet it's surprising they could talk *about* him and not show a hint of recognition. But maybe that's the way we all are. Jesus himself challenged them to explain the words they were bandying about. That surely should have jarred them a little, but they remained as dense as if he hadn't spoken. Shouldn't they have recognised his voice? They knew, too, about the empty tomb. If they didn't trust the report because women delivered it, surely they should have caught something from the men who confirmed the same thing. But they didn't. Jesus himself rebuked them and by reference to the Bible opened their minds. Though he led them from Genesis through Malachi, pointing out the truths about himself, they still didn't catch on.

What kept them from comprehending? So far as we can tell, the disciples heard the words all right, but they weren't able to go beyond the words to where words come from. They talked *about* Jesus rather than listening *to* him. Listening involves more than hearing. It involves sensitivity to nuances words can't convey. A tear trickling down someone's cheek may say far more than thousands of words.

Is this our problem, too? Is our listening problem connected with something else? Does it indicate we are too full of ourselves and what we are doing and thus can't hear what others are trying to say?

For these disciples, all of that changed when Jesus enacted the familiar sign, the 'Aha!', of the breaking of bread. Here we have clear and powerful testimony to the impact an oft-repeated act may exert on inattentive and unresponsive minds and hearts. It awakened recognition of Christ present with them. It stirred recollection of burning hearts on the way. It clarified the scriptures they couldn't comprehend even as Jesus himself explained them. It sent them forth with urgency to tell others.

Each time we break bread together we are summoned anew to this task.

❧❀❧

Once a syphillitic woman knocked on the door at Dorothy Day's Friendship House in Harlem as Dorothy and the other guests prepared to bed down for the night. Dorothy intended to share a double bed with her friend Catherine de Hueck Doherty, but the added guest created a problem.

Dorothy instructed Catherine to sleep in the bathtub while she bedded down with this syphillitic. Catherine, a nurse, protested that syphillis was contagious, and this woman had no nose and running sores. Dorothy replied, 'You have to have faith, Catherine. This is Christ come to us. He will protect me. You have to have faith.'

If we 'saw' the living Christ, we might also find our hearts burning within us as we recalled how he spoke to us as we travelled together down life's road.

E. Glenn Hinson

Inside of me [two contrasting spirits] are wrestling for control. They contend for control of my attitude towards life in general. On one side, there is the flatiron attitude. I hate to take risks; I hate to admit that I don't know what is going on. I want to keep things under control around me; I want an explanation; no surprises please. There is inside of me a wonder-killer. But I also like surprises, I want to keep wonder alive, I love it when my jaw drops, my eyes pop, my knees shake, and I am reduced to amazement. I want my life to be wonder-full. I think that Jesus Christ invites us to transcend our lust to have everything under control and be lifted to the mind-boggling experience of wonder.

Lewis B. Smedes, How Can it be All Right,
When Everything is All Wrong?

Hospitality is one of the richest biblical terms that can deepen and broaden our insight in our relationships to our fellow human beings. Old and New Testament stories not only show how serious our obligation is to welcome the stranger in our home, but they also tell us what guests are carrying precious gifts with them which they are eager to reveal to a receptive host.

When Abraham received three strangers at Mamre and offered them water, bread and a fine tender calf, they revealed themselves to him as the Lord announcing that Sarah his wife would give birth to a son (Genesis 18: 1-15). When the widow of Zarephath offered food and shelter to Elijah, he revealed himself as a man of God offering her an abundance of oil and meal and raising her son from the dead (1 Kings 17: 9-24). When the two travellers to Emmaus invited the stranger who had joined them on the road to stay with them for the night, he made himself known in the breaking of the bread as their Lord and Saviour (Luke 24: 13-35). . .

Thus the biblical stories help us to realise not just that hospitality is an important virtue, but even more that in the context of hospitality, guest and host can reveal their most precious gifts and bring new life to each other.

Henri J.M. Nouwen, *Reaching Out*

We are part of a highly verbal culture. Sounds constantly bombard and dull our ears. Glaring lights vie for our eyes' attention until the retinas lose their natural sharpness. Everything around us takes on a dull uniformity. We experience precious little encouragement to be still and listen, to withdraw and let nature sharpen our hearing and our seeing. When the risen Christ appears to us in the hungry and thirsty, in the cold and naked, in the homeless and imprisoned, as he himself said he appears (Matthew 25: 31-46), we don't recognise him.

We could excuse ourselves for our poor listening much of the time. Life deals us some rough blows, too, enough to dull our memories of the Master's teaching and clog our awareness of his presence. Sickness, sorrow, joblessness, anxiety over family — all of these overwhelm us and we forget. They fill us with ourselves and what we are doing and we can't recognise the Master when he walks alongside us on the road to Emmaus or meets us on the streets of Lantana or Louisville or New York. We're more apt at talking about Jesus than we are at responding to him as he presents himself to us.

I must confess I haven't done well in recognising Christ as the stranger in our midst, but I'm learning from Mother Teresa of Calcutta. Mother Teresa and the Sisters of Charity build their whole ministry to the dying around the perception of Matthew 25: 31-46 that the person whose need we meet *is* Christ. Did Jesus not say, 'Inasmuch as you did it to one of the least of these, my brothers and sisters, you did it to me' (25: 40) or, 'Inasmuch as you did not do it to one of the least of these, my brothers and sisters, you did not do it to me' (45)? The other person, then, is to us the living Christ himself, suffering with them and in them.

E. Glenn Hinson

To do evangelism by extending *shalom* to others is to take God's stance visibly in the world. It confronts the rebellious, hostile world in the out-reaching, open-armed stance of the cross. It embodies and expresses in life and actions the message of reconciliation that we have been entrusted with as ambassadors from Christ. To say 'Shalom' to another person in the name of Christ is the New Testament mission: 'So we are ambassadors for Christ, God making his appeal through us. We beseech you on behalf of Christ, be reconciled to God' (2 Corinthians 5: 20). . .

All who respond to that offer are by its nature commissioned to pass it on. As with mercy and forgiveness, we lack the proof of ever receiving the *shalom* of God if we are not sharing the same with others. For no person whose enmity and alienation has been melted away by hearing God say 'Shalom' can withhold the same loving acceptance from others who are still fighting.

James E. Metzler, *From Saigon to Shalom*

Jesus himself drew near,
And joined them as they walked,
And soon their hearts began to burn,
As of himself he talked:
Draw near, O Lord.

Jesus himself drew near,
And at the journey's end
They could not let him leave them thus:
The stranger was their Friend.
Draw near, O Lord.

A.R. Haberson

Like those two disciples, we, too, Lord, are walking down life's road with signs of your presence all around us. Give us eyes to see, ears to hear, minds to recognise you on our journey.

Like them, we relish our talk about you. But help us also to listen. Forgive our self-preoccupations and self-concerns — and perhaps our self-despisings — which deafen us so that we do not hear your still small voice.

Then help us to recognise you as the stranger in our midst. Make our hearts more tender with your divine compassion. And when you come to us, may we not turn you away. Come to us and abide with us, Lord, and give us joy in ministering to you in your poverty again. Amen.

A Benediction

And although the road is sometimes hard for you, always remember that One walks always by your side. Perhaps that One will be recognised in the person of the stranger for whom the road is harder still. So go in peace to love and serve the Lord. Amen.

A minister of goodwill

God loved the world so much that he gave his only Son. . . to be its Saviour.

As the Father sent me, so I send you.

Jesus said, '"Love the Lord your God with all your heart, and with all your soul, and with all your mind." This is the greatest and the most important commandment. The second. . . is. . . "You must love your neighbour as yourself."'

This is my commandment: love one another, just as I love you.

You have heard that it was said, 'Love your friends, and hate your enemies.' But I tell you: love your enemies, and pray for those who mistreat you.

When they came to the place called 'The Skull', they nailed Jesus to the cross there. . . Jesus said, 'Forgive them, Father! They don't know what they are doing.'

Father. . . I sent them into the world, just as you sent me into the world.

They threw [Stephen] out of the city and stoned him. . . They kept on stoning Stephen as he called on the Lord, 'Lord Jesus, receive my spirit.' He knelt down and cried in a loud voice, 'Lord, do not remember this sin against them!'

(John 3: 16-17; John 20: 21; Matthew 22: 37-39; John 15: 12; Matthew 5: 43-44; Luke 23: 33-34; John 17: 18; Acts 7: 58-60 — all GNB)

'Why', asks Vernon Bartlett, 'why do not governments include a Ministry of Goodwill?' He envisaged representatives of such a portfolio actively fostering friendly, kind, generous relationships between all persons, groups and nations.

It was not a novel idea. Jesus created such a ministry, and appointed all of his followers to carry it out. Its function was to love people.

In English, the word 'love' has lost its clear definition, like a coin whose superscription is worn away by long use. Today, it can denote different things — from the affection which binds a man and woman in lifelong marriage, to hopping into bed with somebody else's spouse; from infatuation with the latest rock star, to preference for a certain sport, or a liking for vanilla slice.

Jesus' Aramaic term for 'love' was so distinctive that the translators had to coin a new Greek word for it. They called it *agape* (noun), *agapao* (verb): 'words unknown outside the New Testament' (Bullinger). *Agape* differs from other Greek words sometimes rendered 'love'. It means a 'voluntary, active attitude of kindness, expressing itself in action rather than sentiment; it is pure *goodwill*'. It wills only good to every person. It can transform people's relationships.

But how can we show goodwill to people we simply do not like — with whom we have no affinity? Samaritans did not like Jews: they despised them. Yet in Jesus' story (Luke 10), only the Samaritan chose to stop and extend tender, loving care to the injured Jew: a vivid example of *agape* in action.

The practice of goodwill in the home and the workplace, in social and industrial and international relationships, would work wonders. One historian believes that if, as Winston Churchill proposed at the end of World War I, the Allies had displayed goodwill by sending shiploads of food and other relief to Germany, instead of imposing crushing reparations, World War II might never have eventuated.

Some would reply that it is not natural to feel such sentiments towards everybody. But *agape* goodwill involves a resolution to allow our *will* to over-ride our feelings. Bullinger's *Greek Lexicon* prints in italics:

Agape. . . chooses its object with a decision of the will, and devotes self-denying devotion to it.

Jesus' vision of a ministry of goodwill might seem like an impossible dream to the unregenerate person. But the regenerate individual has received the Holy Spirit, who makes tall orders possible by reinforcing the will. Paul reminded the Galatians that the Spirit produces *agape* (his word) in those in whom he lives (Galatians 5: 22, GNB). To be Christ's Minister of Goodwill is a privilege not only for the clergy, but for everyone who belongs to him.

Jesus himself embodied to the end the goodwill to which he called his people. On the cross he bore no resentment towards those who were killing him — only *agape*. 'Father, forgive them,' he prayed — the perfect Minister of Goodwill.

❧

Christ has not left for our guidance a code of laws. He has given us instead a compass by which to find our direction.
Sydney Cave, *What Shall We Say of Christ?*

Where people were divided into neighbours and strangers, Jesus regarded all as neighbours. Quite explicitly he included our enemies among our neighbours (Matthew 5: 43-44). He himself refused no contact, however casual. He gave to his disciples a new teaching about loving their neighbours. In his own life and the life of his disciples he substituted for the old comfortable, defined, natural neighbourhood the all-inclusive contacts of a rootless life.
M. Gibbs and T.R. Morton, *God's Frozen People*

Happy is the person who shuns unloving ways,
who is not attracted by apathy or sarcasm,
But finds delight in Jesus' teaching,
testing it out by day and night. . .
Those who love have their taproots in God;
the unloving are rootless.
The Lord can work with the loving people,
but the unloving work their own ruin.
Bruce D. Prewer, *Australian Psalms* (Psalm 1)

It is curious that in so rich a language as English, there is only one word for all the different kinds of love. Martin [Luther King] said many times that the Greeks had three words for it. . . There was *eros* which has come to mean aesthetic or romantic love. *Philia* meant reciprocal love, as between men and women. 'No one,' Martin said, 'could be such a fool as to expect a person to feel that kind of love for an oppressor.'

The third kind of love was *agape*. . . and meant understanding, redeeming goodwill towards everyone. It was disinterested love in which the individual sought not one's own good, but the good of one's neighbour. It was not weak or passive, but love in action: the kind Martin aspired to give his enemies.

Coretta Scott King, My Life with
Martin Luther King Jr

William James was writing as a good psychologist when he said, 'love your enemies!'; mark you, not only those who happen not to be your friends, but your *enemies*, your positive and active enemies. Either this is a mere oriental hyperbole, a bit of verbal extravagance, meaning only that we should, as far as we can, abate our animosities, or else it is sincere and literal. . . If positive well-wishing could attain so supreme a degree of excitement, those who were swayed by it might well seem superhuman beings. Their life would be morally discrete from the life of others, and there is no saying what the effect might be: they might conceivably transform the world.

Harry Emerson Fosdick, On Being a Real Person

A compulsion to love, i.e., to treat all persons with the dignity they deserve as human beings, is the natural compulsion of the true born-again Christian. If conversion results in a salvation experience, a dissolution of guilt and a rise in self-esteem, then the Christian will be constrained by the love of Christ and controlled by a compulsion to treat persons beautifully.

Robert H. Schuller, Self Esteem

In the presence of a superior person — one, let us say, who wins a game we wanted to win, or who writes, paints and preaches better than we can — jealousy is sensitiveness twisted into peevishness, petulance and anger. The only ultimate cure is the right use of the very sensitivity we are wrongly using. As Goethe said, 'Against the superiority of another, the only remedy is love.'

Psychologically healthy persons rejoice in the excellence of others. Objectively interested in whatever they are giving their life to, they are glad when a musician, a teacher, an administrator appears who is better than themselves. Thereby the world is enriched, and if they can admire and so share in the excellence, they are enriched themselves.

Harry Emerson Fosdick, On Being a Real Person

We can stop giving advice and start practising brotherhood where we live. It is more painful, less romantic, but far more effective. We can at least make an effort to bear in our own hearts the burden of the world's hurt. And when we don't know what to do, we can pray.

Luther J. Thompson, Monday Morning Religion

The test of our love of others is our behaviour towards particular people whom we talk, laugh and drink with — the real, raw stuff, the pushing, thrusting, greed-making, fighting, failing, sensual, respectable person who can behave like a cad or a coward on occasion. . . to love these, to be interested in these, is the proof of love.

A.E. Whitham, The Discipline and Culture
of the Spiritual Life

We have to love all sorts of tricky and unpleasant people simply because of the eternal mystery that Jesus loved them enough to die for them. They are extremely unattractive, but they are not all bad and they have dazzling potentialities. . . How are we to love the impossible people we now so thoroughly dislike? There are two methods. We can look into their tired, frightened faces and see the lines engraved by suffering. Watch their dull, hungry eyes in which you can trace sorrows, failures and limitations. And then kneel down and pray for them. You cannot dislike people you have prayed for.

Frederick A. Atkins, *The Durable Satisfactions of Life*

Son (he said)
You are not alone,
I am with you.
I am you.
For I needed another human vehicle to
continue my Incarnation
And my Redemption. . .
I need your hands to continue to bless,
I need your lips to continue to speak,
I need your body to continue to suffer,
I need your heart to continue to love. . .
Stay with me, son.

Michel Quoist, *Prayers of Life*

O brother man, take to thy heart thy brother;
Where pity dwells, the peace of God is there;
To worship rightly is to love each other,
Each smile a hymn, each kindly deed a prayer.

Follow with reverent steps the great example
Of him whose holy work was doing good:
So shall the wide earth be our Father's temple,
Each loving life, a psalm of gratitude.

Then shall all shackles fall: the noisy clangour
Of wild war music o'er the earth shall cease;
Love shall tread out the baleful fire of anger,
And in its ashes plant the tree of peace.

John Greenleaf Whittier

Our Father, who dost desire us to love and to serve one another. . . grant us through this day the gifts and graces which will make us easy to live with.

Grant us courtesy, that we may live every moment as if we were living at the court of a king.

Grant us considerateness, that we may think of the feeling of others even more than our own.

Grant unto us kindliness, that we may miss no opportunity to help, to cheer, to comfort and to encourage another person.

Grant unto us so to live today that the world may be a happier place because we passed through it.

William Barclay, *A Plain Man's Book of Prayers*

Speak thou in my words today, think in my thoughts, and work in all my deeds. And seeing that it is thy gracious will to make use even of such weak human instruments in the fulfilment of thy mighty purpose for the world, let my life today be the channel through which some little portion of thy divine love and pity may reach the lives that are nearest to my own.

John Baillie, *A Diary of Private Prayer*

Grant me, Lord, to spread true love in the world.

Grant that by me and by your children it may penetrate a little into all circles, all societies, all economic and political systems, all laws, all contracts, all rulings.

Grant that it may penetrate the hearts of others and that I may never forget that the battle for a better world is a battle of love, in the service of love. Help me to love, Lord.

Michel Quoist, *Prayers of Life*

O God, bless my enemies and those who have done me wrong. Now as I pray this prayer, let me not still cherish in my heart the resolve to requite them when occasion offers.

John Baillie, *A Diary of Private Prayer*

All-loving — but thy love is stern
And claims not love alone, but deeds;
It little profits if I burn
With rapture, while my brother bleeds;
Further my love with practical intent,
Lest it evaporate in sentiment.

Anonymous, in G.F. Bradbury and J.W.
Hunkin, *Through the Christian Year*

Shine in us Lord, our little love reproving,
That other souls may kindle at the flame;
All the world's hatred, broken by our loving,
Shall bow to love your everlasting name.

Unknown

A Benediction
Go out into the world as a Minister of Goodwill, extending
Christ's agape to every person your life may touch, and may
the Lord of love, Jesus Christ, be with you. **Amen.**

The Saint and the Pharisee

He also told this parable to some who trusted in themselves that they were righteous and regarded others with contempt:

Two men went up to the temple to pray, one a Pharisee and the other a tax collector. The Pharisee, standing by himself, was praying thus, "God, I thank you that I am not like other people: thieves, rogues, adulterers, or even like this tax collector. I fast twice a week; I give a tenth of all my income."

But the tax collector, standing far off, would not even look up to heaven, but was beating his breast and saying, "God, be merciful to me, a sinner!" I tell you, this man went down to his home justified rather than the other; for all who exalt themselves will be humbled, but all who humble themselves will be exalted.'

(Luke 18: 9-14, NRSV)

Saints are many people, but they have this in common: they remind you of Jesus. They love everyone. They know who they are. Saints inhabit every Christian denomination or group. They're people you feel good around: they radiate goodness. They're sinners — indeed more aware of their sins than anyone — but they have had a personal experience of God's grace and forgiveness. Because of that they can't be negative about the personhood (as distinct from the behaviour) of anyone else: they are very *accepting* people.

Here we'll explore just one characteristic of all the saints: they have been cured of 'phariseeism'. Cured? Yes, pharisaism is a spiritual and social disease.

The Pharisees of Jesus' day were 'separatists'. They distanced themselves from evil, segregating themselves from anyone unclean. '"Away" was their directional signal when it came to dealing with evil' (John Claypool). Such evil was mainly of two kinds: heresy and sexual sin.

Now Jesus upset these people because his judgments were against 'sins of the spirit' rather than sins of heterodoxy or sins of the flesh. Not that he made light of these. The truth sets us free, he said. After his pastoral word to the woman caught in adultery — 'neither do I condemn you' — he then adds, 'Go and sin no more.' (The Pharisees — ask them! — always remember the latter, but not the former statement by Jesus to this woman.)

The Pharisees' mindset was to demand repentance before they practised acceptance. With Jesus these were reversed. 'I accept you,' he says to sinners, 'so let's work on change together.'

For the Pharisee, the law is the means of telling the good guys from the bad guys. But, underneath, many Pharisees are jealous of the bad guys who are enjoying their sins, but the Pharisee isn't enjoying righteousness half as much. (Immorality is the morality of those who are having a *better* time!) A Pharisee is a good person in the worst sense of the word. Someone has said there are 'law-breaking sinners' and 'law-keeping sinners' and each is worse than the other! For the saint, whose life is characterised by thankfulness, *gratefulness*, the law is a reminder, codifying a thankful response to the law-giver.

Every Christian is on a journey from sainthood to pharisaism or back the other way. . .

❧❧❧

Lord have mercy on me,
A Pharisee.
Not when I pray,
But surely, surely, thrice a day.
I say,
'See her, see him. How foolish they. . .'
Each one at whom I laugh
Diminishes by half.

So I grow tall
By proving others small.
Lord, pity me
A Pharisee.

Margaret Beidler, 'Pity me'

As Paul came to see it in retrospect, [Pharisees] were exposed to a fatal flaw: the trouble with their outstanding righteousness was that, all too easily, it could be viewed precisely as *their* righteousness. It was a righteousness that could be measured, so that, at a certain point, you could say that you had now achieved it. This meant that it could all too easily come adrift from its original inspiration in devotion to God and become self-sufficient, an end in itself. . . The basic form of complacency, after all, is that people are pleased with themselves.

Simon Tugwell, 'The Beatitudes'

It is, of course, true, whatever denomination you may happen to belong to, that the majority of your good churchgoers will be living under law and not under grace. The human heart is incurably legalistic. . . We prefer the limited demands of an ecclesiastical system, heavy though they may be, to the unlimited demands of genuine surrender to Jesus Christ.

Within its own limits, legalism may produce admirable types of character. The Pharisees were by no means contemptible people; they had a zeal for the law of God, and a devotion to it that would put many Christians to shame. The trouble is that what law can achieve is always limited, since the most that it can effect is modification of character from without, and not transformation from within. That inner transformation can really begin only when we pass from the sphere of law to that of grace, from the status of a servant to that of a son or daughter.

Stephen Neill, *On the Ministry*

Elmer had, even in Zenith, to meet plenty of solemn and whiskery persons whose only pleasure aside from not doing agreeable things was keeping others from doing them.

Sinclair Lewis, *Elmer Gantry*

It is significant that the one born that night was called 'Emmanuel', not 'Pharisee'. The word 'Emmanuel' means 'God with us', while 'Pharisee' means 'the separate one', and when it comes to doing something redemptively about the power of destruction in the world, the difference between 'with' and 'away' is absolutely crucial. . . The approach of Jesus was the utter antithesis to pharisaism. He moved about, not as the Separate One or as a self-righteous purist, but as 'the friend of sinners. . .'

John Claypool, 'The First Christmas: Jesus'

. . .This demonic process has affected every religious order which has ever existed. The escape into canon law has always been an escape from the awful challenge of religion and intimacy combined.

Andrew Greeley, *Confessions of a Parish Priest*

A Pharisee is a righteous person whose righteousness is nourished by the blood of sinners.

Thomas Merton, *Conjectures of a Guilty Bystander*

I have long regarded the year AD 383 as one of the most disastrous turning points in history, since in that year for the first time, in the condemnation of the Spanish heretic Priscillian, the blood of Christians was shed by Christians. . .
. . .In the sixteenth century, we find Francis Xavier, purest and most devoted of Roman Catholic missionaries, writing to the king of Portugal to urge that the Inquisition should be introduced into India as an indispensable aid to the work of evangelisation, and unfortunately securing a favourable answer to his request.

Stephen Neill, *On the Ministry*

When 'righteous' persons determine to do God's will, but are not first born again and awakened to a higher life, they cannot discern what is God's will. . . They believe their own desires and wishes are the will of God.

For example, they refrain from human arrogance, imagining they are humble; but they retain their pride under the guise of the lofty demands of divine truth. . . They refrain from all lust for power and revenge, but they have by no means abandoned the lust for power and revenge. Nor do they in reality become less desirous of power and revenge, but rather more so. For now they can do so completely without regard for others in the name of God. They imagine that when they now seek to force through something, they do so for the sake of the kingdom of God. When they persecute or crush another, they do it thinking that the welfare of the church or of the gospel or of Christianity demands it. The purely human desire for revenge and domination is thus represented under the guise of zeal for morality and the kingdom of God, for what is good and true.

This is satanic. This is hypocrisy. However, hypocrites will never be conscious of it so long as they remain in the unregenerate state.

Hugo Odeberg, *Pharisaism and Christianity*

Many of the insights of saints stem from their experiences as sinners.

Eric Hoffer, *The Passionate State of Mind*

The servants were permitted to hold evening prayer in the kitchen, under Mrs Fairley's indifferent eye and briskly wooden voice. Upstairs, Mrs Poulteney had to be read to alone; and it was in these more intimate ceremonies that Sarah's voice was heard at its best and most effective. Once or twice she had done the incredible, by drawing from those pouched, invincible eyes a tear. Such an effect was in no way intended, but sprang from a profound difference between the two women. Mrs Poulteney believed in a God that had never existed; and Sarah knew a God that did.

John Fowles, *The French Lieutenant's Woman*

All [the publican] knows, from being himself an extortioner, a moneylender, a thief and so forth, is that there are moments when for no reason, because it is not part of the world's outlook, he will forgive a debt, because suddenly his heart has become mild and vulnerable; that on another occasion he may not get someone put into prison, because a face will have reminded him of something or a voice has gone straight to his heart.

There is no logic in this. It is not part of the world's outlook nor is it a way in which he normally behaves. It is something that breaks through, which is completely nonsensical, which he cannot resist; and he knows also, probably, how often he himself was saved from final catastrophe by this intrusion of the unexpected and the impossible — mercy, compassion, forgiveness.

So he stands at the rear of the church, knowing that all the realm inside the church is a realm of righteousness and divine love to which he does not belong and into which he cannot enter. But he knows from experience also that the impossible does occur and that is why he says, 'Have mercy, break the laws of righteousness, break the laws of religion, come down in mercy to us who have no right to be either forgiven or allowed in.' And I think this is where we should start continuously all over again.

Archbishop Anthony Bloom, *School for Prayer*

Healing is the result of love. It is a function of love.

Wherever there is love there is healing. And wherever there is no love there is precious little — if any — healing.

M. Scott Peck, *People of the Lie*

I identify joyfully and painfully with the founder of my contemplative prayer fellowship. Whenever he has written to me, he has always ended his letters: 'With as much love as I have so far received.' He and I know that we have hardly scratched the surface — hardly begun to be filled with all the fullness of God's love.

Peter Dodson, *Contemplating the Word*

The saints, Lord, are profound and simple people, who pray profoundly simple prayers. Like 'Lord, have mercy on me, a sinner.' Their perspective derives from a comparison between themselves and the holiness of God.

The Pharisees, Lord, are profoundly complex people, who pray, 'Lord, I thank you I'm not as bad as so-and-so. . .' Their perspective derives from a comparison between the best in themselves and the worst in others, and any hypocrite can do that.

So, Lord, my simple prayer is this: help me to be more like Jesus, and less like the Pharisees, day by day. Amen.

A Benediction

May your sins be forgiven by Jesus, who loved sinners. May your pride be healed by Jesus, who was meek and lowly. May your self-esteem respond to his gentle acceptance, and may you live all the days of your life in the love of God the Father, the grace of Jesus the Son, and the communion of the Holy Spirit. Amen.

People first

Then Jesus went back to the synagogue, where there was a man who had a paralysed hand. Some people were there who wanted to accuse Jesus of doing wrong; so they watched him closely to see whether he would heal the man on the Sabbath. Jesus said to the man, 'Come up here to the front.' Then he asked the people, 'What does the Law allow us to do on the Sabbath? To help or to harm? To save life or to destroy it?'

But they did not say a thing. Jesus was angry as he looked round at them, but at the same time he felt sorry for them, because they were so stubborn and wrong. Then he said to the man, 'Stretch out your hand.' He stretched it out, and it became well again. So the Pharisees left the synagogue and met at once with some members of Herod's party, and they made plans to kill Jesus.

(Mark 3: 1-6, GNB)

He was known only as 'the man with the withered hand'. Like most of the people whom Jesus helped, this man remained anonymous. We have no case history, no name or address, no details of the problem. We do not even know if the man came seeking healing. We are told only that 'he was there'. Probably he did hope for a cure, because Mark has already told us in his opening chapter that news of Jesus had spread over the whole region of Galilee. Everyone was looking for him; the sick, the deformed, the depressed, the demented, the curious. No wonder the synagogue was crowded on this particular Sabbath.

The enemies of Jesus were there, too. It had not taken long for opposition to be aroused towards this teacher who spoke as no other man spoke, who taught with authority and 'not as the Scribes', who forgave sins, who moved out with compassion even to touch lepers, hideous and rejected. Whenever creative things happen, there are always those who object for a variety of reasons. Some people are threatened by the new or the different just because it is contrary to their own established ways. Sometimes the threat is to position or reputation. Objections can arise from smug self-satisfaction or assumed superiority, or from cynicism, scepticism or sheer jealousy. In some cases, the new thing cuts across a deep-rooted folk wisdom growing out of cultural patterns that are familiar and secure.

The opposition to Jesus was of a more malicious variety. It had the sharp edge and zealous hostility of religious fundamentalism. Jesus' opponents came to the place of worship solely to look for a reason to accuse him. They may even have brought the man with the crippled hand to the synagogue. They certainly knew he was there, for Mark says they were watching Jesus closely to see if he would heal the man on the Sabbath. They could have deliberately set out to use the man to provoke a confrontation.

There are those only too ready to exploit human need for personal, political, financial or even theological reasons. It is a trap that faces all who work with people.

Jesus was aware of all this. He knew the atmosphere was charged with tension and danger. For any number of reasons it would have been prudent to avoid a showdown with the authorities. He was just beginning his public work and people were responding with overwhelming enthusiasm. Surely this was the time to build on this early success, not to stir up antagonism. Furthermore, Jesus could easily have avoided a confrontation. He could have said quietly to the man, 'Look, I've noticed your hand, but it's a bit awkward to do anything about it here. Meet me tomorrow and I'll take a look at it.'

Instead, Jesus made a big issue of the encounter. 'Stand up here in front of everyone,' he said to the man. Why should he choose to expose himself in this manner? Could it be that there were profound issues at stake which must on no account be avoided? Centuries of Jewish tradition had built up a legalistic system, layer upon layer, that had become rigid and oppressive. The purpose of God's law had been totally obscured.

Jesus knew that confrontation over this issue was inevitable and he chose to meet it head on. He threw out a sharp challenge, 'Which is lawful on the Sabbath; to do good or to do evil, to save life or to kill?' This was not an academic question. Jesus was deliberately comparing his intentions with theirs. He was about to perform an act of healing; they were plotting to kill. They saw no contradiction in this; in fact, they thought they were serving God, so utterly distorted was their understanding of his ways.

The question was greeted with silence. Then Jesus, 'deeply hurt as he sensed their inhumanity, looked round in anger at the faces surrounding him' (Mark 3: 5, Phillips). Turning to the man standing there he said, 'Stretch out your hand,' and it was completely restored. The Pharisees immediately went out and conspired to destroy Jesus. They even formed an alliance with their traditional enemies, the Herodians, against this common threat.

There is always an element of risk in acts of mercy and kindness. The risks are not often as dramatic as this, but they are real enough. There is the risk that one's motives will be misunderstood, perhaps suspected. The kindness may be rejected, or the benefactor taken advantage of, considered soft or foolish. There may be physical danger under some circumstances, certainly inconvenience. In these modern times there can be legal implications. If questions of injustice or misuse of power are involved, the hostility of powerful vested interests may be aroused. To care about others is to become vulnerable to such risks.

It does not require a catastrophe to call forth this response of compassion. Not a famine or a flood or a war. Just one man with a deformed hand: one life crippled, physically or emotionally. One ordinary person in need. To the lawyers with their rules, to the religious politicians with their intrigue, to the zealots with their ideologies, to the traditionalists with their prejudice, the plight of one person was insignificant. To Jesus, one life summoned up all the compassion of God.

The healing of the man was no casual event. It was symbolic of a fundamental difference between Jesus' approach to people and the prevailing customs. It exposed a deadly infection that had poisoned the representatives of God. The effect was so intense that they were ready to kill him. Did Jesus think he might win them over? Had his attempt failed? No, he knew what the outcome would be. He was under no illusions. He failed only to the extent that we, today, perpetuate inhuman ways of dealing with persons, especially when clothed in a religious disguise.

It is crucial that contemporary Christians heed the warning; that we hear where the Pharisees were deaf; that we see where they were blind; that we understand where they did not. It is a tragedy beyond comprehension when, having seen this blindness and inhumanity exposed by the Christ whom we profess to follow, we stubbornly set our faces towards the same dead-end path.

❧

Jesus often seems not to understand at all what people are asking him. He seems to be answering quite a different question from that which has been put to him. He seems to be missing the point of the question, not answering the question, but addressing himself direct to the questioner. He speaks with a complex freedom which is not bound by the law of logical alternatives. In this freedom, Jesus leaves all laws beneath him; and to the Pharisees, this freedom necessarily appears as the negation of all order, all piety and all belief.

Dietrich Bonhoeffer, *Ethics*

The indelible message is: people come first. Not systems, not traditions, not rules, not one's own advantage, not even personal safety. These things have their place, but it is not first place. In the fact of a human life in need, other factors are peripheral. The failure of those who claimed to be the people of God to recognise this stirred Jesus to a rare eruption of anger. Their preoccupation with law to the exclusion of all else was an abomination in the eyes of Jesus. This attitude was stifling the work of God when loving and caring were called for.

Myriad forces will conspire to lead us down that same path, many of them influencing us unconsciously: bureaucratic machinery, expediency, impersonal structures, inertia, rivalry, inconvenience, disadvantage to ourselves and personal agendas, to name a few. In the face of this, let us hold clearly before us the picture of one who said, 'Stretch out your hand,' who put his life on the line for an unidentified stranger; one who accorded people the priority intended by their Creator.

Graeme Irvine

What gave him extraordinary personal power was this: that from the Pope to the beggar, from the Sultan of Syria in his pavilion to the ragged robbers crawling out of the wood, there was never a person who looked into those brown burning eyes without being certain that Francis Bernardone was really interested in them individually in their own inner individual life from the cradle to the grave; that they were valued and taken seriously, and not merely added to the spoils of some social policy or the names in some clerical document. . . he treated the whole mob of people as a mob of Kings or Queens.

G.K. Chesterton, *St Francis of Assisi*

In the life and growth of every young church, it seems, there is one perennial disappointment which more than any other grieves and bewilders [us]. . . Before the first generation of converts has passed away, gospel is turned into law. The first fine careless rapture of a new discovery deteriorates into a sorry story of rules of conduct, backsliding and church discipline. . . the church comes to be known not as a community with a new quality of life, but a sect with a lot of unreasonable prohibitions. . . The church itself is never more worldly than when its appeal for humanitarian or political action is based on moralism or guilt.

John V. Taylor, *The Go-Between God*

Bureaucracy is the world of explicitly formulated goals, rules, procedures and givens that define and regulate the place of its 'members'; a world of specialisation and expertise, with the roles of individuals minutely specified and differentiated. . . It is a world that prizes consistency, predictability, stability, and efficiency (narrowly defined) more than creativity and principle. . . The structure, Robert Merton notes, is one that 'approaches the complete elimination of personalised relationships. . .' The more these personalised relationships are eliminated, the less potential there is for reciprocity, response to wants, needs and values. . .

James MacGregor Burns, *Leadership*

The extreme effect of living a role is that persons may become what their role expects them to be. . . Many bureaucrats treat all persons as clients and show no flexibility in meeting the demands of other statuses. Consequently they exhibit little awareness of how to treat others as human beings who have a wide variety of needs and desires.

Russell Heddendorf, 'Status and Role'

There is, regrettably, no in-built guarantee that ecclesiastical authority will provide the most reliable yardstick for judgment. Popes and synods can err grievously, though not inevitably. Would that we were better at discerning the prophets, who occasionally even come disguised as church leaders. . .

Martin Luther King often affirmed that the church's task was neither to dominate the state nor be subservient to it, but to be its conscience. Christian institutions have only occasionally risen to that challenge. . . The balance between solidarity and critique will differ from country to country and from year to year and from Christian to Christian.

Daniel Berrigan S.J., in a letter to his fellow Jesuits

written while on the run and shortly before a spell in Danbury jail (dated 10 April 1970) [wrote]: 'Many of our church leaders are effectively inoculated against Christ and his Spirit. Nothing is to be expected from such men, except the increasing suffocation of the Word. But the real question is not the conversion of cardinals or presidents, but the conversion of each of us.'

Paul Oestreicher, 'Christians as Political Dissenters'

I had gone to pray, that was all. . . 'I'm sorry, Elias,' he replied gravely. 'You have broken the rules. What would happen if we allowed every student to do as he wished? As I am bound by the laws of the church, so you are bound by the rules of the school. You must be punished.'

For the first time, I stood face-to-face with the unbending rules of the church as an institution. I could not understand why strict obedience to a rule was more important than a heart seeking God. Unhappy though I was, I could not fault the principal. He was just a man carrying out his job to the best of his ability. In the end I submitted, more or less quietly, to my punishment: forty days of restriction.

Unfortunately, this would not be my last exposure to the side of the church that seemed to have forgotten the humanity it was intended to serve.

Elias Chacour, *Blood Brothers*

According to Luke 14: 34-35, disciples who give up their life renunciation and return to traditional forms of security are as useless as salt which has lost its taste. In Palestine, salt was not artificially prepared, but was simply dug from evaporated pools near the Dead Sea. It contained many impurities, so if it was rained upon on the way to market, the salt dissolved and what remained was useless. It was thrown away. Be warned, says Luke. Discipleship is a life and death issue, the stakes are high and those who do not make it to the end will be thrown out.

Athol Gill, *Life on the Road*

You are a compassionate God, suffering with us. And we are called to be compassionate, as you our Father are compassionate.

Teach us, Lord, that institutions and compassion do not often successfully mix. It is only when we are powerless that the limitless love of God is demonstrated. It is when we identify with those in need, rather than bending towards them from a privileged position, that they are best helped. May we not rest too much if there are still human beings with tears in their eyes.

Our model for compassion is our Servant-Lord. Save us from the moralism of doing good because that is what is expected of 'good Christians'. Save us, too, from the motivation of guilt: helping the less fortunate because we have so much.

We want to serve you, Lord, from gratitude, and as part of our search for you. Amen.

A Benediction

Send us out into the world, loving Lord, to share one another's burdens and joys, and to carry our crosses together, until that time and that place where all tears are wiped away, poverty is dispelled, prisoners are free, the hungry are fed and the thirsty enjoy the river of life. To you, Lord, and to your sisters and brothers in need we offer our love, our faith and our hope. Glory be to you, Lord Christ, forever and ever. Amen.

46

Peace and justice

The Lord has told us what is good. What he requires of us is this: to do what is just; to show constant love; and to live humbly in fellowship with our God.

But once more God will send us his spirit. The waste land will become fertile, and fields will produce rich crops. Everywhere in the land, righteousness and justice will be done. Because everyone will do what is right, there will be peace and security for ever. God's people will be free from worries; and their homes peaceful and safe.

If only you had paid attention to my commands, your peace would have been like a river, your righteousness like the waves of the sea.

Turn away from evil and do good; strive for peace with all your heart.

. . .love your neighbour as you love yourself.

But the wisdom from above is pure first of all; it is also peaceful, gentle and friendly; it is full of compassion and produces a harvest of good deeds; it is free from prejudice and hypocrisy. And goodness is the harvest that is produced from the seeds the peacemakers plant in peace.

(Micah 6: 8; Isaiah 32: 15-18 — both GNB; Isaiah 48: 18, NIV; Psalm 34: 14; Matthew 19: 19; James 3: 17-18 — all GNB)

Peace without justice is not peace. If a tyrant imposes a type of peace by brute force, there is no real peace, for injustices will still exist. True peace is the result of justice and righteousness. A nation may be at peace with its enemies, but if its people are exploited and cowed, the nation is not at peace.

The early Hebrews lived in a covenant relationship with the Lord God which had certain implications. Part of Israel's commitment to the covenant was to care for the needy and the helpless. A faithful Israel was called to live with justice and integrity. The prophets taught that peace and justice were central aspects of the messianic age. Isaiah pointed out that peace is the result of justice and righteousness and, along with other prophets, he predicted a time when God's anointed, the Messiah, would come to Israel to restore justice and peace. Ezekiel, who promised a covenant of peace, condemned false prophets who pretended there was peace.

'"Because they lead my people astray, saying, 'Peace', when there is no peace, and because, when a flimsy wall is built, they cover it with whitewash. . . those prophets of Israel prophesied to Jerusalem and saw visions of peace for her when there was no peace," declares the Sovereign Lord' (Ezekiel 13: 10, 16, NIV).

We only find true inner peace when we are committed to harmony and justice. It is pointless pursuing our own inner peace if our neighbour is lonely, abused, frightened and tyrannised.

There is little justice in a world that denies food to starving people yet spends millions of dollars on the arms race when enough weapons already exist to blow up the planet. We cannot claim that our world is at peace just because no one is firing nuclear weapons. The injustice that massive outlays of funds on weapons rather than food creates, gives the lie to those who claim we live in an era of peace. Being peacemakers means working for justice in our world.

❧❦

There is no *shalom* where excess and bitter poverty co-exist in neighbourhood and nation, when high production is at the expense of wasted nature and neglected quality of life, when the wealth of one group or country is at the expense of others, where [the money spent] on armaments could do so much to relieve suffering. . .

> Jim Punton, *The Community of Shalom: God's Radical Alternative*

True peace is not merely the absence of tension; it is the presence of justice and a sense of human community.

> Martin Luther King

To take the major share of the world's resources from the daily needs of people and use them to make credible our threat to commit mass murder is wrong. Such an action lets others live in abject squalor so that we may possibly survive a nuclear nightmare. If that is not wrong, then nothing is wrong.

> Gordon Cosby, 'Words of Peace'

The nuclear issue is not a political issue — it is a moral and spiritual issue as well.

> Billy Graham, 'Words of Peace'

A fundamental reality that generally escapes us, even during those fleeting moments when we are forced to think about nuclear war, is that the physical and psychological survival of the Hiroshima victims is largely due to the fact that a world existed beyond the disaster. As the incredible magnitude of the destruction became known, medical supplies and help of all kinds were channelled to the city.

If nuclear weapons are ever used again, and there is increasing reason to believe they will be used, there will be no outside world to come to the aid of the survivors. In other words, the good news about nuclear war is that you will probably be killed; the bad news is that you might survive. . .

Anyone who has witnessed the testimony of the Hiroshima survivors, felt the pain in their words, the sadness in their hearts, and seen the grotesque physical evidence of their experience, cannot help but want to take such a small risk for peace. For me the words of

Rosencrantz and Guildenstern in Tom Stoppard's play echoed this: 'There must have been a time, somewhere near the beginning, when we could have said no.'

Mark Hatfield, 'Human Survival'

Rage will not recede where justice does not prevail. . .
wars will not cease unless greed is compelled to go. . .
peace will not come where righteousness does not reign.

Fay Valentine, 'Peace with Justice'

People who are well-off have very different perceptions of life and a very different theological agenda from those who must worry about survival.

W. Brueggemann, *Living Toward a Vision*

It does not require much insight to realise that the great majority of the world's unpeaceful relationships are between unequal parties and are based on injustice and exploitation.

A. Curle, *Mystics to Militants*

Great shepherd of the sheep, let your peace rest on your world family that there may be an end of cruelty, anger, war, persecution, injustice, exploitation and alienation, and the way of love begin to rule among all humankind.

Bruce Prewer, *Australian Prayers*

Lord, make me an instrument of your peace.
Where there is hatred, let me sow love,
Where there is injury, pardon,
Where there is doubt, faith,
Where there is despair, hope,
Where there is sadness, joy.

Francis of Assisi

A Benediction
May the Lord who is just and merciful
grant you peace,
no matter what your circumstances,

no matter where you live,
no matter who you are.
May his peace fill your mind
and his spirit flood your heart. Amen.

The Lord bless you and keep you,
The Lord make his face to shine upon you
and be gracious unto you.
The Lord lift up the light of his countenance upon you
and give you peace,
In your going out
In your coming in
In your rising up
In your lying down
In your labour and your leisure
In your laughter and your tears,
Until you come to stand before him
In that great day when there is no
sunset and no dawn
In the name of the Triune God, Amen.

I have called you friends

Greater love has no-one than this, than the laying down of one's life for one's friends. You are my friends if you do what I command. I no longer call you servants, because a servant does not know the master's business. Instead, I have called you friends, for everything that I learned from my Father I have made known to you.

'Which commandment is the most important of all?'. . . "'Love the Lord your God with all your heart, with all your soul, with all your mind, and with all your strength." The second most important commandment is this: "Love your neighbour as you love yourself."'

And the scripture was fulfilled that says, 'Abraham believed God, and it was credited to him as righteousness,' and he was called God's friend.

Now a man named Lazarus was sick. . . The sisters sent word to Jesus, 'Lord, the one you love is sick.' . . .Jesus loved Martha and her sister and Lazarus.

. . .a friend of tax collectors and 'sinners'.

Come to me, all you who are weary and burdened, and I will give you rest. . . and you will find rest for your souls.

(John 15: 13-15, NIV adapted; Mark 12: 28,30-31, GNB; James 2: 23; John 11: 1, 3, 5; Matthew 11: 19; Matthew 11: 28-29 — all NIV)

When real friends meet, it's like coming home. Genuine friendship offers each person a place of rest and comfort, a place where it's safe to risk self-disclosure. Real friends remain, even after they have glimpsed the brokenness and the hollowness of shattered hopes and fractured dreams. Acquaintances help us celebrate our 'successes', but genuine friends are there beside us through the 'failures' as well.

Jesus offered real and genuine friendship constantly and consistently. He was known as the friend of 'sinners', even the friend of hated tax collectors. He was known to be a dear and close friend of Mary, Martha and their brother at a time when rabbis did not boast friendships with unmarried women. Jesus called those early disciples into friendship, and was clearly surrounded and supported by an even wider circle of women and men he valued and regarded as friends. We can be assured that our discipleship today includes friendship with our elder brother Jesus, just as that larger group of early disciples was assured of his friendship and love for them.

When asked what was the greatest commandment of all, Jesus singled out a threefold friendship — love of God, love of self and love of neighbours, those fellow travellers along life's journey. As we travel, we can experience the amazing joy of such a threefold friendship entwined through every fibre of life. Without such interconnected relationships, life itself would become lifeless.

We can, therefore, journey on without the fear of being alienated from God, or locked into inner isolation, or separated through hostility from fellow travellers. We travel together in safety, rest and comfort so that the dangerous, tiring and uncomfortable realities of our journey do not overpower us. We keep going then, knowing we are enfolded in God's unfailing threefold love, all the way. All the way home.

❧❀❧

What language shall I borrow
To thank thee, dearest Friend?

Bernard of Clairvaux

Every deed and every relationship is surrounded by an atmosphere of silence. Friendship needs no words — it is solitude delivered from the anguish of loneliness.

Dag Hammarskjöld, *Markings*

God is a compassionate God. This means, first of all, that he is a God who has chosen to be God-with-us. To be able to know and feel better this divine solidarity, let us explore the experience of someone being truly with us.

When do we receive real comfort and consolation? Is it when someone teaches us how to think or act? Is it when we receive advice about where to go or what to do? Is it when we hear words of reassurance and hope? Sometimes, perhaps. But what really counts is that in moments of pain and suffering someone stays with us. More important than any particular action or word of advice is the simple presence of someone who cares. When someone says to us in the midst of a crisis, 'I do not know what to say or what to do, but I want you to realise that I am with you, that I will not leave you alone,' we have a friend through whom we can find consolation and comfort.

Donald P. McNeill, Douglas A. Morrison,
Henri J.M. Nouwen, *Compassion*

Real friendship and genuine community provide a healing and sustaining environment, fostering the life and growth of us human beings.

Morton T. Kelsey, *Caring*

The longest journey
Is the journey inwards.

Dag Hammarskjöld, *Markings*

What a friend!
He is a friend that sticks closer than a brother.
He is a friend of publicans and sinners.
He is the friend who stood betrayed in the Garden. . . Around him stood the soldiers and the hirelings of the high priest.
Before him stood Judas, the betrayer.
'Judas my friend, why are you here?'. . . he called him 'friend!' It is a kindly term. . . signifying closeness of relationship, even of purpose.

He is the friend who received wounds in his hands and his side. . . the friend who laid down his life for his own friends.

But more — he laid down his life for his enemies.

Well we might say, 'What a friend!'

John Robinson, Under His Wings

How long the road is. But, for all the time the journey has already taken, how you have needed every second of it in order to learn what the road passes by.

Dag Hammarskjöld, Markings

I am still waiting for the telephone call which will tell me that my college friend is dead, and I know that even though those of us who love her deeply may not be near her hospital bed, we are nevertheless with her. And I think of a mutual friend who died a few years ago at ninety-three, a great lady of vision and laughter who never lost her ability to change and to go into the unknown, and I feel that she is waiting at the gates, to hold out her hand. . .

Madeleine L'Engle, And it Was Good

Night is drawing nigh. . .

For all that has been — Thanks!

To all that shall be — Yes!

Dag Hammarskjöld, Markings

My loving God and Friend, I am so grateful you are my companion along the way. This journey has indeed seemed long and, at times, neverending. Yet I've needed every second in order to learn from all that has passed by. And I've needed every friend along the way who has comforted me, consoled me and celebrated together with me.

As each new day dawns like the tender unfolding of a fern, may I experience your friendship anew with gratitude and joy. And may your peace and gracious love so enfold us all that our shared journey becomes a sign of hope in the midst of a despairing world.

A Benediction

And now, respond with delight and joy to the One who calls you friend. Go forth and travel, knowing you are not alone, ever. Your journey continues with the sure and deep knowledge that God goes with you and enfolds you in an amazing threefold love, wrapping you round with unbreakable cords designed to hold and sustain you through every step of life's unfolding journey for you. May you grow in understanding and friendly acceptance of your own uniqueness, while enjoying the wonder of diverse yet interconnected friendships with fellow travellers all along the way. Amen.

48

Who is my neighbour?

Then the Lord said, 'I have seen the affliction of my people who are in Egypt. . . and I have come down to deliver them.'

The Spirit of the Lord is upon me, because he has anointed me to preach good news to the poor. . .

For he is our peace, who has made us both one, and has broken down the dividing wall of hostility, by abolishing in his flesh the law of commandments and ordinances, that he might create in himself one new humanity in place of the two, so making peace, and might reconcile us both to God in one body through the cross, thereby bringing the hostility to an end.

And all who believed were together and had all things in common.

I hate, I despise your feasts, and I take no delight in your solemn assemblies. . . Take away from me the noise of your songs; to the melody of your harps I will not listen. But let justice roll down like waters, and righteousness like an everflowing stream.

For which is the greater, one who sits at table, or one who serves? Is it not the one who sits at table? But I am among you as one who serves.

Which of these three, do you think, proved neighbour to the man who fell among the robbers? He said, 'The one who showed mercy on him.' And Jesus said to him, 'Go and do likewise.'

Then the righteous will answer him, 'Lord, when did we see you hungry and feed you, or thirsty and give you drink?. . .' And the King will answer them, 'Truly, I say to you, as you did it to one of the least of these who are members of my family, you did it to me.'

You cannot serve God and mammon.

There was a rich man, who was clothed in purple and fine linen and who feasted sumptuously every day. And at his gate lay a poor man named Lazarus. . . The poor man died and was carried by the angels to Abraham's bosom. The rich man also died and was buried; and in Hades, being in torment, he lifted up his eyes, and saw Abraham far off and Lazarus in his bosom. And he called out, 'Father Abraham, have mercy upon me, and send Lazarus to dip the end of his finger in water and cool my tongue; for I am in anguish in this flame. . .'

Whoever says, 'I am in the light,' while hating a brother or sister is in the darkness still. Whoever loves a brother or sister abides in the light, and in it there is no cause for stumbling.

And I heard the voice of the Lord saying, 'Whom shall I send, and who will go for us?' Then I said, 'Here am I! Send me.'

(Exodus 3: 7-8; Luke 4: 18 — both RSV; Ephesians 2: 14-16, NRSV; Acts 2: 44; Amos 5: 21, 23-24; Luke 22: 27; Luke 10: 36-37 — all RSV; Matthew 25: 37,40, NRSV; Matthew 6: 24; Luke 16: 19-20, 22-24 — both RSV; 1 John 2: 9-10, NRSV; Isaiah 6: 8, RSV)

To be a neighbour is to be closer than just living next door. It is to own a space in our heart for anyone who wants to enter and sit there. It is for the neighbour to enter into the deepest needs of the visitor and if necessary to be actively helpful.

Where does one see neighbourliness in action?

The Christian sees true neighbourliness in God — the Blessed Trinity.

Israel, the chosen people of God the Father, fell on hard times. Through Moses, God asked Pharaoh to let his people go. What he longed for he soon made possible. He gave his chosen ones a plot of land in which to live. He gave them the Law by which they could live with one another. He chastised them when they failed him, yet he never forsook them.

As the Father is, so is the Son.

The second person of the Holy Trinity emptied himself of the fullness of divinity to become one of us, to be a neighbour to all people for all time.

In his first sermon at Nazareth, Jesus proclaimed the good news that the great age had come in which he would journey alongside the marginalised and the disadvantaged, even unto his own death.

In the world, the rich man would not be free from criticism if he ignored Lazarus at his gate. The priest and the Levite, the custodians of the structures of the church, would always come under divine judgment when they separated themselves from the ugly environment in which the unfortunate lived.

Christ broke the middle wall of partition separating the rich and the poor, the holy and the unholy, the lovely and the ugly. He devised the solidarity binding all disciples together as 'new people' leading the way to neighbourliness.

By his final act of self-offering on the cross, Jesus showed that there was no personal limit to the path that he had trod.

As the Son is, so is the Holy Spirit.

Jesus bequeathed to society the Spirit-filled community in Jerusalem — the church. This new community, which was to be God's chosen neighbour to the world, could not grow in neighbourliness unless the Holy Spirit, the third person of the Holy Trinity, were present among its members.

This community *did* care for the poor. They did share possessions and they felt the needs and hurts of the world.

So our model for neighbourliness is God in action.

And, we may now ask, What is required for anyone to be neighbourly?

Firstly, we must evaluate the world in which we live. As people living near to one another, we live in tension and know that something is wrong. Yet our problem is not one of ignorance. The greatest contribution to our stress is our defective will. We war against others. We neglect the small people. We fail to hear the cries of the hurting. Often we even add to their pain by our acquiescence in the corporate evil of the world and by the daily expressions of our own ill will.

We live in the company of thieves and robbers and often we join them. We plunder the property of others. We squander what is our own, ignoring the cries of those who wish to share our bounty — they are the despised poor, the casualties of our selfishness.

Secondly, we must apply our knowledge of Jesus as God's model of neighbourliness.

Jesus had compassion on all those who were in need because he *was* one of the poor — the suffering servant.

Jesus was involved in social service. He cared about those who were not clothed, those who were thirsty, those who were hungry, those who were in prison. He knew that each person needed to be liberated from basic human deprivations, and called upon his followers to assist in this mission.

To follow Jesus is to grow into true neighbourliness. This begins from the heart, which must be pure before God and before each person whom we meet.

There is no place in neighbourliness for filling up the barn to protect ourselves against possible want. Humanly speaking, Jesus must be our example as a neighbour. As he had compassion on the crowd who were hungry and living away from home, so must we reflect his compassion with our gift of fish and barley loaves.

There must be no limit to what we will give if it is necessary to relieve need. Each of us must 'live simply so that others may simply live'.

Jesus also recognised a place for social action in the context of structural oppression. In his mind the structures of the church and the structures of society were intended by God to open the window providing for all a vision of life fulfilled.

Neighbourliness here involves the illumination of the minds of those who are oppressed, so that they may become aware that theirs is an unjust situation in which their rights as members of the human family have been violated.

Such 'conscientisation' and humanisation motivate a process of reflection that must lead to social action to remove the injustice.

Yet the deliverance from bondage does not mark the end of this journey.

If we are to express neighbourliness to those in need, we must not stop short when there has been liberation from hunger and oppression. The disadvantaged must be translated from the situation of human want to an environment where there is human love impregnated with the love of God. Every person must be liberated from the hold of evil to become a member of God's kingdom of love.

True neighbourliness demands living within the space in God's heart and allowing others to live within the space of our heart.

❧❧

The mystery of God's love is not that he takes our pains away, but that he first wants to share them with us.

Donald P. McNeill, Douglas A. Morrison,
Henri J.M. Nouwen, *Compassion*

Jesus did not stand alongside the haughty and rich. Rather he stood on the side of the hungry, thirsty and naked, strangers and prisoners, harlots and publicans. All these fall in the category of the 'poor', for they have no one to stand on their side.

Orlando Costas, *The Church and its Mission*

Our way lay from one to another of the most wretched dwellings, reeking with horrible odours. . . In a room in one of these places. . . there lay, in an old egg-box which the mother had begged from a shop, a little feeble, wasted, wan sick child. With his little wasted face, and his little hot, worn hands folded over his breast, and his little bright, attentive eyes, I can see him now, as I have seen him for several years, looking steadily at us. . . There he lay, quite quiet, quite patient, saying never a word. He seldom cried, the mother said; he seldom complained; 'he

lay there, seemin' to wonder what it was a' aboot'. . .
There he lay looking at us, saying, in his silence. . . 'Will
you please tell me what this means, strange man?'

Charles Dickens

We know, of course, that the church has always suffered
from the tensions of society. It ought not to surprise us
to see coming out of the same land a movement of
domination and exploitation together with the message of
freedom imbedded in the gospel. What is hard to take,
however, is the way that the values undergirding the
imperialistic philosophy and practice of these nations make
their way into the church, distorting the gospel sometimes
beyond recognition.

Orlando Costas, *The Church and its Mission*

Falsehood is not found among them; and they love one
another, and from widows they do not turn away their
esteem; and they deliver the orphan from him who treats
him harshly. And those who have give to those who have
not, without boasting. And when they see a stranger, they
take that one into their homes and rejoice as if a member
of their own family had arrived; for they do not call them
brothers or sisters after the flesh, but after the spirit and
in God.

Aristides

They dwell in their own countries, but simply as sojourners.
As citizens, they share in all things as if foreigners. Every
foreign land is to them as their native country, and every
land of their birth as land of strangers. . . They are in
the flesh, but they do not live after the flesh. They pass
their days on earth, but they are citizens of heaven.

Diognetus

Justice, not power, is the essence of the state. Remove
justice and what are kingdoms but gangs of criminals on
a large scale? What are criminal gangs but petty
kingdoms? A gang is a group of people under the command of a leader, bound by a compact of association, in

which the plunder is divided according to an agreed convention. The point is that justice cannot be had where the true God is not worshipped.

Robert Webber, *The Secular Saint*

We must listen to the poor, exist with them, try to stand in their shoes; and then be willing for them to take a full share in leadership and decision-making. That would mean uncomfortable changes for each of our churches. The church must risk losing its image of respectability.

David Sheppard, *Bias to the Poor*

We, the privileged, should ask, Why are others so different from us? Why are we without pain and they suffer? In looking at us, the hurting say that it is bad enough that individually we should make our contribution to the world's pain, but more damnable is it when we band together as corporate thieves. We manipulate and hurt through decisions around a board table or in the chambers of government to reap a harvest of gain for ourselves and provide a famine and a desert for those who suffer.

Economically and politically, the powerless are so imprisoned within their deprivations that they become paralysed and unable to help themselves while we try to protect ourselves at any cost against disease, the world, the flesh and the devil.

John Rymer

The tension remains between being a church of the area and being a church which is different from the area in the right kind of way; believing and worshipping Christians will want to share what is to them the best news in the world with their neighbours.

David Sheppard, *Bias to the Poor*

Nevertheless the church reaffirms the primacy of her spiritual vocation and refuses to replace the proclamation of the kingdom by the proclamation of forms and of human liberation; she even states that her contribution to liberation is incomplete if she neglects to proclaim salvation in Jesus Christ.

Pope Paul VI

It is a great gift to bring out love, even greater than loving.

Ann Todd

Break through your shell of selfishness.
If you do not
know yourself,
you will never know
others.
Selfishness is the deepest root
of all unhappiness
— your own and
— that of the whole world.
It feeds an insatiable hunger
that first eats up
everything belonging to others
and then causes a creature
to devour itself.

Dom Helder Camara, *Hoping Against All Hope*

. . .The Bishop said that he had just seen a terrible sight: in front of the cathedral was a woman with three small children and a baby clinging to her neck. He saw that they were fainting from hunger. The baby seemed to be dead. He said: 'Give the baby some milk, woman!' 'I can't, my lord,' she answered. . . Finally because of his insistence, she opened her blouse. Her breast was bleeding; the baby sucked violently at it. And sucked blood. . . The bishop knelt down in front of the woman, placed his hand on the baby's head, and there and then vowed that as long as such hunger existed, he would feed at least one hungry child each day.

Leonardo Boff, Clodovis Boff, *Introducing Liberation Theology*

Worldly holiness

(J.G. Davies)

All the saints greet you, especially those of Caesar's household.

What shall I bring to the Lord, the God of heaven when I come to worship him? Shall I bring the best calves to burn as offerings before him?. . . No, the Lord has told us what is good. What he requires of us is this: to do what is just, to show constant love, and to live in humble fellowship with our God.

He opened the book and found the place where it was written, 'The Spirit of the Lord is upon me, because he has anointed me to preach good news to the poor. He has sent me to proclaim release to the captives and recovery of sight to the blind, to set at liberty those who are oppressed, to proclaim the acceptable year of the Lord. . .' And he began to say to them, 'Today this scripture has been fulfilled in your hearing.'

Do you think you are a king because you compete in cedar? Did not your father eat and drink and do justice and righteousness? Then it was well with him. He judged the cause of the poor and needy; then it was well. Is not this to know me? says the Lord.

And the King will answer, 'Truly, I say to you, as you did it to one of the least of these members of my family, you did it to me.'

In that day not a bell on a war-horse but shall be inscribed, 'Holy to the Lord,' and the pots in the house of the Lord shall be like the bowls before the altar. Every pot in Jerusalem and Judah shall be holy to the Lord of Hosts.

What God the Father considers to be pure and genuine

religion is this: to take care of orphans and widows in
their suffering and to keep oneself from being corrupted
by the world.

And the Word became flesh and dwelt among us, full
of grace and truth.

(Philippians 4: 22, RSV; Micah 6: 6,8, GNB; Luke 4: 18-19, 21;
Jeremiah 22: 15-16 — both RSV; Matthew 25: 40 NRSV; Zechariah
14: 20-21, NEB; James 1: 27, GNB; John 1: 14, RSV)

The word 'spiritual' must surely be one of the most ambiguous in the Christian vocabulary. A preacher known to
me was accused by some members of his congregation as
'too practical', with the strong implication that therefore he
was not spiritual enough. This, intended as a criticism, was
received by him as a compliment. There are Christians who
respond to any suggestion that the affairs of the church might
be conducted in a more businesslike way as unspiritual.

In short, some who claim to be more spiritual than their
fellows are among the unkindest, most arrogant, most
judgmental, most self-righteous people one could meet.
The old Puritan had people like this in mind when he
said of a cantankerous brother, who claimed to be spiritual,
'I will not say, "the zeal of the Lord's house hath eaten
him up," but it doth seem to have devoured the greater
part of his good manners.' Then there was a little girl
who prayed, 'O Lord, make all the bad people good, and
all the good people nice.' There are some spiritual people
whose behaviour negates the gospel they profess.

In recent years, the church has been greatly occupied
with discovering the kind of spirituality which fits the
twentieth century, and one of the changes which has made
the work of the clergy more difficult has been the insistence that the church should be involved in practical
service to the community in which it is placed, with no
thought of any possible advantages to itself through increased membership. It is ministry entirely without
strings attached.

This has been good and healthy, but in some cases has
gone too far, substituting social service for the church's

primary task of evangelism, forgetting the dictum that such a church is like a body without a soul, while the church that neglects such a service is like a soul without a body.

To anybody unfamiliar with what the Bible has to say about this kind of thing, the reference of Paul to the 'saints in Caesar's household' in Philippi seems like the ultimate incongruity. The locus of Christian service is not so much the precincts of the church, but the world in which we live, and move, and have our being.

In the Bible, there is no such distinction, as is commonly made, between 'material' and 'spiritual'. It was Archbishop William Temple who reminded us that Christianity is the most avowedly materialistic of the world's greatest religions. God created the world; it belongs to him; it is the scene of his activity; it is the property location for the Christian life, where we Christians are called to express our discipline and devotion.

What the Hebrews had in mind when they spoke of 'the world' was not simply a physical entity. They meant a lived-in world, a world of human decisions and mistakes, of hopes and frustrations. When God made his final revelation of himself it was described by John in these terms: 'The Word became flesh, and dwelt among us.'

So a spirituality for the twentieth century must be incarnational. The Creator God is to be met and known and worshipped, not by turning our backs on history, but through obedience to facts and events, physical facts, economic facts, political and international events. When the Word became flesh, he became involved in everything human, with nothing left.

So a Christian spirituality for our day involves his followers in human need, wherever it exists.

The Christian must be concerned with justice (a great word among the Old Testament prophets), hunger, housing for the homeless, poverty and peace. 'Is not this to know me,' says the Lord. For these are his concerns, and we must share them if we are to be his disciples.

❧

We have to seek a worldly holiness, i.e. sanctity is to be so understood that it involves acceptance of and involvement in the world, in the realm both of I-Thou and I-It. Secular existence is the locus of the encounter — the holy gives it meaning and rescues it from sheer absurdity. Indeed, one cannot have a 'spiritual' life apart from one's life as a human being in the world. . . Hence, to live a true 'religious' life means to live a truly human life, and this means to live a life truly responsive to the holy, and this, in turn, means to live a life truly responsive to others and to one's total situation. . . we can say that to be a fully mature person and to be a saint are the same thing.

J.G. Davies, *Every Day God*

The sacred is understood as the depth of the secular, or, to put it another way, the secular becomes transparent, so that in and through the multiplicity of things and activities belonging to this world, we become aware of the one creative Source that holds them all together and maintains them in being. . .

I might illustrate the difference between the two by recalling two chapels that I visited in the past two years. One was the Chapel of the Transfiguration at the foot of the Rocky Mountains in Wyoming. At the east end, instead of a reredos, there is a plate glass window affording a view of the mountain peaks. Superimposed on these, as one looks out is the altar cross. This symbolism does indeed speak of God in the world, present in the majesty of his creation. Yet perhaps to the contemporary person, on vacation from the city, it all seems rather romantic and unreal, and one has the impression that this chapel is more of a tourist attraction than a contemporary place of worship.

The other chapel was the Chapel of Industry, part of the new Coventry Cathedral. Here again a clear expanse of window opens out, but the view is of the factories and industrial installations of one of England's most up-to-date cities. The symbolism also speaks of God in the world, but here he is seen in the human efforts and the human relations that twine together in the complex structure of an urban society.

John Macquarrie, *God and Secularity*

On the other hand, we have the religious person who is not ethical. In an old 'Moocher's Map', passed from hand to hand a century ago with its conventional signs to indicate the nature of the reception likely to meet the tramp at various doors, there is one which appears only occasionally. The interpretation, given by the vagrant composer, is 'religious but kind'. There is a world of criticism in the 'but'. The picture of soulless piety is, of course, a caricature of religion, as is also the person who is kind because it is a religious duty to be kind — and how we hate to be shown dutiful kindness.

Edgar Primrose Dickie, God Is Light

I once visited a prison where an instruction was exhibited, admittedly yellow with age. In effect it said that I was not to converse with the prisoner about his or her case or past or family or future, but was to confine myself to 'spiritual subjects'. How, in Bible terms, can you divorce a soul from case, family or future? I broke the regulations in the name of God.

George F. Macleod, Only One Way Left

I am not supposed to be a gilt-edged spook with wings, making a holy hum, one-half human and one-half angel. I am supposed to be a normal, natural, down-to-earth human, full of creation's practical spirit — the thirteenth chapter of Corinthians dressed up in modern clothes.

Howard Butt, The Velvet-covered Brick

The second thing that is being discovered (in the House Church Movement in the UK) is the meaning of holiness. By uniting the words 'holy' and 'common', hitherto defined as opposites, Christianity created something entirely new and, in that juxtaposition, the religion of the Word stands or falls. By taking the Holy Communion from the cathedral to the scullery, the 'offence' of Christian holiness is once more made unequivocal. . .

There is a still deeper reason why what appears to be self-evident, taking religion into politics, is so controversial. That is because most of us are only half-converted to the justification for it, and we take out our uneasiness on other people. . . what is the biblical basis for involvement in politics at all. . .? Notice that I said the biblical basis, and not merely the New Testament basis. For precisely the trouble so often is that we isolate the teaching and example of Jesus. We lift him out of the stream of history, and then conclude that he was not involved in it — and that we need not be either. But Jesus came, as he himself makes abundantly clear, as the last word of a response to God in history, which he was there not to negate but to fulfil. What that response was had been hammered out in the blood and sweat of the Old Testament story.

John A.T. Robinson, *On Being the Church in the World*

It is precisely at the point where the word 'spiritual' makes its appearance that many contemporary Christians think that they have entered the realm of unreality, of otherworldiness and, therefore, of irrelevance. . . [Paul saw that] the person who was truly spiritual acknowledged that the God who had taken human form, and had thereby made sacred the bodies of humans, was the Lord of life, of our minds and of our bodies. Likewise John saw the need for definition, and for a test of Christian spirituality. He opposed any notion of the 'spiritual' that was not fully explicable in terms of the incarnation (1 John 4: 15). . . and, looking at him (Jesus Christ), we are forced to the conclusion that the 'spiritual' is as material as the incarnate Christ.

Bruce Kendrick, *The New Humanity*

Jesus was not crucified in a cathedral between two candles, but on a cross between two thieves; on the town garbage heap; at a crossroad so cosmopolitan that they had to write his title in Hebrew and in Latin and in Greek (or shall we say in English, in Bantu and in Afrikaans?); at the kind of place where cynics talk smut, and thieves curse, and soldiers gamble. Because that is where he died. And that is what he died about. And that is where the church should be. . .

George F. Macleod, *Only One Way Left*

Father, forgive me for wanting a private sign, when your public sign, Jesus Christ, awaits my discovery. I seek so haltingly to follow and serve him, because I have caught a glimpse in him — of how wide the horizons of worship and service really are. Forbid it that I should try to be so heavenly-minded that I am no earthly use, or try to be more spiritual than he found it necessary to be. Give me a deeper awareness of the needs of other people; make me more sensitive to how they feel, even as my Master was. Help me to do my daily work, whatever it is, and however filled with drudgery, as my service to him. And let my worship encompass the attempt to meet the needs of other people, and heal their hurts.

We are all what we are because you are mindful of us, because you created us and recreated us in Jesus. Lord, because of all your bounty it is impossible that I should seek to live only for myself. You are calling me to be a steward of your goodness, saying to me in so many ways, 'Freely you have received, freely give.' Amen.

Forgive us if we label others, if we substitute slogans for thought, and estimate our fellows without first-hand knowledge of them. Forgive us because we fail to see people because we are preoccupied with abstractions like 'principles' and 'justice' and 'tradition'; when we are more intent on being right than reconciled. Forgive us, too, when we refrain from judgment for the wrong reasons — through fear of recrimination or lack of sensitiveness. May it become our passion, as it is yours, to enter into fellowship with others, to win people not for our party labels, but for the truth. Save us when we isolate ourselves in self-righteousness, when we prefer to win an argument than to make a friend, and when we exalt order and safety over the good of the human person.

W.B.J. Martin, *Acts of Worship*

A Benediction

Now the God of all grace who has called you to his eternal glory in Christ, after you have suffered for a little while, support, strengthen, and establish you. To him be the power forever and ever. Amen.

1 Peter 5: 10-11, NRSV

As righteous as a beermug

Righteousness and justice are the foundation of your throne. . . O Lord.

With what shall I come before the Lord and bow down before the exalted God? Shall I come before him with burnt offerings, with calves a year old? Will the Lord be pleased with thousands of rams, with ten thousand rivers of oil? Shall I offer my firstborn for my transgression, the fruit of my body for the sin of my soul? He has showed you, [O mortal], what is good. And what does the Lord require of you? To act justly and to love mercy and to walk humbly with your God.

I hate, I despise your religious feasts; I cannot stand your assemblies. . . Away with the noise of your songs! I will not listen to the music of your harps. But let justice roll on like a river, righteousness like a never-failing stream!

Is not this the kind of fasting I have chosen: to loose the chains of injustice and untie the cords of the yoke, to set the oppressed free and break every yoke? Is it not to share your food with the hungry and to provide the homeless with shelter — when you see the naked, to clothe them, and not to turn away from your own flesh and blood? Then your light will break forth like the dawn, and your healing will quickly appear; then your righteousness will go before you, and the glory of the Lord will be your rearguard. Then you will call, and the Lord will answer; you will cry for help, and he will say: Here am I. If you do away with the yoke of oppression, with the pointing finger and malicious talk, and if you spend yourselves on behalf of the hungry and satisfy the needs of the oppressed, then your light will rise in the darkness, and your night will become like the noonday. The Lord will guide you always.

Blessed are those who hunger and thirst for righteousness, for they will be filled. . . Blessed are those who are persecuted because of righteousness, for theirs is the kingdom of heaven.

(Psalm 89: 14; Micah 6: 6-8; Amos 5: 21,23-24 — all NIV; Isaiah 58: 6-11, NIV/NRSV; Matthew 5: 6,10, NIV)

When we hear the word 'righteous' today, it is quite likely that we associate it with vague notions of unworldly piety. Thus someone described as righteous is pictured as highly religious, law-abiding and scrupulous in the extreme. (We may in our own minds even add the word 'self' before the 'righteous'.)

Yet in Old English, one meaning of 'righteous' was much more ordinary and earthy. Something or someone that acted according to their true nature could have been described as righteous. Thus a beermug that held the beer well, and was good to use, might be called 'righteous'. So too might a mayor, a wife, a sheep dog, a hammer or a law.

The Bible's picture of righteousness is rather closer to this than it is to a head-in-the-clouds piety. For us today, being righteous means being what God created us to be. . . children who reflect the Father's likeness. For God is a righteous God, and his righteousness is not abstract. He acts to maintain and restore righteousness in all things. That is what his justice is. . . action taken to restore righteousness.

The idea that we can be righteous by disengaging from the dirt and struggle of everyday life is totally foreign to that biblical way of thinking. It would be akin to putting a fine pewter beermug onto a mantelpiece, keeping it beautifully polished, but never actually using it. It may draw a great deal of admiration. It may even be described as a thing of beauty. But by definition it is not a 'righteous beermug' until it is taken down and used as it is meant to be used.

❧❦❧

Christians, like Christ our head, are filled and made rich by faith. . . This faith is our life, our righteousness, and our salvation: it saves us and makes us acceptable, and bestows upon us all things that are Christ's. . .

Although Christians are thus free from all works, we ought in this liberty to empty ourselves, take upon ourselves the form of a servant. . . be found in human form, and to serve, help and in every way deal with our neighbours as we see that God through Christ has dealt and still deals with us. . . Each ought to think: 'Although I am unworthy and condemned, my God has given me in Christ all the riches of righteousness and salvation without any merit on my part, out of pure, free mercy, so that from now on I need nothing except faith which believes that this is true. Why should I not therefore freely, joyfully, with all my heart and with an eager will do all things which I know are pleasing and acceptable to such a Father who has overwhelmed me with his inestimable riches? I will therefore give myself as a Christ to my neighbour, just as Christ offered himself to me. . .'

From faith thus flow forth love and joy in the Lord, and from love a joyful, willing and free mind that serves one's neighbour willingly and takes no account of gratitude or ingratitude, of praise or blame, of gain or loss.

Martin Luther, *Freedom of a Christian*

T: The trouble with the youth of today, George — they just don't have time for the holy words of Jesus.

G: Very true, Trev.

T: They'll help the poor, mind.

G: Oh yes, they'll help the poor.

T: And they'll speak out for the captives, all right.
And work to rid the world of blindness.

G: Yes, that as well.

T: And fight for the oppressed of the world, of course.

G: Don't need to tell me, Trev — they'll fight for the oppressed all hours of the day, it seems.

T: And yet, do you know what they don't have time for, George?

G: What's that Trev?

T: They don't have time for the holy words of Jesus. Makes you weep, doesn't it?

Simon Parke, 'The Holy Words'

I went about, covetous of riches, and I found not Jesus. I ran in wantonness of the flesh, and I found not Jesus. I sat in companies of worldly mirth, and I found not Jesus. In all these I sought Jesus, but I found him not. For he let me know by his grace that he is not found in the land of soft living.

Therefore I turned another way, and I ran about in poverty, and I found Jesus, poorly born into the world, laid in a crib and wrapped in cloths. I wandered in the suffering of weariness, and I found Jesus weary in the way, tormented with hunger, thirst and cold, filled with reproofs and blame. I sat by myself alone, fleeing the vanities of the world, and I found Jesus in the desert, fasting on the mountain, praying alone. I went the way of pain and penance, and I found Jesus bound, scourged, given gall to drink, nailed to the Cross, hanging on the Cross, and dying on the Cross.

Richard Rolle, fourteenth century

Jesus never commanded his disciples to think, to contemplate, to consider, to read, to study, to reflect, to ponder; his words were active: feed, heal, go, seek, give, find, sow, plant, build.

Anne Rowthorn, *The Liberation of the Laity*

Christians who believe in a neat 'order is of God, conflict of the devil' formulation would do well to ponder that in countries where Christians are not so materially and politically benefitted by the social order as in the West, this neat distinction is implausible. Thus black Christians in South Africa. . . and German members of the Confessing Church during the Second World War took it for granted that the social order is not wholly from God.

J.A. Walter, *A Long Way from Home*

More helpful than all wisdom is one draught of simple human pity that will not forsake us.

George Eliot, *The Mill on the Floss*

We are not made for justice from our fellows, but for love, which is greater than justice, and by including supersedes justice. Mere justice is an impossibility, a fiction of analysis. . . Justice to be justice must be much more than justice. Love is the law of our condition, without which we can no more render justice than a person can keep a straight line, walking in the dark.

George MacDonald

God of justice and righteousness, we admit that we do not burn with the same sense of justice and righteousness as you intend. We who benefit in so many ways from injustice; we who seek so often to limit righteousness to appearances; we pray that you will change these hearts of stone into hearts of flesh so that, by your grace, we may begin to display the family likeness of you, our righteous and just Father.

Eternal God and Father, by whose power we are created and by whose love we are redeemed: guide and strengthen us by your Spirit, that we may give ourselves to your service, and live this day in love to one another and to you; through Jesus Christ our Lord. Amen.

Australian Prayer Book

A Benediction
In love and in faith,
May we follow thee,
With self-denial, steadfastness, and courage. . .
Give us
A pure heart
That we may see thee,
A humble heart
That we may hear thee,
A heart to love
That we may serve thee,
A heart of faith
That we may live thee.

Dag Hammarskjöld

51

The childlikeness of God

For to us a child is born, to us a son is given; and the government will be upon his shoulder, and his name will be called 'Wonderful Counsellor, Mighty God, Everlasting Father, Prince of Peace'.

Now the birth of Jesus Christ took place in this way. When his mother Mary had been betrothed to Joseph, before they came together, she was found to be with child of the Holy Spirit; and her husband Joseph, being a just man and unwilling to put her to shame, resolved to divorce her quietly. But as he considered this, behold, an angel of the Lord appeared to him in a dream, saying, 'Joseph, son of David, do not fear to take Mary your wife, for that which is conceived in her is of the Holy Spirit; she will bear a son, and you shall call his name Jesus, for he will save his people from their sins.'

At that time the disciples came to Jesus, saying, 'Who is the greatest in the kingdom of heaven?' And calling to him a child, he put him in the midst of them, and said, 'Truly, I say to you, unless you turn and become like children, you will never enter the kingdom of heaven. Whoever becomes humble like this child is the greatest in the kingdom of heaven. Whoever receives one such child in my name receives me, but if any of you causes one of these little ones who believe in me to sin, it would be better for you to have a great millstone fastened round your neck and to be drowned in the depth of the sea.'

And they were bringing children to him that he might touch them; and the disciples rebuked them. But when Jesus saw it he was indignant, and said to them, 'Let the children come to me, do not hinder them; for to such belongs the kingdom of God. Truly, I say to you, whoever does not receive the kingdom of God like a child shall not enter it.' And he took them in his arms and blessed them, laying his hands upon them.

When the time had fully come, God sent forth his Son, born of woman, born under the law, to redeem those who were under the law, so that we might receive adoption as children. And because you are children, God has sent the Spirit of his Son into your hearts, crying, 'Abba! Father!'

(Isaiah 9: 6; Matthew 1: 18-21 — both RSV; Matthew 18: 1-6, NRSV; Mark 10: 13-16, RSV; Galatians 4: 4-6, NRSV)

In the image of God we were created. Not just as adults, but as children also, we mirror God's nature.

A God who chooses to become human. A God who knows what being a child is. A God who chooses vulnerability, entering the world from the womb of a woman, living and growing in the world through the stage we call childhood. Growing at last to maturity.

Who else but a God who shares our childlikeness would affirm a child as the symbol of the kingdom of God? What kind of a God is it who calls us to become as a child to understand wisdom? Who but a childlike God would warn us that our judgment comes in the measure that we brutalise, neglect or damage a child? Who but a God of youthfulness would make a child the host at the great banquet feast of the King?

The prophecy is there. A little child shall lead them. What is this strange paradox we confront; the powerless is the most powerful, the victim is the judge, the guest is the host?

This kind of God takes a flute and plays for us in the market place, inviting us to dance. A dancing God then? A playful God, a laughing, joyous, celebrating God? For just as the child in us remains, no matter what our age, so also does the child in us reflect the childlikeness of the God who created us. A God full of surprises.

There are few theological writers who can penetrate so quickly into the heart of the mystery of life as a child. As we get older, we become more verbose, more pompous, more inclined to make simple things more complex than they need to be. The incomprehensibility of God, the unfathomable nature of God, the God beyond God, become subjects of our reflection. We may be more learned but less wise.

Jesus seemed clear about the role of children. They, he said to his disciples once, when he placed a child in the midst of them, are the ones who are bearers of the kingdom. Meditate upon that for a moment. Children open our eyes to the presence and claim of the kingdom of God. Something in them — vulnerability, acceptance, spontaneous gratitude, trust and delight in the givenness of things, enables them to reflect the light of God's purposes to us.

Reflect a little more. In a child there is always openness to the Other, a twofold relationship of giving and receiving, of offering and responding, of willingness on one side and grateful acceptance on the other.

'Unless you become as a child,' Jesus said, 'you will not enter the kingdom of God.' What Jesus meant by this statement is elusive and even frightening. We echo the bewilderment of Nicodemus, 'Can we enter our mother's womb a second time and be born?' (John 3: 4).

Perhaps, then, a child gives off that light which points us to God, a God who is simple, direct in his unswerving regard for us, always inviting us to new discoveries, welcoming us into the vast mystery of his vulnerability, love and suffering.

The childlikeness of God is more than a metaphor. Part of the divine nature is forever childlike, forever spontaneously reaching out, forever being creative and active and searching. The Christian claim about incarnation is founded on the conviction that all that we are is taken up into the very being of God and transformed, renewed, recreated beyond imagining. An unexpected, unpredictable God is a childlike God.

Our struggle should be to remain young enough to understand this childlike God. . .

❧

He started to re-arrange the paints and straighten up the mess.

'Do you feel that you must put them in a certain order?' I asked.

'Oh yes,' he said. 'There are twelve brushes and twelve colours.'

He laughed.

'Do you think they should always be in a certain order?' I asked.

'Oh yes,' he said with a grin. 'That is, unless they are all mixed up.'

'Then either way is all right?'

'In here,' he said, 'remember, in here, it's all right just to be.'

Virginia Axline, *Dibbs in Search of Self*

Be not lax
in celebrating.
Be not lazy
in the festive service of God.
Be ablaze with enthusiasm.
Let us be an alive,
burning offering
before the altar of God.

Hildegard of Bingen

In the light of the incarnation, childhood can no longer be regarded as merely a provisional and a preparatory episode. . . Our theology of childhood concentrates on the continuous now of the child's life. . . A child at any age may be wholly human and wholly God's.

The Child in the Church

If the kingdom is already granted to children, it is not because of any subjective qualities we may suppose them to possess. . . The kingdom is theirs because objectively they are weak and helpless. The lowliness, that left to themselves they would die — these are their title deeds to the highest place in the kingdom of God.

The Child in the Church

The extravagant gesture is the very stuff of creation. After the one extravagant gesture of creation in the first place, the universe has continued to deal exclusively in extravagances, flinging intricacies and colossi down aeons of emptiness, heaping profusions on profligacies with ever fresh vigour. The whole show has been on fire from the word go!

Annie Dillard, *Pilgrim at Tinker Creek*

What is this darkness? What is its name? Call it: an aptitude for sensitivity. Call it: a rich sensitivity which will make you whole. Call it: your potential for vulnerability.

Meister Eckhart

We are the 'mother' of Christ when we carry him in our heart and body by love and a pure and sincere conscience. And we give birth to him through our holy works which ought to shine on others by our example.

Francis of Assisi

I, God, am your playmate. I will lead the child in you in wonderful ways, for I have chosen you.

Mechtild of Magdeburg

When we say God is 'eternal', we mean God is eternally young.

Meister Eckhart

Come, Love! Sing on! Let me hear you sing
this song — sing for joy and laugh, for I
the Creator am truly subject to all creatures.

Mechtild of Magdeburg

It is our helplessness a child sees, even when we cannot recognise it. And when a child moves to give us comfort, instinctively and without premeditation, we know that it is true that we are dependent, weak and needy creatures. In the end these little ones, with the strength of their compassion, can bring to naught the brittle might of the powerful.

Focus on the Child

We die on the day
when our lives cease to be illumined
by the steady radiance
renewed daily
of a wonder
the source of which
is beyond reason.

Dag Hammarskjöld, *Markings*

Eternal God:
You have created a world in which the small things are of as much worth as the large and important. The song of children, their wonder and delight, the gladness with which they greet the day, their total commitment, their enthusiasm are signals of transcendence. Let them point us unerringly to you in the celebration of life. Amen.

Let us always remember, O God,
the human person
is the form
and the fullness of creation.
In humankind
God brings to fullness all his creation.
God created humankind
so that we
might cultivate the earthly
and thereby create the heavenly;
humankind should be the banner of divinity.

Hildegard of Bingen

O thou with whom is the fountain of life, from whom cometh every good and perfect gift, whose strength is made perfect in weakness, be near to us to quicken our faltering praise, to assist our stammering prayer and to strengthen our feeble understanding of thy Word, that those things which we do may set

forth thy glory and magnify thy holy name. *Through Jesus
Christ our Lord. Amen.*

O Christ child,
    look at me —
    old but not wise,
    experienced but still bewildered,
    established but deeply uncertain,
    hungering but not yet after righteousness.

Look at you —
    young but filled with God's Spirit,
    newborn but at home in the world,
    just begun but greeting the world trustingly,
    without guile, seeking the good
    and loving it with your whole heart.

O childish God,
    give me of your wisdom,
            your hope,
            your joy,
that I may be young again in spirit
and so enter the door of the kingdom
you hold open for me. Amen.

    Look upon us and hear us, O Lord our God,
    and assist those endeavours to please thee which
    thou thyself hast granted to us; as thou hast
    given the first act of will, so give the completion
    of the work; grant that we may be able to finish
    what thou hast granted us to wish to begin;
    through Jesus Christ our Lord. Amen.

                Mozarabic Sacramentary, seventh century

A Benediction

    *May the God of hope
    fill you with all joy and peace in believing,
    so that by the power of the Holy Spirit
    you may abound in hope.*

*And may Almighty God bless you
the Father, the Son and the Holy Spirit.* Amen.

Romans 15: 13, RSV

52

There is no life except through death

My God, my God, why have you abandoned me?
I have cried desperately for help,
but still it does not come.
During the day I call to you, my God,
but you do not answer;
I call at night,
but get no rest.

So many troubles have fallen on me
that I am close to death.
I am like all others who are about to die;
all my strength is gone.
I am abandoned among the dead;
I am like the slain lying in their graves,
those you have forgotten completely,
who are beyond your help.
You have thrown me into the depths of the tomb,
into the darkest and deepest pit.

Joseph said to his brothers, 'Don't be afraid; I can't put myself in the place of God. You plotted evil against me, but God turned it into good, in order to preserve the lives of many people who are alive today because of what happened. You have nothing to fear. . .'
I felt the powerful presence of the Lord, and his spirit took me and set me down in a valley where the ground was covered with bones. . . He said to me, 'Mortal man, can these bones come back to life?' I replied, 'Sovereign Lord, only you can answer that!' He said, 'Prophesy to

these bones. Tell these dry bones to listen to the word of the Lord. Tell them that I, the Sovereign Lord, am saying to them. . . I am going to put breath into you and bring you back to life. Then you will know that I am the Lord.'

Martha said. . . 'I know that even now God will give you whatever you ask him for.'. . . Jesus said, 'I am the resurrection and the life. Those who believe in me, even though they die will live; and whoever lives and believes in me will never die. Do you believe this?'. . . He called out with a loud voice, 'Lazarus, come out!' He came out, his hands and feet wrapped in grave cloths, and with a cloth around his face. 'Untie him,' Jesus told them, 'and let him go.'

The hour has come for the Son of Man to receive great glory. I am telling you the truth: a grain of wheat remains no more than a single grain unless it is dropped into the ground and dies. If it does die, then it produces many grains. Those who love their life lose it; those who hate their life in this world will keep it for eternal life. Whoever wants to serve me must follow me, so that my servant will be with me where I am. And my Father will honour anyone who serves me.

By our baptism we were buried with him and shared his death in order that, just as Christ was raised from death by the glorious power of the Father, so also we might live a new life. For since we have become one with him in dying as he did, in the same way we shall be one with him by being raised to life as he was. . . For whoever has died is freed from sin. Since we have died with Christ, we believe that we will also live with him.

We felt that the death sentence had been passed on us. But this happened so that we should rely, not on ourselves, but only on God, who raises the dead. From such terrible dangers of death he saved us, and will save us; and we have placed our hope in him that he will save us again.

At all times we carry in our mortal bodies the death of Jesus, so that his life also may be seen in our bodies. . . One died for everyone, which means that all share in his death. He died for all, so that those who live should no longer live for themselves, but only for him who died and was raised to life for their sake. . . Even though it was in weakness that he was put to death on the cross, it is by God's power that he lives. In union with him we also are weak; but. . . when I am weak, then I am strong.

Those who wept as they went out carrying the seed will come back singing for joy,
as they bring in the harvest.

But you, God's people, will be happy and sing as you do on the night of a sacred festival. You will be as happy as those who walk to the music of flutes on their way to the Temple of the Lord.

(Psalm 22: 1-2; Psalm 88: 3-6; Genesis 50: 19-21; Ezekiel 37: 1, 3-6 — all GNB; John 11: 22, 25-26, 43-44; John 12: 23-26; Romans 6: 4-5, 7-8 — all GNB/NRSV; 2 Corinthians 1: 9-10; 4: 10; 5: 14-15; 13: 4; 12: 10; Psalm 126: 6; Isaiah 30: 29 — all GNB)

I am not in parish ministry at the moment, so during the last three years I have conducted just four funerals. A Christian lady in her fifties died of an asthma attack. An unhappy young man put a gun into his mouth and blew the top of his head off. Another mixed-up young fellow gassed himself in his car. And a Christian man in his mid-sixties died of complications after heart surgery. On each of these very different occasions I read the same words from Jesus: 'I am the resurrection and the life.'

In Ezekiel's well-known vision where he saw a valley covered with dry bones, he is commanded to predict their resurrection. Those bones rattled into life. The Lord similarly commanded the dead body of Lazarus to come back to life.

But we can die before our death. Indeed, life comprises many deaths — separation from loved ones, the break up of a romance, our children 'leaving the nest', the loss of a friend, or a pet, or a job. Some of the mystics, with their deep objective sense of sin and their insights into the ways of the divine healer, talk about God infecting us with a wound of love. We are still seeking God, even perhaps with deep longing, but the way is dark and hard. At these times (in Catherine de Hueck Doherty's words) we must fold the wings of the intellect, and open the door of the heart. Our loving Father-God has not forsaken us. He is there in the darkness. He can see, if we can't.

John of the Cross believed the dark night is God's gift to those whom he most desires to purify and draw into the light of his presence.

When the seed, in Jesus' short parable, is put into the ground, and the earth is heaped onto it, there is a dying before germination and life. Imagine you're the seed. The feeling of entombment in the earth is awful — it's black, lonely, cold, dark and damp. But the Father-Gardener knows what he's doing. And with him there is always resurrection at the other side of Calvary. (So don't ever, ever, let any person or event crucify you that can't resurrect you!).

The biblical stance during these death experiences is hope. Not optimism ('things will get better') or pessimism ('things can only get worse'); but hope, which rests on the promise that whatever happens, God is with us (as he was with his people in the past).

Archbishop Oscar Romero of El Salvador, gunned down as he preached at mass during Lent, 1980, left a legacy of hope for his people, which has strengthened them through the years of slaughter and hardship that have followed. The hope shines even when the world looks hopeless. 'We are living in a black night,' he once told his people in the midst of violence and suffering, 'but Christianity discerns that beyond the night the dawn already glows. The hope that does not fail is carried in the heart. Christ goes with us.'

❧❧

The experience of the dark night of the soul is a common theme in mystical literature. . . The most characteristic note is that of a frustrated quest for the divine Presence. . . [Then there] is a union of self-distrust with self-condemnation. . . A third dominant trait is loneliness, the bitterness of isolation both from God and others. . . A fourth note is. . . spiritual weariness and discouragement. . . Various evil moods ensue, not the least of which is the exasperation of helplessness.

Georgia Harkness, *The Dark Night of the Soul*

A grain of wheat, says Jesus, remains a solitary grain unless it falls into the ground and dies, but if it dies it bears a rich harvest. The occasion was that pregnant confrontation with the group of Greeks who were in Jerusalem for the festival — representatives of the great world beyond the tiny province of Judea and its introverted conflicts. Their search for Jesus came as another temptation to short-cut the way to the world's renewal and have a mission without a cross. But though his soul was thrown into turmoil, the bait was refused. The seed died. And then began the proliferation. He who was uniquely the Son of God will now bring many sons and daughters to glory through his sufferings (Hebrews 2: 10).

John V. Taylor, *The Go-Between God*

To each one of us Christ is saying: If you want your life and mission to be fruitful like mine, do as I. Be converted into a seed that lets itself be buried. Let yourself be killed. Do not be afraid. Those who shun suffering will remain alone. No one is more alone than the selfish. But if you give your life out of love for others, as I give mine for all, you will reap a great harvest. You will have the deepest satisfactions. Do not fear death or threats; the Lord goes with you.

Oscar Romero, 1 April 1979, a year before
he was shot while preaching at mass

You yearn to rise again? This also is legitimate and appropriate. But I have to ask you one other question: Did you ever reach the depths?

Not only the depth of any inward or outward misery, but the depth where we must acknowledge that we can no longer help ourselves, that no one else can help us, that there is absolutely no help save God's mercy?

In this depth, God's mercy has already reached out for you, has already found you, and you will experience that it will lift you to the highest heights.

> Karl Barth, a sermon delivered in Basle
> prison, in *Deliverance to the Captives*

God has not created anything which is in itself injurious or evil, or which can harm any of his creatures if rightly used. Likewise all pain and suffering is a means of growth and of deepening our spiritual life (Romans 8: 18). . . The real victory is not that we should be saved from pain and suffering or death and evil, but that, by the grace of God, we may change pain into ease, the cross and death into life, and evil into good. We must through much trouble enter into the kingdom of God (Acts 14: 22). The real value of ease cannot be appreciated without having known pain, nor of sweetness without having tasted bitterness, nor of good without having seen evil, nor even of life without having passed through death.

> Sadhu Sundar Singh, *The Spiritual Life*

Old Testament scholar Bruce Rahtjen took leave from academia to serve as a hospital chaplain in a ward for dying children. Out of his heart-rending experience with those children and their families — during which he became painfully aware of the limits of his ability to find words to answer their questions about suffering, justice and death — Rahtjen was forced to add a new rite to his pastoral and liturgical resources: the sacrament of silence.

> Charles E. Wolfe, 'Willing to Die'

We must be still and still moving
Into another intensity
For a further union, a deeper communion
Through the dark cold and empty desolation.

> T.S. Eliot, *Four Quartets*

One of the best and hardest things about praying is the way it opens me up to the cross. It isn't so much that I choose the cross. Instead, the cross chooses me. . . C.S. Lewis puts it well: 'The cross comes before the crown, and tomorrow is Monday morning.' Sometimes it is in the sheer Mondayness of things that I experience the cross. . .

[But] just when I think the glory of the resurrection is very unlikely, I find myself standing in the garden with Mary Magdalene after all. Suddenly, where I least expect it, he is alive and calling me by name. The Lord seems closer when we stop pretending to be powerful and admit how wounded we are. Then he comes to us, crucified and risen. He can hold us tight. We touch him. We grasp him. To this real Master we cling, this vulnerable Lord with the wounds still open in his hands and side.

Emilie Griffin, 'A Different Wisdom'

It is because the word of Christ has this power [to raise dead Lazarus, John 11: 1-45] here and now that we can believe it will have the same power hereafter. . . The evangelist agrees with popular Christianity that the believer will enter into eternal life at the general resurrection, but for him this is truth of less importance than the fact that the believer already enjoys eternal life, and the former is the consequence of the latter.

C.H. Dodd, *The Interpretation of the Fourth Gospel*

We become strongest when we are weakest. I have said this to thousands of young people more often than I have said any other single thing, and in thousands of lives I have seen light break into life from this truth.

John R. Mott, 'Seven Principles'

The spirit cannot die — in no circumstances, under no torment, despite whatever calumnies, in no bleak places.

Franz Marc, in *Dying We Live*

'Little deaths, big resurrections'; by this I mean that a personal disappointment or miscalculation, a 'little death', can be the occasion of a 'big resurrection,' the emergence of new possibilities, new hopes, new life, in ways far beyond our calculation or miscalculation. . . We discover that although grace did not seem apparent it was still there, transforming for good what we were fearful had only been for ill.

Robert McAfee Brown, *Creative Dislocation*

All our anguish (even if we have been partly responsible for aggravating it ourselves) is itself part of God's grace, a mark of his intimacy.

R.D. Williams, *The Wound of Knowledge*

It is a strange and severe mercy that calls us to live without props. . . But if we are to be weaned from the breasts of romanticism and emotional fundamentalism to the true emotion of loving God for himself; and if we are to be truly healed, so that the individual wounds of our personal unconscious and the barbaric archetypes of the collective unconscious are touched and transfigured by this 'fearful symmetry' of grace operating through the depths of loving contemplation of God, then we must be ready to enter the alternating currents of hurt and healing, desolation and consolation, darkness and light, finding God in all things. . . For he is Lord; Lord of light and darkness; and he does not play games. . . The love of God is our only healing, and it is for that glorious and terrible vocation that we are born and born again.

Philip Seddon, *Darkness*

We cannot go around despair to hope. We have to go right through despair. We will never know what hope is until we have tasted real despair. . . Jesus says 'No' to death, 'Yes' to life. . . Out of the grave of despair Jesus comes to us, as he came out of his place of despair, the tomb. He encounters us [because] he suffered despair too.

Henri Nouwen, 'The Journey from Despair to Hope'

You say you are more disposed to cry, 'Miserere!' than 'Hallelujah!'. Why not both together?

John Newton, *Letters*

Lord, the pain is severe, the terror of dying is sometimes un-bearable, the darkness is frightening, and I am tempted to abandon faith in your mercy. When the light flickers, and dusk settles over my mind and emotions, and I wonder about the sense of any commitment to your love, teach me again about your presence in the dark night. You wound to heal. You allow me to be severed from my alternatives to ultimate security, so that I may, beyond the pain of grief and loss, experience the reality of eternal joy. I am faced at these times with a choice between death and death: death to all that is not God and good, or a slow extinction of my true self as it is submerged in unreality.

So, with Jesus, I lay down my life to receive it again. I lay it down of my own free will. This charge I too have received from my Father.

May your holy name be praised, for ever and ever. Amen.

A Benediction
After you have suffered for a little while, the God of all grace, who calls you to share his eternal glory in union with Christ, will himself perfect you and give you firmness, strength and a sure foundation. To him be the power for ever! Amen.

1 Peter 5: 10-11, GNB

Postlude

The desert. . . is a place in which the providence of God is experienced in circumstances where human strength and ability reach their limits. It is a place in which people are made aware of human fragility and the stark reality that without the basics of water and food, all human life is brought to naught. The desert is no respecter of wealth or position. It reduces people to a naked dependence on God and a recognition of creatureliness as the basis of trusting God. The desert is also a place that best affirms all the gifts of life as 'daily bread' from the hand of God.

Paradoxically, the desert is also a place of testing by the elements and demons and can become the land of God-forsakenness. . .

To be dependent on God is to be humbled and so the desert is a place where the pride of humankind is stripped away. Any created idols fall away and the awareness of being a creature before God is felt in the silence of worship. The meaning of the desert is silence, simplicity and humility. . .

[In] the foundational years of Israel's faith and culture, the landscape provided the atmosphere to God's revelation of himself. It helped people learn how to revere him as a great and awesome God. It brought people into a sense of creatureliness and dependence on the gifts of God and out of this feeling grew the kind of faith looked for by God.

The desert was, also, the natural environment to learn that while human life naturally moves towards society dominated by city values, it does so at the risk of losing the immediacy of desert faith. For that reason Moses says, 'Remember how the Lord led you all the way in the desert.'

Cavan Brown, *Pilgrim Through This Barren Land*,
Albatross, 1991, pp. 54, 151 and 157

Abbreviations

Abbreviations of versions of the Bible used in this book

Barclay:
William Barclay, *The New Testament: a new translation*, Collins, 1969

GNB:
Good News Bible, the Bible in Today's English Version, The American Bible Society, 1976

JB:
Jerusalem Bible, Darton, Longman and Todd, 1968

KJV:
The Holy Bible, King James Version, 1611

LB:
The Living Bible, Tyndale House, 1971

NEB:
The New English Bible, OUP and CUP, 1970

NIV:
Holy Bible, New International Version, International Bible Society, 1973

NRSV:
New Revised Standard Version Bible: The New Oxford Annotated Bible, OUP, 1991

Phillips:
J.B. Phillips, *The New Testament in Modern English*, MacMillan, 1958

REB:
Revised English Bible, OUP/CUP, 1989

RSV:
Revised Standard Version, Thomas Nelson, 1952

Bibliography

Other sources used in weekly readings

Week 1

Anthony Bloom, *Meditations on a Theme*, Mowbrays, 1972, pp.15-16

Dietrich Bonhoeffer, *Life Together*, SCM, 1954, p.75

Rex Chapman, in *The Hodder Book of Christian Prayers*, Tony Castle (comp.), Hodder and Stoughton, 1986, p.101

T.S. Eliot, 'Choruses from the Rock', *Selected Poems of T.S. Eliot*, Penguin, 1948, p.105

Richard Foster, *Freedom of Simplicity*, Triangle/SPCK, 1981, pp.57-58, 89

Richard Foster, *Celebration of Discipline*, Hodder and Stoughton, 1980, p.94

Henry Gariepy, *Portraits of Perseverance*, Victor, 1989, pp.35, 51

Thomas Kelly, *A Testament of Devotion*, Hodder and Stoughton, 1941, pp.108-109

Albert Osborn, *The Silences of Christ*, Salvationist Publishing and Supplies Limited, pp.10,49

Week 2

St Anselm, *Prayers*, in *The English Spirit*, Paul Handley et al (comps), Abingdon, 1987, p.18

St Anselm, *St Anselm's Proslogion*, M.J. Charlesworth (tr.), OUP, 1965, p.111

Gerhardt Ladner, *Theologie und Politik vor dem Investiturstreit*, Wissenschaftliche Buchgesellschaft, 1968, p.11

William Law, *A Serious Call to a Devout and Holy Life*, Dent, 1906, p.1

Henri J.M. Nouwen, *The Way of the Heart*, Seabury, 1981, p.31

Evelyn Underhill, *Concerning the Inner Life*, Methuen, 1947, pp.9-11

Evelyn Underhill, *The Parish Priest and the Life of Prayer*, A.R. Mowbray, 1937, pp.1-2

Week 3

Ciro Alegria, *The Golden Serpent*, New American Library, 1963, pp.151-152

David Cairns, *In Remembrance of Me*, Geoffrey Bles, 1967, pp.22-23

Amy Carmichael, in *The Hodder Book of Christian Prayers*, Tony Castle (comp.), Hodder and Stoughton, 1986, p.27

Donald Coggan, *Convictions*, Hodder and Stoughton, 1978, pp.248-249

Dennis Coon, *Introduction to Psychology*, West, 1986, p.233

Peter C. Craigie, *The Daily Study Bible: Ezekiel*, St Andrew Press, 1986, p.47

G.G. Findlay, *The Expositor's Bible: Galatians*, Hodder and Stoughton, 1889, p.159

John A. Mackay, *The Presbyterian Way of Life*, Prentice-Hall, 1963, p.162

Eugene H. Peterson, *A Long Obedience in the Same Direction*, IVP, 1980, pp.162-163

Week 4

John Bunyan, *The Pilgrim's Progress*, Zondervan, 1967, p.110

John Calvin, *Institutes of the*

Christian Religion, The
Westminster Press, 1960, p.704
Barry Chant, Spindles and the
Children, Tabor, 1985, p.152
Thomas Chisholm, 'Great is Thy
Faithfulness', The Hymnal,
Aylesbury, 1978, No. 73
Francis of Assisi, Through the Year
with Francis of Assisi, Collins
Fount, 1987, p.125
Leo Harris, God Heals Today,
Crusade, no date, p.36
Julian of Norwich, Revelations of
Divine Love, Hodder and
Stoughton, 1987, p.55
C.S. Lewis, The Lion, the Witch and
the Wardrobe, Lion, 1987,
pp.130-131
John Pollock, John Wesley, Hodder
and Stoughton, 1989, pp.250-252
Oral Roberts, The Fourth Man and
Other Famous Sermons, Oral
Roberts, 1951, p.19
Robert Schuller, Success is Never
Ending: Failure is Never Final,
Nelson, 1988, p.244
Charles Spurgeon, Lectures to my
Students, Zondervan, 1954,
pp.164-165
J.R.R. Tolkien, Lord of the Rings,
George Allen and Unwin, 1969, p.75
Thomas Watson, A Body of
Divinity, Banner of Truth, 1986,
p.69

Week 5
Augustine of Hippo, in Love Song,
Sherwood Wirt (ed.), in Decision,
June 1971, p.8
Ivor Bailey, 'Live and Let Love', a
sermon preached from Maughan
Church, Adelaide, 9 July 1972
Leslie F. Brandt, A Book of Christian
Prayer, Kingsway, 1978, p.10
The Cloud of Unknowing, in
Michael Cox, Handbook of Christian
Spirituality, Harper and Row,
1985, p.139
Gerard Manley Hopkins, Poems by
Gerard Manley Hopkins, OUP, 1948,
p.188
Frank Laubach, Learning the

Vocabulary of God: A Spiritual
Diary, Lutterworth, 1956, pp.59-60
Frank Laubach, Letters by a Modern
Mystic, Lutterworth, 1957, p.30
Brother Lawrence, The Practice of
the Presence of God: the best rule of a
holy life, being conversations and
letters of Brother Lawrence,
Epworth, no date, pp.6-7
Walter Lippmann, 'A Preface to
Morals', Time, 1964, p.188
Thomas Merton, New Seeds of
Contemplation, New Directions,
1961, pp.282-284
St Patrick's Lorica, in Frank
Laubach, Learning the Vocabulary of
God: A Spiritual Diary,
Lutterworth, 1956, p.42
Sadhu Sundar Singh, The Spiritual
Life, Christian Literature Society,
1926/1986, pp.13-14
W.E. Sangster, The Pure in Heart,
Epworth, 1954, pp.242-243
A.W. Tozer, 'Love's Final Test',
The Life of Faith, 20 October 1960

Week 6
Ronald Allen and Gordon Borror,
Worship: Rediscovering the Missing
Jewel, Multnomah, 1982, p.24
John E. Burkhart, Worship,
Westminster, 1982, p.15
Oswald Chambers, My Utmost for
His Highest, McClelland and
Stewart, 1935, p.6
James R. Spruce, Come, Let Us
Worship, Beacon Hill, 1986,
pp.104-106
Jack R. Taylor, The Hallelujah
Factor, Broadman, 1983, p.172
William Temple, in Richard
Foster, Celebration of Discipline,
Harper and Row, 1978, p.138
James B. Torrence, in Ray
Anderson, Theological Foundations
for Ministry, Eerdmans, 1979, p.363
A.W. Tozer, Whatever Happened to
Worship?, Christian Publications,
1985, p.82
Stephen Winward, Reformation of
Our Worship, John Knox, 1965, p.50

Week 7
Bernard of Clairvaux, 'Jesus the Very Thought of Thee', *Australian Hymn Book*, Collins, 1977, No. 126
Richard Foster, *Celebration of Discipline*, Hodder and Stoughton, 1980, pp.140-141
Isobel Kuhn, *In the Arena*, Lutterworth, 1959, p.192
Frank Laubach, *Learning the Vocabulary of God*, Lutterworth, 1956, pp.22-23
Brother Lawrence, *The Practice of the Presence of God*, Conversation Four, Epworth, no date, p.23
John Samuel Bewley Monsell, 'Worship the Lord in the Beauty of Holiness', *Australian Hymn Book*, Collins, 1977, No. 382
Henri J.M. Nouwen, *Making All Things New*, Harper and Row, 1981, p.85
Don Postema, *Space for God*, Bible Way, 1983, pp. 179,16
Oswald Sanders, *Enjoying Intimacy with God*, Moody, 1980, p.23
A.W. Tozer, *Knowledge of the Holy*, Christian Publications, 1961, p.95
Charles Wesley, 'Love Divine, All Loves Excelling', *Australian Hymn Book*, Collins, 1977, No. 148

Week 8
An Australian Prayer Book, The Standing Committee of the General Synod of the Church of England in Australia, 1978, p.75
A.S.T.D. Newsletter, Loughborough University of Technology, Issue No. 7, Autumn 1979
Augustine of Hippo, *Confessions*, Book X, Chapter XXVII, *The Library of Christian Classics*, Vol. VII, John Baillie, et al (eds), SCM, 1955, p.224
John Baillie, *Christian Devotion*, OUP, 1962, p.42
John Donne, 'Batter My Heart, three-personed God', in *The Rinehart Book of Verse*, Alan Swallow (ed.), Holt, Rinehart and

Winston, 1965, p.91
Meister Eckhart, in *Meister Eckhart*, R.B.Blakeney (tr.), in *The Choice is Always Ours: An Anthology on the Religous Way*, Dorothy Berkley Phillips (ed.), Harper and Row, 1960, p.4
Max Scheler, *On The Eternal in Man*, Archon Books, 1972, pp.251ff

Week 9
W.H. Auden, hymn verse from *Sing Alleluia*, Collins, 1987, p.65
Paul Claudel, in Pierre-Yves Emery, *Prayer at the Heart of Life*, Orbis, 1975, p.35
Pierre-Yves Emery, *Prayer at the Heart of Life*, Orbis, 1975, p.84
Monica Furlong, *Contemplation Now*, Hodder and Stoughton, 1972, p.108
Hildegard of Bingen, *Meditations*, versions by Gabriele Uhlein, Bear and Company, 1983, p.40
Martin Israel, in I. Neville Ward, *Friday Afternoon*, Epworth, 1982, p.46
Ogden Nash, in *The Penguin Book of Comic and Curious Verse*, J.M. Cohen (ed.), Penguin, 1956, p.159
Nicephorus the Solitary, in *Writings of the Philokalia*, Faber, 1979, p.32
Eric O. Springsled, *Simone Weil and the Suffering of Love*, Cowley Publications, 1986, pp.66, 75
Thomas Traherne, *Centuries*, Mowbray, 1975, p.109
The Way of a Pilgrim, Helen Bacovcin (tr.), Image, 1978, p.34
Simone Weil, *Waiting on God*, Collins, 1977, pp. 75, 150

Week 10
Augustine of Hippo, in *Hodder Book of Christian Prayers*, Tony Castle (comp.), Hodder and Stoughton, 1986
Dietrich Bonhoeffer, *The Cost of Discipleship*, Macmillan, 1949, p.101
E.M. Bounds, *The Weapon of Prayer*, Baker, 1931, p.97

Leslie Brandt, 'James 1', *Epistles Now*, in Mildred Tengborn, *Sometimes I Hurt*, Concordia, 1986, p.6

Oswald Chambers, *My Utmost for His Highest*, Chambers, 1935, p.262

Dick Eastman and Jack Hayford, *Living and Praying in Jesus' Name*, Tyndale House, 1988, p.28

Francois Fénélon, *Let Go*, Whitaker, 1973, p.30

George Matheson, 'O Love That Wilt Not Let Me Go', *Australian Hymn Book*, Collins, 1977, No. 525

Katharina von Schlegel, 'Be Still My Soul', *Australian Hymn Book*, Collins, 1977, No. 48

A.W. Tozer, *Keys to the Deeper Life*, Zondervan, 1957, p.23

Week 11

Matthew Bridges and Godfrey Thring, 'Crown Him with Many Crowns', *Australian Hymn Book*, Collins, 1977, No. 163

Tony Cupit, *Peace I Leave with You*, Baptist Resource Centre, Victoria, 1988, p.75

Terry Falla, *Be our Freedom Lord*, Lutheran Publishing House, 1982, p.182

Frederick Pratt Green, 'Christ is the World's Light', *Australian Hymn Book*, Collins, 1977, No. 191

M. Scott Peck, *The Different Drum*, Simon and Schuster, 1987, pp.13-15

St Patrick's Breastplate, in *Lion Book of Christian Prayers*, Lion, 1983, p.22

R. Sider and R. Taylor, *Nuclear Holocaust and Christian Hope*, Hodder and Stoughton, 1982, p.21

John Stott, in 'Calling for Peacemakers in a Nuclear Age', *Christianity Today*, February 1980, p.44

R.V.G. Tasker, *The Gospel According to St John*, Tyndale, 1960, pp.168-169

Week 12

Aristotle, *Nichomachean Ethics*, VIII, 1, Martin Ostwald (tr.), Bobb-Merrill, 1962

Dietrich Bonhoeffer, *Life Together*, SCM, 1954, pp.9-10

Rodney Clapp, 'The Celebration of Friendship', *The Reformed Journal*, August 1989, p.11

Samuel Crossman, 'My Song is Love Unknown', *Australian Hymn Book*, Collins, 1977, No. 256

Robert Frost, 'Death of a Hired Man', in *Robert Frost's Poems*, p.165, in Don Postema, *Space for God: The study and practice of prayer and spirituality*, Bible Way, 1983

Interviewee, 'The Friendship Paradox', *Partnership*, in Rodney Clapp, *op cit*

Henri J.M. Nouwen, *Reaching Out*, Fount, 1980, pp.139-140, 140-141

Don Postema, *Space for God, op cit*, pp.34-35

Lewis B. Smedes, *Caring and Commitment: Learning to live the love we promise*, Harper and Row, 1988, p.46

Week 13

Robert Banks, *All the Business of Life: Bringing theology down-to-earth*, Albatross, 1987, p.134

James L. Crenshaw, *A Whirlpool of Torment: Israelite traditions of God as an oppressive presence*, Fortress, 1984, p.118

Gordon MacDonald, *Ordering Your Private World*, Highland, 1985, p.140

Huub Oosterhuis, *Your Word is Near: Contemporary Christian Prayers*, N.D. Smith (tr.), Paulist, 1968, p.17

Frank Rees, unpublished sermon

Brother Roger of Taizé, *The Wonder of a Love*, Journal 1974-1976, Mowbray, 1981, pp.105-106

Paul Tillich, 'Spiritual Presence', in *The Eternal Now*, Scribners,

1956, p.88
Paul Tillich, 'In Everything Give Thanks', in *The Eternal Now*, Scribners, 1956, pp.184-185

Week 14
Henri Blocher, *In the Beginning*, IVP, 1984, p.56
Lyndon Bowring, unpublished speech, August 1987
Peter Brierley, *Vision Building*, Hodder and Stoughton, 1989, pp.32-33
Lee Iacocca, in Robert Waterman, *The Renewal Factor*, Bantam, 1988, p.111
Indian proverb, in *Chambers Book of Business Quotations*, Martin H. Manser (comp.), Chambers, 1987, p.48
Information Sheet, The Carpenters' Shop, Longbenton Estate, Newcastle-upon-Tyne, 4 September 1987
Charles Inge, in Ray Willsmer, *The Basic Arts of Marketing*, Business Books, 1984, p.147
Grace Hopper, *Cobol Computer Language*, in Renewal Magazine, 1988, p.10
John Naisbitt, *Re-inventing the Corporation*, Futura, 1986, p.20
Peter Neilson, 'Life and Work', Church of Scotland magazine, 1988
Oxford Concise Dictionary, Oxford
Samuel Zwemer, in Peter Brierly, *Vision Building*, Hodder and Stoughton, 1989, p.186

Week 15
C. Bryant, *The River Within*, DLT, 1983, p.143
J. Gardner, in G. MacDonald, *Rebuilding Your Broken World*, Thomas Nelson, 1988, p.80
Robert Frost, 'The Road Not Taken', in Louis Untermeyer, *The Road Not Taken*, Holt, Rinehart and Winston, 1962, p.271
J. Gunstone, *Free in Christ*, Daybreak, 1989, p.9

John J. Newman, 'The Pillar of the Cloud', in *The Australian Hymn Book*, Collins, 1977, No. 494
Julian of Norwich, in R. Llewelyn, *Enfolded in Love*, DLT, 1980, p.197
G. O'Collins, *The Second Journey*, Paulist, 1978, p.90
M. Scott Peck, *The Different Drum*, Simon and Schuster, 1987, pp.56,94
John Powell, *The Christian Vision*, Argus Communications, 1984, p.11
A. Van Kaam and S. Muto, *Am I Living a Spiritual Life?*, Dimension Books, 1978, pp.49,91-92, 133
David Watson, *Through the Year with David Watson*, Hodder and Stoughton, June 13
Simone Weil, *Waiting on God*, Collins, 1956, p.88
H.A. Williams, *Tensions*, Mitchell Beazley, 1976, pp.109, 111, 115

Week 16
Sheila Cassidy, *Prayer for Pilgrims*, Collins, 1980, p.30
John Claypool, *The Preaching Event*, Word, 1980, p.126
Henry Drummond, *The Ideal Life*, Hodder and Stoughton, 1897, pp.214, 216
Dag Hammarskjöld, *Markings*, Faber, 1966, p.169
Caroline Jones, *The Search for Meaning*, ABC/Collins Dove, 1989, pp.10, 11, 15, 9
Thomas Kelly, *A Testament of Devotion*, Hodder and Stoughton, 1961, p.107
R. Langmead, 'Lord let me see', in *Be Our Freedom, Lord*, Terry Falla (ed.), Lutheran Publishing House, 1981, p.346
Denis Lant, *First Steps in Prayer*, Carey Kingsgate, 1944, p.32
Alan Richardson, *Preface to Bible Study*, SCM, 1943, p.111
Steve Turner, 'Noise', in *Up to Date Poems 1968-1982*, Hodder and Stoughton, 1983, p.39
Jean Vanier, *The Broken Body*, St Paul Publications, 1988, pp.80-83
Elie Wiesel, *Five Biblical Portraits*,

University of Notre Dame Press, 1981, pp.38-39

Week 17
William Blake, 'A Poison Tree', in *Oxford Dictionary of Quotations*, OUP, 1953, p.76
William Blake, 'Proverbs of Nell', in *Oxford Dictionary of Quotations*, OUP, 1953, p.77
Carl Burke, *Treat me Cool, Lord*, Fontana, 1969, p.78
Abbot John Chapman, in *The Hodder Book of Christian Quotations*, Tony Castle (ed.), Hodder and Stoughton, 1982, p.223
David Clines, 'Beyond all Proportion', *The Harvester*, July 1989
Francois Fénélon, in *The Hodder Book of Christian Quotations*, Tony Castle (ed.), p.229, and in W.H. Auden and Louis Kronenberger, *The Faber Book of Aphorisms*, Faber, 1964, p.87
Thomas Fuller, in *The Hodder Book of Christian Quotations*, Tony Castle (ed.), No. A159
Fynn, *Mister God, This is Anna*, William Collins, 1974, p.152
George Herbert, 'Bitter Sweet', in *The Poetical Works of George Herbert*, James Nisbet and Co., 1865, p.218
Martin Luther King, in *Famous Prayers*, Veronica Zundel (ed.), Lion, 1983, p.122
C.S. Lewis, *Prayer: Letters to Malcolm*, Geoffrey Bles, 1964
C.S. Lewis, *Till We Have Faces*, Geoffrey Bles, 1956
Terence Rattigan, *In Praise of Love*, Hamish Hamilton, 1973, p.51
Veronica Zundel, 'Put a Name', in *A Touch of Flame*, Jenny Robertson (ed.), Lion, 1989, p.128

Week 18
Augustine of Hippo, *The Confessions of St. Augustine*, F.J. Sheen (tr.), Sheed and Ward, 1943, p.105
Karl Barth, *Church Dogmatics, The*

Doctrine of Creation, T & T Clark, 1961, pp.606,625
'Be Thou My Vision', Irish traditional, Mary Elizabeth Byrne (tr.), *Australian Hymn Book*, Collins, 1977, No. 542
Harry Blamires, *The Will and the Way: A study of divine providence and vocation*, SPCK, 1957, p.67
John Calvin, *Institutes of the Christian Religion*, in Paul Helm, *The Callings*, Banner of Truth, 1987, pp.58-59
Diane Davis, 'God Has Called You', in *Celebration*, Jeanne Harper (ed.), Hodder and Stoughton, 1986, No. 70
D.H. Lawrence, 'What is He?', in *The Collected Poems of D.H. Lawrence*, Heinemann
Gordon MacDonald, *Ordering Your Private World*, Highland, 1985, pp.30,33-37,51-52
M. Basil Pennington, *Called: New Thinking on Christian Vocation*, Seabury, 1983, p.14
Denis de Rougement, *The Christian Opportunity*, Holt, Rinehart and Winston, 1963, p.37
Charles Wesley, 'Forth in Thy Name', in *By Heart: A Lifetime Companion*, J. Bowden (ed.), SCM, 1984

Week 19
Walter Brueggemann, *The Prophetic Imagination*, Fortress, 1978, pp.45-46
Arthur Clutton-Brock, source unknown
Kahlil Gibran, source unknown
Norman C. Habel, *The Book of Job*, The Cambridge Bible Commentary on the New English Bible, CUP, 1975, pp.227-228
Lesslie Newbigin, *Honest Religion for Secular Man*, Westminster, 1966, p.93
Henri J.M. Nouwen, source unknown
David Wenham, *The Parables of Jesus: Pictures of Revolution*,

Hodder and Stoughton, 1989,
pp.12-13

Week 20
Beatrice, in Dante, *Divine Comedy,
Purgatorio,* XXXII: 72, Penguin,
1955
Nicholas Bielby, 'Elijah on Horeb',
An Invitation to Supper, Outposts,
London, 1978
William Blake, 'A Vision of the
Last Judgement', *Complete
Writings of William Blake,* Geoffrey
Keynes (ed.), OUP, 1966, p.611
Gerard Manley Hopkins, 'Carrion
Comfort', *Poems,* W.H. Gardner
and N.H. Mackenzie (eds), OUP,
1967, pp.99-100
St John of the Cross, 'Living Flame
of Love', Stanza II, 16, *The
Complete Works of St John of the
Cross,* E. Allison Peers (tr. & ed.),
Burns and Oates, 1964, Vol III
John Keble, *The Baptist Hymn Book,*
Psalms and Hymns Trust, 1964,
No. 76
Stephen Prickett, *Words and the
Word: Language, Poetics, and
Biblical Interpretation,* CUP, 1986,
p.224
Alfred, Lord Tennyson, *In
Memoriam,* i: 20-24, OUP, 1982
John Greenleaf Whittier, 'Dear
Lord and Father of Mankind',
Methodist Hymn Book, 1933, No. 669

Week 21
Matthew Arnold, 'Quiet Work', in
The Batsford Book of Country Verse,
R.S. Thomas (ed.), Batsford, 1961,
p.78
Henry Ward Beecher, in
*Encyclopedia of Religious
Quotations,* Frank S. Mead (ed.),
Revell, 1965, p.386
Dom Helder Camara, *A Thousand
Reasons for Living,* DLT, 1981, p.42
Leonardo da Vinci, *Notebooks
(c.1500),* Jean Paul Richter (tr.), in
*The International Thesaurus of
Quotations,* R.T. Tripp (ed.),
Harper and Row, 1970, p.708

Clarence Day, *This Simian World,*
1920, p.5
Diary of a Welsh Swagman, William
Evans (ed.), Sun Books, 1977,
pp.41, 55, 180
*Encyclopedia of Religious
Quotations,* Frank S. Mead (ed.),
Revell, 1965, p.472
George Herbert, 'Teach me my
God and King', in H.L. Gee,
Another Cheerful Day, Methuen,
1949, p.148
Paul Marshall, 'Work and Rest',
Reformed Journal, June 1988, p.13
President Ronald Reagan was
supposedly joking with reporters,
April 1987
John Ruskin, *Time and Tide,* 1867,
p.5
Voltaire, *Candide,* 1759, 30 in *The
International Thesaurus of
Quotations,* R.T. Tripp (ed.),
Harper and Row, 1970, p.708
Denis Waitley, *The Joy of Working,*
Ballantine Books, 1985, pp.90-91
Booker T. Washington, address,
Atlanta Exposition, 18 September
1895, in *The International Thesaurus
of Quotations,* R.T. Tripp (ed.),
Harper and Row, 1970, p.708

Week 22
Dr. E. Berg, in Tony Cupit, *Peace I
Leave with You,* Baptist Resource
Centre, Victoria, 1988, p.28
John Claypool, 'The Things that
Make for Peace', unpublished
sermon preached on 7 October
1979
Tony Cupit, *Peace I Leave With
You,* Baptist Resource Centre,
Victoria, 1988, p.49
John Gladstone, 'The Christ Who
Brings a Great Calm', sermon
preached in Yorkminster Park
Baptist Church, Toronto
Colin Morris, *Mankind My Church,*
Hodder and Stoughton, 1971,
pp.136-137
Horatio G. Stafford, 'When Peace
like a River', in *Worship and Service
Hymnal,* Hope Publishing

Company, 1966, No. 283
John Stott, *Issues Facing Christians Today*, Marshall, Morgan and Scott, 1984, p.101
U.S. Bishops' Pastoral Letter, 'The Challenge of Peace: God's Promise and our Response', CTS/SPCK, 1983, p.80
Carolyn Weatherford, 'Missions and Peace', the Sunday School Board of Southern Baptist Convention, January 1984, p.7
John Greenleaf Whittier, 'Dear Lord and Father of Mankind', *The Baptist Hymn Book*, Psalms and Hymns Trust, 1964, No. 50

Week 23
An Australian Prayer Book, Anglican Information Office, 1978, pp.35-36
Steve Brown, 'Leadership', *Christianity Today*, Fall 1985, p.77
Lyman Coleman, Denny Rydberg, Richard Peace, Gary Christopherson (eds), *Serendipity New Testament for Groups*, Serendipity House, 1986, p.247
P.T. Forsyth, *Christian Perfection*, Hodder and Stoughton, 1899, p.106
E. Stanley Jones, *Conversion*, Hodder and Stoughton, 1960, pp.187-188
E. Stanley Jones, *Victory Through Surrender*, Abingdon, 1966, pp.32-33
Sören Kierkegaard, *Purity of Heart Is to Will One Thing*, Harper and Brothers, 1956, p.205
George W. Robinson, *Hymns II*, IVP, 1976, p.106
John Sanford, *The Kingdom Within*, Paulist, 1970, p.125
Charles Wesley, *Hymns II*, IVP, 1976, p.88

Week 24
Harry Blamires, 'Where Do We Stand Against Current Idolatries?', in *Where Do We Stand?*, Servant Books, 1980, p.121
Robert McAfee Brown, *Creative Dislocation*, Abingdon, 1980, p.114
Frederich Buechner, *Wishful Thinking*, Collins, 1973, p.40
John Carmody, *Towards a Male Spirituality*, Twenty-third Publications, 1989, pp.11-13
John Claypool, 'God for Each of Us', Chapter 20 in *The Light Within You*, Word, 1983, p.197
Graham Houghton, 'Idolatry and the Image of God', unpublished paper, SAIACS, Bangalore, India, pp. 21-22, 23
St John of the Cross, *The Collected Works of St John of the Cross*, Kieran Kavanagh & Otilio Rodriguez (trs), Institute of Carmelite Studies, 1976, p.67
Sadhu Sundar Singh, *The Spiritual Life*, Christian Literature Society, 1986, p.49
Jim Wallis, *The New Radical*, Lion, 1983, pp.154-155
Rowan Williams, 'Dark Night, Darkness', in Gordon Wakefield (ed.), *A Dictionary of Christian Spirituality*, SCM, 1983, p.104

Week 25
John Baillie, *A Diary of Private Prayer*, OUP, 1936, p.105
Book of Prayers For Students, SCM, 1921, pp.97, 99
Daniel Jenkins, *The Christian Belief in God*, Faber, 1964, p.32
Alan Jones, *Soul Making*, SCM, 1985, p.128
W.B.J. Martin, *Five Minutes to Twelve*, Collins, 1947, p.133
D.T. Niles, *The Preacher's Task and the Stone of Stumbling*, Harper and Brothers, 1963, p.72
Wayne E. Oates, *The Psychology of Religion*, Word, 1973, pp.73-74
John Oman, *Grace and Personality*, CUP, 1942, pp.14-15
John A.T. Robinson, *Twelve New Testament Studies*, SCM, 1962, p.54
Francis Thompson, in *A Diary of Readings*, John Baillie (ed.), OUP, 1955, Day 276

H.A. Williams, 'Theology and Self-Awareness' in *Soundings*, A.R. Vidler (ed.), CUP, 1962, p.72

Week 26
John Ernest Bode, 'O Jesus, I have Promised', *Australian Hymn Book*, Collins, 1977, No. 514
Athol Gill, *Life on the Road*, Lancer, 1989, p.293
John Goldingay, 'Preaching on the Stories in Scripture', *Anvil*, Vol. 7, No. 2, 1990, pp.106-107
Archibald D. Hart, *The Success Factor*, Power Books, 1984, p.187
Jon Mohr, 'Find us Faithful', Birdwing Music, 1987
Gordon Moyes, *Discovering the Young Church*, Albatross, 1989, p.132
J.I. Packer, *Knowing God*, Hodder and Stoughton, 1973, p.31
M. Scott Peck, *The Different Drum*, Simon and Schuster, 1987, pp.229-230
J.B. Phillips, *Making Men Whole*, Fontana, 1955, pp.86-87
John Stott (ed.), *Free to be Different*, Marshalls, 1984, p.155

Week 27
Ambrose, *De Virginate*, in Louis Bouyer, *The Spirituality of the New Testament and the Fathers*, Vol.1, Seabury, 1963, *p.458*
Ambrose, *Explan. Psalm*, in Cheslyn Jones et al (eds), *The Study of Spirituality*, SPCK, 1986, p.132
Augustine of Hippo, *Soliloquies*, in Louis Bouyer, *op cit*, p.470
David Campbell, 'A Song and a Dance', *Anthology of Australian Religious Poetry*, Les A. Murray (comp.), Collins Dove, 1986, p.134
Carlo Carretto, *Letters from the Desert*, DLT, 1972, pp.73-74
Cassian, *Conferences*, in Louis Bouyer, *op cit*, p.318
Glenn Clark, *Windows of Heaven*, Arthur James, 1959, p.174
Evagrios, 'On Prayer', *The Philokalia*, Vol.1, G.E. Palmer et al

(trs), Faber, 1979, p.58
Kahlil Gibran, *The Prophet*, Heinemann, 1974, p.94
A.D. Hope, 'Australia', *Anthology of Australian Religous Poetry*, op cit, p.228
G.A. Studdart Kennedy, 'A Song of the Desert', *The Unutterable Beauty*, Hodder & Stoughton, 1964, p.60
Anthony de Mello, *One Minute Wisdom*, Gujarat Sahitya Prakash, 1985, p.200
Thomas Merton, *The Wisdom of the Desert*, New Directions, 1960, p.3
Henri J.M. Nouwen, *The Way of the Heart*, DLT, 1981, pp.27-28, 30-31, 34-35
Origen, *Hom.27 on Numbers*, in Louis Bouyer, *op cit*, p.293
Bruce Prewer, 'Hunger and Thirst', *Australian Psalms*, Lutheran Publishing House, 1979, pp.74-75
Bruce Prewer, 'Without you, life is desert', *Australian Prayers*, Lutheran Publishing House, 1983, p.29

Week 28
Teilhard de Chardin, *Hymn of the Universe*, Collins Fount, 1979, pp.86-87
Egyptian 13th century BC, in Barbara Greene and Victor Gollancz, *God of a Hundred Names*, Victor Gollancz, 1962, p.235
Kenneth Leech, *True Prayer*, Sheldon Press, 1980, p.176
Karen Manton, unpublished journal, 1988
Thomas Merton, *Thoughts in Solitude*, Farrar, Strauss and Giroux, 1982, p.19
Henri J.M. Nouwen, *Reaching Out*, Collins, 1976, pp.35-36
Brother Roger of Taizé, *Letter from the Desert*, Les Presses de Taizé, 1984, p.11
Brother Roger of Taizé, *And Your Deserts Shall Flower*, Les Presses de Taizé, 1983, pp.1, 31

Antoine de Saint-Exupéry, *The Little Prince*, Piccolo Books, 1983, p.75

John Shea, *Stores of God*, Thomas More Press, 1978, pp.158,151

H.A. Williams, *The True Wilderness*, Collins Fount, 1986, pp.28, 30

Week 29

Dietrich Bonhoeffer, *Ethics*, Macmillan, p.77

Herbert Butterfield, *Christianity and History*, G. Bell and Sons Ltd, 1950, p.75

Joy Davidman, *Smoke on the Mountain*, Hodder and Stoughton, 1959, p.120

Austin Farrer, *Love Almighty and Ills Unlimited*, Fontana, 1966, p.174

T.R. Glover, *The Jesus of History*, SCM, 1929, p.190

Brian Hession, *The Gentle Step*, Peter Davies, 1958, p.176

C.S. Lewis, *The Problem of Pain*, Fount, 1940, p.103

William Temple, *Readings in St John's Gospel*, St Martin's Library, Macmillan, 1961, p.247

Malcolm C. Tolbert, *Broadman Bible Commentary*, Vol. 9, 1970, p.122

Dean Vaughan, Robert Louis Stevenson and St Basil, in *With One Voice*, G. Hedges (ed.), 1970

Edward Young, in *Elbert Hubbard's Scrapbook*, Wm. H. Wise & Co., 1923, p.169

Anonymous German Pastors, in *I Was In Prison*, Dorothy F. Buxton (ed.), SCM, 1939

Week 30

George Appleton, *Journey for a Soul*, Collins, 1974, pp.47, 49

Dom Helder Camara, *A Thousand Reasons for Living*, DLT, 1981, p.53

Teilhard de Chardin, in George Appleton, *Journey for a Soul, op cit*, p.48

Douglas MacArthur on his 75th birthday, quoted in Carroll E. Simcox, 'The Gift of Aging', *The Christian Century*, 2 December 1987, p.1090

J.O. Sanders, 'Age is in attitudes – not arteries', *The Reaper*, June/July, 1989, p.3

Carroll E. Simcox, 'The Gift of Aging', *op cit*, p.1091

Nahum Tate and Nicholas Brady, 'Through all the changing scenes of life', *Australian Hymn Book*, Collins, 1977, No. 30

Week 31

Thomas Aquinas in *Uncommon Prayers*, Cecil Hunt (ed.), Hodder and Stoughton, 1963, p.120

Karl Barth, *Church Dogmatics*, III, 1, T & T Clark, 1958, p.589

Karl Barth, *Deliverance to the Captives*, SCM, 1961, pp.122-123

Rudolf Bultmann, *This World and Beyond*, Lutterworth, 1960, p.81

Sören Kierkegaard, in *The Prayers of Kierkegaard*, Perry D. LeFevre (ed.), Phoenix, 1956, p.48

Hans Küng, *On Being a Christian*, Collins, 1977, p.361

Carl Michalson, *Faith for Personal Crises*, Scribners, 1958, pp.161-163

Joachim Neander, 'All my hope on God is Founded', *The Methodist Hymn Book*, Methodist Conference Office, 1933, No. 30

Johann Andreas Rothe, 'Now I have Found the Ground Wherein. . .', *The Methodist Hymnbook, op cit*, No. 375

Charles Wesley, 'Lord, in the Strength of Grace. . .', *The Methodist Hymn Book, op cit*, No. 594

Walt Whitman, in *The Oxford Dictionary of Quotations*, OUP, 1956, p.568

Week 32

The Book of Offices, Methodist Publishing House, no date, p.132

Joost De Blank, *Uncomfortable Words*, Longmans, Green and Co., 1985, pp.9f, 8

Richard Foster, *Celebration of*

Discipline, Hodder and Stoughton, 1980, p.76

Martin Luther, *Martin Luther: Selections from his Writings,* John Dillenberger (ed.), Doubleday, 1961, p.24

Michel Quoist, *Prayers of Life,* Gill and Son, 1963, p.94f

J. Aulay Steele and A.J. Campbell, *The Story of the Church,* Vol. III, the Church of Scotland Committee on Youth, 1954, p.89f

Jim Wallis, *The Call to Conversion,* Collins, 1981, p.28f

David Watson, *Discipleship,* Hodder and Stoughton, 1981, p.24

Charles Wesley, *Australian Hymn Book,* Collins Liturgical Publication, Sydney, 1977, No. 408

John Wesley, 'Self Denial', *Sermons on Several Occasions,* Vol. I, Hayman Bros and Lilly, no date, p.682f

Week 33

John Macquarrie, *The Humility of God,* SCM, 1978, pp.37-41

Mag Oleson, 'Forward', in *The Australian Baptist,* 15 November 1978

Pulpit Resource, Mediacom Associates Inc., Vol. 7, No. 2, April-June 1990, p.26

Margaret Spufford, 'Journey through Pain', *The Tablet,* 25 March 1989, p.344

David Watson, *Fear No Evil: A personal struggle with cancer,* Hodder and Stoughton, 1984, p.136

John Williams, 'Random Writings', in *Church and Nation,* 20 February 1985, p.35

William H. Willimon, 'When Bad Things Happen', *The Christian Century,* February 1989, pp.198-199

Bruce Wilson, 'The God Who Suffers': A Re-examination of the Theology of Unjust Suffering, *St Mark's Review,* No. 140, Summer 1990, pp.21, 31

Week 34

Hendrikus Berkhof, *Christian Faith: An introduction to the study of the faith,* Eerdmans, 1979, p.464

Leonardo Boff, *The Way of the Cross – Way of Justice,* John Drury (tr.) Orbis, 1986, pp.13-14

Dietrich Bonhoeffer, *The Cost of Discipleship,* SCM, 1971, pp.78-79

C.W. Everest, *Baptist Hymnal,* Psalms and Hymns Trust, 1962, No. 510

Terry Falla, *Be Our Freedom Lord,* Lutheran Publishing House, 1981, p.279

Robert G. Kemper, *The New Shape of Ministry: Taking accountability seriously,* Abingdon, 1979, p.142

Donald B. Kraybill, *The Upside-Down Kingdom,* Herald Press, 1978, pp.296-297

David Watson, *Discipleship,* Hodder and Stoughton, 1981, p.187

John H. Westerhoff, *Building God's People in a Materialistic Society,* Seabury, 1983, p.33

Week 35

Martin Luther King, *The Trumpet of Conscience,* Harper and Row, 1968, p.76

D. Paton and C. Long (eds), *The Compulsion of the Spirit – A Roland Allen Reader,* Eerdmans, pp.105, 106, 113

L. Richards and G. Martin, *Lay Ministry: Empowering the People of God,* Zondervan, 1981, pp.13,18

R. Stevens, *Liberating the Laity,* IVP, 1985, pp.23, 33, 34, 69

John Stott, *One People,* Fleming Revell, 1982, pp.25-26

E. Trueblood, *The Company of the Committed,* Harper and Row, 1980, pp.20, 39, 40, 60, 62

Week 36

Charles E. Hummel, *Tyranny of the Urgent,* IVP, 1980, pp.4, 5, 6, 8

D.G. Kehl, 'Burnout: The Risk of Reaching Too High', *Christianity Today,* 20 November 1981, p.26

Thomas Kelly, *A Testament of Devotion*, Hodder and Stoughton, 1967, pp.67, 68, 72, 73
Patty Kennedy, 'You are Here', Mercy Publishing, 1985
Gordon MacDonald, *Rebuilding Your Broken World*, Highland Books, 1988, pp.193,195
David Seamands, *Healing Grace*, Victor Books, 1989, p.26

Week 37

Thomas Aquinas, in *Great Souls At Prayer*, Allenson & Co., 1937, p.42
John Baillie, *Invitation to Pilgrimage*, Penguin, 1960, p.31
Herman Bavinck, *Our Reasonable Faith*, Baker, 1984, pp.26-30
Benedict, in *A Book of Services and Prayers*, Congregational Church in England and Wales, 1968, p.272
F.C. Happold, *Mysticism*, Penguin, 1970, p.122
Frances Ridley Havergal, in 'I Bring My Sins to Thee', *The Methodist Hymn Book*, Methodist Conference Office, 1933, No. 520
Evelyn Underhill, *The Spiritual Life*, Hodder and Stoughton, 1956, pp.99,100
Charles Wesley, 'Christ Whose Glory Fills the Skies', *The Methodist Hymn Book*, Methodist Conference Office, 1933, No. 924

Week 38

Sydney Carter, 'Lord of the Dance', in *The Australian Hymn Book*, Collins, 1977, No. 183
John R. Claypool, 'A Benediction', in his sermon, 'As you go', in *Crescent Hill Sermons*, Crescent Hill Baptist Church, Louisville, Kentucky, Vol. X, No. 7, 19 September 1971
John R. Claypool, *Tracks of a Fellow Struggler: How to handle grief*, Word, 1974, p.35
James D.G. Dunn, explaining Romans 8: 37, in *Word Biblical Commentary, Volume 38A, Romans 1-8*, Word, 1988, p.512

Terry Falla, *Be Our Freedom, Lord*, Lutheran Publishing House, 1981, p.271
Richard Keen, 'How Firm a Foundation', in *The Australian Hymn Book*, Collins, 1977, No. 491
Mary O'Hara, *The Scent of the Roses*, Fontana/Collins, 1981, p.265
Mary Peters, 'Through the Love of God our Saviour', in *The Baptist Hymn Book*, Psalms and Hymns Trust, 1962, No. 590
Gardner C. Taylor, *How Shall They Preach*, Progressive Baptist Publishing House, 1977, p.89
John V. Taylor, *The Go-Between God: The Holy Spirit and the Christian Mission*, SCM, 1972, p.78
Paul Tillich, *The Courage To Be*, Fontana/Collins, 1962, p.49

Week 39

Augustine of Hippo, in *The Hodder Book of Prayers*, Tony Castle (ed.), Hodder and Stoughton, 1986, p.18
Amy Carmichael, 'Make Me Thy Fuel', in Gene Denler, *The Fruit of Adversity*, Navigators, 1961, p.10
Joni Eareckson, *Joni*, Zondervan, 1976, p.5
Ruth Bell Graham, *It's My Turn*, Fleming H. Revell Company, 1982, p.169
Helen Keller in *The Faith of Helen Keller*, Jack Belck (ed.), Hallmark, 1967, p.19
Susan Perlman, 'If You Want Life, Expect Pain', *The Vineyard*, November 1988, p.13
Michel Quoist, *Prayers of Life*, in David Watson, *Fear No Evil*, Hodder and Stoughton, 1984, p.132
Corrie Ten Boom, in Peter Kreeft, 'When God Allows Suffering', *Charisma*, January 1987, p.77
A.W. Tozer, in David Watson, *Fear No Evil, op cit*, p.121
David Watson, *op cit*, pp.132, 138

Week 40
Augustine of Hippo, in *Readings in Christian Thought*, H. Kerr (ed.), Abingdon, 1966, p.57
Benedict, in David Konstant, *Jesus Christ The Way, The Truth, The Life*, Collins, 1981, p.74
Catherine of Siena, in *Readings in Christian Thought*, H. Kerr (ed.), Abingdon, 1966, p.127
Frederick Franck, in *The Book of Angelus Silesius*, Frederick Franck (tr.), Bear and Company, 1985, p.28
Dag Hammarskjöld, *Markings*, Leif Sjoberg and W.H. Auden (trs), Faber, 1964, p.169
William James, *The Varieties of Religious Experience*, Collier Macmillan, 1961, p.160
Caroline Jones, 'What Australians Believe about God', *Age: Good Weekend Magazine*, 25 March 1989, p.33
Thomas à Kempis, *The Imitation of Christ*, Grosset and Dunlap, pp.251,253
D.H. Lawrence, in *A Christian's Prayer Book*, Peter Coughland et al (eds), Cassell, 1972, p.208
James E. Loder, *The Transforming Moment*, Harper and Row, 1981, pp.86-87
Henri J.M. Nouwen, *The Way of the Heart*, DLT, 1981, pp.25-32
Pope Paul VI, in David Konstant, *op cit*, p.67
Mary Caroline Richards, in Wynn Davis, *The Best of Success*, Great Quotations Publishing Company, 1988, p.161
Angelus Silesius, in *The Book of Angelus Silesius*, Frederick Franck (tr.), Bear and Company, 1985, p.104
David Suzuki, *Metamorphosis – Stages in a Life*, Allen and Unwin, 1987, Preface
Kanzo Uchimura, *The Complete Works, Vol. III, Alone with God and Me*, Kyobunkwan, 1972, pp.86, 87, 88
Allan Watts, *The Way of Liberation*,

Weatherhill, 1983, p.21
John Wesley, 'And Can It Be', *The Australian Hymn Book*, Collins, 1977, No. 138
Olive Wyon, in *The Lord of the Journey*, Roger Pooley et al (eds), Collins, 1986, p.282

Week 41
Leslie F. Brandt, 'Psalm 139', *Psalms/Now*, Lutheran Publishing House, 1976, pp.211-212
Dom Helder Camara, *A Thousand Reasons for Living*, DLT, 1981, p.103
Thomas Carlyle, in *Oxford Dictionary of Quotations*, 1985, p.127
Maxie Dunman, *Alive in Christ*, Abingdon, 1982, p.51
Archibald Hart, *The Success Factor*, Power House Books, 1984, pp.50, 43-44
Archibald Hart, *Unlocking the Mystery of your Emotions*, Word, 1989, p.158
Michael Hollings, in Henri J.M. Nouwen, *Reaching Out*, Collins, 1975, p.11
David Lonsdale, 'Authority: the Sources of Abuse', *The Way*, October 1989, pp.327-328
Henri J.M. Nouwen, *Making All Things New*, Harper and Row, 1981, pp.36-37
Henri J.M. Nouwen, *Reaching Out*, Collins, 1975, pp.40-41
Lewis B. Smedes, *How Can It Be All Right When Everything Is All Wrong?*, Pocket Books, 1982, pp.81-82
John Stott, *Free to be Different*, Marshalls, 1984, p.155

Week 42
A.R. Haberson, 'Jesus himself drew near', *Keswick Hymnal*, Marshall, Morgan & Scott, c.1940, No. 364
E. Glenn Hinson, unpublished, 1989, pp.5-6
James E. Metzler, *From Saigon to Shalom*, Herald Press, 1985, pp.107-108

Henri J.M. Nouwen, *Reaching Out*, Fount, 1980, pp.64-65
Lewis B. Smedes, *How Can It Be All Right When Everything Is All Wrong?*, Pocket Books, 1982, pp.72-73

Week 43
Frederick A. Atkins, *The Durable Satisfactions of Life*, Nisbet, 1925, p.25
John Baillie, *A Diary of Private Prayer*, OUP, 1968, pp.13,38
William Barclay, *A Plain Man's Book of Prayers*, Collins Fontana, 1959, p.36
Vernon Bartlett, *Tuscan Retreat*, Chatto & Windus, 1964, p.164
C.F. Bradbury and J.W. Hunkin, *Through the Christian Year*, OUP, 1933, p.164
Ethelbert W. Bullinger, *Critical Lexicon and Concordance*, Longmans Green, 1924, p.469
Sydney Cave, *What Shall We Say of Christ?*, Hodder & Stoughton, 1938, p.182
Harry Emerson Fosdick, *On Being a Real Person*, SCM, 1943, pp. 147, 138
M. Gibbs and T.R. Morton, *God's Frozen People*, Collins Fontana, 1964, p.87
Coretta Scott King, *My Life with Martin Luther King, Jr*, Hodder and Stoughton, 1969, p.72
Bruce D. Prewer, *Australian Psalms*, Lutheran Publishing House, 1979, p.19
Michel Quoist, *Prayers of Life*, Gill & Son, 1967, p.50
Robert H. Schuller, *Self Esteem*, Key-Word Books, 1982, p.161
Luther J. Thompson, *Monday Morning Religion*, Broadman, 1961, p.77
A.E. Whitham, *The Discipline and Culture of the Spiritual Life*, Hodder and Stoughton, 1938, p.182
John Greenleaf Whittier, *Baptist Hymn Book*, Psalms & Hymns Trust, 1962, No. 662

Week 44
Margaret Beidler, 'Pity Me' (Luke 18: 10-13), in *Faith at Work*, October 1977
Archbishop Anthony Bloom, *School for Prayer*, DLT, 1970, pp.8-9
John Claypool, 'The First Christmas: Jesus', sermon preached in Northminster Baptist Church, Jackson, Mississippi, 23 December 1979
Peter Dodson, *Contemplating the Word*, SPCK, 1987, pp.55-56
John Fowles, *The French Lieutenant's Woman*, Pan Books, 1987, p.54
Andrew Greeley, *Confessions of a Parish Priest*, Pocket Books, 1986, p.341
Eric Hoffer, *The Passionate State of Mind*, 1954, p.9
Sinclair Lewis, *Elmer Gantry*, Panther, 1927, 1961, p.319
Thomas Merton, *Conjectures of a Guilty Bystander*, in *Through the Year with Thomas Merton*, T.P. McDonnell (ed.), Image, 1985, p.8
Stephen Neill, *On the Ministry*, SCM, 1952, pp.101,120
Hugo Odeberg, *Pharisaism and Christianity*, Concordia, 1962, pp.100-101
M. Scott Peck, *People of the Lie: The Hope for Healing Human Evil*, Simon & Schuster, 1983, p.44
Simon Tugwell, 'The Beatitudes', in *Modern Spirituality: An Anthology*, John Garvey (ed.), DLT, 1986, p.61

Week 45
Dietrich Bonhoeffer, *Ethics*, SCM, 1971, p.14
James MacGregor Burns, *Leadership*, Harper, 1978, pp.295-296
Elias Chacour, *Blood Brothers*, Kingsway, 1987, p.94
G.K. Chesterton, *St Francis of Assisi*, Doubleday, 1957, pp.96-97
Athol Gill, *Life on the Road*, Lancer, 1989, p.77

Russell Heddendorf, 'Status and Role', in *Christian Perspectives on Sociology*, Stephen A. Grunlan & Milton Reimer (eds), Zondervan, pp.97-98

Paul Oestreicher, 'Christians as Political Dissenters', *The Way*, April 1988, pp.132, 133, 136, 137

John V. Taylor, *The Go-Between God: The Holy Spirit and the Christian Mission*, SCM, 1975, pp.153,161

Week 46

W.B. Brueggeman, *Living Toward a Vision*, United Church Press, 1976, p.30

Gordon Cosby, 'Words of Peace', in *The Student*, January 1984, The Sunday School Board of Southern Baptist Convention, p.14

A. Curle, *Mystics to Militants*, Tavistock, 1972, p.3

Billy Graham, 'Words of Peace', in *The Student*, January 1984, The Sunday School Board of Southern Baptist Convention, p.14

Mark Hatfield, 'Human Survival', in *The Student*, January 1984, The Sunday School Board of Southern Baptist Convention, p.9

Bruce Prewer, *Australian Prayers*, Lutheran Publishing House, 1983, p.130

Jim Punton, *The Community of Shalom: God's Radical Alternative*, Frontier Youth Trust, 1980, p.4

Foy Valentine, 'Peace with Justice', in *The Student, op cit*, January 1984, p.15

Week 47

Bernard of Clairvaux, 'O Sacred Head Sore Wounded', *Australian Hymn Book*, Collins, 1977, No. 255

Dag Hammarskjöld, *Markings*, Alfred A. Knopf, 1965, pp.8, 58, 81, 89

Morton T. Kelsey, *Caring*, Paulist, 1981, pp.87-88

Madeleine L'Engle, *And It was Good*, Harold Shaw Publishers,

1983, p.203

D.P. McNeill, D.A. Morrison, H. J.M. Nouwen, *Compassion*, Doubleday, 1982, pp.13-14

John Robinson, *Under His Wings*, S. John Bacon, pp.74-75

Week 48

Aristides, in Robert E. Webber, *The Secular Saint*, Zondervan, 1979, p.84

Leonardo Boff, Clodovis Boff, *Introducing Liberation Theology*, Paul Burns (tr.), Orbis Books, 1987, pp.1-2

Dom Helder Camara, *Hoping Against All Hope*, Matthew J. O'Connell (tr.), Orbis Books, 1984, p.55

Orlando Costas, *The Church and its Mission*, Tyndale House, 1974, pp.13, 243

Charles Dickens, in *The Speeches of Charles Dickens*, R.H. Shepherd (ed.), Michael Joseph, pp.196-197

Diognetus, in Robert E. Webber, *op cit*, 1979, p.140

D.P. McNeill, D.A. Morrison, H.J.M. Nouwen, *Compassion*, Doubleday, 1982, p.18

Pope Paul VI, Apostolic Exhortation *Evangelii Nuntiandi*, Saint Paul, 1976, p.37

David Sheppard, *Bias to the Poor*, Hodder and Stoughton, 1983, pp.56-57, 217

Ann Todd to Ingrid Bergman, in *Dawn Through Our Darkness*, Giles Harcourt (comp.), Collins, p.179

Robert E. Webber, *op cit*, pp.192-193

Week 49

Howard Butt, *The Velvet-covered Brick*, Harper and Row, 1973, p.106

J.G. Davies, *Every Day God*, SCM, 1973, p.216

Edgar Primrose Dickie, *God is Light*, Hodder and Stoughton, 1958, p.79

Bruce Kendrick, *The New Humanity*, Collins, pp.66, 68, 69

George F. Macleod, *Only One Way Left*, The Iona Community, 1964, pp.90, 38

John Macquarrie, *God and Secularity*, Westminster, 1977, p.63

W.B.J. Martin, *Acts of Worship*, Abingdon, 1960, p.132

John A.T. Robinson, *On Being the Church in the World*, SCM, 1960, pp.96,111

Week 50

An Australian Prayer Book, Anglican Information Office, 1978, p.68

George Eliot, *The Mill on the Floss*, Vol. II, William Blackwood and Sons, p.343

Dag Hammarskjöld, *Markings*, Leif Sjoberg and W.H. Auden (eds), Alfred A. Knopf, 1966, p.214

Martin Luther, *Martin Luther: Selections from His Writings*, John Dillenberger (ed.), Anchor Books, 1961, pp.75-76

George MacDonald, in *George MacDonald: An Anthology*, C.S. Lewis (ed.), Geoffrey Bles, 1946, p.24

Simon Parke, 'The Holy Words', in *Act Justly*, CAFOD & Christian Aid, Collins, 1987, p.24

Richard Rolle, in *Selected Works of Richard Rolle*, G.C. Heseltine (ed.), Longmans, Green & Co., 1930, p.85

Anne Rowthorn, *The Liberation of the Laity*, Morehouse-Barlow, 1986, p.67

J.A. Walter, *A Long Way From Home*, Paternoster, 1979, pp.193-194

Week 51

A Book of Services and Prayers, Independent Press Ltd, 1959

Virginia Axline, *Dibbs in Search of Self*, Victor Gollancz, 1966

The Child in the Church, British Council of Churches Consultative Group on Ministry with Children, British Council of Churches, 1984, pp.14,15,16

Annie Dillard, *Pilgrim at Tinker Creek*, 1975, p.9

Meister Eckhart, in Matthew Fox, *Original Blessing*, Bear and Company, 1983, pp.157,122

Francis of Assisi, in Matthew Fox, *Original Blessing, op cit*, p.221

Denham Grierson, *Focus on the Child*, Dove Communications, 1979, p.61

Dag Hammarskjöld, in *Focus on the Child*, Dove Communications, 1979, p.16

Hildegard of Bingen, in *Meditations with Hildegard of Bingen*, Gabriele Uhlein (ed.), Bear and Company, 1983, pp. 88,128

Mechtild of Magdeburg, in *Original Blessing, op cit*, pp.222, 278

Week 52

Karl Barth, *Deliverance to the Captives*, in *The Australian Baptist*, 6 September 1989

Robert McAfee Brown, *Creative Dislocation*, Abingdon, 1980, p.51

C.H.Dodd, *The Interpretation of the Fourth Gospel*, CUP, 1958, p.148

T.S. Eliot, 'East Coker V', *Four Quartets*, in Philip Seddon, *Darkness*, Grove Books, 1983, p.14

Emilie Griffin, 'A Different Wisdom', in *Praying*, National Catholic Reporter Publishing Company, No. 17, p.39

Georgia Harkness, *The Dark Night of the Soul*, Abingdon, 1945, pp.24-27

Franz Marc, in Gollwitzer et al, *Dying We Live: The final messages and records of some Germans who defied Hitler*, Collins, 1956/1960, p.8

John R. Mott, 'Seven Principles', in Robert Mackie, *Layman Extraordinary: John R. Mott 1865-1955*, Hodder and Stoughton, 1965, p.101

John Newton, in Philip Seddon, *Darkness*, Grove Books, 1983, p.8

Henri J.M. Nouwen, 'The Journey from Despair to Hope', in *Praying, op cit*, No. 17, pp.4-7

Oscar Romero, in James R. Brockman, 'Archbishop Romero's Spirituality,' in *Praying*, March-April 1990, pp.9, 8

Philip Seddon, *Darkness*, Grove Books, 1983, pp.20, 24

Sadhu Sundar Singh, *The Spiritual Life*, Christian Literature Society, 1926/1986, p.22

John V. Taylor, *The Go-Between God*, SCM, p.106

R.D. Williams, *The Wound of Knowledge*, DLT, 1979, p.161

Charles E. Wolfe, 'Willing to Die', in *Exegetical Resource*, Logos Productions, Vol. 5, No. 2, April-June 1990, p.8

Contributors

Personal profiles of contributors

George Appleton, born in 1902, spent many years as a clergyman in London and Asia before becoming Anglican Archbishop of Perth in 1963 and then of Jerusalem and the Middle East from 1968 to 1974. Married to Marjorie, he has had a busy and productive retirement in Oxford, especially with various writing assignments.

Susan Bjorndal has a background in nursing and home missions, and is currently an intern in a church in Vancouver, Canada. This involves her in counselling, Bible teaching and Sunday school, as well as speaking at meetings and retreats. She is interested in a variety of sports and her favourite pastime is reading.

Vaughan Bowie is a lecturer at the University of Western Macarthur, Milperra Campus in Sydney. He has a commitment to social justice issues, especially youth homelessness, and has written *Coping with Violence: a guide for human services*. His wife, Deirdre, lectures in music.

Peter Brierley is European director of MARC Europe, a Christian training and research organisation. Previously he worked as program director of the Bible Society and as a statistician in the Cabinet Office. He is the author of *Vision Building* and the editor of the *UK Christian Handbook* and other like volumes. He likes reading, doing mathematical puzzles and making models. He is married with four children and lives in London.

Chris Bullard is the senior minister for the Church of Christ in Overland Park, Kansas, USA, where he has served since 1977. He is an avid reader of mystery novels and attempts to play golf. He is married to Maxine and has three children.

Eva Burrows is General of the Salvation Army. She has responsibility for evangelical and social work in ninety-three countries. She previously served in Zimbabwe, Great Britain and Ireland, Sri Lanka and her home country, Australia. Her leisure interests are classical music concerts and reading.

Peter Burnham is a Churches of Christ minister and for the past twelve years has been chaplain to Toorak College, Victoria. His interests are in religious education, the Buddhist faith and the history of Christianity in Japan. He is currently writing a thesis on the history of the Churches of Christ ministry in Australia. Married to Sue, who teaches Japanese at Toorak College, they often visit Japan, taking groups of students.

Barry Chant is an author, speaker and teacher and has written books on theology, church history and family life, and children's stories. He is founder and president of Tabor College, a multidenominational Christian education centre in South Australia. He and Vanessa have three children and five grandchildren.

Dorothy Clack has been proprietor of a secretarial services agency, editorial assistant of the *Australian Baptist* and later an editor with the Australian Baptist Board of Christian Education. In retirement, she is involved in Bible study, writing, telephone counselling, word processing, gardening and music.

David Cormack is an international consultant working in the areas of business and mission. He has written a number of books, notably on time management, team work, conflict and reconciliation, change and excellence. He is married with three sons, and is a deacon in the Scottish Baptist church.

Howard Crago pastored in Victorian churches for twenty-five years, and for eighteen years was publication director of the Federal Baptist Board of Christian Education. He has lectured internationally, authored six books, and written 'A Saturday Reflection' in the Melbourne *Age* since 1976. His hobby is amateur radio.

Rowland Croucher has pastored churches in NSW, Victoria and British Columbia. For the past eight years he has ministered to clergy, church leaders and their spouses, first with World

Vision, now with John Mark Ministries. He is currently pursuing a ministry to ex-pastors, part of which involves a major research project exploring why they leave pastoral ministry. He and Jan are a 'clergy couple' with four children and two grandchildren.

Tony Cupit has recently joined the staff of the Baptist World Alliance in the USA. An Australian Baptist pastor, he has had overseas service in Papua New Guinea and a period as general superintendent of the Baptist Union of Victoria. He has held committee positions with a number of international bodies, and is an author and speaker. He and Margaret have three children.

Graeme Garrett is senior lecturer in theology at the College of Ministry, St Mark's National Theological Centre, Canberra. He is an ordained minister of the Baptist Church and has been a pastor at Collins Street and Box Hill Baptist churches in Melbourne. Prior to taking up his present position he was principal of Burgmann College in the Australian National University. He and Pam have two adult daughters.

Ken Gnanakan is the founder of ACTS Institute in Bangalore, India, and Executive Director of ACTS Ministries. Apart from his executive responsibilities, he is a Bible teacher, conference speaker, theologian, musician, evangelist and writer. He studied in India, Australia and London. His ministry often takes him far from his home in Bangalore, where he resides with his wife Prema and two children.

Peter Grant is married to Lynne, and they live in Hobart with their three children. After ten years with Scripture Union in Tasmania, he has lately been a freelance writer, part-time minister and part-time jam-maker. His interests include bushwalking, folk music, reading and writing.

Denham Grierson, a Uniting Church minister, is a member of the United Faculty of Theology, Melbourne, where he holds an ecumenical lectureship in the field of education. He is also executive secretary of the Victorian Council of Christian Education, and is the author of a number of books on congregational life and the mission of the church.

Alan Harley is a Congregational minister in New South Wales. He is president of the Australian Fellowship of Congregational Churches, and also the national director of the Asia Evangelistic Fellowship. He returned to Australia from Canada around 1980 after twenty years there as a pastor, evangelist, editor and teacher.

Glenn Hinson is a professor of church history at the Southern Baptist Theological Seminary, Kentucky. A native of Missouri, he has also taught at Wake Forest University, St John's University, The Catholic University of America, and the University of Notre Dame. He is married and has two children. His hobbies include carpentry and hiking.

Graham Houghton was born in New Zealand. In 1965 after studying at the Bible College of New Zealand, Graham went as a missionary to India. He then studied at the University of California, Los Angeles (UCLA). After a time as principal of Madras Bible Seminary, he became principal of the newly-established post-graduate South Asia Institute of Advanced Christian Studies in Bangalore. Graham and his wife Carol have a daughter, Kushi.

Graeme Irvine, as president of World Vision International since 1989, leads a Christian humanitarian organisation carrying out 6 000 projects in more than ninety countries. Following an eighteen year career with the YMCA in Australia, he joined World Vision of Australia as executive director in 1968. He moved to California in 1975 to take responsibility for World Vision's field ministries, and later served as vice-president for international relations in Geneva. Graeme and his wife, Fran, have two daughters.

Samuel Kamaleson has been with World Vision for sixteen years. His present position is vice-president-at-large, with responsibility for pastors' conferences in Third World countries. He and his wife Adela have three children and three grandchildren. His hobbies are jogging, gardening and raising aquarium fish. He has written four books and recorded three albums as a soloist.

Tom Keyte was ordained to the Baptist ministry in 1934, served various Baptist churches in Victoria and six years as the first general superintendent of the Baptist Union of Victoria. He retired from full-time ministry in 1972, but further served part-time in team ministry for eleven years. He and his wife Jean have three children.

Fergus MacDonald is currently General Secretary of the National Bible Society for Scotland, having had a long association and various senior committee positions with the United Bible Societies. He is a minister of the Free Church of Scotland, with former pastorates in Scotland and Peru. He is married with four daughters and one son.

Graham Mackay is a member of Armidale Uniting Church, NSW, and is engaged in part-time theological studies with special interest in various aspects of spirituality and its relationship to personality types. He is associate professor in Education at the University of New England and runs an educational coaching centre. He has four children and is interested in the Arts, especially music, and finding time for triathlons.

Ken Manley was the pastor of Epping Baptist Church in Sydney until he became the principal of Whitley College — the Baptist college of Victoria — in 1987. He has lectured at Baptist colleges in Adelaide and Sydney and is the author of books and articles on church history. He is married to Margaret and they have two married daughters.

Jill Manton has been a member of the pastoral team at Ashburton Baptist Church for the past four years, where her ministry has a particular emphasis on spiritual formation. She taught within the secondary school system. Later she took an MA in Biblical Studies and developed a ministry of biblical teaching within the local church. More recently she has undertaken study and training in spiritual direction and an increasing amount of her time is spent in this area. She is widowed, with three adult children.

Peter Moonie is a parish minister in the Uniting Church, currently serving in Ocean Grove, Victoria. He is a former farmer, studied in Melbourne, California and Boston, and has ministered in Victoria, Tasmania, New Hampshire and Massachusetts. He is a founding member of the Australian

Fellowship for Church Growth, is married to Eileen, and they have three adult children.

Peter Newall is a Uniting Church minister, retired and working assiduously at spiritual formation by way of writing, giving seminars, making cassettes and offering direction; all within his 'Paschal Ministries'. He remains grateful to God for W. Amadeus Mozart and eighteenth century music generally; and gardens and travels.

George Peck was, until his recent death, president of Andover Newton Theological School in Massachusetts. An Australian by birth, he was ordained and pastored in Queensland, before missionary experience in India. He undertook further study at London and Harvard universities, and was dean of Andover Newton for nearly twenty years prior to becoming president.

Gordon Preece is married to Susan and has three energetic children. He has been an Anglican minister in Sydney, and Ethics lecturer at the New South Wales Baptist Theological College. He is now doing PhD studies at Fuller Theological Seminary, California, in the area of work and vocation.

Stephen Prickett is Regius Professor of English Language and Literature at the University of Glasgow. Until 1990 he held the Chair of English at the Australian National University in Canberra. He has also taught at the universities of Minnesota and Sussex and at Smith College, Massachusetts, as well as authoring a number of books on religious literature. He is married with two children and two cats, and lives in a seventeenth century farmhouse in Renfrewshire.

Robin Pryor is a Uniting Church minister in Melbourne. He has a special concern to build up eldership, and a socially-aware spirituality. He is researching and publishing on spiritual formation for ministry, spirituality and personality, and stress and support in ministry, and is involved in retreat leadership for ministers and other Christian leaders. He was formerly a demographer at the Australian National University, and with the United Nations.

Frank Rees studied and pastored Baptist churches in Melbourne before pursuing doctoral studies at the University of Manchester on the relationship of doubt and faith in the Christian journey. Then followed seven years as pastor of the Hobart Baptist Church in Tasmania. He is now professor of systematic theology at Whitley College, Melbourne. He is married to Merilyn, and they have three children.

Julie Renner, a trained group worker, has a special concern for the empowerment of women. She is a part-time theological student and serves as a deacon in her local church. Julie lives with her husband, Geoff, and their three children in the southern foothills of Melbourne's Dandenong Ranges.

Mike Robinson has pastored Baptist churches in New South Wales and Victoria for twenty-two years, and is currently at Bathurst Baptist Church. He and his wife Bev have three children and a grandchild. His hobby is flying.

Stuart Robinson grew up in Brisbane and served for fourteen years as a missionary in Bangladesh. Since 1983 he has been senior pastor of Blackburn Baptist Church in Melbourne. He holds a number of tertiary qualifications. He is married to Margaret and has three children.

Doug Rowston coordinates and teaches Life Studies (including religious education) at Prince Alfred College in South Australia. A Baptist minister with a PhD in New Testament, Doug has also taught in a theological college. He was married to Sue, who died in 1984, and has a son and a daughter. He is interested in theology, cricket, football and music. In 1988, he married Rosalie. They enjoy doing the garden together, walking their Corgi dog and teaching Sunday school.

John Rymer is Anglican Dean of Auckland. An Australian by birth, he has studied in Queensland and London and taught in New South Wales and New Zealand. He is chairman of the board of World Vision in New Zealand, and a member of the international board. He is married with two grown-up daughters.

Samuel Southard was, until recently, senior professor of pastoral theology, Fuller Theological Seminary. His present interests are writing and research, with some time for organic gardening. His most recent publications are *Theology and Therapy* (Word, 1989) and *Death and Dying: A Bibliographic Survey* (Greenwood, 1991). He is currently working on 'A Pastoral Theology of the Gospels'. He is married to Donna, a graphic designer. His two daughters are Pamela Roesel and Melanie Southard.

Grace Thomlinson, formerly a secondary school music teacher, is currently coordinator of the Church and Christian Relations Unit at World Vision of Australia. She also lectures in Ethics and Old Testament at the Bible College of Victoria, and is involved in choral ministry at Blackburn Baptist Church with her husband Geoffrey.

Kevin Yelverton is now the pastor of a Baptist church in Geelong, Australia, after ministering to churches in New Zealand. He received his undergraduate training at the New Zealand Baptist Theological College, and gained his DMin from Northern Baptist Theological Seminary, Illinois. Kevin currently serves as secretary of the Baptist World Alliance Commission on Christian Leadership. Married to Cherry, they have two children.

Norman Young is professor of systematic theology at Queen's College, University of Melbourne, and teaches within the United Faculty of Theology (Uniting Church, Anglican and Jesuit). Ordained a minister in the Methodist Church, he headed up that church's negotiations for church union, and maintains a strong ecumenical commitment, being a member of dialogue groups with Roman Catholics in Australia and at the international level. Married to Barbara, they have two sons. His hobbies are gardening and golf.

Veronica Zundel is a freelance writer who contributes regularly to Scripture Union notes. She is compiler of the Lion anthologies *Famous Prayers, Christian Classics* and *Faith in Her Words*, a book of women's poetry; and author of *Life and other Problems* (a collection of her magazine columns) and *Going Out*, a book on dating. She married Ed Sirett in 1989 and they live in London.